Arab Elites

Arab Elites

Negotiating the Politics of Change

edited by
Volker Perthes

LYNNE
RIENNER
PUBLISHERS

BOULDER
LONDON

Published in the United States of America in 2004 by
Lynne Rienner Publishers, Inc.
1800 30th Street, Boulder, Colorado 80301
www.rienner.com

and in the United Kingdom by
Lynne Rienner Publishers, Inc.
3 Henrietta Street, Covent Garden, London WC2E 8LU

Library of Congress Cataloging-in-Publication Data
Arab elites : negotiating the politics of change / Volker Perthes, editor.
    p.   cm.
    Includes bibliographical references and index.
    ISBN 1-58826-266-9 (alk. paper)
    1. Arab countries—Politics and government—1945–   2. Elite (Social
sciences)—Arab countries.   3. Heads of state—Succession.   I. Perthes,
Volker.
    DS39.A685 2004
    320.9176'7'090511—dc22

                    2004003803

British Cataloguing in Publication Data
A Cataloguing in Publication record for this book
is available from the British Library.

Printed and bound in the United States of America

The paper used in this publication meets the requirements
of the American National Standard for Permanence of
Paper for Printed Library Materials Z39.48-1992.

5 4 3 2 1

Contents

Acknowledgments   vii

1   Politics and Elite Change in the Arab World
    Volker Perthes   1

Part 1   New Rulers in Power

2   Jordan: Between Regime Survival and
    Economic Reform
    André Bank and Oliver Schlumberger   35

3   Morocco: Reconciling Continuity and Change
    Saloua Zerhouni   61

4   Syria: Difficult Inheritance
    Volker Perthes   87

Part 2   Succession Looms

5   Egypt: Succession Politics
    Gamal Abdelnasser   117

6   Saudi Arabia: Dynamism Uncovered
    Iris Glosemeyer   141

Part 3   System Preservation and the Cooperation of New Elites

7   Algeria: System Continuity Through Elite Change
    Isabelle Werenfels   173

8   Tunisia: Economic Transformation and
    Political Restoration
    Steffen Erdle   207

Part 4   Elite Change Under Domination

9   Lebanon: Building Political Dynasties
    Rola el-Husseini   239

10   Palestinian Territories:
     From State Building to Crisis Management
     Hans-Joachim Rabe   267

Part 5   Conclusion

11   Elite Change and Systems Maintenance
     Volker Perthes   301

Bibliography   309
The Contributors   327
Index   329
About the Book   344

Acknowledgments

This book results from the work of the Elite Change in the Arab World research project at the Stiftung Wissenschaft und Politik–German Institute for International and Security Affairs (SWP) in Berlin. The two-year project, which began in 2001, brought together a group of European and Arab scholars to research common concepts, issues, and approaches to elite change in various Arab countries.

The goal of the project was not to produce a comprehensive overview of the Arab world, but to focus on cases that reveal something about social and political change in the region at large. Although none of our project members could carry out fieldwork in Iraq, events since March 2003 would have quickly dated any study of Iraqi elites.

The Elite Change project and this book would not have been possible without the generous support of the Ford Foundation and the Thyssen Foundation, both of which funded the project from 2001 through 2003, and the United States Institute of Peace, which contributed funding for the last year of the study.

We also gratefully acknowledge the support of Mahdi Abdul Hadi, Sadiq Jalal al-Azm, Bradford Dillman, Abdulhadi Khalaf, Bassma Kodmani, Gudrun Krämer, Heinz Kramer, Giacomo Luciani, Ulrich Wurzel, and others who in one way or another helped us organize our thoughts and refine our approaches. Also, without the patience, assistance, ideas, and indulgence of friends and colleagues from Arab countries who must remain anonymous, much of our work would have been lacking. Special thanks go to Imke Ahlf-Wien, research assistant at SWP, whose management and coordination were essential to the success of the project. Her ability to make the Arab members of the project feel at home in the cold of Berlin was invaluable. Thanks also to Pia Littmann, Imke's successor as research assistant, who patiently helped to bring the project to a close, and to Robin Surratt, whose copyediting improved our German- and Arabic-laced English.

None of these persons carries any responsibility for the deficiencies of this book. In many respects, elite change in the Arab world has just begun. Research on this topic remains a work in progress.

Politics and Elite Change in the Arab World

Volker Perthes

Regime change and the quality of governance in various Arab countries have come to the fore as major topics in the international policy debate, particularly so in the United States under the administration of George W. Bush. There is little doubt that leadership personnel and the manner in which Arab leaders rule their states and societies also have an impact on how these countries fare in an increasingly globalized world. Why, however, should one study elites or the changes in and among elites in Arab states? Do "elite" and "elite change" denote a particular normative or political background? Why should the focus be on the particular group of countries that constitute the Arab world? Is it relevant to study the change of elites in that region in the first place? If so, which theoretical assumptions should guide such research?

A comparative study of the Arab world focusing on its elites—or more precisely in this case, on its politically relevant elites—and on change among them necessarily proceeds from general underlying assumptions. First, one must assume that there are enough similarities and interdependencies among the Arab states that will lend themselves to useful insights from a comparative perspective. Second, one must assume that change among elites is actually taking place or will occur at some point at roughly concurrent times. It is obvious that in the Arab world a generation of leaders—not just a couple of septuagenarian prime decisionmakers—is gradually disappearing, and a new political elite is emerging.

It is also assumed that this "changing of the guard" will affect political dynamics in the region. This assumption implies that national politics are important. Political outcomes, in other words, are to a large extent shaped by the agendas and strategies of political actors in addition to being influenced by global and regional structures and developments, and by constraints that limit the capabilities of individual states. This study thus takes an actor-oriented approach, assuming that political elites indeed matter. The

1

state remains the primary framework for social and political action, but, as Charles Tripp notes, it must not be divorced "from the individuals and groups which in fact hold the power of decision."[1]

Elites are a sociopolitical reality. They are the people, as Harold Lasswell has put it, "who get most of what there is to get."[2] That goes for politics as much as for the economy and other areas of social life; in many cases, they take the most in every instance. There is nothing normative in this statement or in the critical analytic approach taken here: the elite are not necessarily the best or the brightest nor are they always those who should rule or should have certain privileges. Such elitist notions, with theoretical foundations in Plato's *Republic* and Pareto's sociology, too easily lend themselves to authoritarian or even totalitarian systems and rulers. Our approach is also not normative in the sense of proposing what elites should do in their respective states: One may wish, for example, that Arab leaders would move their countries toward democracy, pluralism, or social equality. This research, however, is about the agendas and political projects of these leaders, as well as other members of the elite, in regard to the socioeconomic and political challenges their countries face. Finally, studies of elites should not be normative or even ideological in the sense of claiming that the ruling or politically relevant elites have gained their positions as a result of some equitable and pluralist form of competition. For most of the Arab world, this is certainly not the case.

Elite studies experienced something of a renaissance in the mid-1980s and into the 1990s, to a great extent because of the transformation processes of authoritarian systems in Latin America and, even more so, in the former socialist countries. The crucial role of political elites in democratic transitions is commonly acknowledged by those researchers interested in transition processes as such,[3] and it has became a focal point of elite studies.[4] There has been more than one attempt to find common ground between studies that focus on elites and those that focus on the masses or class actors in order to better understand the interaction of leaders and the masses that shaped the democratization processes in Latin America and Eastern Europe. Mass action has often been a driving force in elite policies.[5] Michael Burton, John Higley, and others have explored the relationship between certain types of elites—consensual, fragmented, or divided—and regime types, as well as the chances of transition from one regime type to another. They conclude that the emergence of consolidated democracies requires "unity in diversity"—that is, a situation in which the groups comprising the elite agree on the rules of the game.[6] In regard to some of the former socialist countries of Eastern Europe, the Caucasus, and Central Asia, it has recently been noted that some of the elite who ruled these countries under socialism have survived the breakdown of those regimes and managed to retain their political elite status.[7]

Political failure evidently does not directly or necessarily lead to a loss of status.

Contrary to the claim that in this renaissance of elite studies "hardly any country . . . has not been the site of at least one recent elite study,"[8] the fact is that the Arab world has largely been ignored. Most studies of elites and emerging elites in the Arab states were done in the 1960s and 1970s, some even in the early 1980s. Little wonder that most of this work is heavily influenced by the modernization paradigm, which was dominant at that time. These studies—focusing mostly on the formation of a broad range of young elites, their social and professional backgrounds, socialization, political alignments, and worldviews—reflect the more or less revolutionary political and socioeconomic transformations that the region underwent beginning in the mid-1950s.[9] Frequently they are analytical, but tend to be more apologetic than critical, particularly in regard to the military. They generally stress the role of the new salaried middle classes as a social stratum promoting technological change and social modernization, and some even hail the civil and military functionaries who constituted this stratum as "the principal revolutionary and stabilizing force."[10] The optimism surrounding the role of the man on horseback receded considerably, practically as well as theoretically, with the unfolding of the long and often agonizing experiences with Arab rulers of military origin and army-backed regimes.

Because of the longevity of Arab regimes, academic interest in the political elites of the Arab world began to decline at the end of the 1970s. Thereafter students of political sociology occasionally took a look at new or reemerging elite segments, particularly the entrepreneurial elite and professional groups, or at emerging social alliances between these strata and state bureaucracies or state bourgeoisies.[11] Such interest in the role of Arab political elites usually surfaced in the context of studies concerning economic and political adjustment or liberalization processes, for which transition and "third-wave" (of democratization) literature often provided the conceptual framework. In a sense, however, everyone took for granted the continuity of the existing regimes and the ruling strata. Studies from the 1970s, or with respect to that period, remained largely valid in their characterization of the ruling elite up to the late 1990s. At present, these studies offer a basis for comparison of this older elite with the younger elite who have emerged or are positioning themselves for substantive political roles.

Despite the recent interest in elite studies, no general theory of elites and political change exists on which this book could rely, and it is not going to fill that gap. At best, the essays here furnish elements of a theory of limited reach that helps in explaining the relationship between elite change and political and socioeconomic changes in Arab countries. They may, nonetheless, be useful to students of other regions.

The Focus on Elite Change in the Arab World

It took the deaths in 1999 and 2000 of four Arab heads of state—King Hussein of Jordan, King Hassan II of Morocco, Amir Isa of Bahrain, and President Hafiz al-Asad of Syria—to make outside observers alert to the prospect of a wide-ranging change of leadership in the Arab world. By 2009 the leadership map of the region will differ substantially from the one a decade prior, and the difference will be considerably greater than that between the maps of 1999 and 1989 and even of 1979. Arab regimes have been extremely stable over the past three last decades or so: In 1999, the average term in office of prime decisionmakers was more than twenty years. Change at the leadership level will hence be regionwide, and the effects of such parallel change on domestic developments and on the regional and international relations of individual Arab states are well worth studying.

Academic and media observers have tended to focus on who will follow the top decisionmakers in individual states; in some cases, due to the longevity of some leaders, such questions have been studied for more than a decade.[12] Other studies have dealt with the problems of succession,[13] or with successful succession processes, and, consequently, with the personalities of new leaders.[14] The upcoming changes of the guard will go much deeper, however. Mainly because of the autocratic and personalized nature of many Arab regimes, there has been little change in the second and third circles of decisionmaking elites. Long-standing leaders have retained trusted advisors and ministers or commanded a pool of trusted aides whom they rotate in and out of government positions. Also, from the 1970s (and sometimes 1960s) to the late 1990s in Egypt, Syria, Morocco, and within the Palestine Liberation Organization (PLO), there was about as much change at the top of tolerated opposition parties and factions as at the top of the respective regimes.[15] Accordingly, a real generation gap has emerged between the political elite and the majority of the population in most Arab countries. Consider that up to three-fourths of the population in Arab states is less than twenty-five years of age. In 2003 the majority of Libyans, Egyptians, Iraqis, and Saudis, among others, had no active memory of a regime other than the one in power. Also, the historical events and symbols frequently invoked in public discourse by many of these regimes mean little to younger generations. Future changes at the top and within the wider elite are likely to reduce that gap and be reflected in new (or renewed) discourses and symbols closer to the experiences of the younger generations.

In some country studies, scholars have addressed such issues as the social and professional backgrounds of future leadership elites.[16] The effects of multiple parallel successions in the region, however, and questions pertaining to the development of a broader political elite have not yet been systematically examined.

The Politically Relevant Elite

The subject of the research presented here is the politically relevant elite (PRE). This stratum comprises those people in a given country who wield political influence and power in that they make strategic decisions or participate in decisionmaking on a national level, contribute to defining political norms and values (including the definition of "national interests"), and directly influence political discourse on strategic issues. The PRE thus encompasses the political elite, defined as those top government, administrative, and political leaders "who actually exercise political power"[17] or "persons whose strategic position in large and powerful organizations and movements enable them to influence political decisionmaking directly, substantially, and regularly."[18] The PRE reaches, however, beyond the political elite to include groups and segments that contribute to political processes or influence them from various sidelines. "Temporary elites"[19]—people who gain a position of political relevance but do not maintain elite status once their job is done—should not be conceptually excluded from this group. The same applies to ad hoc leaders of mass movements—the arouch in Algeria, for example—who, as John Peeler has argued in the case of Latin America, become elites the moment they lead.[20]

The concept of politically relevant elites also extends beyond today's common understanding of "political class"—those, in Tom Bottomore's words, who "exercise political power or influence, and are directly engaged in struggles for political leadership."[21] The PRE encompasses such functional segments as government, administration, and the military and may include individuals or groups who are not competing for political leadership, but rather use their influence to set or influence political agendas and define the themes of national discourse. These latter are opinionmakers rather than decisionmakers, advisors and *éminences grises* or lobbyists. Top businessmen, members of the media, and religious leaders, among others, are not per se considered part of the PRE; they are only included if their contribution to political processes is considered relevant. Generalizations are difficult, as relevance depends on the political structures as well as on the political culture of the different Arab states. Although religious leaders are certainly part of the PRE in Saudi Arabia or, for completely different reasons, in Lebanon—defining the legal framework in the former and, often enough, community interests in the latter—they cannot be considered politically relevant in Tunisia. Prominent journalists may have real influence on political agenda setting in Lebanon and, perhaps, in Kuwait and

Egypt, but for the time being they do not in Iraq and Syria. Similarly, the political relevance of deputies and members of shura councils, party functionaries, military officers, and government ministries is not the same from country to country. Which groups are considered part of the PRE must be established through a structural analysis of the political systems in each state.

The PRE concept includes opposition or dissenting voices once they are relevant to political processes. It is not necessary to theoretically juxtapose a "ruling elite" and a "counterelite," which would create a sometimes problematic and rather artificial distinction between those who are "in" and those who are "out." The criterion is relevance, as defined above, not membership in a ruling coalition or appointment to a formal office. Position alone does not guarantee a person political relevance; sometimes even position coupled with wealth do not translate into political power or influence. On the other hand, a full-fledged parliamentary democracy is not required for political forces that oppose a given government or differ with its agenda to gain a voice or some measure of influence on political processes. These forces might be competitors who play by the rules of the game or challengers who do not accept these rules or are not allowed to play the game in the first place. Take for example Lebanon, where members of the political oligarchy, even if they strongly oppose the president or the prime minister, still compete for political and material resources and are never actually "out." Even in some of the Arab monarchies rulers or parts of the ruling elite try to accommodate or integrate dissenters in one way or another. In these and other cases, even opposition leaders based outside the country may have real influence on decisions and discourses within the country. Algeria's Hocine Ait-Ahmed is an example of an influential challenger; it would be difficult to defend the claim that this veteran party leader has lost relevance in Algerian politics by being in exile. He is certainly not, however, among the core decisionmakers.

A model of three concentric circles highlights the different degrees of influence within the PRE (see Figures 2.1, 5.1, and 7.1 as exemplary illustrations).[22] The first (or inner) circle comprises the core elite—those who make decisions on strategic issues. In the second circle one finds an intermediate elite—groups and individuals who exert considerable influence on or make decisions of lesser political importance, but do not have the power to make decisions on strategic issues unless these are delegated to them. The third circle comprises what may be referred to as the subelite—less influential elites capable of indirectly influencing strategic decisions or contributing to national agenda setting and national discourses through their position in the government and administration, interest organizations and lobbies, the media, or other means. The boundaries between the circles are not hard and fast or hermetically sealed: Political elites have always been "somewhat elastic formations with unclear boundaries."[23] Movement into and out of the PRE, and between its circles, is indeed a major feature of social mobility and political change, and it is as such the center of interest here.

Issues and Approaches

This comparative look at politically relevant elites in the Arab countries focuses, where possible, on emerging or new elites. The dominant theme of change concerns change within elites and of elite settings as well as changes in the domestic and external environments that affect or are affected in some way by change on the elite level. Change includes everything from minor modifications of existing constellations to major, systemic transformations.

The case studies in this book deal with three related clusters of questions or issues that also denote three different levels of analysis: the human actor, the regional or international environments, and the nation-state. The first cluster pertains to the structure and composition of Arab PRE per se, which concerns identifying the politically relevant individuals and groups and those who have emerged or are about to emerge as part of this elite. The focus here is on the circulation of elites—the exchange of personnel—and on their attitudes and behavior. Given the longevity of regime elites in the Arab world, the question of what characterizes "new" or "emerging" is of particular importance: What is the scope of the changes taking place?[24] Can one speak of broad change in the sense that large numbers of positions in the first, second, and third circles change hands, or are these changes rather narrowly restricted to the most prominent or some of the more prominent elite members? How deep is such change? Is change within an elite purely generational, that is, is the new or emerging elite a mere reproduction or a younger version of the incumbent elite? Is that change structural—involving new political forces or new social strata or segments, and shifts in class or ethnic composition—or a new political or social balance of power? Further, can one detect changes in the dominant attitudes and values of a country's PRE, and what kind of effects do such changes have on that elite's behavior?

The second cluster of issues considers the interrelation between elite change and developments in the regional and international environment of the states in question. Elite change does not take place in a void. The political elites of the Arab world must deal with new regional and international structures—such as the World Trade Organization and the Euro-Mediterranean Partnership—that tend to penalize noncooperation more than the international system did when the outgoing generation of leaders came to power. In some cases, external players have explicitly demanded that incumbent political elites change or be exchanged.

Evolving regional and global circumstances do not act as absolute constraints on what the PRE of a given country can do in terms of regional and international relations, but they have to be taken into consideration. Analytical caution should prevail, however. There is no reason to assume that new elites will necessarily promote more peaceful solutions to interstate conflicts, take regional cooperation more seriously, or allow a higher degree of direct foreign interference in personnel and policy decisions simply because, when compared to their predecessors, they have a more civilian background, more exposure to the West, greater appreciation of the means and effects of globalization, and can count the Madrid and Oslo processes as part of their formative experience.

The third cluster of questions focuses on the relationships between the formation of new elites and socioeconomic as well as structural political changes. One should not presume that the emerging elites of the Arab world will necessarily follow a liberal economic agenda, let alone a liberal political one. Generation change on the elite level could, however, speed reforms: There is little doubt that the longevity of some regimes, such as that of Hafiz al-Asad in Syria or of Hosni Mubarak in Egypt, and the ossification of the Syrian and Egyptian elites explain to some extent the resistance to reform seen in both countries in the 1990s.[25] To the extent that reforms are enacted by a core elite, and structural changes occur, there arises a need for new qualifications within the broader elite. That is, reform and structural change will create pressures that may expedite further generation change and most certainly have an impact on recruitment patterns and elite composition, particularly in the second and third elite circles.

Identifying the PRE

A comparative project of this kind must allow for academic pluralism in the various contributions that form its whole. Consequently, for example, some authors stress the sociological aspects of elite change more than others, while some approach it from a political economy perspective or pay special attention to the relevance of external factors. Putting such foci aside, however, the study of each country involves identifying its politically relevant elite.

For a critical analytic perspective, one cannot be content with a purely institutional or positional approach that defines the political elite as the group of people whose members occupy the ten, twenty, or fifty or so top executive or representative positions in the official or constitutional structure of a given polity in a certain period. In a study of the Palestinians, one author included within the "political elite" the president of Palestine, anybody who held at some point a position in the council of ministers, the president of the Palestinian Legislative Council, the heads of committees in the parliament, the heads of parties, and the leaders of major public institutions.[26] Obviously, a major portion of those called the politically relevant elite here will be found in such official positions. One must consider, however, that many ministers in Arab (and other) countries do not participate in strategic decisions and have only limited influence on dominant discourses. Thus, to avoid being deceived by rank and formal position, it is necessary to examine the structure and workings of the political system, including where and how strategic decisions are made, in order to pinpoint possible positions and persons of influence outside the official framework. Key decisions may be made in formal or informal bodies that do not actually have constitutional or even legal bases.

To overcome the shortcomings of approaches that concentrate on formal position alone, structural analysis of political systems and decisionmaking processes is essential. Generalizations should be avoided: While most of the governments of the Arab states can be characterized as autocratic, decisionmaking structures, even at the highest (or core-elite) level, are not all the same. A few countries—among them Egypt, Tunisia, and Syria under the rule of Hafiz al-Asad—look like "presidential monarchies," where strategic questions rest firmly in the hands of the prime decisionmaker. Even in such authoritarian countries, however, presidents do not make their decisions alone. Corporatist institutions often play a role; ruling parties or security apparatuses might have a say in decisions.

In some countries, decisionmaking structures are more consultative and consensus oriented, sometimes explicitly so: Consider the Lebanese constitution, which sets out three presidencies designed to share and balance decisionmaking powers between the three main confessional groups, or the family councils in the Gulf monarchies. In still other cases there exist more or less informal bodies that are consulted on strategic decisions, hold veto power over such decisions, or actually make them collectively. Examples include the Saudi Royal Council, or Algeria's self-recruiting military junta, which forms a collective leadership with more power than the president or the government.[27] Similarly, the so-called *qiyada filastiniyya* (Palestinian leadership), a group of ministers, political and military cadres, and advisors surrounding the Palestinian Authority leader Yasser Arafat, is consulted on strategic issues, but it does not, as a body, have veto power.[28]

Even more variance exists with respect to structures comprising the second and third circles of the PRE. In Egypt or Syria, to give but two examples, the ruling party has a role to play in decisionmaking. In Jordan opposition party leaders, including Islamists, are also part of the PRE, and they have a voice even if parliament is suspended. In Lebanon, and to some extent in Egypt and Morocco, the media (and individual journalists) have some influence on agenda setting and public discourse. Religious leaders have a say in policy debates in countries as different as Egypt, Lebanon, and Saudi Arabia, but virtually no input in Algeria or Tunisia. Business associations have gained weight in several countries; trade unions have lost clout in most.

While a body of reliable literature exists on the political structures of Arab states, actual decisionmaking processes often remain opaque. Theoretically, a researcher would have to trace the processes that lead to decisions on relevant issues; identify the groups and institutions that try to influence and succeed in influencing debates on particular issues; and establish at what level disputes are solved, compromises are sought, or conflictual outcomes are determined. Practically, such research will only be possible to a limited extent. At times one will only be able to note that powerful networks have an influence on key decisions, but it will be too difficult to ascertain their structures or members.

Beyond political systems analysis, identifying the PRE requires relying on expert opinion, or the so-called reputational approach, which is an indispensable tool.[29] This may mean asking a group of knowledgeable observers from inside and outside the country who, according to their judgment, plays a relevant role with regard to strategic decisions. Method clearly meets content here, as people, even in systems with little transparency, tend to "know" who is in charge, who is influential, or who or which institutions and bodies can largely be disregarded. Such knowledge is of practical importance to citizens trying to solve individual or collective problems vis-à-vis the state but which cannot for whatever reason be solved through official, institutional channels; this knowledge is generally built on experience. A reputation of being influential, powerful, close to a top decisionmaker, an éminence grise, and so on is more than having a whiff of fame; it can be a real asset that facilitates access to material and symbolic resources and, thereby, increases political weight, or "capital." It is one feature among others that distinguish the elite from the masses.

Identifying emerging elites requires examining career and recruitment patterns. Elites are never, even in revolutionary situations, totally exchanged. In most of the Arab states, incumbent elites significantly influence the formation of the new elite that will replace them. Although recruitment patterns change over time, such as to meet new economic, foreign policy, or other challenges, it is usually possible to identify the incubators, as it were, where emerging elites are trained or prepare themselves for political careers. Parliament, as Rola el-Husseini and Gamal Abdelnasser point out, is a place to hone one's political skills in Lebanon and in Egypt. The Moroccan parliament, the shura council in Saudi Arabia, and some other legislative bodies may attain such a role in the future, or at least become places in which to vet ideas and thus influence political discourse.[30] In Algeria, Egypt, Morocco, and Syria, administration, particularly being in the position of a *wali* or a *muhafiz* (regional governor), is an important training and recruitment site for ministerial careers. The military remains a pool for future leaders in most countries, with the notable exception of the Gulf monarchies. Some leading families in Jordan, Lebanon, or Saudi Arabia have provided PRE members over two, three, or more generations.

Modernizing young leaders are likely to look for elite incubators outside the established structures of state, party, and leading families. Consider the role of the Economic Consultative Council in Jordan or the Syrian Computer Society in Syria in the modernization efforts of Abdallah II or Bashar al-Asad, respectively.[31] Also, in countries that undergo economic reform and adjustment processes, nationals who have made a career in international organizations stand a good chance of parachuting into key government positions. In general, the contributors to this book follow qualitative rather than quantitative analysis. All contributions are based on extensive fieldwork, particularly on semistructured or informal interviews with members of the PRE and other resource persons. The object of analysis defines the researcher's method to quite some extent. Members of political elites are less easily accessible than members of broader societal elites; and one can hardly expect the political leadership of a country to fill in the questionnaire of some curious researcher. While the ability to grasp changing realities through quantitative analyses must not be overestimated in the first place, sociobiographical data, even of a sample of incumbent PRE members and young recruits to the second and third circles, can help discern patterns of elite formation and their modification over time. Saloua Zerhouni's examination of Morocco provides a particularly useful example.[32]

Some of the chapters also present portraits of individuals, biographies of incumbents and emergent elites, or sketches of proto- or ideal-type PRE members. Such analysis helped the authors organize their ideas, and it may help others understand the politicocultural environment of the polities in question. Future developments will determine whether a researcher was able to skillfully sift through the available information to plausibly judge whose lives make representative biographies, who is a promising young leader, or where the line should be drawn between the first, second, and third circles of the PRE.

Identifying Agendas and Strategic Themes

A study on elite change must be concerned with the agendas of new and emerging PRE. Agendas, or political projects, should be understood as the concretized and prioritized interests of actors within a given temporal and spatial framework. Although incumbent elites can be judged by their track record, such evaluation of emerging or young elites will necessarily be limited. One therefore must rely, to a large extent, on discourse analysis—critical examination of "speech acts" that reflect the opinions and attitudes of emergent as well as incumbent members of the elite. Discourse is not merely a reflection of attitudes, however. It is also practice—it is an essential part of agenda setting; it helps one recognize friend and foe; and it can redefine norms and institutions, challenge existing political configurations, or shield those in power against the claims of contenders.[33] To discern elite discourses, the contributors to this book have relied on personal interviews and discussions, published and unpublished statements, speeches, publications, and other materials.

Political culture had to be taken into account in identifying and selecting relevant materials. For example, in a country such as Lebanon, with a media-oriented culture, members of incumbent and emerging elites generally make efforts to publish books or articles. In Saudi Arabia and other Gulf states, oral communication remains essential; for example, Crown Prince Abdallah and other Saudi leaders set agendas by publishing their addresses to select gatherings. Emerging elite members in the Gulf are more likely to rely on their word being spread through formal meetings or informal gatherings, such as the *diwaniyya*s of Kuwait. Here, even researchers may have to rely more on what they can hear than on what they can read.

In order to focus their analysis, the authors generally identified a limited number of relevant, strategic themes concerning their country of study. The assumption here is that impending elite change will be reflected in the political debates and discussions about these strategic themes and thus in elite discourse. The strategic themes are those of national importance, so they vary from country to country. European Union (EU) association, for example, and the liberalization measures that are to go along with association would certainly be considered strategic themes in countries that are about to negotiate agreements with the Europeans. They are contested within the PRE in Egypt and Syria, but not in Lebanon or Tunisia. In Lebanon, relevant themes include relations with Syria and the future of the confessionalist system. In Jordan, the questions of "normalization" of relations with Israel and of domestic relations between Palestinian Jordanians and Transjordanians are disputed and highly relevant. In the major oil-producing countries, questions of rent distribution, subsidies and taxes, and adjustment because of decreasing oil income may have similar relevance.

One should keep in mind that political science and other social sciences are not exact sciences. This book does not, therefore, offer irrefutable prophecies, statistics, or comprehensive quantitative data. A researcher may easily determine statistically that the emerging elites in a given country are better educated, more urban, or more civilian than their predecessors, or that more of them are women. The value of such findings is, however, rather limited unless it can be translated into judgments and hypotheses about future political developments. In more than a few cases, such hypotheses can be based on anecdotal evidence rather than statistical or sociobiographical material.

Comparative Observations and Prospective Hypotheses

Political systems of Arab states vary, and comparative studies help to identify their differences. What these systems share, however—and this, again, underscores the relevance of studying elites and elite change in the region—is the elitist nature of political participation: Royal councils, shura councils, the Lebanese parliament with its confessionalist representation (indeed, the assemblies of most Arab countries), the Economic Consultative Council in Jordan, and other bodies are explicit means for integrating a wider, politically relevant elite into decisionmaking processes. In the past, republican regimes, like those in Syria, Egypt, Algeria, and elsewhere, have tried to hide their elitism behind a populist facade. Practically, however, by treating their population as "the masses," rather than as citizens, they never left any doubt that decisionmaking powers were concentrated and should remain in the hands of a narrow, self-recruiting elite.

Elite Structure and Composition

The social and professional profile, as well as the historical experiences, of the new and emerging Arab leaders as of 2003 was considerably different from those of the political elites that emerged in the 1960s and 1970s (or even earlier in some of the monarchies). According to Manfred Halpern, these earlier elites were "a core of salaried civilian and military politicians, organizers, administrators, and experts,"[34] that is, technocrats from either the military or the bureaucracy. The old commercial and land-owning bourgeoisie were no longer considered part of the political elite, and an entrepreneurial class had yet to emerge.

The breadth and depth of elite change in the Arab world has and will continue to vary by country. In Jordan, Morocco, and Syria, where prime decisionmakers have relatively recently been replaced by their sons, a large percentage of people within the first, second, and third circles of the PRE have been exchanged. Except in Morocco, where some Islamists have moved into the third elite circle, these changes were not necessarily structural or deep in the sense that new political forces or new social segments entered the scene. In Jordan King Abdallah II's recruitment of members of the business elite into leading political functions has brought more depth to postsuccession elite change, at least in the first and second circles, than that witnessed in Syria.

Algeria has experienced wide-ranging change, particularly in the third circle, and Isabelle Werenfels notes that its core elite has seen the replacement of "one generation of the revolution by a younger generation of the revolution."[35] These changes were partially structural, as the elite became more civilian. In Lebanon, many of the prewar and war elites have left the scene, and there has also been structural change: there are now fewer notables in the PRE, more businesspeople, and, at least in the third circle, more civil society actors than before. Also, most of the war elite militia leaders have been removed in one way or another, and some of the politicos who owe their positions solely to Syria may well experience the same fate if Syria's dominance in Lebanon fades. In Tunisia, the pre–Ben Ali elite has been totally replaced, but the new elite is basically a reproduction of the old in terms of socioprofessional composition and basic political philosophy. In Egypt, wide-ranging change can be expected once a successor to President Husni Mubarak comes to office, and it is likely to be at least partly structural—more civilian and probably with a strong business component. In Iraq, the war launched in 2003 by the United States and Britain was the driving force engineering wide-ranging elite change, from abroad. In the Palestinian territories, change is likely to be more constrained, even after the death or removal of Yasser Arafat, not least so because not everybody in the political elite derives his (or, in some cases, her) power directly from the president. Structural change will largely depend on Israeli-Palestinian developments. In Saudi Arabia, changes in the third circle have been relatively broad, including the co-optation of members of hitherto unrepresented social segments. Change in the first and second circles may come in doses. The death of a leader will lead to changes of position, but not necessarily to wide-ranging replacements of members of the PRE.

In general, as Arab societies have become more complex and diversified, the socioprofessional profile of new and emerging PRE has broadened, and PRE members have increased in number. Military officers are likely to be less dominant than they were in the final decades of the twentieth century. Even in Algeria, where the military firmly holds on to power, the president is now a civilian, and the institution of the presidency has been strengthened.[36] Overall, there will still be a military element in most PRE. Today's military officers, however, differ in many respects from the officer generation of largely rural origin that graduated from the military academies in the 1950s and 1960s and had a social revolutionary agenda.[37] Arab military officers in the early twenty-first century can generally be seen as a stability-oriented element. At the same time, their interactions with the political leadership and with the public have changed: With respect to Egypt, for instance, it has been noted that younger officers tend to be less antidemocratic, less suspicious of the outside world, and more open to participating in public policy debates than the elder generation, which was used to the military being secluded from civil society.[38]

Managers and politicians. Relatively speaking, the country studies in this volume indicate that there are fewer military personnel, medical doctors, and teachers among the new elites than was the case in earlier times. Engineers, who formed an important element of the incumbent Arab political elites, are still to be found in large numbers among the newcomers, but their professional experience is increasingly in the private rather than the public sector. There is also a growing number of representatives of the liberal professions, and more people with management and business backgrounds. Overall, the new PRE of most Arab countries are or will be largely of urban middle-class origin.

One can no longer speak of emerging political elites in Arab states without a reference to private business and its more traditional and new entrepreneurial sectors. In some countries, expatriates who are prepared to invest their skills and their capital in their homeland have entered or may enter the fold. Observers have noted that since the late 1980s, the offspring of the bureaucratic and military classes, or state bourgeoisie, of Arab states with more or less etatist development courses have turned into new entrepreneurs or joined the business class.[39] Egyptian Gamal Mubarak is representative of this trend, which is also evident among the sons of Algerian, Libyan, Saudi, and Syrian policymakers and generals. As possible contenders for political influence and power, these young men must be taken as seriously as members of the reinvigorated and more self-confident "traditional" business classes that have reestablished themselves in the course of economic liberalization.

During the last three decades or so, the pattern in the Arab republics and monarchies has been to attain political influence, which could then be used to acquire wealth or establish a business, not the reverse. Cases such as Lebanon's Rafiq al-Hariri, a businessman who gained political power, remain impressive exceptions to the rule. More of these may lie in the future, but such a pattern would presuppose the emergence of more competitive political systems.

One can therefore assume that the number of true politicians—who in the Weberian sense live for politics, rather than from politics[40]—and their relevance in the political lives of Arab countries, will increase, if only slowly. In contrast to the rather apolitical type of technocratic functionary simply occupying a government position, such a politician would act as a power broker, stand for a political program, and even act as and be perceived as the representative of a particular constituency or of social or economic interests. This latter type has always existed in Lebanon. As Husseini illustrates in her contribution, since the end of the civil war there has been an increase in politicians who do not come from the traditional bourgeoisie and who are attempting to push themselves into the foreground of the political stage via entrepreneurial success or civil society activities. In Morocco, former prime minister Abd al-Rahman Youssoufi represents an ideal-type politician. Most of his life, he opposed the monarchical regime that eventually co-opted him to form a government of alternation. Zerhouni explains how his appointment, which preceded the death of Hassan II and the accession of Mohammed VI, represented a partial political opening of the system. While the number of politicians in the PRE increased, bureaucratic and technocratic cadres remained dominant. It is noteworthy that Youssoufi's successor, Driss Jettou, is a technocrat, though one with a private sector background.

Politicians—in the "true" sense—are also to be found in the political elites of Algeria, Egypt, and Jordan. Even with agendas out of step with their government's, they can occasionally influence or determine public discourse. So far, however, they have not entered the inner circle of the PRE. In Saudi Arabia, as Iris Glosemeyer explains, the Consultative Council has become a forum for the emergence of a group of politically relevant "bourgeois"—that is, nonprincely—politicians. In Syria, a group of independent politicians and civil society actors stepped forward after the accession of Bashar al-Asad. Once they threatened to become a politically relevant factor, their movement was quickly cut down to size. Steffen Erdle argues that in Tunisia under Zine al-Abidine Ben Ali, politicians have disappeared from the politically relevant elite. In these cases and others, it is safe to infer that an increase in the number or weight of "politicians" within a country's PRE usually attests to the movement of the political system toward plurality and competitiveness.

The knowledge factor. In general, the percentage of PRE members with undergraduate degrees or doctorates, many of them from universities in Europe or the United States, is on the rise. In the 1970s and 1980s a number of universities were established in Arab countries. These schools provide opportunities for upward social mobility, and their graduates are now competing for jobs and positions with graduates who studied abroad. Upward mobility through national universities, however, may have its limits. In all likelihood, persons with "foreign" degrees will continue to have better chances of being recruited into the technocratic segments of the PRE, and incumbent elites will continue to send their sons and daughters to universities abroad or to universities with Western curriculums within their countries as a means of reproducing themselves—that is, passing on their elite status to their offspring.[41]

In the republican systems, membership in the regime party may still be indispensable for recruitment into the first or even the second circle of influence. Party membership—or membership in the royal family in a country like Saudi Arabia—is no longer sufficient in and of itself for gaining a position of political relevance. What counts beyond loyalty or membership are qualifications and knowledge—a degree that certifies technocratic competence, training, or professional experience abroad, or, generally, skills that correspond (functionally or at least symbolically) to the challenges of the globalized flow of information and goods. Thus, among the newer recruits into the PRE of Arab countries, one finds increasing numbers of jurists (such as Algerian prime minister Ali Benflis), economists with experience in international financial institutions (such as Palestinian finance minister Salam Fayad, Lebanese economy minister Bassel Fuleihan, or Syria's minister of economy and trade Ghassan al-Rifa'i), or managers (such as Moroccan prime minister Driss Jettou and Jordanian prime minister Ali Abu Raghib). In contrast to some expectations that the new elites of Arab states would, among other things, also be more female,[42] the proportion of women within positions of political relevance has not substantially increased.

Generation matters. When speaking of new or emerging elites, one should keep in mind that the concept of "youth" varies in the different Arab countries. Incumbent elites have begun to or are about to give way to a younger generation in most Arab states, but this does not mean that the new PRE represent the same generation throughout the entire Arab world. In Bahrain, Jordan, Morocco, and Syria, the death of the long-standing head of state precipitated a far-reaching exchange of leaders in their sixties and seventies with persons in their thirties and forties. In Saudi Arabia one can expect that positions currently held by septuagenarians and octogenarians will be taken over by "younger" princes in their fifties and sixties once the incapacitated monarch passes away.

At any rate, the historical experience of emerging PRE differs from that of the incumbent generation, and the fact that it is closer to that of the majority of the population may be of considerable importance given the relative youth of Arab societies. More often than not, generations can be defined clearly in relation to historical moments; the members of the generation may also perceive themselves as being marked by shared historical experience: they would then, to borrow a concept from Marxist class theory, constitute a generation "for itself" rather than only "in itself."[43]

This may have been the case for the generation that ruled Syria, Lebanon, and Egypt in the years following their independence, and it certainly holds for the so-called generation of the revolution in Algeria, defined by participation in the struggle against French colonialism. This generation, which includes, to date, the president of the republic and most leading military officers, has long managed to successfully exclude members of postrevolutionary generations from positions of real power. At the same time, they have worked to transfer their revolutionary legitimacy to their offspring, sometimes literally, as by establishing the Organisation Nationale des Enfants des Chouhada (National Organization of the Children of Martyrs).[44]

In Egypt and Syria, politicians of largely the same age group have tried to define themselves by the 1973 Arab-Israeli war. Egyptian president Mubarak and other military officers and former military officers who had a leading role in that war are generally referred to as *jil uktubir* (the October generation).[45] For many of their age group and of their somewhat younger cohorts, however, in Egypt, Iraq, Jordan, Syria, and Palestine this generation has remained what Palestinian author Saïd Aburish (himself born in 1935) has called the "generation of despair"[46]—a generation that never recovered from the psychological wounds of the 1967 war. In many respects, this is a pan-Arab generation that generally—to the extent that generalizations are possible—has sought and hoped for a strong Arab leadership that would create "parity" with Israel. Many of its members, from the Gulf to North Africa, perceived the Arab world as part of the anti-imperialist camp, believed (for some time at least) in socialist development models, and did not view democracy or civil rights as political priorities. Iraqi political scientist Isam al-Khafaji has aptly characterized the basic attitudes of political activists from that generation: "The belief that imperialism would try to forestall any attempt to overcome underdevelopment, whether through direct intervention or through local agents . . . reinforced the perception that a strong state with a strong army was an essential prerequisite for genuine development. Hence the easiness with which liberal and even reformist ideas were dismissed or discredited among the populace."[47]

In the 1970s increasing direct or indirect oil rents allowed for an enormous expansion of the state and public sectors throughout the region and for rapid social mobility for great numbers. Many who had entered professional life by that time, among them a substantial number of left-leaning *soixante-huitards* (adherents to the ideals of the worldwide 1968 student protests), remember the era as their golden years. In Egypt, pupils and university students at the time of the 1973 October War and those who served as conscripts have alternatively been dubbed *jil al-wasat* (the generation of the middle) and *jil al-sahwa al-islamiyya* (the generation of the Islamic awakening). The older members of this age group benefited from the oil boom. For the somewhat younger members, who graduated and entered professional life in the late 1970s and early 1980s, the bust of oil prices and the economic crises of the 1980s and 1990s were decisive in determining their future and their outlook. Although benefiting from the expansion of secondary and university education, many of them found career opportunities blocked by members of the preceding generation clinging to power and positions of influence. By the late 1990s, few of this generation had made it into the first or second circle of political relevance. A substantial part of those politically active sought Islamic alternatives to the regimes in power.

In most Arab countries, political developments in the next two or three decades will likely not be determined by the generation of the middle, which in many respects is a generation between two dominant others. It is no coincidence that Egypt's al-Wasat party—whose name references not only a centrist course between moderate Islamist and liberal approaches, but also the generation of its founders—has not been licensed to participate in politics. One should rather expect the generation of Bashar al-Asad, Abdallah of Jordan, Mohammed VI, and Marwan Barghouthi to take the lead. The historical experience of this elite generation differs considerably from that of the outgoing PRE. It is, generally speaking, not the experience of the East-West conflict, of the great Arab-Israeli wars, of experimentations with socialism, or of the oil boom. It is instead one of the end of bipolarity, U.S. hegemony, protracted recession, debate about globalization, the post–1991 Arab-Israeli peace process, and civil war in Algeria. In many Arab countries, this generation could be called the generation of sons—the offspring of those who shaped the history of the Arab world during the last quarter or more of the twentieth century. In the case of the Palestinians, these emerging leaders represent the intifada generation, certainly a generation in and for itself, whose members generally share the experience of violent conflict with the Israeli army and struggles for power and influence with the incumbent Palestinian leadership around Arafat—*al-khityar* (the old man), as he is so often referred to in the Palestinian territories.[48]

Regional and International Factors

Much of the historical experience that defines Arab elite generations is related to external factors. The relationship between elite change on the one hand and the regional and international relations of Arab states on the other has crosscutting effects: Elite change affects these relations, and external factors affect the composition and behavior of local elites.

For starters, change at the top can trigger shifts in bilateral relations; often a change of the guard helps to improve such relations. This has definitely been the case for Bahrain and Qatar, where new leaders found a way to settle a long-standing territorial dispute by simply accepting the decision of the International Court of Justice. In the case of Jordan and Syria, the accession of two young leaders at roughly the same time also helped improve bilateral relations. These cases primarily reflect the personal nature of Arab regimes and, consequently, of inter-Arab relations. Jordan's case is telling: The death of King Hussein allowed his successor, Abdallah, to turn a new page with Syria, where he found a like-minded young leader in Bashar al-Asad, who was then still in training to succeed his father. Abdallah's ascension also cleared the way for better relations with Saudi Arabia and Kuwait, whose leaders decided to bury their animosity toward Jordan with the death of Hussein, the man responsible for Jordan's pro-Iraqi neutrality during the Gulf War.

What these situations illustrate is a change in personnel, not a change in pattern. There is, in other words, no guarantee that a personal falling out or a conflict over issues of regional policy between, say, the Jordanian and the Syrian leaders, would not seriously disrupt bilateral contacts and relations. To institute structural change in inter-Arab relations, the new leaders and their teams would have to depersonalize their countries' bilateral relations, insulating state institutions that deal with day-to-day foreign relations from the power games at the leadership level. Such a move would allow functional cooperation to stand on its own administrative and economic feet. Authoritarian and highly centralized regimes may not necessarily be less peaceful or more aggressive than democracies or pluralistic systems, as is sometimes claimed in a vulgarized form of the "democratic-peace" theorem,[49] but they are definitely less able to cooperate. Sustainable regional and international cooperation, particularly in multilateral frameworks, needs the broader participation of societal actors and necessitates the delegation of decisionmaking powers to lower-level officials. It cannot be guaranteed through a mere change at the top of the hierarchy.[50]

In speaking of the regional relations of Arab states, one should not forget that the leadership generation that dominated Arab and Middle Eastern policies throughout the last quarter of the twentieth century did manage to introduce some continuity into regional politics. Although these elites failed to foster stable cooperative relations, settle the dominant regional conflict, or implement a system of cooperative security, they did prove capable of containing the civil wars of Algeria, Lebanon, Sudan, and Yemen, preventing these crises from turning into regional wars. Also, Arab-Israeli wars have been shorter and less destructive than might have been expected considering the depth of enmity and the longevity of the conflict.

The new generation of leaders obviously lacks similar experience in conflict administration. Regarding the Arab-Israeli conflict, there is little reason to expect that the replacement of one leadership generation by another will by itself make it easier to civilize the conflict, or help resolve issues of contention. In Israel, the change from the generation of Yitzhak Rabin and Shimon Peres to Benjamin Netanyahu's postindependence generation did not at all make Israel more peaceful or cooperative. In a similar vein, some Israelis are likely deceiving themselves (and others) when they claim that all that is needed to settle the conflict with the Palestinians is the exit of Arafat and the accession of a younger generation.[51]

The new leaders of Jordan, Morocco, Syria, and Bahrain have all enjoyed something of a honeymoon in terms of the regional environment, and in most cases future new leaders are likely to experience a similar beginning. National interests usually dictate greeting a new team in a neighboring country with high hopes of good relations. One cannot, however, exclude the possibility that significant changes within the PRE of a country might negatively affect regional relations. This is most likely to happen in the case of nonconstitutional or revolutionary change or in the case of weak and inexperienced leaders coming to power. To build and broaden their domestic base, they might engage in hypernationalistic discourses or in activities that their neighbors or relevant international players find provocative, or that challenge the regional balance. The same might occur when regional players try to take advantage of the assumed or de facto weaknesses of a newcomer.[52]

Perhaps a more daunting prospect for the new and emerging Arab elites will be dealing with the changing external challenges summed up under the heading "globalization": speedier flows of information and finance, increased competition based on global standards, and a premium on openness and the ability to cooperate regionally and internationally. Those who miss the globalization train will pay the high costs ensuing from the lack of economic efficiency. Although all Arab political elites will have to face these challenges, they have the option of responding to them in different ways. The Syrian leadership, to give but one example, could decide to go slow in negotiating an association agreement with the European Union, or even do without such an association. This would probably be done at a loss, however, passing up access to European resources and risking a further relative decline of competitiveness in comparison to regional neighbors.

In general, the new and emerging elites of the Arab world are more prepared to deal with the challenges of globalization and economic openness than their predecessors were. Many of them see cooperation with Europe as a strategic choice. At the same time, these young elites do not want to relinquish what they perceive as national or regime interests. The Maghreb states in particular, because of their dependence on the EU, have tried to strengthen cooperative relations with the United States in an attempt to limit the influence of Europe over and within them.

In the regional geopolitical context, the Arab-Israeli conflict and the peace process continue to be of great relevance for the young elites in Palestine—where Israeli occupation and the struggle over how to deal with it dominate all other political issues—and also for those young elites in the countries neighboring Israel and in the Gulf. In Algeria, by contrast,

"Palestine" is a nonissue for most political groups, with the exception of the Islamists. Rather, domestic policy and relations with Europe and the West in general carry much more weight. In Egypt, Jordan, Lebanon, and Syria, however, the intifada and the Arab-Israeli conflict are consistently topics of domestic debate and conflict. Abdelnasser even argues that the course of Arab-Israeli events will be the main determinant for the type and political outlook of Egypt's post-Mubarak PRE. In Jordan contesting elements of the PRE have garnered substantial public support under the banner of fighting normalization with Israel. In Lebanon, the military tension that Hizballah tries to sustain along the Lebanese-Syrian-Israeli border area is a major point of contention between the supporters of the liberal economic course set out by Hariri and Syria's men within the country's political elite.

In Syria, the leadership elite around Bashar al-Asad are more aware than their predecessors of the economic necessity of settling the conflict with Israel; at the same time, they use conflict to bolster the popularity of the young president. Bashar al-Asad, without discarding his father's realpolitik approach, has developed a more provocative, hard-line discourse when speaking of Israel and the Arab-Israeli conflict. This has disturbed foreign observers, but it appeals to many of the younger generation, not only in Syria but also in other Arab countries. With respect to Israel and the future of the peace process, the general attitude of the emerging PRE across the Middle East seems to be to legitimize radical methods while remaining pragmatic about the substance of an acceptable settlement.

Changing regional relations and new forms of integration into the regional and international environments are factors in elite change that should not be overlooked. Thus, in the countries that share a front or a border with Israel, recent heightened tensions with Israel have affected the balance of forces within the core elite, generally to the advantage of less reform-oriented elements. At the same time, any decision to launch a cooperative scheme—Euro-Mediterranean, Arab, or other—is a strategic choice that will influence the recruitment of leadership personnel, at least on the technocratic level, and thus the composition of emerging PRE. In Egypt, for instance, the decision to enter into negotiations over an association agreement with the EU led to the installation of a revamped foreign and economic policy team, much as occurred in an earlier era concerning the decision to wage peace with Israel.

Peace between Israel and the Palestinians and Palestinian statehood would no doubt precipitate major changes within the Palestinian PRE. Confrontations with Israel, the first agreements between the PLO and Israel, and the establishment of proto-state structures had a decisive impact on elite formation. By the end of the first intifada (1987–1993), a relatively young local elite had emerged that could not be ignored once the Oslo process was on track. With the establishment of the Palestinian Authority, this largely secretive, underground elite stepped forward, and diaspora leaders returned. A new national (not just local) political and economic elite emerged with the creation of ministries and other public bodies and the election of representatives to the legislative council. The elites associated with these institutions had interests in trade and investment policies and relations with Israel.[53]

Arafat, as Hans-Joachim Rabe points out in this volume, was able to dominate elite structures thanks to the agreements with Israel and financial aid from abroad. By the fall of 2000, the failure of Arafat and his team to bring about a withdrawal of the Israeli army from at least most of the occupied territories encouraged a young guard of newly emerging local leaders and leaders of the first intifada to launch the al-Aqsa intifada. This second uprising was not only an attempt at ending the Israeli occupation, it also aimed to "weaken and eventually displace" the Palestinian old guard, the historic leadership around Arafat.[54]

Since George W. Bush became president of the United States, and particularly since the events of 11 September 2001, the question of forced regime change or elite change from abroad has become a major topic in regard to Palestine and, of course, in regard to Iraq. In the Palestinian case, major external forces agreed to press for reforms that implicitly or explicitly included the demand for the prime decisionmaker, Yasser Arafat, to leave the scene or agree to being relegated to a position of much less importance. Parts of the emerging Palestinian elite obviously desire a change at the top, but they have no interest in becoming or being perceived as an instrument of a U.S. or an Israeli agenda. Repeated Israeli sieges of Arafat's headquarters have served to strengthen his legitimacy and abort attempts to initiate reforms from within Palestinian institutions. The U.S. mission to Iraq has not only removed Saddam Hussein and his clique from power. The ensuing "de-Baathization" was in fact an attempt to enforce a wide-ranging exchange of the political elite. By the time this book was finalized, a post-war PRE was emerging in still undecided struggles for power and positions, and for the soul of Iraq.

Leaders and commentators in other Arab countries began to ask which country's leadership would "be next on the list," after the Bush administration succeeded in replacing the regime in Baghdad. Maybe they need not fear too much. Among other things, the Palestinian and Iraqi cases demonstrate the limits of direct external pressure. Policy shifts are often externally induced, which may speed or otherwise affect elite change. Short of an inappropriate degree of force or outright war, however, such pressure will likely not succeed in bringing about a change in the political leadership of any country in the region. Western policymakers should realize that even a forced removal of local elites would not necessarily yield more open or more efficient political and economic systems.

Modernity First:
The New Elites and Their Domestic Agendas

Decisions concerning economic reform that are in one way or other induced by external factors can indeed have wide-ranging effects on elite settings. Even half-hearted starts in that direction can lead to significant changes among top political personnel. In Egypt's case, the reform efforts of the early 2000s brought a new prime minister to power who symbolized that new departure: someone with a managerial background rather than a loyal party functionary. Within the last decade or so, the governments of Algeria, Egypt, Jordan, Morocco, Saudi Arabia, Syria, and Tunisia have all placed emphasis on securing the skills and knowledge of technocrats with economic expertise or have at least tried to incorporate businesspeople and private sector representatives into formal decisionmaking or consultative structures. In most Arab countries, however, business elites have gained influence mainly or only in the realm of economic policy decisionmaking. With the notable exceptions of Lebanese prime minister Rafiq al-Hariri and Moroccan prime minister Driss Jettou, few businesspeople have acquired leading government positions. If and when economic liberalization proceeds, Arab governments will need the expertise of increasing numbers of people qualified in business management, banking, and international trade law.

New business elites have benefited from changing economic policies or have been able to take advantage of such opportunities as, for example, the sanctions against Iraq, the emergence of new technologies, particularly in the information sector, or the space that has gradually been opened for private institutes of higher education in most of the countries studied here. Thus far, business elites have not asked for any real share in political power nor have they been encouraged to do so. The Arab regimes have allowed these groups wealth and a certain economic power, but they have also seen to it that they remain in the outer circles of political relevance.

Overall, the emerging leadership generation in the Arab world is clearly more business friendly than the outgoing generation. Not all of this generation will make the emergence and success of private business as much a priority as Jordan's young king and his team apparently seek to do, but on the other hand few of them share the enthusiasm for etatism and public sector dominance that the outgoing elites possess. In a sense, the pressures of globalization and the orientations of the newcomers reinforce each other. At the same time, a larger presence of business-oriented technocrats within the PRE may increase the confidence of local, expatriate, and foreign investors and thus propel them forward through initially slow and gradual moves toward economic liberalization.

The emerging elites' historical backgrounds and the era in which they were socialized make many of them less apprehensive of political pluralism than the dominant elites of the last thirty years have been. To many of them, single-party states and streamlined media are somewhat outmoded. The denial of competing groups' interests can no longer be pursued once economic liberalization and privatization become issues of public debate. Expectations about the depth of reforms and the structural political changes associated with the emergence of new regime elites should, however, remain guarded. Bahrain, on which there is no chapter in this book, may serve as an example of a new ruler's attempt to renegotiate a political pact with the people. The cases of Jordan, Morocco, and Syria, however, demonstrate that generational change at the top will not automatically lead to far-reaching political reform. Also, as the Tunisian case, among others, underlines, modern discourses and the willingness of a Western-oriented regime elite to embrace technical modernization and economic opening need not be accompanied by political liberalization.

Some of the young leaders have reminded Western audiences and domestic critics that they are not willing to "apply the democracy of others upon ourselves," as Syria's Bashar al-Asad put it. "We have to have our [own] democratic experience," he continued, "which is special to us, which stems from our history, culture, civilization and which is a response to the needs of our society and the requirements of our reality."[55] Morocco's young king Mohammed had a similar message for those who expected him to rapidly democratize his country. "My rhythm is the one of Morocco. . . . It is not necessarily the same rhythm certain observers, with arrogance and ignorance, wish to impose upon us."[56]

Most of the new leadership elites are likely to use the authoritarian instruments of the states they inherit or take over in order to firmly establish themselves. Their priority is clearly economic reform and technical modernization. Jordan, Morocco, and Syria, with largely new PRE, and Algeria with its "nationalist reformers," are indicative in this respect. At least in the first and second circles, their discourses with regard to democracy or political reform are similar. Some argue that democracy, or democratization, cannot be a priority as long as they must fend off resistance— from bureaucracies or from interest groups—to any reform they seek to implement. Others make use of classical modernization theory propositions concerning what degree of prosperity or literacy must be achieved before one actually could, or should, speak of democratization.[57] Still others argue that their respective societies are simply not ripe for democracy: Wouldn't the Islamists be the winners under the circumstances?

Given these outlooks, when new elite teams take charge in other countries of the region, rapid democratic transformations should not be expected. More probable is a gradual and cautious process of pluralization. This would likely include more liberal and open debates, fewer restrictions on the media and the use of information systems, a greater variance of political views and agendas within legislatures and assemblies, and more elections involving representative bodies. Pluralization would stop, however, at elections for the highest decisionmaking positions or measures with the potential of bringing about a change of regime or a substantial recomposition of the PRE through the ballot box.

In most Arab countries, regime elites have shown a remarkable ability to control the pace and scope of political change. Steps toward economic and political reform have been taken from above, basically system maintenance operations, rather than by societal forces applying pressure on the regime.[58] Little seems to have changed in this respect with changes at the top in some countries. The relatively wide-ranging reforms introduced to the political system in Bahrain have been as much a regime affair—or, more concretely, a process designed by the new amir and the crown prince—as have the more gradualist paths embarked on by Bashar al-Asad in Syria or Mohammed VI in Morocco.[59]

Given that change within the Arab PRE continues to be fostered mainly through recruitment and co-optation from above, rather than through elections, it is not surprising that many second-circle PRE see things largely the same as their countries' prime decisionmakers and core elites see them. Zerhouni, observing Morocco's "neo-makhzanian" officials, notes that many of them have little to say about political reform. In Algeria, to give another example, only "radical democrats" and "Islamist reformers"—according to Werenfels's characterization—put political reform high on their agenda; none of them has made it into the first circle of influence. In a number of countries, explicit prodemocracy activists have had no chance thus far to enter even the third circle.

As a matter of fact, democracy is not high on the agenda of any group of actors that otherwise are forces pushing for change. Businesspeople in most Arab countries have become vocal in demanding economic reform and liberalization. As mentioned, however, they have in most cases abstained from openly calling for political liberalization, let alone democratization. A study of Egyptian businessmen found that they have been "either unconcerned with, or not particularly averse to, the kind of moderate political authoritarianism" that the regime of Husni Mubarak represents.[60] Similar judgments have been elicited from Palestinian and North African business elites.[61]

Even the new generation of businesspeople in the Arab world does not seem to count democracy among their primary interests. A small survey conducted in 2001 at a regional meeting of young entrepreneurs and managers from eight Arab countries clearly revealed the political priorities of this stratum: economic liberalization first, followed by reform of the training and education systems of their countries. Democracy and political liberalization would be appreciated, but they only came in third or even fourth place among participants from countries neighboring Israel, where higher priority was given to the Arab-Israeli conflict.[62] In some countries, individual representatives of the business class who have a more far-reaching agenda have been warned to keep their political ambitions within limits. The arrest and subsequent trial in the summer of 2001 of two Syrian deputies, both with business backgrounds, was a case in point. Both had clearly transgressed the mandate that they, according to the view of the regime leadership, were supposed to fulfill as deputies and representatives of the entrepreneurial stratum.

Most of the countries examined here have societal forces that have been calling or campaigning for such political reforms as more transparency, respect for human rights, and a transformation to democracy. With few exceptions (the Palestinian territories being one) such voices are either to be found within the third circle of the PRE or outside it entirely. Foreign observers who (legitimately) pay much attention to those who seek more substantive changes than the incumbent elites do should be cautious not to overrate the influence of these groups and individuals.

It is striking, in a sense, that neither the clamp-downs on prodemocracy or human rights activists in Egypt, Syria, Tunisia, and other states nor the repeated postponement of elections in Jordan have led to protests of any consequence or threat to the regimes in power. Certainly, none of them led to popular reactions as strong as those triggered in most of these countries by the continued Israeli occupation and policies in the Palestinian territories. Algeria and Lebanon digress from this picture somewhat. Both are countries with highly differentiated, partly fragmented political elites; in both cases, there is no single, patrimonial leader; and radical prodemocracy movements have been able to influence strategic discourses and thereby contribute to national agenda setting to an extent. The overall state of affairs in the Arab countries may be partly explained by repression, but one must not overlook the fact that the constituency for substantial political reform within and around the PRE is still quite limited.

There is as yet also little external pressure on Arab states to embark on thoroughgoing political reforms. While the "elites appear to be modern but not democratic," writes Lisa Anderson, "the masses are angry." There is no guarantee that democratizing Arab countries would remain friendly. Rather, democratization processes could unleash new nationalisms, ethnic conflicts, or anti-American and anti-Western political ideologies.[63] Most probably, therefore, the United States as well as the European Union will be content if new, friendly Arab regimes and regime elites do exactly what they have placed at the top of their agenda—modernize their economies and their administrations while refraining from risking domestic and regime stability and well-established international relations by putting themselves and the systems as such to a sudden democratic test of popularity. In fact, many governments, while often deploring the lack of democracy in Arab countries, have appreciated the continuity inspired by authoritarianism in the Arab world.[64] This appreciation of what one might call a "lid-on stability" may actually contribute to the ills that the same Western governments are deploring in the Arab world and the Middle East: the lack of accountability and good governance; the lack of regional cooperation; and, of course, the anger of much of the young generation.

This book, in the chapters that follow, presents case studies of nine Arab countries.[65] Following the comparative approach that was outlined above, the authors identify the respective politically relevant elite, scan changes within the structure and composition of that elite, examine the elite's agenda, and analyze the interrelation between elite change, policies, and, where applicable, external influences. The first three chapters deal with Arab states where changes at the top have recently taken place, and relatively young leaderships are now in power. Bank and Schlumberger in their article on Jordan demonstrate how the renewal of the PRE has supported a new ruler's changing policy priorities: Jordan has become more business oriented, and new, hand-picked elite members represent the king's technocratic and business-minded orientation. Zerhouni shows that the succession from Hassan II to Mohammed VI has not led to broader power sharing. The new leadership has been able to adapt to new discourses on, among other things, democracy and human rights, but neither the mode of recruitment into the PRE nor the attitudes of most of the first-circle PRE have undergone significant change. In the Syrian case, the renewal of the wider political elite, which the new president and his team have brought about, seems to have been of major importance for the gradual strengthening of the power of an heir. The fact that the reproduction of Syria's elite was largely conducted from the center, however, may well account for the limits of political change.

The two chapters that follow deal with countries where a succession at the top will occur in a not too distant future and where the succession question occupies much of the interest of the domestic public and international partners. In his contribution on Egypt, Abdelnasser makes a case to revise the prevalent picture of a stagnant elite that does not allow for change. He also shows that the outcome of the succession process will largely depend on the regional situation, not the least of which is the state of the Arab-Israeli conflict and peace process. Analyzing the case of Saudi Arabia, Glosemeyer also rejects the image of stagnancy, demonstrating that the combination of actors that form the PRE is up for changes and that no segment of the incumbent or emerging elite is able to escape the impact of globalization.

Algeria and Tunisia provide two cases of countries where elite change, economic transformation, and political systems continuity seem to reinforce each other. Werenfels, in her contribution on Algeria, demonstrates the attempt of the incumbent PRE to extend the revolutionary legitimacy it claims to its offspring. She also argues that a substantial increase in the number of relevant political players has actually fragmented the elite, made alliances of new elite segments improbable and, hence, political change less likely. In the Tunisian case, as Erdle makes clear, the authoritarian system is relying on, and has quite successfully co-opted, social actors who usually would be seen as agents of change, namely the educated middle classes, reform-minded technocrats, and young business elites. Thus, by presenting itself as a facilitator of development and modernization, and as a protector against both globalization and Islamism, the regime elite has been able to reassert its control over society.

The last two case studies deal with elite change under foreign domination. Husseini, dealing with Lebanon, demonstrates how a new, partly recycled political elite has consolidated itself since the end of the civil war, and how it has managed, so far, to block the way for emerging elite aspirants. To the observer, elite politics in today's Lebanon seem very much like a replay of patterns that marked the development of that country after independence and before the first breakdown of the system in 1958. The main difference seems to be Syria's dominance, and the emergence of an elite segment that owes its political capital solely to its ties with the Syrian leadership. Rabe, in his chapter on Palestine, shows how a national elite has tried to informally expand the limited field of action opened to it with the Oslo Accords and the establishment of the Palestinian Authority. He also demonstrates how the breakdown of the peace process has contributed to multipolarization of the elite, and how Arafat's attempt to establish and maintain a centralized system has largely failed.

The book closes with a short conclusion that highlights some of the comparative evidence from the country studies, particularly the remarkable correspondence in most of these cases of elite change and reproduction on the one hand, and systems maintenance on the other.

Notes

1. Tripp, "States, Elites and the 'Management of Change.'"
2. Lasswell, *Politics,* p. 13.
3. See, among others, O'Donnell, Schmitter, and Whitehead, *Transitions from Authoritarian Rule;* Przeworski, *Democracy and the Market;* Bos, "Die Rolle

von Eliten"; Gill, *Dynamics of Democratization;* McFaul, "The Fourth Wave of Democracy and Dictatorship."

4. See Higley and Burton, "The Elite Variable in Democratic Transitions"; Higley and Moore, "Political Elite Studies at the Year 2000"; Peeler, "Elites, Structures, and Political Action."

5. See, for example, Etzioni-Halevy, "Elites and the Working Class"; Peeler, "Elites, Structures, and Political Action," p. 242.

6. Fields, Higley, and Burton, "A New Elite Framework"; Burton and Higley, "The Study of Political Elite Transformations"; Higley and Lengyel, "Elite Configuration After State Socialism."

7. See, among others, Adam and Tomšič, "Elite (Re)configuration"; Higley and Lengyel, "Elite Configuration After State Socialism." Both titles deal with Russia, Eastern Europe, and the Balkans. On political transition processes and the elites in the former Soviet republics of Central Asia and the Caucasus, see Tismaneanu, *Political Culture and Civil Society.*

8. Higley and Moore, "Political Elite Studies at the Year 2000," p. 176.

9. See, among others, Lenczowski, *Political Elites in the Middle East;* Tachau, *Political Elites and Political Development in the Middle East;* Heradstveit, *Arab and Israeli Elite Perceptions;* Zartman, *Political Elites in Arab North Africa.*

10. Halpern, *The Politics of Social Change;* Hurewitz, *Middle East Politics.*

11. See Bahout, *Les entrepreneurs syriens;* Blin, "Les entrepreneurs palestiniens"; Gotowicki, "The Military in Egyptian Society"; Longuenesse, "Ingenieurs et médecins dans le changement social"; Perthes, "Bourgeoisie and the Ba'th"; Picard, "Arab Military in Politics"; Springborg, "The Arab Bourgeoisie"; Zaki, *Egyptian Business Elites.*

12. See, among others, Drysdale, "The Succession Question in Syria"; Henderson, *After King Fahd;* Legrain, "Les 1001 successions de Yasser Arafat"; Peterson, "Succession in the States of the Gulf Cooperation Council"; Abdul Aziz and Youssef Hussein, "The President, the Son, and the Military."

13. See Faath, *Konfliktpotential politischer Nachfolge;* Cantori, "Political Succession in the Middle East."

14. See, for example, Taheri, "Les átouts d'Abdallah"; Willis, "After Hassan"; Ghadbian, "The New Asad"; Khalaf, "The New Amir of Bahrain."

15. This, of course, is also largely a reflection of the authoritarian nature of the regimes, or the dominant political culture, in the entire political scene. As a rule, when conflicts have erupted within these parties and organizations, the groups have split rather than change leaderships.

16. See Waterbury, "Whence Will Come Egypt's Future Leadership?"

17. Bottomore, *Elites and Society,* p. 7.

18. Higley and Moore, "Political Elite Studies at the Year 2000," p. 176.

19. See Obeidi, "Elitenstruktur in Libyen."

20. Peeler, "Elites, Structures, and Political Action," p. 242.

21. Ibid.

22. This is not the first and will not be the last time this model is used for such purposes. For an earlier (1975) use, see Bill, "The Patterns of Elite Politics in Iran."

23. Burton and Higley, "The Study of Political Elite Transformations," p. 182.

24. On the scope, width, and depth of elite change, see Higley and Lengyel, "Elite Configuration After State Socialism."

25. On Egypt, see Kienle, *A Grand Delusion;* on Syria, see Perthes, *The Political Economy of Syria.*

26. See Hilal, *Takuin al-nukhba al-filastiniyya.*

27. See Isabelle Werenfels's chapter on Algeria in this volume.

28. See Hans-Joachim Rabe's chapter on Palestine in this volume.

29. See in general Moyser and Wagstaffe, *Research Methods for Elite Studies.*

30. See Saloua Zerhouni's chapter on Morocco and Iris Glosemeyer's chapter on Saudi Arabia in this volume. On the changing function of parliaments in the Arab world, see Baaklini, Denoeux, and Springborg, *Legislative Politics in the Arab World.*

31. See André Bank and Oliver Schlumberger's chapter on Jordan and Volker Perthes's chapter on Syria in this volume.

32. See Saloua Zerhouni's chapter on Morocco in this volume.

33. Asbach, "Von der Geschichte politischer Ideen."

34. Halpern, *The Politics of Social Change,* p. 52.

35. See Isabelle Werenfels's chapter on Algeria in this volume.

36. Ibid.

37. See, among others, Batatu, "The Egyptian, Syrian and Iraqi Revolutions."

38. See Soltan, "The Military and Foreign Policy."

39. See, among others, Perthes, "Bourgeoisie and the Ba'th"; Waterbury, "Twilight of the State Bourgeoisie?"

40. Weber, "Politics as a Vocation."

41. It is noteworthy that the number of foreign (European, Euro-Arab, U.S.) private universities in the Arab world has substantially increased since the mid-1990s. Traditionally, there have been the American University in Cairo and the American University of Beirut. Additional "American universities" of various origins and quality are to be found in Dubai, Jordan, Lebanon, and at least two places in the United Arab Emirates. In Syria, a Euro-Arab private university is about to be established.

42. In a report on the Middle East Institute's 1999 annual conference, "Leadership for a New Century," Elizabeth Fernea was quoted as stating, "Future leaders will be those who focus on poverty, unemployment, corruption, and health care, and will be drawn from both sexes since the perception of women's place in society has changed." *Middle East Institute Newsletter,* November 1999.

43. According to Mannheim, there is indeed an analogy between the phenomena of class and generation. Belonging to the same class or to the same "generation unit" means sharing a common location in social and historical processes, and it limits the members of that group "to a specific range of political experience." Mannheim, "The Problem of Generation," p. 291.

44. See Isabelle Werenfels's chapter on Algeria in this volume.

45. See Gamal Abdelnasser's chapter on Egypt in this volume.

46. Aburish, *Saddam Hussein,* p. 139.

47. Khafaji, "War as a Vehicle."

48. See Hans-Joachim Rabe's chapter on Palestine in this volume; see also Shikaki, "Palestinians Divided."

49. The still debated democratic peace theorem holds that democracies do not fight each other, not that they are per se more peaceful than others. See Brown, Lynn-Jones, and Miller, *Debating the Democratic Peace.*

50. For a more detailed argument, see Perthes, *Vom Krieg zur Konkurrenz.*

51. Ehud Barak, after being voted out of office, became an early proponent of this after-Arafat view. See his editorial, "It Seems Israel Has to Wait for a New Palestinian Leadership," *International Herald Tribune,* 31 July 2001.

52. The accession of Hamad bin Khalifa in Qatar is a case in point. First, Hamad accelerated the constitutional process of succession by overthrowing his

father—an act certainly not appreciated by the aging rulers of other Gulf monarchies. Second, along with Hamad came a new ruling elite that nurtured ambitious foreign policy and media projects, such as simultaneously cultivating good relations with Iraq and Israel, and establishing an uncensored satellite news channel that aggressively covered other Gulf countries. Hamad and his new team also made it clear that they would not be patronized by Saudi Arabia. In the judgment of many of their neighbors, they tried to grab more regional and international weight than Qatar deserved. Their actions upset the ruling elites of the other states of the Gulf Cooperation Council, with relations bottoming when Qatar accused Saudi Arabia and the United Arab Emirates of having lent support to a counter coup attempt by Hamad's deposed father. The accusation, it seems, was not totally baseless.

53. See Hilal, *Takuin al-nukhba al-filastiniyya*, pp. 59–63.

54. See Shikaki, "Palestinians Divided."

55. Inaugural speech, as quoted in *Syria Times,* 18 July 2000.

56. Interview, *Le Figaro,* 4 September 2001.

57. See Saloua Zerhouni's chapter on Morocco, André Bank and Oliver Schlumberger's chapter on Jordan, and Volker Perthes's chapter on Syria in this volume.

58. See, among others, Krämer, "Liberalization and Democracy in the Arab World"; Perthes, "The Private Sector, Economic Liberalization and the Prospects of Democratization"; al-Najjar, "Waqi' wa-mustaqbal al-awda' al-siyasiyya."

59. See Khalaf, "The New Amir of Bahrain."

60. Zaki, *Egyptian Business Elites,* p. 226. The picture does not seem to differ much for the businesspeople of other Arab countries.

61. See Hilal, *Takuin al-nukhba al-filastiniyya;* Dillman, "Facing the Market in North Africa."

62. See Perthes and Spapperi, "The Young Entrepreneurs of the Arab World."

63. Anderson, "Friendly Arab Democracy: Dismal Prospects," *World Policy Journal* 18, no. 3 (Fall 2001) (Internet edition).

64. See also Dunn, "The Coming Era of Leadership Change."

65. This is not a "handbook" on the Arab world or its leadership personnel, and it was therefore never supposed to give a comprehensive picture of all Arab countries. Comparative evidence can be drawn even from a limited sample. Regrettably, however, there is no article on Iraq, which doubtless forms an important case: Fieldwork in Iraq on such a highly political issue as the elite was seen as too difficult, or even dangerous; and we did not want to depart from our common approach—studies based on extensive fieldwork, that is—and make do with a contribution that would solely rely on secondary sources.

Part 1

New Rulers in Power

2

Jordan:
Between Regime Survival and Economic Reform
André Bank and Oliver Schlumberger

Jordan stands in line with the other Arab countries of Bahrain, Morocco, and Syria in having experienced changes in its head of state in the late 1990s.[1] It was in February 1999 that Prince Abdallah bin Hussein bin Talal acceded to the Hashemite throne. King Hussein, only days before his death, had designated Abdallah as his successor, thereby dispelling any aspirations that long-standing crown prince Hassan bin Talal, Hussein's brother, might have had. Although it would be an exaggeration to speak of intradynastic rivalries, the nomination of a young and politically inexperienced successor—in comparison to the new leaders of the above-mentioned countries— did come as a surprise. Abdallah II's accession ushered in new dynamics in elite recruitment patterns and in the composition of the politically relevant elite.

In Jordan, elite change in the first and second circles of influence is managed exclusively by the king, whereas the composition of contesting elite segments in the third circle depends on prevailing public opinion.[2] The relative weight of different elite segments in the first and second circles depends on the importance of strategic issue areas as perceived by the leader: The recent inclusion of economic specialists through newly institutionalized channels is remarkable, but the influence of older and more security-oriented segments continues, increasing as the regional political climate, as reflected in strengthened domestic opposition, becomes more tense.

Politically Relevant Elites in Jordan:
Context and Framework

Jordan is a polity in which the king, the ultimate source of power and legitimacy, acts as the arbiter of last resort in instances of competing social interests, as is typical of political systems dominated by neopatrimonial types of sociopolitical relationships.[3] As such, Jordan fits within the larger structure of neopatrimonial polities that shaped Arab politics in the last several decades of the twentieth century. Given the clientelist networks and patronage systems typical of neopatrimonialism, it is imperative to look at the role of such regimes' political leaders and the policies they pursue. This is even more relevant when the leadership in such a context changes.

Despite their power, neopatrimonial leaders need loyalists in order to maintain their uncontested and privileged position "above" society. Thus, looking at leaders alone is insufficient in attempting to understand the political processes in such systems. Rather, as Charles Tripp notes, "the significance of this phenomenon" can be seen to lie in the fact that neopatrimonialism also is "a preeminent instrument of elite maintenance."[4] In order to better grasp the more complex structures of political rule in Jordan, it is this aspect of the interplay of neopatrimonial political structures, on the one hand, and the dynamics of elite change in a situation of leadership change, on the other, that is the focus here. On a more abstract level, there are two ways of looking at patterns of political rule and its exercise: While a focus on neopatrimonialism as a regionwide phenomenon implies a more structure-oriented viewpoint, the focus on political elites as selected and recruited by a political leader, obviously, is at the heart of a more actor-centered perspective. The choice here is to approach the question of elite change after succession within the framework of the neopatrimonial Jordanian monarchy, but within this framework to also take a close look at the changes and continuities within the PRE. Thus the focus is on political actors, acknowledging the importance of human agency, but analyzing them as acting within an overarching neopatrimonial political system. In essence it is an examination of human behavior within structures that work as constraints on the range of options from which actors can choose.

In this chapter, we will examine three key aspects of Jordan's PRE within the context of changing leadership. First, where dynamics are susceptible to shifting and change seems imminent, it is conceivable that opposition groups might be attracted to the idea of challenging long-established political elites. Second, it has to be clarified if (and to what extent) those who implement policies are still able to do so effectively after a change at the top of a regime that might result in changes in policy priorities. Third, under conditions of leadership change some crucial aspects of elite dynamics might in fact be the most interesting because they concern the upper echelons of powerful decisionmaking circles: Do key players remain in charge of their previous responsibilities or are they replaced? How is the balance between various elite factions maintained in order to avoid political instability in the face of leadership change? What happens to policy priorities: Is continuity a strategy to keep the said balance stable, or do external or internal developments require adjustments within the hierarchy of issue areas? In the latter case, one would expect certain members of the core elite to gain more influence than others, who, by contrast, would lose some of their former standing according to political necessities as perceived by the new leader. In Jordan after 1999, the situation was somewhat extraordinary in the sense that a new king faced the problem of not having been well established as the uncontested *primus supra non-pares* (first above non-equals) within the complex fabric of national elites. Abdallah, therefore, had to create new loyalties and allegiances, instead of simply sustaining old and accepted ones. Intraelite struggles for political influence and power would seem likely to emerge in such a context, thus requiring a strong leader to maintain stability.

Elites and Institutions

As in any authoritarian polity, repression or the threat thereof has been a vital instrument in the hands of political leaders in Jordan since its inception. Thus, the upper ranks of the military, the various divisions of the security services (*mukhabarat*), and the police forces inevitably form an important part of the PRE. These are the backbone of the dynasty when legitimation strategies fail. Given the sensitivity of their areas, insight into this part of the political elite is extremely difficult to obtain.[5] Despite its authoritarian character, however, Jordan's political system has at the same time been one of the most open and liberal when compared with those of other Arab countries. Relying on blunt repression for maintaining stability would therefore be politically problematic and possibly delegitimizing for the new king.

Jordan's bicameral parliament—with a directly elected lower house (Chamber of Deputies) of 104 representatives[6] and a royally appointed 40-member upper house (Senate)—has traditionally played a role in the recruitment and positioning of the people upon whom Hashemite monarchs have relied.[7] Under King Hussein, the Senate in particular was a pool of potential advisors and officeholders upon whose loyalty the monarch was able to count and who, in fact, were often rotated in and out of government office, to and from the Senate. Likewise, the Speaker of the Chamber of Deputies was a figure close to real power with a reliable link between the court and the legislature. Thus, unlike in a democratic environment, the Speaker has tended to speak not only on behalf of the parliament, but also to communicate to parliament the interests of the court, essentially performing functions of mediation on the one hand and control on the other. The lower house has been less politically relevant.

Although multipartyism formally exists, political parties as formal bodies do not possess much influence.[8] They have primarily served their leaders as vehicles for individual rent seeking, with very limited active memberships and not much to offer in terms of political programs. Jordan's political parties, thus, have functions profoundly different from those of parties in democracies. The same applies to the legislature as an institution: Although the parliament debates and endorses legislation, can question individual ministers, and criticizes government decisions on certain issues, the scope for opposing or vetoing royal decisions and royally approved policies is limited at best. This pertains especially to issues sensitive to regime maintenance and the reign of the Hashemite dynasty, including questions regarding internal and external security, such as the conclusion in 1994 of a peace treaty with Israel, regional policies, and restrictions on civil and political liberties on the domestic front.

Likewise, interest groups, such as business organizations and professional associations, do not per se play a large role in politics, and their members cannot be said to belong automatically to the PRE. This does not exclude the possibility of individual members of such groups being involved in the political arena and even entering decisionmaking circles, thus becoming members of the PRE. Yet, in such cases, it is personal affiliation, rather than institutional factors, that result in a representative of an interest group gaining influence and power. As a rule, the strength and closeness of his or her personal ties to members of the core elite or to the king himself determine the degree of influence a given individual can expect to wield politically. Thus, it is difficult to ascribe a certain influence or power to any institution as such. Rather, it is the individual personality, his or her social offspring—family status in society, contact to key decisionmakers, and so on, plus geographical background (East Bank versus West Bank)—that are key to understanding who wields what degree of influence in which circles of the PRE. This finding reaffirms a long-known fact: In neopatrimonial polities, any purely positional approach to the study of elites is unlikely to bear out real power structures, because the latter are more often than not determined by extrainstitutional alliances and affinities, *wasta* (informal personal relations for mutual benefit),[9] and clientelist ties.[10]

Recruitment Patterns: Old and New

In neopatrimonial settings, a change at the helm is likely to have an impact on the composition of and the recruitment patterns for the PRE. Various studies validate this general hypothesis.[11] The "old" recruitment pattern in

Jordan was one of reshuffling incumbent political elites. Parallel to this, a "new" recruitment mechanism has been developed, involving the creation of a formal institution staffed by informal means—a phenomenon we call formalized informality. In this context, under King Abdallah the Economic Consultative Council (ECC) has become the primary new channel for entering the PRE. The new mechanism has not, however, been used to the exclusion of the old one. Rather, there are links between reshuffling and formalizing informality.

Reshuffling of Incumbent Elites

As is the case in every succession, King Abdallah's primary goals at the start of his reign were to stabilize his position and to extend as far as possible his political room to maneuver in order to pursue his own policy priorities. To no one's surprise, Abdallah attempted to achieve this through a strategy of guaranteeing continuity in certain areas and initiating changes in others. Continuity is evidenced in Abdallah's continuous and permanent rotation of members of the PRE into different political positions.[12] In this regard, Abdallah, like his father, seems to rely on a reservoir of loyal politicians who held various official posts at different times during Hussein's reign. Former prime minister Zaid al-Rifa'i, the son of four-time prime minister Samir al-Rifa'i, is a case in point.

Zaid al-Rifa'i was a close friend of King Hussein, and he retains strong links to the royal family. Despite rumors that he had been involved in various corrupt activities, he maintains a high degree of influence as Speaker of the Senate and the "grand old man" of Jordanian politics. Rifa'i and several other loyal politicians exemplify part of a select pool of people who have circulated, usually for long periods of time (in this case, for about four decades), through the different circles of the PRE. This strategy of reshuffling prevents individual elite members from building patronage networks strong enough to become autonomous and operate beyond the king's grasp. Such alternative power bases would be a threat to the king's claim of uncontested rule. Two examples from the early period of Abdallah's reign serve to illustrate this phenomenon.

Samih Battikhi, head of the General Intelligence Department (GID), enjoyed an elevated standing within the PRE. As a royal advisor, he became powerful enough to publicly oppose the prime minister, leading some commentators to nickname Jordan "Battikhistan."[13] At this point, royal tolerance came to an end. In November 2000, after weeks of heated debate behind the scenes, Battikhi was replaced by Major General Sa'd Khair, the second in command of the GID and who was considered rather apolitical. Battikhi's fall was part of a wider reshuffling within the security apparatus during this period.

Battikhi's dismissal was somewhat related to an affair involving Mustafa Hamarnah, director of the Center of Strategic Studies (CSS) at the University of Jordan in Amman. Hamarnah is a well-known personality who had turned the CSS into one of the most successful fundraising non-governmental organizations (NGOs) in the country. In July 1999 Hamarnah resigned his post, reportedly after Battikhi exerted pressure; the president of the university was then ordered to close the CSS. It was speculated in the local media that the CSS had angered Battikhi by publishing an opinion poll showing a dramatic decrease in the popularity of former prime minister Abd al-Ra'uf Rawabdah, a conservative tribal figure whom Battikhi had wanted to remain in that post. Hamarnah refused to go quietly; by summer 2000 he was publicly criticizing Battikhi, who at that time was at odds with the new prime minister, Ali Abu Raghib. After a discussion of the matter between Abdallah and Hamarnah, the CSS was reopened and its director reinstated. Shortly thereafter, Battikhi resigned and was appointed to the Senate. Hamarnah, in turn, was nominated to the board of a newly established committee for the privatization of the Jordanian media.[14] He thus entered the Jordanian PRE while keeping his position at the CSS. This allows him to continue claiming to be an NGO activist struggling for democratization, especially vis-à-vis foreign donor institutions,[15] while simultaneously acting as a royally appointed decisionmaker.[16]

Formalizing Informality

The pattern of elite circulation or reshuffling in Jordan should not be confused with structural change; rather, it should be analytically separated from it. In contrast to elite reshuffling, structural elite change is an exchange, at least a partial one, of structurally different elite segments. That is, segments with different backgrounds and political priorities enter the PRE or lose their standing within the elite. King Abdallah, through the institutionalization of a new channel into the PRE, has pursued a strategy of gradual elite change implemented from above; this was particularly evident in 1999 and 2000. In comparison to his father's approach, this institutionalization is a trait and new feature of Abdallah's rule.

In November 1999 Abdallah invited more than 150 leading representatives of the private and public sectors to the Dead Sea Retreat, a two-day seminar. In December he created the Economic Consultative Council as an advisory body for economic policy planning.[17] The ECC has twenty members, and the king presides over it. For an economy in which the state has been the main employer and most powerful economic agent for decades, it is remarkable that the ECC was in its initial composition dominated by fourteen representatives of the private sector. Who are these appointees? What are their educational and professional backgrounds and worldviews?

What do they consider to be Jordan's policy priorities, and what is of lesser relevance on their agenda?

Ghassan Nuqul is vice chairman of the Nuqul Group, a family business with twenty-seven companies and 5,000 employees (2,800 in Jordan) that dominates the paper and packaging market in the Middle East and North Africa.[18] Fadi Ghandour is the cofounder and CEO of Aramex, an international shipping company with several thousand employees worldwide. Karim Ka'war entered the ECC as president of the Ideal Group of companies and headed int@j, the Jordanian information technology association.[19] The only woman in the ECC is Suhayr al-Ali Dabbas, who was born in Damascus but hails from a Salti family and serves as the general manager of Citibank in Jordan. Fawaz Zu'bi was born in 1956 and is from the northern city of Ramtha. He founded and still owns the Adritec Group, which deals in irrigation equipment. When he joined the ECC, Zu'bi was also president of the newly founded Young Entrepreneurs Association (YEA).[20] Salah al-Din al-Bashir, in his mid-thirties, worked as a legal advisor on international affairs in Amman. He holds a doctorate in civil law from McGill University in Montreal and a master's degree from Harvard Law School. Last but not least, Bassem Awadallah is not an entrepreneur, but he belongs to this group because he studied business administration and is a former head of the economic unit at the royal court. During his tenure as rapporteur of the ECC, he personalized the link between the ECC and the court and was arguably the most powerful representative of this new economic guard.

It is striking that these new PRE members are all between the ages of thirty-five and forty-five and thus belong to the same generation as King Abdallah (who was born in 1962).[21] Another similarity is their educational background. Almost all hold a degree in business or economics from universities abroad, primarily the United States or Great Britain, and speak English fluently. Yet another common element is that they are successful businesspeople oriented toward international markets. They are active in various fields, including information technologies, banking and finance, and industry. In contrast to a large part of the older elite under King Hussein, this "Generation Abdallah" has been socialized during the economic crisis that began in the late 1980s and by the Arab-Israeli peace process (and its subsequent failure). They represent Jordanian economic "success stories," symbolizing young, self-confident "winners" in globalization and have internalized the currently fashionable neoliberal jargon. Their agenda is thus primarily economic—the far-reaching economic and technological transformation of Jordan and its integration into the globalized world economy. They therefore desire the abolition of trade barriers, privatization of state-owned enterprises (SOEs), and increased investments in the education sector as well as in information technologies.[22]

In contrast to their economic policy priorities, the young ECC members lack any concrete ideas on political participation. Democracy and human rights are seen, at best, as secondary issues that might get on the agenda in some distant future, after successful economic reforms. This indifference regarding genuine political reform, however, is sometimes veiled by a strategic rhetoric of reform. Thereby, they attempt to meet the conditionalities of international donors, on whom Jordan's economy is still largely dependent. Questions of regional and foreign policy, such as Jordan's role in the Israeli-Palestinian conflict or the Iraqi situation, are predominantly viewed from an economic perspective: An Israeli-Palestinian peace treaty as well as an end to UN sanctions against Iraq would increase Jordanian opportunities in intraregional trade.[23]

At first glance, it is not surprising that an institution like the ECC, with an explicitly economic task, is dominated by persons with strong economic backgrounds. This certainly reflects King Abdallah's "prioritization of the economy."[24] Yet, the ECC's mandate is not restricted to economic affairs. It extends into such areas as education, water management, administrative and institutional reforms, legislation, and planning. In other words, what has begun in Jordan is a vast project of transformation for development, with the majority of the members of the most influential economic decisionmaking body having newly acceded to positions of direct political influence. This marks a significantly strengthened business focus among the political elite. Through the creation of the ECC as a "superbody," Abdallah has brought into the political elite a handpicked group of people of his own leanings. In addition to being loyal because they were appointed and are dependent on the king's directives, the members of this new guard are also seen as being better able to implement the king's policy priorities than are the older elites. At the same time, the formation of the ECC might be interpreted as a mechanism for overcoming resistance to reform from within the ranks of the conservative establishment, such as the central administration or the security apparatus.

There are, however, two aspects of elite recruitment consistent with King Hussein's earlier politics. First, the king alone determines, in an informal way, whom to grant influence, hence the composition of the ECC in a process that can be characterized as formalized informality. Second, the composition of the new guard reflects the continued privileged status of certain families in Jordan. Most members belong to families that are well known and have been politically influential in the Hashemite kingdom for decades. Through their connections and educational and professional backgrounds, these "children of powerful fathers" were able to attain positions that brought them to Abdallah's attention. The influence of traditional families is also apparent among those members of the ECC who are not representatives of the Generation Abdallah. They either belong to wealthy families of Palestinian descent, for example Sabih al-Masri, one of the richest businessmen in Jordan, or they are, like Kamal al-Sha'ir, part of the tribal conservative establishment.[25] So even in regard to the ECC, the newly designed instrument for elite change, there is evidence that Abdallah's choice of personnel takes into consideration traditional coalitions as well as overall social balance.

Linkages Between
Reshuffling and Formalizing Informality

The picture of recruitment mechanisms in Jordan under King Abdallah drawn so far has analytically separated reshufflings of incumbent elites from the new and rather specific formalized informality embodied in the ECC. These patterns can, however, interrelate: Muhammad Halayqa, for example, was appointed to the ECC in late 1999, while an undersecretary at the Trade and Industry Ministry. He headed Jordan's delegation during the fall 2000 negotiations for a free trade agreement with the United States. Just thirty years old at the time, he very much symbolized the new guard. A few months later, he climbed farther up the ladder to become Jordan's national economy minister in the government of Ali Abu Raghib, increasing his influence in the decisionmaking process, mostly in the field of economic reform. In a cabinet shuffle in August 2002, however, Halayqa lost his post (without an official reason provided) and was replaced by Samir Tawil, another newcomer.[26] Halayqa was not completely ousted, as he remains on the board of the Executive Privatization Commission Council.[27] Thus, although new members can enter the inner elite circles through the royally designed recruitment channel of the ECC, once there they are subject to the pattern of reshuffling. It appears that Abdallah's selected group of newcomers is not exempt from the dominant neopatrimonial features of elite manipulation and reshuffling. This hints at the persistence of systemic structures even when rulers and other core political personnel change.

Despite this general finding of system maintenance, the new recruitment channel via formalized informality has led to changes in relations between some institutions. Since there are no indications that the ECC might be abolished any time soon, it seems that Abdallah has added a new body to Jordan's institutional landscape. Creating the ECC while at the same time retaining all other political bodies brought about a shift in the relative influence of institutions and elite segments and contributed to an increasing complexity of the PRE. It appears that the role of the ECC as an advisory body has come at the expense of Senate members, on whom King Hussein had primarily relied. Abdallah's role as the ultimate arbiter between elite factions is still unchallenged, but mediation to keep his rule stable and flexible remains a difficult undertaking. One may conclude that

Abdallah successfully initiated elite change in the sense of bringing into the PRE a structurally different segment. After three years, however, the conventional neopatrimonial pattern of reshuffling appears to dominate the situation-specific strategy of formalizing informality.

The Composition of Jordan's Politically Relevant Elite

Based on the model of three concentric circles of influence, the first, or inner, circle of Jordan's PRE comprises core decisionmakers who can influence strategic issues of national relevance. These are, most of all, related to economic reforms and security of the state and, to a lesser degree, foreign policy. The second circle consists of those individuals who have an impact on decisionmaking in the field in which they specialize. Belonging to the third circle, by contrast, depends on various criteria. On the one hand, the third circle represents segments responsible for implementing decisions taken in the first and second circles. On the other hand, it includes opinionmakers, loyal to or opposed to regime policies, who are able to influence the political agenda on certain issues. Overall, this "power map"—to borrow a term coined by Robert Springborg[28]—can necessarily be no more than a heuristic attempt to portray the three circles of the Jordanian PRE in late 2002. Being a snapshot of a particular moment in time, the picture can neither claim validity as an exact representation of Jordan's elite constellations in the past nor in the future.

The First Circle

This empirical analysis of the PRE's composition is based on the assumption that Jordan's system of rule can be adequately understood as neopatrimonial. From this structural determinant follows the observation that the Hashemite king is the central agent, de jure and de facto, at the center of the core elite.[29] This means that all members of Jordan's PRE are dependent on Abdallah's will and his priorities. The king can potentially dismiss any individual elite member in the first two circles if necessary to maintain the character of the neopatrimonial authoritarian regime.

Closest to Abdallah presumably is Sa'd Khair, head of the General Intelligence Department who was appointed in late 2000. In contrast to his predecessor, Battikhi,[30] Khair is considered to be absolutely loyal to the Hashemite leader.[31] Further, his clientelist networks do not appear to be as tightly knit and strong as Battikhi's, who, at least in Abdallah's perception in 1999 and 2000, were able to threaten the king's position of dominance.[32] The other heads of the military, security, and police forces also belong to the first circle of the PRE, but it is difficult to determine their absolute and relative influence, as they represent those sectors within the PRE that are most sensitive to regime survival and stability.

It is clear that Prime Minister Ali Abu Raghib (since June 2000) belongs to the first circle. Raghib, a liberal businessman, was Abdallah's personal choice and pursues the king's policies. Former ECC member Bassem Awadallah was appointed planning minister in late 2001, and since that time has been the most outspoken proponent of the king's economic reform agenda. He, however, has only little influence on state security policies and so is to be located between the first and second circles. One can interpret the incorporation of the new guard as well as the dismissal of Battikhi as chief of the GID in 2000 as a sign of the growing strength of the reformists among the core decisionmakers. This tendency was counterbalanced, however, with the nomination of Fayez Tarawneh as chief of the royal court. Tarawneh belongs to a southern, Transjordanian tribe, thus representing those parts of society on which the Hashemites have traditionally relied as their primary power base.[33] He superseded the more liberal-minded Abd al-Karim Kabariti. These choices reflect Abdallah's efforts to strike a balance between the new, reform-oriented segments of the core elite and the conservative establishment.

Shifts in the power relations within the PRE, including within the first circle, are the result also of altered political realities. Demonstrations since September 2000 in response to the al-Aqsa intifada led the king to rely more on traditional elite segments than before. In this tense domestic atmosphere, Abdallah consulted the most experienced politicians about how to contain potential threats from within the country.[34] In this context, Zaid al-Rifa'i seems to have gained particularly in political weight. Thus, while the elite segments that make up the core elite remain relatively stable, their respective influence varies according to the political situation (see Figure 2.1).

The Second Circle

The second circle of the Jordanian PRE is characterized by a higher degree of permeability and fluctuation than the first circle. A number of newcomers have entered this part of the PRE who are able to influence strategic decisions in various fields related to the economy as well as questions of information technology (IT) and administrative reform. National Economy Minister Samir Tawil, Information and Communications Technology Minister Fawaz Zu'bi, and Trade and Industry Minister Salah al-Bashir are prominent examples. Bashir is married to Rim Badran, who, as head of the Jordan Investment Board and daughter of former Prime Minister Mudar Badran, is another example of this group, as is Karim Ka'war, ambassador to the United States since May 2002. Other members of the PRE who

Figure 2.1   Mapping Power: Jordanian Politically Relevant Elites, 2002

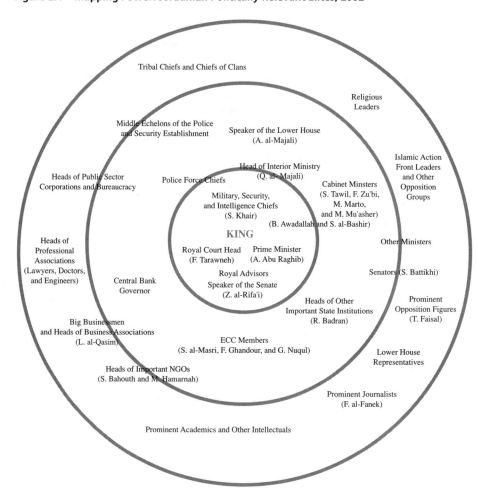

Notes: The idea of mapping elites in concentric circles was first suggested by James A. Bill, "The Patterns of Elite Politics," p. 23, and was further developed by Peter Pawelka, *Herrschaft und Entwicklung.* Political relevance in Jordan depends on the personal standing of an incumbent elite rather than on the formal institutional post he or she occupies. Thus in mapping the Jordanian PRE, the model has been modified to include individual incumbent elites rather than formal institutions only.

Incumbents and their positions are as follows: *Bassem Awadallah,* planning minister; *Rim Badran,* director general, Jordan Investment Board; *Sima Bahouth,* director, Queen Noor Foundation; *Salah al-Bashir,* trade and industry minister; *Toujan Faisal,* former deputy, House of Representatives, prominent opposition figure; *Fahd al-Fanek,* journalist for the *Jordan Times* and the *Daily Star; Fadi Ghandour,* ECC member and CEO of Aramex; *Mustafa Hamarnah,* director of the Center of Strategic Studies and board member, media privatization council; *Sa'd Khair,* head of the General Intelligence Department; *Qaftan al-Majali,* interior minister; *Michel Marto,* finance minister; *Sabih al-Masri,* ECC member with diverse business interests domestically and internationally; *Marwan Mu'asher,* foreign affairs minister; *Ghassan Nuqul,* ECC member and vice-chairman of the Nuqul Group; *Laith al-Qasim,* head of the Young Entrepreneurs Association of Jordan; *Zaid al-Rifa'i,* Speaker of the Senate; *Samir Tawil,* national economy minister; and *Fawaz Zu'bi,* information and communications technology minister.

entered the second circle through the recruitment channel of the ECC include Ghassan Nuqul and Fadi Ghandour. The primary source of influence of this group is competence in questions of economic policy. As advisors they are able, due to their skills and business know-how, to assert some influence on the decisionmaking process. Even more importantly, they are Abdallah's personal choices. For the time being, it is likely that they will keep their positions as long as they are deemed helpful to the king's economic policy pursuits.

With the pro-Palestinian demonstrations in Jordan, the issue of state security gained in importance, particularly after the intensification of protests in 2001. Tensions were not restricted to the capital—specifically, the Wihdat refugee camp or the campus of the University of Jordan—but also took place in other parts of the country, notably in the southern city of Ma'an, which experienced bread riots in 1989 and 1996.[35] Demonstrations in January 2002 took place almost contemporaneously with a reshuffling at the Interior Ministry, which included the appointment of Qaftan al-Majali to head it. The selection of Majali, who belongs to an influential southern tribal family, can be seen as a concession to the frustrated southerners. At the same time, Majali's reputation as a "hard-liner if necessary"[36] points to an assumed willingness of the police forces to exert firm control in tense circumstances. Abd al-Hadi al-Majali, of the same clan, also belongs to the second circle of PRE. With a strong Transjordanian power base, he figures among the country's most experienced politicians and has served as Speaker of the Chamber of Deputies, among other posts.

Thus, the second circle is made up of individuals who can bring their influence to bear in one of the policy fields that dominates the Jordanian political agenda under King Abdallah. The different ministers and advisors in this circle are specialized in economic questions or issues related to security and foreign policy.

The Third Circle

The third circle of the Jordanian PRE is composed of a multitude of segments that can be divided into three broad categories: implementers of regime policies, regime-loyal individuals, and opposition, or contesting, elites. The implementers consist of the large majority of parliamentarians, primarily in the lower house, who are not able to exert political influence that extends beyond their official mandate.[37] Their main duty is to rubber-stamp decisions made by the king and the PRE of the first circle and, to a lesser degree, of the second circle. With the dissolution of parliament in summer 2001 and the subsequent "temporary laws" issued by royal decrees, the influence of deputies on smaller policy corrections in the lawmaking process further declined. The upper echelons of the public sector corporations and state-owned enterprises also belong to this group. They exert influence when it comes to enforcing regime policies on the ground, particularly with regard to the strategic issues of economic reform and state security. Tribal chiefs perform similar tasks as "local strongmen."[38] Of particular importance in this context is their role as distributors of rents and patronage through clientelist networks from the PRE to the people living in the country's rural areas.

The regime-loyal segment of this circle is made up of individuals who, though in general loyal to the Hashemite regime, at times criticize certain regime policies. Fahd al-Fanek is a case in point. As one of Jordan's leading journalists, he writes for the semiofficial *Jordan Times* and for the Lebanese *Daily Star*. With his decades-long experience as a writer, Fanek has gained a reputation as an important opinionmaker, above all concerning identity politics and the relationship between Transjordanians and Palestinians. In general, he belongs to the camp that moderately prioritizes East Bankers' rights over those of the Palestinian population. He thus represents a position to which many Transjordanians, including some PRE members (among others, Zaid al-Rifa'i and Fayez Tarawneh), similarly adhere.

Well-known figures of public life, such as former planning minister Taher Kana'an and Taher al-Masri are other examples of this segment. Masri, the brother of ECC member Sabih al-Masri, was in the early 1990s Jordan's first and, so far, only prime minister of Palestinian origin, but he has lost most of his former power. By contrast, other members of this segment, such as Sima Bahouth and Laith al-Qasim, are on the rise. Bahouth, executive director of the Queen Noor Foundation, one of the most prominent representatives of the so-called NGO sector in Jordan,[39] has recently been appointed by the king to the national committee of Jordan First (al-Urdunn Awwalan), a campaign initiated in fall 2002 to strengthen the unity of Jordanians in times of regional crises.[40] Qasim succeeded Fawaz Zu'bi as head of the increasingly important Young Entrepreneurs Association.

The opposition, or contesting, elite segments of the third circle of influence, are not contesting in the sense of being antisystemic; in fact, they explicitly accept Hashemite rule. They differ from the regime loyalists, however, in their degree of opposition to regime policies. More important, they have not held privileged positions within the first and second circles nor are they likely to ever be included in them (unlike Taher al-Masri or Taher Kana'an). The most obvious opposition elites in Jordan are the moderate Islamists. Relative to Islamists in other Arab countries, Jordan's are well-integrated and partially co-opted into the system of rule,[41] but the Hashemite regime cannot totally control such groups as the Muslim Brotherhood or the Islamic Action Front.

Professional associations were at the forefront of massive protests against Israel's renewed occupation of the West Bank and Gaza. Some of their members have become the main actors in the so-called antinormalization front.[42] These committees can rely on strong support from large parts of the Jordanian population, above all from the nonprivileged social strata of Palestinian descent that are affected most by the country's economic crisis and the subsequent structural adjustment programs.[43] The antinormalization front, with its clear anti-Israel stance, was able to establish a counterdiscourse among the Jordanian public that was contrary to the official pro–peace treaty position. Even in a neopatrimonial authoritarian setting, groups outside the core elite are sometimes able to put issues on the agenda that the regime cannot afford to ignore.

It must be underlined, however, that the opposition in Jordan, except for the Islamic Action Front, remains extremely weak.[44] Although political parties are allowed to operate, they barely influence decisionmaking and agenda setting in the kingdom. In contrast, individuals of a certain standing in the contesting elite can put pressure on the regime. For example, Toujan Faisal, Jordan's first female parliamentarian (1993–1997), has established a reputation as a women's rights' activist and an outspoken critic of regime policies.[45] In March 2002 she sparked a political scandal when she published an open letter in which she accused Prime Minister Abu Raghib of personally enriching himself and his family. Faisal was subsequently sentenced to eighteen months in prison by a state security court in May 2002 on charges of "seditious libel" and "spreading information deemed harmful to the reputation of the state."[46] This harsh judgment elicited loud criticism in the Western media, highlighting the deliberalization of civic freedoms in the kingdom. In order to limit damage to Jordan's image as an allegedly liberal country, King Abdallah issued a decree in June 2002 releasing Faisal; her conviction, however, was allowed to stand. This illustrates that there are incidences when the regime will respond to "shaming." In this case, Abdallah was more concerned with Jordan's image than with silencing an opposition figure. At the same time, he underlined his role as the ultimate arbiter by keeping Abu Raghib as prime minister, thus ensuring that a loyal politician remained in a key position within the PRE.

Analyzing Major Policies

A number of political priorities and possible changes therein have become evident under the rule of King Abdallah. From 1999 until late 2002 the primary issues of concern were economic policy, internal security, and foreign policy. All three are central to political stability, and changes in them could have repercussions on or be influenced by elite change.

Eagerness for (Partial) Economic Reform

A shift in Jordan's policy priorities has been more than obvious since the first days of King Abdallah's reign. In his early speeches, in spring 1999, he put the need for far-reaching reform of Jordan's economy at the top of his personal political agenda. This economic activism dominated official rhetoric well into 2001. Although during the later years of King Hussein's reign, regional politics and the effects of the 1994 peace treaty with Israel had been the central elements in regime rhetoric, this changed entirely with the advent to power of the new king. Since then, the official discourse has almost exclusively hovered around economic and technological development. Through public appearances, speeches, and the media, King Abdallah has successfully created an image of a highly motivated leader, working harder than anyone else in the country for economic and social improvements.

This one-sided discourse of the regime and the rise of the new guard are functional in various respects. First, they serve Jordan's international reputation, especially with regard to the international financial institutions and the country's Western allies. Activism in the field of economic reform and the dominant rhetoric of Abdallah and the PRE promoted via the ECC correspond neatly with the vocabulary of international donors and help create the image of a liberal Jordan. Second, in domestic politics the neoliberal discourse serves to legitimize the king's policies by signaling to the Jordanian public his intent to undertake wide-ranging modernization. This new rhetoric is illustrated by the New Jordan (al-Urdunn al-Jadid) campaign, which was omnipresent in newspapers and on billboards throughout the country.

Rhetoric aside, some major economic reforms have been implemented. On the external side, there are now laws concerning intellectual property rights, arbitration, and antitrust regulations, which were preconditions for Jordan's accession to the World Trade Organization (WTO) in January 2000. In October 2000 Jordan became the fourth country to reach a free trade agreement with the United States.[47] Furthermore, since the beginning of the Barcelona process in 1995, Jordan has been a member of the Euro-Mediterranean Partnership Initiative.[48] On the domestic front, most economic policies are based on Jordan's agreements with the International Monetary Fund.[49] Tight monetary and fiscal policies have helped keep inflation low and allowed for sensible debt management.[50] New Qualifying Industrial Zones (QIZ) have been set up,[51] and at the Red Sea port of Aqaba, a Special Economic Zone (SEZ) came into operation in January 2001. Although aimed at attracting foreign direct investment, little concrete investment had materialized at the time of writing.

Of Jordan's economic issues, privatization ranges among the most important. While for almost two decades successive governments paid lip service to privatization, only since the late 1990s have significant divestments been made. Since 1999 sell-offs have included a 40 percent stake in the Jordan Telecommunications Company to a consortium of France Télécom and the local Arab Bank, and the government's holdings in the two largest industrial companies, the Jordan Phosphate Mines Company and the Arab Potash Company.[52] The state, through a multitude of mechanisms, however, remains in control of partially privatized entities, so its capacity to supervise the economy is still high.

This reluctance to fully privatize mainly stems from a desire to control strategic parts of the economy in order to avoid the emergence of alternative power bases, and from fear of unemployment and its social and possible political consequences. Since regime stability can seriously be threatened by large-scale dismissals from state-owned enterprises and the bureaucracy, members of the PRE explained that dismissed employees needed to be absorbed by other public institutions.[53] Here it is obvious that at least some of the PRE, contrary to the neoliberal view expressed by the Bretton Woods institutions, see one of the essential functions of the state as providing and allocating resources to larger parts of society. So, more than a decade after continuous structural adjustment, Jordan still displays features of a "rentier state of second order," or a "semirentier."[54] In such settings, the state exerts patronage in that it distributes jobs and money in exchange for loyalty from its citizens. Large-scale privatization would endanger if not entail a total breach of the implicit social contract that has been the base of regime stability for decades. In sum, the issue of privatization has been addressed to a certain extent, but without the state losing much of its influence on the economy.

In November 2001 the government presented the Plan for Social and Economic Transformation, which was designed to stimulate private investment and improve public services.[55] Administrative reform is a prominent feature of the plan, because red tape and corruption are rampant, with employment largely based on tribal affiliation and wasta. The anticorruption unit at the Justice Ministry, however, is said to exist as mere window dressing, protecting the "big fish" and not tackling real problems. Nothing has altered the "general sense among the Jordanian public that financial and administrative corruption is prevalent in the civil service at the highest and lowest levels."[56] The ECC in mid-2000 drafted recommendations for administrative reform, such as the introduction of a merit-based system of remuneration and staffing,[57] but the document is unclear about how this should be done.

All in all, the depth of the economic reform process initiated by King Abdallah constitutes an important departure from King Hussein's policies. At the same time, economic reform remains partial because it does not touch upon the clientelist organization of power structures on which neopatrimonial rule and the constellation of the PRE in Jordan essentially rest.

Guaranteeing State Security: Depoliticization and Deliberalization

The dominance of Abdallah's modernization discourse can be interpreted as a strategy to monopolize the public sphere and fill it with issues such as economic development and technological innovation. This serves the purpose of tamping down expectations and debates about such political topics as democratization, discussion of which were prominent in Jordan during the early 1990s. This "return of classical modernization theory,"[58] stipulating that democracy will follow after socioeconomic prerequisites have been fulfilled,[59] serves to depoliticize public debate. Maghraoui makes a similar point for the Moroccan case: "Economic imperatives have been used strategically, across the board, to delay political reform."[60] Depoliticization can thus be interpreted as a preemptive strategy of the state and its elites to justify the absence of more concrete political reforms.

After 2001 this soft "survival strategy"[61] was relegated to the background, and more directly repressive features came to the fore. The pro-Palestinian demonstrations after the outbreak of the al-Aqsa intifada in September 2000, though partially tolerated as a "safety valve" for the regime, were nevertheless flanked by a huge police force. Security agents carefully noted whether the protesters touched red lines defined by the regime, such as the peace treaty between Jordan and Israel. In Amman in 2001 as well as in Ma'an in 2002, security forces carried out major clampdowns on demonstrations, which led to the deaths of some policemen and protesters and to hundreds of arrests.

In addition to such repression, the perpetual postponement of parliamentary elections confirms the trend of deliberalization. In August 2001 the king dissolved the parliament that had been elected in 1997. Elections were then scheduled for November 2001; these were postponed in summer 2001, to an unspecified date in 2002, on the ground that the new system of electronic identification cards would not be ready on time.[62] Apparently, the regime feared that the effects of the intifada and Jordan's precarious economic situation would likely have led to greater numbers of Islamists and "antinormalizers" in parliament, despite the fact that regime-loyal politicians are clearly privileged by the electoral system. In August 2002 the king once again postponed elections, this time to spring 2003, citing the tense regional situation as the main reason for his decision.[63] The elections were finally held in June 2003 and resulted in a landslide victory for proregime candidates.

The temporary laws issued by royal decree since August 2001 have curtailed political liberties. The events of September 11 have served to accelerate this tendency: since that time, more than one hundred regulations have been passed concerning "state security." In short, the regime has further restricted freedom of association and of the media. Amendments to the penal code have prompted greater self-censorship by all newspapers. The new code includes measures allowing for the closure of newspapers and for fines and even prison terms for journalists who are accused of "disrupting society's basic norms by promoting deviation from what is right." Under the new regulations, any activity that potentially threatens the "integrity of the state"—a vague notion that can be interpreted as it best suits the regime's purposes—can be prosecuted.

The obvious shift away from an almost exclusive focus on economic reform in the early years of Abdallah's reign and toward an enhanced concern with state security is also expressed in the Jordan First campaign launched in fall 2002: In essence, it calls on the nation to unite behind Jordan's interests in times of precarious regional situations.[64] Of course, Jordanian interests are what the king defines as such. Jordan First, more so than New Jordan, which symbolized a fresh start represented by the newcomers in the PRE, presents evidence of depoliticization and deliberalization.

Continuity in Foreign Policy

The partial "economicization" of the PRE under King Abdallah has not altered the basic parameters of Jordanian foreign policy. Jordan remains a reliable Western ally. With the executed trade agreement with the United States and accession to the WTO, the kingdom seems to have deepened its relationship with Washington.[65] Jordan's relations with its Arab neighbors, notably Syria, have also improved. The personal animosity between King Hussein and Hafiz al-Asad had resulted in a "cold peace," but their sons have reached a marked détente. Since 1999 Jordan has also improved ties with the Gulf states, Egypt, Turkey, and with Iraq, on which Jordan entirely depends for its oil.[66] It is important to stress that the improvement of ties with various regional states is to a large extent intended to enhance economic relations. At the same time, Jordan is concerned with not becoming too dependent on any one state in the region. With the second intifada, however, Jordan necessarily became increasingly involved regionally and urged the United States to take a more active role as an arbiter. Jordan's military and economic weaknesses and its geopolitical location between the two hot spots of Israel/Palestine and Iraq necessitate a constant balancing act.[67]

In sum, Jordan's foreign policies remain primarily reactive and dependent on external influences. Its rapprochement with its neighbors was not the result of the partial elite change that has taken place within the PRE since 1999. Rather, changes in policy have been caused by the replacement of the central figure in the political system and the evolution of the regional political landscape.

Conclusion

Elite change in Jordan has emerged under Abdallah II as bearing the distinct imprint of the new king as well as being shaped by structural continuities despite the change in leadership at the top. In elite politics, the situation has not been "business as usual," but rather "more business than usual" in that the core elite has been reshaped in such a way that private business and economic expertise have been significantly enhanced and made more central in the first and second circles of the PRE.

Under Abdallah elite members who represent economic expertise have grown in number, and their power has increased in the first and second elite circles when compared to King Hussein's reign. It is not only in comparisons across time but also across countries that Jordanian PRE have come to be shaped more by businesspeople and economists than those in other Arab countries that have undergone successions. Compared to Syria and Morocco, Jordan stands out because the policy priorities of the new leader appear to be shaped more by an awareness of the need for sound economic policies than are those of his fellow heads of state. Therefore, the fact that business elites and economic experts have gained more influence under Abdallah than they have elsewhere in the Arab world is not surprising.

The question that arises from this finding concerns causes and symptoms: Has a new team been installed to solve old problems, or have new approaches to problems necessitated new elite segments because the established ones did not possess the necessary know-how? The findings here hardly leave any doubt: It is the person of the new ruler who has established his own policy priorities (primarily economic recovery) that are different from the ones his father had pursued (primarily national and regional stability).[68] Parts of the old elite were not familiar with the language, politics, and strategies that the new king deems necessary for dealing with the country's problems. Thus, Abdallah created a new elite segment. Its members had already proven their ability to operate successfully in a free market environment, knew the language of globalization that would appeal to foreign donors, were personal friends and acquaintances of the ruler and therefore enjoyed the king's trust, and were flexible enough to undertake political decisionmaking. The inclusion of new elite segments has been the intentional choice of a neopatrimonial leader. The approaches that this new segment uses to address Jordan's pressing economic problems, however, are not an invention of the new king, but rather bear the imprint of globalized capitalism as symbolized by Jordan's commitments to the International Monetary Fund (IMF).

It has become clear more recently, however, that an exclusive focus on economic policies and the pragmatic worldview this implies with regard to the regional and international scene is not enough to maintain political stability. Jordan has two precarious neighbors—Israel and Iraq—and, most importantly, has to cope with its Palestinian majority, who remain strongly attached to their brethren in the Israeli-occupied territories. This situation may explain why in 2001 and 2002, with the al-Aqsa intifada, the focus of King Abdallah's elite politics shifted back toward a renewed inclusion of older and more experienced advisors. What began as an entirely new dynamic in the first and second circles of elites can still be considered a new element of elite politics, but it has since been diluted by a recourse to patterns known from Hussein's reign and from other neopatrimonial systems.

In political systems of personal rule, change in the first and second circles of the PRE comes about exclusively from above, orchestrated by the ruler himself. Change in third-circle opposition elites is subject more to prevailing public opinion and societal interests. Opposition elites, although nonexistent in the first two circles, cannot be entirely repressed or controlled since regimes, as a rule, are not ready to give up the semblance of legitimacy.

Although altered policy priorities can significantly influence the composition of elites, the polity's structure continues to influence elite politics in terms of recruitment and composition. This applies especially to the pattern of continuously reshuffled core elites. Changes in domestic and international politics—here the foreign intervention in Iraq and domestic opposition to the regime's normalization policies toward Israel—have an influence on the degree of power that individual elite members and elite segments wield at a given moment. The more precarious the regional political landscape, the more influential are the security-related segments of the PRE.

It follows that the power of individual elite members and, indeed, entire elite segments, cannot be depicted as static. Rather, the dynamic process of shifting degrees of power and influence among the PRE within the first and second circles is crucial for overall political stability. The maintenance of power in the hands of the ruler is the ultimate goal; all foreign and domestic policies, including the handling of domestic PRE, are subject to its primacy. This primacy leaves unfounded the hope that leadership change, resulting in changed PRE, might pave the way to democratization. Also, the composition of the newly integrated elite segments clearly contradicts any such scenario. Even a casual look at the socioeconomic background of the newly included PRE reveals that they are recruited from among long co-opted families with strong traditions of loyalty to Hashemite rule. The new elite, by virtue of their focus on economics and business, are instrumental in staving off societal demands for greater political liberalization. As noted, the regime's rhetoric follows the assumptions of early modernization theory: economic development as a goal dominates demands for political liberalization to the extent that the new king can afford to significantly deliberalize the polity without incurring any dangerous loss of legitimacy.

Despite a precarious regional situation and a lack of tangible economic success, the Jordanian political system will remain stable, with the regime successfully safeguarding its neopatrimonial character for the foreseeable future. Those developments that might lead to instability are compensated for by the revitalization of older politicians experienced in striking a balance between granting limited leeway for autonomous societal action and the degree of repression necessary to maintain stable authoritarian rule.

Notes

We would like to thank Holger Albrecht, Aron Buzogány, Heinz Kramer, Rolf Schwarz, and the Elite Change in the Arab World working group at the Stiftung Wissenschaft und Politik in Berlin for their invaluable comments. Thanks are also due to the editors of *Arab Studies Journal* at Georgetown University, where we first published the results of our research on Jordan, on which this chapter builds.

1. On these processes in the Middle East and North Africa, see, inter alia, the briefs in *Middle East Policy* 9, no. 3 (September 2002), pp. 105–123, which were originally presented as papers at the annual meeting of the American Political Science Association, September 2001, San Francisco.

2. On the three-circle model used here, see the introductory chapter in this volume.

3. Neopatrimonialism implies the existence of a political leader who holds ultimate power and exercises it by often informal means of patronage networks and clientelist relations incorporating loyalists of that leader's choice. For more on the concept of (neo)patrimonialism, see the standard text, Bill and Springborg, *Politics in the Middle East,* esp. pp. 136–175. See also Eisenstadt, *Traditional Patrimonialism,* and Theobald, "Patrimonialism," pp. 548–559.

4. Tripp, "States, Elites, and the Management of 'Change,'" p. 220.

5. Analysis here is therefore restricted to information available in local media as concerns this segment of the elite and roughly forty-five interviews conducted during two research trips to Jordan in fall 2000 and spring 2001. On the role of the army, see Bligh, "The Jordanian Army," pp. 13–20.

6. This figure is since July 2001. Before that, the Lower House comprised eighty members.

7. For a historical overview of legislative institutions in Jordan, see Baaklini, Denoeux, and Springborg, *Legislative Politics,* pp. 133–168.

8. For the role of political parties in Jordan, see Lust-Okar, "The Decline of Jordanian Party Politics," pp. 545–569.

9. On the prevalence of wasta in Jordanian society, see Sakijha and Kilani, *Towards Transparency,* and Sakijha and Kilani, *Wasta: The Declared Secret.* For a more conceptual effort on wasta, refer to Cunningham and Sarayrah, *Wasta: The Hidden Force.*

10. On the various aspects of clientelism as a concept and on its application, see Eisenstadt and Lemarchand, *Political Clientelism.*

11. See for Egypt, among others, Pawelka, *Herrschaft und Entwicklung;* for the Palestinian Authority, see Brynen, "Dynamics of Palestinian Elite Formation," pp. 31–43, and Brynen, "Neopatrimonial Dimension of Palestinian Politics," pp. 23–36; for various African cases, see Bratton and van de Walle, "Neopatrimonial Regimes," pp. 453–489.

12. Migdal subsumes such appointments and removals under the "Big Shuffle" and "Nonmerit Appointments." See Migdal, *Strong Societies and Weak States,* pp. 214–223. In the case of Jordan, Piro has analyzed these shufflings—he calls them "elite circulation"—with regard to the five biggest state-owned enterprises (SOEs) during Hussein's reign. According to him, "Elite circulation has been one of the strategies employed by King Hussein to preserve his base of power. While much of this circulation has taken place at the ministerial level, positions on the boards of Jordan's SOEs have played a similar role. The board members of the 'Big 5' reads like a who's who of Jordan's largest and influential families." See Piro, *The Political Economy,* p. 81.

13. See Henderson and Pasch, "Jordan," p. 4.

14. *Star,* 16 November 2000.

15. For a general overview of the relationship between foreign donors and democracy-promoting NGOs in the Middle East, see Carapico, "Foreign Aid for Promoting Democracy," pp. 379–395.

16. These examples are taken from Schlumberger and Bank, "Succession," p. 56.

17. Following the establishment of the ECC, two more economic forums were held: Dead Sea II in March 2001 and Aqaba I in September 2002. Regarding elite change, it is the initial composition of the ECC that is of primary importance and therefore our focus here.

18. Francesca Sawalha, "Nuqul Group's 50 Years: A 'FINE' Way to Run a Business," *Jordan Times,* 1–2 November 2002.

19. For more information on the Jordanian IT association, see www.int@j.com.

20. The Young Entrepreneurs Association is an initiative of mainly young Jordanian businesspeople that differs from traditional chambers of commerce and industry in that it represents the younger generation and new technologies (such as information technologies). In 2000 the association published "Jordan Vision 2020," policy recommendations for doubling Jordanians' per capita income within the next two decades. For more information on this ambitious project, see www.jv2020.com.

21. For a theoretical elaboration of the "generation factor," see Mannheim, "The Question of Generation," pp. 276–322.

22. On the role of IT in Jordan, see Cunningham, "Factors Influencing Jordan's Information Revolution," pp. 240–256.

23. Interviews conducted before the 2003 war on Iraq.

24. See Milton-Edwards and Hinchcliffe, "Abdallah's Jordan," p. 30.

25. Kamal al-Sha'ir is chairman of Dar al-Handasah Consulting Engineers and former head of the Finance and Economic Committee of the Jordanian Senate.

26. Samir Tawil was in his mid-thirties and an undersecretary when he was appointed national economy minister. He holds a bachelor's degree in business and accounting from the University of Jordan and a degree in accounting from the University of Illinois. He sits on the board of directors of the Arab Bank, the Jordanian Petroleum Refinery Company, and the Social Security Corporation.

27. See *Jordan Times,* 17 October 2002.

28. Springborg, *Family, Power, and Politics.*

29. By law, the king's dominant position stems from, among other things, the fact that Jordan's political system is essentially "Hashemite and dynastic" (National Charter, 1991, para. 1). There are no built-in mechanisms in the constitution that could subjugate the king to a system of checks and balances to constrain his power. As commander in chief of the armed forces, he also controls the apparatuses that are decisive in maintaining the security of the state. The king can dissolve the government, including dismissing the prime minister, as Abdallah did in June 2000. He can also, without justification, dissolve parliament, as happened in summer 2001. Abdallah then essentially ruled via royal decrees.

30. In August 1999 Abdallah authorized a crackdown on the activities of the Palestinian Islamist group Hamas, forcefully expelling some of its leading figures to Qatar. Reportedly, this move resulted from Battikhi's strong influence on the inexperienced king, who, just days before, had publicly declared that he was opposed to such an action. With Battikhi's dismissal, similar interference in Abdallah's leadership authority is unlikely to recur. He has managed to establish himself safely on the throne.

31. Interview with a member of the second circle of the PRE.

32. This seems to be a typical feature in regimes that have recently experienced a succession. In Morocco, King Mohammed VI dismissed Driss Basri, the former interior minister and strongman of the ancien régime under Hassan II. See Saloua Zerhouni in this volume, "Morocco."

33. For a recent overview of the relationship between the Hashemite rulers and the Jordanian tribes, see Brand, "Al-Muhajirin w-al Ansar," pp. 279–306.

34. Interview with a member of the second circle of the PRE. On the Palestinian issue, Abdallah's wife, Rania, is generally considered an asset. The young and educated queen, who is of Palestinian descent, led a solidarity march during the al-Aqsa intifada on 9 April 2002.

35. See Sana Kamal, "Ma'an Erupts Again," *Middle East International,* 8 February 2002, pp. 16–18, and "The King's Quest," *Middle East International,* 8 November 2002, pp. 10–12. Also see Ryan, "Peace, Bread and Riots," pp. 54–66.

36. Interview with a Jordanian journalist.

37. For an overview of the composition of Jordan's deputies, refer to Hourani and Yassin, *Who's Who.*

38. The term is from Migdal, *Strong Societies and Weak States,* pp. 238ff.

39. On the problem of categorizing NGOs in authoritarian Arab regimes, see Carapico, "NGOs, INGOs, GO-NGOs and DO-NGOs," pp. 12–15. On the political limits of NGOs in Jordan, see Wiktorowicz, "Civil Society as Social Control," pp. 43–61, and "The Political Limits," pp. 77–93.

40. "'Jordan First' Will Be Working Plan to Promote Loyalty," *Jordan Times,* 31 October 2002.

41. See Krämer, "Integration of the Integrists," pp. 200–226; Robinson, "Can Islamists Be Democrats?" pp. 373–387.

42. This front opposes the normalization of Jordan's relations with the state of Israel as exemplified in the 1994 peace treaty. See Scham and Lucas, "Normalization and Anti-Normalization," pp. 54–70.

43. On the link between the "losers" of the economic reforms—that is, the poor majority of the population as well as the wage-dependent middle classes—and their participation in antinormalization protests, see Schlumberger and Bank, "Succession," pp. 53–55.

44. See Dieterich, "Weakness of the Ruled," pp. 127–148.

45. For other aspects of Toujan Faisal's political activities, see Brand, *Women, the State, and Political Liberalization,* pp. 145–149.

46. See Schwedler, "Don't Blink."

47. For more details on the free trade agreement, see www.jordanusfta.com.

48. For a critical account of the Euro-Med Initiative and its possible consequences for the Arab states, see Schlumberger, "Arab Political Economy," pp. 247–268.

49. In July 2002 the IMF approved a $113 million stand-by credit for the period 2002–2004. See the IMF website at www.imf.org/external/np/sec/pr/2002/pr0231.htm.

50. For in-depth analysis of Jordan's economic policies since the initiation of structural reforms in 1989, see Schlumberger, "Jordan's Economy in the 1990s," pp. 225–253.

51. The QIZ offer duty- and quota-free access to U.S. markets for products manufactured by "qualifying" enterprises. The most important criterion is that there be a Jordanian and Israeli share of the value added. For details, see Riad al-Khouri, *Qualifying Industrial Zones as a Model for Industrial Development: The Case of Jordan and Its Implications for the Middle East Region,* Friedrich Ebert Foundation, Amman, 2001.

52. Other fields affected by the privatization process are transportation, the postal service, the national airline, some state-owned media, water management, energy, and electricity. For a complete list of privatization projects in Jordan, see Economic Intelligence Unit, Country Profile 2002, Jordan, London, 2002, pp. 21f.

53. Prime Minister Abu Raghib is said to have told this to the ECC concerning the Jordan Phosphate Mines Company, one of the large public sector dinosaurs. Interviews with ECC members.

54. For the concept of the rentier state, see the contributions to Beblawi and Luciani, *Rentier State.* On rentierism in Jordan, see Brand, "Economic and Political Liberalization," pp. 167–188, and Brynen, "Economic Crisis," pp. 69–97.

55. Kamal Sha'ir, "The Plan for Social and Economic Transformation: Ingredients for Long-Term Success, *Jordan Times,* 7 November 2002.

56. Henderson and Pasch, "Jordan," p. 14. In a recent contribution, Beverly Milton-Edwards and Peter Hinchcliffe put it similarly, stating "that revolutionary new thinking advocating genuine reform may not figure too strongly in the King's entourage." See Milton-Edwards and Hinchcliffe, *Jordan,* p. 121.

57. Economic Consultative Council, Tahdith wa tatwir al-qita' al-'amm (Modernization and development of the public sector) (unpublished paper, Amman, June 2000).

58. See Schlumberger and Bank, "Succession," p. 63.

59. See the famous contribution by Lipset, "Some Social Requisites," pp. 69–105.

60. Maghraoui, "Depoliticization," p. 25.

61. The term is taken from Brumberg, "Survival Strategies," pp. 73–104.

62. The German company responsible for the cards repeatedly asserted that the system worked.

63. "Parliamentary Polls Postponed Until Spring," *Jordan Times,* 16 August 2002.

64. Because of its inclusive character, this campaign rallied most of the relevant social forces behind the regime. A notable exception are the nonmoderate Islamists who, in turn, risked being excluded from participation in other fields. See "King Chairs 'Jordan First' Committee Meeting," *Jordan Times,* 1–2 November 2002.

65. This enables the Jordanian regime to further attract foreign rents, a decisive prerequisite for domestic stability. See Brand, "In Search of Budget Security." A similar argument is pursued by Bouillon, "Walking the Tightrope," pp. 1–22.

66. See Sasley, "Changes and Continuities," pp. 36–48.

67. See Chesnot, "La Jordanie," pp. 129–143.

68. An alternative structural explanation would be that neoliberal international pressure was strong enough to force the king to alter the country's overall economic policy orientations. Yet, if this had been the case, one would have expected King Hussein to have initiated the changes his son has implemented since 1999. Neoliberalism reached the Arab world well before the end of the 1990s.

3

Morocco:
Reconciling
Continuity and Change

Saloua Zerhouni

After four decades of authoritarian rule under King Hassan, in July 1999 Morocco experienced a smooth succession with the ascension of King Mohammed VI to power. Like his Arab counterparts King Abdallah in Jordan and President Bashar al-Asad in Syria, the young king seemed full of promise for change and a desire to move his country toward economic liberalization and democratization. Indeed, the new king affirmed his attachment to the constitutional monarchy, the multiparty system, the establishment of rule by law, and the safeguarding of human rights. While keeping some of his father's "old guard" appointees, during the first three years of his reign Mohammed VI brought in a new generation of elites composed mainly of people from his close circle of friends, the "court clique," and technocrats. Changes at the core of the regime were also accompanied by transformations in the composition of the second and third circles of the politically relevant elite.[1]

The new elite configuration in Morocco should be seen in the context of the political opening that was set in motion in the last decade by King Hassan, who recognized the necessity of preparing conditions for a smooth succession. Also since the early 1990s domestic opposition and international pressures had led the regime to adopt measured political, social, and economic reforms aimed at democratizing the political system.

Changes in the composition of the politically relevant elite, however, will not have a substantial impact on political liberalization unless they are also accompanied by changes in elite attitudes and behavior.[2] Indeed, elite attitudes toward political power have tended to be characterized primarily by concern for their own interests. The monarchy has played a vigorous role in the perpetuation of elite *immobilisme* (stasis), employing various means of manipulation. The monarchy at the same time created a clientelist network in which economic self-interest became part of elite members' shared values. The attitudes of elite members toward the monarchy have contributed gradually to the emergence of a culture of passivity and political apathy. This culture has not been, and in the long run will not be, in favor of establishing democracy.[3]

For a long time, Moroccan political culture has been shaped by an entrenched authoritarian rule around the central power of the *makhzan,* that is, the monarchy and its hegemonic state apparatus.[4] Makhzan is constantly present in the collective consciousness of Moroccans and tends to be associated with an absolute authority that should not be contested.[5] As defined by Micheaux Bellaire, this brand of "despotic authority" has maintained a certain social disorder in order to maintain the power to arbitrate.[6] To survive, this kind of authority has sustained a set of allegiances and has succeeded, over the years, in converting allegiance into submission by creating a culture of obedience and stigmatizing any form of political dissent. In addition, Hassan II employed Islam and tradition to sustain this culture.[7]

It is the contention here that elite change in Morocco will not lead to a change in the political system or, more specifically, in the power structure. That is, a more liberal monarch and a relative change in the personnel of the PRE does not mean more democracy. Morocco's political culture is simultaneously the source of the regime's strength and of its weakness. Its strength is evident in its continuity, but its weakness becomes apparent when the regime gives the impression of implementing changes for moving toward modernity. The power and practices of the neo-makhzan—the new king and his court clique and appointees—are evident in the modes of recruitment and political behavior among the elite. Yet, this analysis should be nuanced. The process of political liberalization initiated by Hassan II allowed for more freedom of expression and for the entry of new political actors into the circles of influence. Because of limited resources, however, increases in the number of the elite might make it more difficult to maintain the current clientelist system. It is also likely that political liberalization will create a new set of attitudes among the elite. Thus, a culture of political participation might slowly evolve within the traditional makhzanian culture.[8]

The Moroccan Monarchy and Interelite Relations

One way of understanding recent political developments in Morocco is to examine the behavior and relations between the monarchy and other political actors involved in the process of change. The monarchy is the main component of the political system and the center around which all political actors revolve. While holding firmly to power, the monarchy has occasionally made concessions, aimed at more openness, in the face of national and international pressures. Over the years, King Hassan managed changing situations and political challenges through the use of repression, co-optation, and consensus. These strategies were all part of the so-called *politique de ficelle* (literally, politic of the string),[9] which rested on the king's ability to ensure the stability and continuity of the regime without completely cutting ties with the opposition.

King Mohammed has thus far maintained if not reinforced the centrality of the monarchy, through a more liberal style, thus guaranteeing his predominance in politics. The formation of royal committees charged with important dossiers is one method he has adopted. This institutionalization of royal powers has a dual function: on the one hand, it is an important tool for controlling the elite by seeming to give them a voice in decisionmaking as well as regulating their integration into the political system; on the other hand, it is a way of affirming the preeminence and the efficiency of the monarchical institution. Thus, the evolution of the political system under Mohammed VI is more about continuity than change. The young king merely reproduces monarchical dominance by using a more liberal approach or style, which is characteristic of the neo-makhzan.

Hassan II:
Between Monarchical Dominance and Liberalization

The rule of King Hassan was characterized by alternating phases of authoritarianism and liberalization. While demonstrating a certain willingness to modernize the regime, Hassan II remained keen on preserving its central role in the political system. The first constitution in 1962 established a multiparty system and delineated the powers of the parliament and the government. Yet, as *amir al-mu'minin* (commander of the faithful), the king continued to hold disproportionate prerogatives that subordinated the parliament and the government. The constitution grants the king broad powers that ensured him an active role in political life. The discretionary power of appointment allowed the king to reward supporters or punish challengers or co-opt them, thus consolidating the patterns of a clientelist politic, not those of democracy.[10] Thus, the orchestration of this clientelist system provided the king with a reservoir of loyalists.

The supremacy of the monarchy was maintained by other means as well, such as by forming alliances with the rural elite[11] or neutralizing the urban elite.[12] It has also managed to retain control of the army, the police, and the technocratic state apparatus. Over the years, it has placed itself in a role of arbiter and manipulator of the elite. The fragmentation among the elite as well as their *immobilisme* also played an important role in preserving the king's dominance. A number of scholars have located the role of the elite in Morocco within a persistent pattern of political behavior structured by the monarchy. In 1970, Waterbury proffered,

Following independence, most nationalist politicians genuinely wanted
and sought real collective responsibility for national policy. As the throne
held them off and coaxed them into the royal stables one by one, they tac-
itly came to accept a total lack of individual or collective responsibility
for national affairs, all the while protesting the contrary. They are too dis-
illusioned to fight the regime themselves and too attached to its benefits to
renounce it.[13]

That said, the relationship between the monarchy and other members
of the PRE has been marked by cycles of conflict and consensus, depending on how actors behaved during crises and on whose interests were at
stake. The history of this relationship was one of confrontation when the
issue was sharing power, and consensus when common interests were concerned or when the integrity and stability of the country were raised. The
nature of this relationship and elite attitudes and behavior significantly
influenced the political evolution of the country. In the past, regime crises
led to either blockage or opening of the political system, depending on how
the monarchy and other political forces, particularly the opposition parties,
reacted.[14] Three main periods can be distinguished.

The first period (1962–1975) was characterized by confrontation,
repression, and authoritarianism, with the dominance of the monarchy reinforced by intraelite conflict. The inability of opposition political parties,
mainly Istiqlal and Union Nationale des Forces Populaire (UNFP), to agree
on certain issues resulted not only in disputes among themselves, but also
with the monarchy.[15] Because of such fragmentation, the king was able to
manipulate this segment of the second circle of the PRE, with whom he had
a strong disagreement over the distribution of power.

The second phase (1975–1992) started with Hassan II taking a strong
stand on Morocco's claim to the Western Sahara. His mobilization of
Moroccans behind a national cause contributed to restoring the centrality of
the monarchy and the emergence of a consensus between the monarchy and
the opposition parties.[16] The leftist Union Socialiste des Forces Populaires
(USFP)[17] changed its strategy from criticism and boycott and agreed to
operate as a "constructive opposition" in the parliament. Censorship was
lifted on the press, and the king released a number of political prisoners. In
the late 1980s, however, liberalization was interrupted, with the king placing restrictions on the opposition and occasionally banning their newspapers when they criticized the government.

Although profound differences remained regarding political choices
and economic and social issues, the monarchy and the opposition reached
an implicit consensus about the importance of normalizing political life and
participation of the opposition in the existing system. This led to the third
period (1992–1999) that was characterized by consensual interactions
between the monarchy and opposition leaders from the Istiqlal and left-

wing parties. These parties, part of a united front known as the Koutla al-Democratiya (the Democratic Bloc),[18] drafted a memorandum to the king in which they requested direct universal suffrage in parliamentary elections. Hassan II reacted in March 1992 by stating his intention to revise the constitution and hold free elections. For the first time, the opposition parties were consulted and involved in revising the constitution. A series of reforms were introduced after the constitutional revision of 1992. For instance, the powers of the parliament were enhanced by giving it the right to set up committees of inquiry if a majority of the chamber voted to do so. The Constitutional Council[19] and the Social and Economic Council[20] were established. Minor restrictions on the powers of the monarchy were also introduced, including (Article 35) preventing the king from dissolving the parliament during states of emergency.[21]

Following legislative elections in 1993, Hassan II held negotiations with Koutla leaders in an attempt to form a new government. The royal offer was rejected mainly because Hassan II wanted to keep the most important ministries, commonly referred to as *ministères de souveraineté* (sovereign ministers), under his control.[22] Despite the failure of the first round of negotiations, dialogue still informed the relationship between the two protagonists. It is out of this context that the 1996 constitutional revision resulted. All the opposition political parties voted for the amendments introduced, because they satisfied some of the demands presented in their memorandum. One of the most important reforms was the abolition of indirect suffrage of members of the Chamber of Representatives and reinforcement of the executive powers of the prime minister. Relatively transparent local and national elections were held in 1997.[23] One year later, the king succeeded in convincing Abderrahman Youssoufi, leader of the largest opposition party, the USFP, to head a government of *alternance*.[24] Formed in 1998, the government was primarily drawn from opposition parties that had largely been excluded from power in the past.[25] The new government announced an ambitious program of reforms in the social, political, and economic spheres, symbolizing a new era in relations between the monarchy and the opposition parties.

These discernible periods in the history of relations between the monarchy and the opposition parties demonstrate the importance of consensual relations with the elite if political change is to be initiated and maintained. During the 1970s and the 1980s the relationship between the monarchy and the opposition parties was highly confrontational. The change in relations during the 1990s, whatever the tactics or strategic motives behind it, brought about a measure of political liberalization. Still, the change in the nature of relations did not mean a change in the nature of the regime. Although this process of "democratization" allowed more space for political participation, freedom of expression, and respect for human rights and liberties, it was accompanied by a rejuvenation of the role of the monarchy in the political arena.

Mohammed VI's Liberal Style: Reinventing the Monarchy

With the ascension of Mohammed VI, some observers spoke of a new era in the political history of Morocco. Indeed, the new king brought with him a new style to the monarchical institution and presented the image of a leader with conceptions of political, social, and economic issues different from those of his father. In his second address to the nation in August 1999, Mohammed VI affirmed his attachment to the principles of constitutional monarchy, respect for human rights, and individual liberties. He called for a new conception of authority based on accountability and proclaimed that defining a new status for women and fighting against corruption and poverty were his top priorities.

The atmosphere of dialogue and consensus that characterized the late 1990s has framed the current relationship between the monarchy and the political elite. Mohammed VI confirmed the government of alternance and has not interfered in the internal affairs of the political parties. He has urged reform of the electoral law to ensure more representativeness. He has also called upon Moroccans to take elections seriously. The first legislative elections held under Mohammed VI, in September 2002, and orchestrated by Interior Minister Driss Jettou occurred under relatively transparent conditions. Many observers perceived them as an important moment for the prospect of democratization in Morocco.[26]

The aftermath of the 2002 elections, however, reveals that the potential for meaningful democratic change remains limited. First, there appear to have been no major changes in the composition of the political elite. A large majority of incumbent parliamentarians were reelected despite implementation of a revised voting system designed to broaden representation; the *scrutin de liste* (suffrage based on an electoral list) still reflects an elite that remains to a certain degree discredited and without a solid social base. This is clearly the case of the socialists, who are still the major force in the parliament in spite of criticism directed against them during the period of alternance. Their failure to implement parts of their program or present solutions to some of Morocco's urgent problems, such as unemployment, alienated part of their base. Despite the emergence of the Islamic party, the Party of Justice and Development (PJD), as a political force,[27] as well as the election of thirty-five women,[28] the 2002 elections did not lead to any radical shift in power. The king selected Driss Jettou as prime minister although he was not a member of the parliamentary majority that included the USFP and the center-right Istiqlal. Additionally, Mohammed VI appointed, as had been the tradition, the ministers of interior, foreign affairs, and Islamic affairs. Politically speaking, these appointments represented a step backward in the process of democratic transition that the king had called for. Youssoufi's successor had no party affiliation, and his appointment—a surprise—created tension among the political elite. The appointment of Jettou reconfirmed the traditional supremacy of the monarchy and its position as the only significant force in the decisionmaking process.

King Mohammed VI has proven astute at using political unity and consensus to his advantage. He describes himself as a "democrat,"[29] appropriating the discourse of democracy and human rights and expressing genuine concern about poverty, which are important elements for building legitimacy and maintaining power. The king's focus on economic issues and unemployment has made him popular among Moroccans. Mohammed VI has also succeeded in marginalizing his critics by ignoring them instead of using repressive measures against them as Hassan II did against his. The most telling example is Mohammed VI's reaction to the provocative letter sent to him by Abdessalam Yassine, the leader of the Islamist group al-'Adl wa-l-Ihsan.[30] In this letter, Yassine acknowledged the goodwill of the new king toward his people. At the same time, he recommended that the king use his father's fortune to pay off Morocco's financial debt and deal with the problems of poverty.

Parallel to these declared democratic intentions, the king has reinforced his powers through the creation of royal committees on strategic issues. Hassan II started a trend of the monarchy asserting monopoly control over key matters, and under Mohammed VI this tendency has markedly increased.[31] While power was established through the personification of authority under Hassan II, with the succession, there is an "institutionalization" of royal powers. Whether the rationale behind this tendency is modernization of the monarchical institution, more efficiency, or tighter control over the decisionmaking process, it is clear that it is leading toward a hybrid system, here meaning a combination of royal committees and state institutions with the same functions. This is exemplified by the establishment of a number of royal committees dealing with investment, tourism, education, reform of the family code, and human rights, although there are ministries already in charge of those issues. Moreover, there are no rules delineating the function of these committees in relation to state institutions.

The royal committees have also played a part in Mohammed VI's strategy for elite integration. To guarantee continuity of the regime, the current monarchical institution has adopted the strategy of elite co-optation, which was practiced by his father. What is new, however, is Mohammed VI's integration of new groups from civil society that emerged as the result of political liberalization. A symbolic sign of this attempt at integration is the appointment of one of the most "radical" Moroccan activists, Ibrahim

Serfaty, to head the National Bureau of Energy. In early 2002 Mohammed VI created the Royal Institute of Amazigh Culture and appointed as its head Mohammed Chafik, an important actor in the Berber movement. The Amazigh question therefore became part of the palace's political monopoly. More recently, human rights activist Driss Benzekri was made general secretary of the royal Consultative Council on Human Rights.

Mohammed VI's brand of elite integration and the hybrid character of the political system are likely to have negative effects on the liberalization process because they serve mainly the goals of the neo-makhzan. In the long run, state institutions will be undermined instead of reformed and strengthened. In a best-case scenario, the result will be a strong and rejuvenated monarchy with weak "democratic institutions." It is in this context of monarchical dominance and attempts at democratic experimentation that one finds the dilemma of change and continuity as it relates to the composition of the PRE in Morocco.

The Moroccan PRE

In Morocco, the king has traditionally had the discretionary power to recruit members of the elite, and with the latest succession this mode of recruitment has not changed.[32] The appointment of members of the PRE and the advancement of individual careers are still regulated at the level of the central power. With King Mohammed VI, the composition of the PRE has undergone a number of changes in membership. Within the first weeks of his reign, the new king dismissed Driss Basri, interior minister since 1979 and considered the "right hand" of the late king. As part of the makhzan elite, Basri had come to symbolize the authoritarian rule of Hassan II. Basri's dismissal was a sign of Mohammed VI's intention for change. The young monarch also made new appointments in the royal cabinet, army, Islamic institutions, government, public sector, and provincial and regional administration. In looking at the relationship between elite change and political transformation, it is important to consider whether change in the PRE is limited to simply replacing individuals or whether the personnel changes go beyond that and into the realm of changes in attitudes and behavior of the PRE.

Linking social background and attitudes has been a topic of debate in elite studies. Some scholars argue that the link is valid; the behavior of elites may well derive from their attitudes, which in turn can be traced to their social background.[33] Thus, examining the educational, social, and professional backgrounds of the makhzan elite among palace, government, and provincial and regional administration personnel can assist in assessing their attitudes and behavior.

Change and Continuity in the Composition of the PRE

In Morocco, the monarchy had been the core around which elites coalesced. The politically relevant elite comprise single and collective actors, including the political elite, economic and business groups, senior officials in the administration, civil society activists, religious organizations, and the military. Access of individual members to the first and second circles of the PRE as well as their degree of influence on the decisionmaking process depends on their closeness or distance from the center of power—the monarchy—and the interests they defend or represent. Education, family ties, and wealth constitute important resources for elite membership. Yet, as John Waterbury notes, "Neither education nor wealth are criteria for membership in the elite, although most members tend to be educated or wealthy or both. Access to the elite is through co-optation."[34]

The first, or inner, circle of the PRE comprises, apart from the king, who is the prime decisionmaker, counselors and members of the royal cabinet. The members of this inner circle are recruited from among highly educated individuals who hold or have held positions in the executive branch and are considered successful.[35] The king's counselors, or advisors, are experts in their specialties. They supervise and assess the work of the ministers and serve, at the same time, as a bridge between the palace and the members of the second and third circles of the PRE. Some observers consider the king's advisors a "shadow government." All strategic decisions are made within this inner circle. For example, among such decisions have been those involving reform of the education system, for which the late king appointed a royal committee. Decisions on reform were made in this committee, and the parliament confirmed them. Mohammed VI initiated measures for further economic liberalization. He also appointed committees to take charge of tourism and investment, two of his top priorities.

With Mohammed VI's ascendance, the monarchical institution appears to have been rejuvenated. Though the new king kept most of his father's counselors, he has also brought in new people. Most of them belong to his generation and were his classmates. Two changes stand out: for the first time, the king has brought in a female advisor and appointed a palace spokesperson. To a certain extent, these changes reflected the desire of the new king to project an image of a modern monarchy that intends to have better communicate with the people.[36]

The second circle of the PRE included senior army officers, representatives of "official Islam" or Islamic institutions, government ministers in charge of important portfolios, officials from various public institutions, the business elite, and leaders of political parties of the national movement (principally Istiqlal and the USFP). The army has always represented an important segment of the second circle of elite, but information about this institution remains difficult to attain. Since the creation of the Forces Armées Royales (FAR) after independence, the monarchy has tried to maintain control of the military. Hassan II attempted to strengthen the relationship between the palace and the military by integrating senior army officers into the royal patronage network. In the 1960s the political influence of the army began to increase. In 1963 two generals were assigned nonmilitary ministerial posts. After the 1971 and 1972 coup attempts, the army's role in politics changed considerably, with Hassan II adopting a strategy of keeping the military "busy, dependent and divided."[37] Since 1975 the Western Sahara conflict contributed to keeping the FAR away from politics. Hassan II has over the years concentrated all important military powers,[38] reorganized the FAR, and began to recruit outside the traditionally rural and Berber elements that had come to dominate the officer corps of the military. The political role of the army did not change during the 1980s and the 1990s. Contrary to speculation that it would be revived after the death of Hassan II, there are not yet signs of an increase in the military's influence. The army remains a significant force, but it is more concerned with protecting its established interests than in expanding them. The attitude of the army toward power, like other political actors in Morocco today, is in favor of the status quo.

Mohammed VI has not made many personnel changes in the composition of the army. He appointed Col. Maj. Hamidou Laanigri as director general of the National Intelligence Service (DST), and he promoted two other generals in the army. The lack of changes made in the army can be explained by the fact that the military has been a powerful interest group that has the capacity and the means to resist change even at the individual level. Calls for rooting out corruption in the military were met with deaf ears on the part of the king.[39] The status quo of the army might also be explained by the fact that the monarchical institution is still waiting for the appropriate moment at which to introduce changes, most probably after resolving the Western Sahara conflict. It may also well be that the king does not deem change in military personnel necessary.

Mohammed VI has also not moved to alter the composition of Islamic institutions. This constitutes a desire for continuity in the area of the monarchy's most "sacred" source of legitimacy. Indeed, as of July 2002 only three new appointments had been made—in the presidency and the secretariat of the Supreme Council of Ulama. The council was established by King Hassan and has been under the control of the monarchical institution. The palace and the council have represented themselves as the guardians of Islam in the face of secularism and radicalism. In addition, after the 2002 elections, the Religious Affairs Ministry underwent a change with the appointment of Taoufiq Ahmed, an apolitical figure with a Sufi background, to head it.[40] His appointment was revealing in terms of a strategy to maintain a certain political balance and in that it appears to be an attempt to promote moderate, nonpolitical Islam. In the context of the growing influence of the Islamists and demands for reform from women's organizations, the appointment of somebody with the profile of Ahmed Taoufiq can be viewed as part of a conscious attempt on the part of Mohammed VI to steer Morocco toward the path of moderation concerning religious matters.

The third circle of the PRE has experienced the most substantial changes under Mohammed VI, in particular the segment of *walis* (heads of regions) and governors. To weaken Driss Basri's network, the product of his twenty-two years as interior minister, Mohammed VI set about replacing governors and walis. In this regard, eighty-seven appointees have been employed over three years to fill seventy-six positions, a rather high turnover. In addition to walis and governors, the third circle includes influential members of parliament, representatives of prominent NGOs, and leaders of the political parties commonly called *les parties de l'administration,* notably the Rassemblement National des Indépendants (RNI), Union Constitutionnel (UC), and Mouvement Populaire (MP). These parties were created by the regime and are thus supportive of its politics. They have been part of the makhzan elite that the monarchy has used in order to control and manipulate political life. New actors entered the third circle, among them entrepreneurs, Islamists, and journalists.

It should be kept in mind that some PRE are not confined to one circle. Some individuals hold more than one office, and there is movement toward and away from the inner circle. For instance, the king recruited counselors from among competent and successful government ministers or members of the parliament. Not all members of a group of elites would necessarily occupy the same circle. The degree of change in personnel varies from one institution to another. These changes do not, however, represent elite rejuvenation. Rather, elite change in Morocco should be considered partly as an exchange of personnel and to some extent a structural one, especially at the level of the third circle.

In order to deal with Morocco's economic problems, members of the technocratic elite have been increased in all three circles of the PRE. The number of elite members from political parties and civil society has been rising. The configuration of elites has also been changed by the inclusion of new actors such as the Islamists and by the increase in the relative influence of some segments of the PRE, such as entrepreneurs, businesspeople, and technocrats.

In the long run, the broadening of the elite and the access of new actors to the PRE might contribute to the breakdown of the clientelist network established by the monarchy. A lack of the resources needed to satisfy the increasing numbers of the monarchy's clients might lead to a change in the attitudes of Moroccan elites toward power. As Waterbury contends, "When the numerical size of the Moroccan elite increases significantly, and it will, we may expect as a necessary consequence that the elite have to readapt its style and behavior to fit the new circumstances or risk bursting apart at the seams. Relatively intimate personal relations sustained by an underlying social homogeneity will become increasingly difficult to maintain with a massive influx of elite aspirants of widely varied educational and social backgrounds."[41] Ultimately, one might expect that the rise in the number of members of the PRE is likely to lead to less immobilisme and to more participation in the decisionmaking process.

Mohammed VI's Appointees: More Recycling than Renewal

As noted, a relative change of the core elite and members of the second and third circles of the PRE accompanied the advent of the new leadership. Indeed, within the first three years of his reign, King Mohammed VI appointed 241 people to high positions.[42] In addition to the changes he made in the monarchical institution, the army, Islamic institutions, and provincial and regional administrations, the new king reshuffled the government of alternance on 6 September 2000 and reduced the number of ministers from forty-one to thirty-three. Following the 2002 legislative elections, Mohammed VI formed a new government with thirty-eight ministers. Twenty-nine senior officials and sixty-four ambassadors were appointed. Based on the sheer number of appointments, one might assume that major changes have taken place in the makeup of the PRE or get the impression that there has been elite renewal. The social backgrounds of recently appointed PRE indicated otherwise. The evidence can be drawn from looking at three segments of the PRE that were affected by changes in their ranks: the monarchical institution (they represent here seven people); government ministers (72); and senior officials (29).

The members of the chosen sample do not consist of a socially homogeneous group; they are not from the same age or ethnic groups. They had varied educational experiences, ranging from Moroccan to French or American systems of education, and different sociopolitical backgrounds. A common characteristic among them is that none of them attended traditional religious institutions, such as al-Qarawiyin. The appointees also have some characteristics that differentiate them from Moroccan elites of the 1970s and the 1980s. Contrary to the emphasis in William Zartman's study in the 1980s, it is no longer the case that most of the elite have Fassi origins. The majority of the appointees in this sample have urban origins and are concentrated in Rabat and Casablanca.[43]

Higher education is another common denominator among members of the core elite and the second-circle elites who comprise the sample. In Morocco, education is becoming more and more a prerequisite for elite status. The tendency to go to France and pursue advanced studies is a dominant characteristic among them. About 70 percent of the recently appointed PRE in the monarchical institution, the government, and public institutions continued their studies in France, while close to 21 percent did so in Morocco, and the rest studied in the United States. One can, therefore, conclude that these elites have largely Francophone tendencies.[44]

Age, which can be considered an indicator of generation, varies widely among the new appointees. One-third of the members of the sample—108 appointees—are thirty-five to forty-five years old. These appointees were educated after independence and socialized in the 1970s and 1980s. As noted above, this era was characterized by the passage from a period dominated by confrontation and repression to a more stable one, in part resulting from a national consensus on the Western Sahara. These appointees can be considered an emerging new generation, likely to move into decisionmaking positions in coming years.[45] Half of the appointees are between forty-five and sixty years of age, which demonstrates a lingering tendency to reshuffle among the established members of the elite. The rest are sixty years old or older, representing, more or less, King Hassan's old guard.

In terms of professional background, the tradition of hiring people from the education sector is being eroded by the selection of a growing number of bureaucrats and technocrats. The majority of the appointees have never held an electoral mandate at the local or national level and do not belong to any political party. Finally, it is worth mentioning that women are no longer excluded from positions of power and authority; almost 7 percent of the appointees in the sample here are women. Even though this is not a significant percentage, it is a positive sign of change in the composition of this elite.

In regard to renewal among the personnel of the PRE, only 11 percent of the sample are newcomers. The new elite tend to be journalists, professors, or directors of technical schools. The "recycled" appointees (89 percent, who held appointments under Hassan II, that is, Hassan II's makhzan) tend to be members of parliament, leaders of political parties, government ministers, or senior officials.[46] Thus the recent new appointments represented recycling, not renewal. The practice of "rotation," also used by King Hassan, has enabled the monarchy to prevent the creation of a competing center of power. Moreover, most rotated appointees are bureaucrats or technocrats, with no political background or history as local or national representatives. The high number of technocrats and bureaucrats among the core elite and second circle of the PRE can be explained by the fact that Mohammed VI does not want to surround himself with politicians, particularly those who lack the technical skills for implementing economic liberalization. Politicians are also likely to have aspirations of power sharing. The selection of Driss Jettou—a technocrat with experience in the economic field—as prime minister highlights the tendency of Mohammed VI to surround himself with technocrats who are perceived as likely candidates for dealing with Morocco's economic problems. This openness toward a technocratic elite reveals the king's strategy of directing attention to economic issues and away from political matters. Indeed, such political questions as the distribution of power and accountability have been eclipsed by a depoliticization of the political field.[47]

Perceptions of Change Among the PRE

Identifying the views that members of the PRE have concerning political change, including its meaning to them, sheds light on possible new elite attitudes toward power.[48] Such change is viewed by most of the PRE as a necessity given the current context. There is, however, a consensus concerning the value and importance of retaining a monarchical regime. One can, therefore, infer that the PRE's perception of political change does not necessarily imply a change of regime. The preeminence of the monarchical regime is not questioned or challenged even by the progressive opposition. Members of the PRE do not contest the nature of the regime perhaps because they have come to believe that the monarchy is the most appropriate type of regime to rule the country, or because they fear worse alternatives (such as the army or the Islamists), or because the status quo better serves their interests. The current attitudes of elites severely limit the prospects of political change and thus perpetuate the makhzan strategy of "change in continuity," whereby the regime appropriates new discourses in order to adapt itself to new situations without inherently changing the structure of power. That said, it is possible to identify how change is conceptualized among members of the Moroccan elite from political, economic, and cultural perspectives.

The Political Perspective

This perspective mainly reflects the perception of members of the third circle of the PRE and the emerging elite, who are self-promoted (or self-recruited) as opposed to appointed. These include leaders of left-wing political parties, influential NGOs, and representatives of the Islamic movement. Among them, change is conceived primarily as part of a necessary transformation in the political system, stressing a more balanced distribution of power between the monarchy and other political actors. This would entail the enlargement of the space allotted for political participation as well as the achievement of a consensus in relation to the rules of politics. The idea of a monarchy that reigns but does not govern is emphasized. They also make reference to the importance of a system in which representative institutions, notably the parliament, are responsible for enacting laws and can exercise its full power. Also emphasized is the need to bring certain key issues into the open for national debate. In this regard, for instance, women's status and women's rights have thus far been debated in the closed circles of the *ulama,* without consideration of the more liberal suggestions formulated in the so-called Program for the Integration of Women (Plan d'Integration de la Femme) presented by Said Saadi, the minister who was in charge of family affairs in the government of alternance.

This political perception of change was nicely articulated by a party leader in these terms: "The key for change is political not economic; it is a political transition that can help introduce economic and social reforms."[49] In the same vein, a leader of an influential NGO asserted, "Change means having a space not only for expressing our views and discontent, but also a space through which we communicate ideas and suggestions that are taken seriously and translated into concrete programs."[50] What one gathers from such opinions is that change can be implemented only according to a set of norms and principles that are clearly still lacking in the current context.

The Economic Perspective

The economic perspective emphasizes the relationship between political change and economic development. This approach, primarily based on the modernization theories of the 1950s and the 1960s, stressed the correlation between economic development and the establishment of a stable and democratic system of government. The PRE members who advocate an economic approach are predominantly technocrats in the second circle. One senior official bluntly asked, "What does democracy mean for someone who is hungry?" He added, "We have six million Moroccans who are detached from reality. A change in the electoral law does not mean much for almost 70 percent of Moroccans, a percentage that corresponds to the rate of illiteracy in the country. When we have different economic conditions, democracy will follow."[51]

This appears to be the approach favored by the core elite as well. As mentioned, Mohammed VI has moved in this direction, initiating a process of social and economic reform and launching new programs in the agriculture, tourism, and investment sectors. He has appointed technocrats to key positions and has demonstrated a tendency to subordinate political issues to economic ones. He has also established a number of committees in order to deal with economic issues, for example, creating the Hassan II Fund for Economic and Social Development and the Regional Bureaux of Investment. These institutions work closely with the new king and contribute to the maintenance of the king's preeminence in the political scene.

The Cultural Perspective

The cultural perspective reflects, quite interestingly, the views of members of the PRE who were previously university professors and who were appointed by Mohammed VI to key ministries or hold influential positions in left-wing political parties. They are generally second and third circle decisionmakers. Opinions of this segment of the PRE have converged on three main points.

First, political change is tantamount to the elaboration of a culture of citizenship. An advisor to the prime minister put it directly, "Change means that each Moroccan citizen considers himself or herself as a full actor of change on a daily basis. This individual consciousness is the only way to have a stable and democratic Morocco. We need a new culture, a culture of citizenship that might lead to a change at all levels. We need to have citizens who assume their responsibilities; this requires a change in the mentalities and in the way of dealing with different problems."[52]

Second, change will require a "new conception of time." There is considerable awareness among the PRE about the importance of taking into account globalization and the challenges of the twenty-first century, and time has become a major element in how the elite measure change. One of the strongest criticisms against the government of alternance concerns its slow pace in implementing reforms. Prime Minister Youssoufi was perceptively criticized for his use of the expression "Il faut laisser le temps au temps" (literally, "We should let time take its natural flow").[53] For one senior official, "The amplification of the inherent drawbacks of administrative technocracy is related to bad management of time, which is closely related to the Moroccan conception of time. I would like to stress that the Moroccan conception of time is different from the universal one. We have our own approach, which is typically Moroccan. What can normally be accomplished in two years in an established country will take four years in our country."[54]

Third, members of this segment of the PRE stress the importance of establishing trust between the monarchy and the political elite. Given the tumultuous history of the relationship between the monarchy and the opposition, who are currently in power, a climate of mistrust and ambiguity still lingers. For one advisor of the prime minister, change is, most of all, "a question of trust. . . . The prime minister should place his trust in his partners, and the king should have confidence in the prime minister. An inclusive strategy of political actors in the decisionmaking process is one of the prerequisites of change."[55]

It therefore appears that perception of change among members of the PRE varies according to their position or status, relative influence, and social background. There is also a collective consciousness among members of the PRE who belong to the second and third circle about the importance of change in the makhzanian culture. Many of them emphasize the necessity of a culture of participant citizenship.

Elite Perceptions of Their Role in the Transition Process

Elite perceptions of their role in the process of political liberalization provide insights into possible changes in elite attitudes toward power. These perspectives also help identify whether the relative change in the composition of the elite, since the earlier political opening of the 1990s and the advent of King Mohammed, have led the members of the PRE to a more active role in the political system. Based on the views of some members of the PRE, three main categories of elites can be distinguished: a loyalist elite, an elite in a crisis of reproduction and renewal, and an emerging and active elite.

A Loyalist Elite

There is an awareness among the PRE concerning the role that they have to play in the process of political change. Still, most senior officials in the first and second circles do not perceive themselves necessarily as harbingers of change. When speaking about their role in the liberalization process, they evoke the role of the monarch and his initiatives as the catalysts for political and economic liberalization. Most take no note of his or her own actions in these areas. Rather, they consider themselves executors of the will of the king.[56] The lack of initiative and the *attentisme* (inertia) are still dominant characteristics of the behavior of these members of the PRE.

Some aspects of change in this group's discourse and behavior have been noted. Indeed, in the discourse of the majority of the senior officials interviewed, social issues—poverty, the disabled, women's status, and so on—were the focus. All of these issues have been raised by King Mohammed. Apparently, the elite are more responsive to those issues because the king is interested in them. One senior official stated, "There is the attitude of the 'boss,' and the others will follow."[57] Therefore, changes in discourse and attitude are the result of adherence to the king's will or strategy. One can infer that this segment of the PRE constitutes more or less an acquiescent elite.

This last point reveals the kind of ambiguities still present in the political atmosphere of Morocco. It resulted from the long period of inertia among the elite during a large portion of Hassan II's reign. The vestiges of his authoritarian rule are apparent in the way these elites do not see themselves as directly involved in the decisionmaking process. One advisor of the prime minister alluded to how the elite are absorbed by the monarchical system and hence feel like followers rather than initiators. For him, "In the period between 1959 and 1976, the regime adopted a strategy of repression against the opposition. Between 1976 and 1996, a strategy of integration was implemented by using political corruption and institutions like the parliament and local councils. The members of this elite pursued their own interests and became auxiliaries of the makhzan. The regime created its own elite, and consequently, an elite which is not independent cannot change the system."[58]

An Elite in a Crisis of Reproduction and Renewal

Most members of the PRE are aware of the lack of reproduction and renewal in their ranks. The practice of recycling among the king's appointees can be considered an expression of the stagnation in the composition of the first and second circles of the PRE. This is also the case of another segment of the third circle, notably the party elite. Most of the conventions of the political parties have not led to any changes in the leadership of central committees. This is a general characteristic of all political parties, left and right. At the USFP's 2001 gathering, Youssoufi was reelected as leader of the party, and many members of the central committee retained their positions. The same applies to the leaders of the RNI and MNP, Ahmed Osmane and Mahjoubi Ahardan, respectively. It seems that the party elite are in a crisis of renewal either because the parties are unable to attract younger and more competent people or because the leadership of the parties have adopted a strategy of exclusion to maintain power. The recent emergence of associations operating in the social and economic fields and the dynamism of the civil society in general have also contributed to the problem by siphoning away potential new party members.

The problem of elite reproduction was stressed by many interviewees. Although the emerging entrepreneurial class and new actors in civil society, including the Islamists, have given the PRE a bit of new blood, the political elite in general remains in a crisis that requires urgent solutions. The political system in Morocco has not allowed for the emergence of new elites who can manage the institutional, social, and economic changes that Morocco requires. Given this crisis, members of different segments of the elite consider that a change in the composition of the elite is a prerequisite for any meaningful political change to occur. Such change should touch on all circles of power, starting at the local and regional levels and including political parties, trade unions, and the parliament.

PRE members also emphasize the importance of change in the mode of elite recruitment, which at the moment constitutes an obstacle for elite renewal. Family ties and wealth have largely regulated elite composition. The same fortunes, and consequently the same families, have dominated politics and economics. According to one advisor to Prime Minister Youssoufi, "A change in elite is related to a transformation of Moroccan society, moving away from clientelism to a culture of competence and meritocracy. It is not a generational problem or one of elite mobility, it is rather up to the capacity of the society to create and allow for real competition between different institutions and political actors."[59]

The interviewees emphasized also the importance of having new attitudes toward power. Morocco's elite have limited themselves to a role of criticizing the makhzan or obeying its rules without taking political action. According to the leader of a left-wing political party, "The elite is going through a crisis that I can qualify as 'an existential crisis.' . . . Elite and political actors should get involved and act as full actors of change in order to influence the orientation of the country."[60]

An Emerging and Active Elite

Some members of the PRE perceive themselves as full actors of change in Morocco. The members of this group constitute a minority and come from assorted segments of the elite: left-wing political parties and civil society organizations, the political opposition within the left-wing parties (for example, the socialists), and the Islamic movement.

These PRE members emphasize their role in political life and how they can contribute to change. Social issues, particularly education, are among their most important preoccupations. While speaking about their agenda, they refer to a social project, *projet de société,* instead of a program. Their strategy for change differs from group to group. For the more moderate groups, it is important to influence the decisionmaking process from within the political system by participating in its institutions. More radical groups prefer to participate outside such institutions, unless down the road the monarchy makes acceptable concessions. The more radical groups want major reforms in the overall political arena, in which they want to participate. For an influential member of al-'Adl wa-l-Ihsan, "The makhzanian system is an evil one and is corrupted; that is why we don't want to participate in this system."[61]

These members of the PRE are, regardless of their impact, indicative of the gradual emergence of a new kind of elite, one that is more conscious of its role in the political arena. The opening of the 1990s, change in the monarchy, and the new discourse, attitudes, and priorities provide an ideal context and a more appropriate atmosphere for broader participation in politics. Yet, whether this group will influence the ongoing process of liberalization will depend on its capacity to remain outside the system of co-optation.

The Dilemma of Change and Continuity

In Morocco change in elite attitudes and behavior have significantly affected the progress of political liberalization. The views of politically relevant elites about change and their perceptions of their own role in this process reveal that there are elements of continuity and change. Indeed, continuity and change characterize the Moroccan political system as a whole.

Continuity is evident in the long-standing nature of the regime. The king remains the institutional and political center of the system and the core around which elites coalesce. Decisions are still highly concentrated at the level of the monarchical institution, and most of the reforms that have so far been adopted, whether concerning education, the economy, or tourism, were the result of a royal initiative. While there have been positive signs of change and democratic intentions, Mohammed VI has reinforced his central role through the further institutionalization of monarchical powers. As stated, the "modernization" of the monarchical institution is leading toward a hybrid system of monarchical control and elite integration into the political system. In order to guarantee the continuity of the regime, the monarchy has consistently relied on a strategy of elite co-optation. What is new under Mohammed VI is the integration of the groups that have emerged as a result of the ongoing process of political liberalization. As opposed to Hassan II, Mohammed VI is co-opting an elite that is drawn more and more from a dynamic civil society.

Change is obvious in a number of areas. There is, for example, a growing role of civil society and the media as a result of more freedom of expression. The media has begun to raise a number of issues to the level of national debate, including corruption, women's rights, immigration, poverty, and unemployment. Even some issues that were considered taboo under Hassan II are now openly discussed. Criticism of the government and parliament can now be found on the front pages of most newspapers. Even the army has recently been criticized (though in a rather timid way) for corruption in its ranks. In the field of human rights, there have also been positive signs, notably the release of political prisoners and the creation of a committee for compensation. Overall, many aspects of change are clearly noticeable. Yet, the process of political, economic, and social reforms launched in the early 1990s remains incomplete. There has been no constitutional reform concerning the distribution of power among the monarchy, the government, and other political actors. The Moroccan constitution still favors the monarchy and the concentration of power in it.

Continuity and change also characterize the composition of the Moroccan elite. One can speak of changes in leadership style and priorities, but there have been no major changes in the composition of the core elite. Because of the "depoliticization" of the political field, the new members of the PRE are concerned more with economic liberalization than they are with the institutionalization of democracy. There is clearly a focus on investment, tourism, and economic relations with Europe and the United States. Members of the first circle of the PRE are primarily associated with this trend. Apart from a small number of newcomers, who were recruited from among friends and classmates of King Mohammed, the new monarch retained most of his father's old guard. Overall, the core elite consists of a conservative social group oriented toward economic reform but not political change. Its members tend to be part of the "loyalist" segment of the elite, whose interests lies in the political status quo.

In the second circle of the PRE, there is a continuous reshuffling. It is difficult to speak about a renewal of this elite segment; rather it is characterized by a recycling of its members. The faces that headed public institutions under Hassan II also head them under Mohammed VI. Most of the members of this circle of the PRE are by no means actively involved in the promotion of democracy. The authoritarian political culture of Hassan II's reign remains in the memory of an elite that is not yet ready for change. Their technocratic orientation and loyalty make them something of an "executive" grouping in the purely economic sense of the word. As part of the makhzan elite, they are more likely to advise the king and execute his instructions and directives.

Change in the composition of the third circle of the PRE is more obvious. Though there were no major changes in the composition of parliament following the 2002 elections, there is an emerging and more liberal elite from within civil society, left-wing parties, and the media that, while a minority, is willing to play an active role in politics and leave an imprint on the process of liberalization. If there is a new elite on the verge of entering the circles of influence, one question must be asked: To what extent will this generation of newcomers have an impact on the more conservative segment of the elite or vice versa? To answer this question, it is once again important to put the political centrality of the monarchy into perspective. The absorptive capacity of the monarchical system will persistently activate itself and react appropriately, co-opting and integrating any part of the elite that is willing to challenge its legitimacy and attempt to establish solid democratic institutions and government.

Change in the elite will not lead necessarily to a change in the system. Change in Morocco is more about continuity. Nevertheless, this analysis should be nuanced. The growing number of elites could lead to a breakdown in clientelist networks because of the lack of resources needed to keep it operating. In addition, the political opening of the 1990s that allowed for more participation and involvement in Morocco's political life may pave the way for the emergence of a participatory culture and a greater sense of initiative, already noticeable, among certain members of the third circle. In the long run, the combination of these two factors can have a major impact on the process of liberalization.

Notes

The author thanks Iris Glosemeyer, Azzedine Layachi, and especially Driss Maghraoui for their comments on a draft of this chapter.

1. For a theoretical formulation of the concept of politically relevant elites, see Volker Perthes's introductory chapter in this volume.

2. In their study of the third wave of democratic transitions, a number of scholars have stressed the importance of the role played by political elites. See, O'Donnell, Schmitter, and Whitehead, *Transitions from Authoritarian Rule*. Elites are not, however, the only factor in such transitions. Others include the level of economic development, mass action, and international pressure. On the role of the elites, see Higley and Gunther, *Elites and Democratic Consolidation*.

3. On the lack of ideology and the shared value of economic interest, see Tessler, "Morocco: Institutional Pluralism and Monarchical Dominance," p. 72. Until recently, little attention has been paid to the values to which elites adhere; their commitment to democracy was considered secondary. See Rustow, "Transitions to Democracy"; Huntington, "Will More Countries Become Democratic?"; Karl, "Democracy by Design: The Christian Democratic Party in El Salvador." Samuel Huntington and Terry Lynn Karl argue that democracy has been an unintended consequence and that political elites viewed democracy as a means of realizing other objectives. Other scholars think differently on elites' normative commitment to democracy. Scott Mainwaring, in "Transitions to Democracy and Democratic Consolidation," p. 309, argues that "in Latin America, democracy has worked only where political elites saw it as a best solution, not as an instrumental means of securing some of their interests."

4. The literal meaning of makhzan is "storage." It was used historically to refer to the sultan's court and retinue, the regional and provincial administration, the army, and all persons linking these institutions to the general population. The makhzan's task was the collection of taxes, and when certain groups resisted, it turned to coercive measures. The notion of "makhzan" and its meaning have changed over time. It has also variously been used to refer to the state apparatus; the services that the state provides to its citizens, such as education, health care, and other forms of economic and social development; and all persons in the service of the central power (the monarchy) and with official and unofficial (religious, military, economic, or political) authority. Cherifi, in *Le Makhzen politique au Maroc*, p. 15, refers to the makhzan as "une structure, un style de gouvernement, un système et une institution" (a structure, a style of government, a system and an institution). For more on the makhzan, see Bourqia, "The Cultural Legacy of Power in Morocco"; Claisse, "Le Makhzen aujourd'hui"; and Waterbury, *The Commander of the Faithful*.

5. See Bourqia, "The Cultural Legacy of Power in Morocco."

6. See Bellaire, "L'Administration au Maroc."

7. On the cultural foundations of Moroccan authoritarianism, see Hammoudi, *Master and Disciple*.

8. This study is based on data that have been gathered through semidirective interviews with thirty-five members of the PRE. It also benefits from the analysis of interviews conducted with academics, journalists, and people who are closely connected to the PRE or facilitate contact with them. Some of them hold official positions but they have no real influence on the decisionmaking process.

9. The opposition, especially members of the left, used this expression to describe their relationship with Hassan.

10. According to the constitution, the king has the right to appoint the prime minister and other cabinet members. He can dissolve the parliament and rule single-handedly by declaring a state of emergency.

11. See Leveau, *Le fellah marocain, défenseur du trône*.

12. Waterbury, *The Commander of the Faithful*.

13. Ibid., p. 158.

14. For instance, the process of political opening was interrupted in 1965, when Hassan declared a state of emergency after the failure of political parties to reach an agreement concerning their participation in a *gouvernement d'union nationale* (government of national union). This process was put back on track in the mid-1970s with the emergence of a "national consensus" concerning the monarchy's claim to the Western Sahara. Since 1975, Morocco has asserted territorial claim over the Western Sahara, the former Spanish colony (1884–1975) that was ceded by Spain to Morocco and Mauritania without the consent of Western Saharans. For more on the Western Sahara dispute, see Zoubir and Volman, *International Dimensions of the Western Sahara Conflict*.

15. In one example, in 1962 the Union Nationale des Forces Populaire, the Communist party, and the Moroccan Workers Union opposed the constitution, while the Istiqlal party supported it.

16. Phosphate deposits and potential income from fishing along the Western Sahara coastline also colored the picture.

17. The USFP was created in 1975 after a schism in the UNFP in 1972. For more details on the evolution of political parties in Morocco, see Khatibi, *L'Alternance et les Partis Politiques*.

18. The Koutla was composed of four political parties: the PI, USFP, Partie du Progrès et du Socialisme (PPS), and the Organisation de l'Action Démocratique et Populaire (OADP).

19. This council replaces the Constitutional Chamber of the Supreme Court. It is composed of twelve members with nine-year terms, six of which are appointed by the king, three appointed by the president of the House of Representatives, and three members appointed by the president of the House of Counsellors. The chairman of the Constitutional Council is selected by the king from among the members appointed by him (as per Article 79 of the constitution).

20. This council is an advisory body for the government and the parliament.

21. Hassan II previously declared a state of emergency, under which he concentrated all power in his hands, dissolved the parliament, and assumed the duties of the prime minister. He ruled in this manner from June 1965 until July 1970.

22. These ministries are interior, justice, Islamic affairs, and foreign affairs. See Tozy, "Political Changes in the Maghreb."

23. See Daoud, "Maroc: les élections de 1997."

24. In liberal democracies, alternance means the emergence of opposition par-

ties to power as a result of their success in free and transparent elections. For alternance in the Moroccan context, see Boudahrain, *Le nouveau Maroc politique, quel avenir?* pp. 61–73. Many interpretations were given to the king's initiative on alternance. For some observers, it pointed to the possible evolution of a more pluralistic political system but also to Hassan preparing conditions for a smooth succession. For others, such as Michael Willis, it was "a cynical attempt to tempt critics of the system or in the system itself so they compromise themselves." According to this thesis, "unable to find quick solutions to Morocco's multiple economic and social problems for which they have long berated previous administrations, the new government will discredit itself, lose power and no longer be able to effectively criticize the Makhzan which will reassume full power after the perceived failure of the alternance experiment" (Willis, "After Hassan," p. 118).

25. The government of alternance was a coalition drawn from a parliamentary majority formed by seven parties: Front des Forces Démocratiques (FFD), Istiqlal, Mouvement National Populaire (MNP), Partie Social Démocrate (PSD), PPS, Rassemblement National des Indépendants (RNI), and USFP.

26. On the results of the 2002 elections, see www.afrol.com/News2002/mor029_poll_results.htm and www.elections2002.ma (accessed on 12 October 2002).

27. From nine seats in 1997 to forty-three seats in 2002.

28. Up from four in the 1997 legislature.

29. Youssoufi relays, "At our first working session, the king said, 'You must know I'm a democrat.' That's reassuring." Howe, "Morocco's Democratic Experience."

30. Yassine asked Mohammed to use some of his father's fortune to pay off Morocco's debts and to relieve poverty. For the text of the letter, see http://abbc.com/yassine/memo.htm, accessed on 17 September 2002.

31. In 1994 Hassan created a consultative council for following social dialogue.

32. As mentioned earlier, according to Article 24 of the constitution, the king appoints the prime minister. It is upon the prime minister's recommendations that the king appoints the other ministers, as the king may terminate their services. Article 30 outlines the king's role as commander in chief, permits him to make civil and military appointments, and reserves his right to delegate such powers.

33. Frederick W. Frey, in *The Turkish Political Elite,* p. 157, doubts the existence of causal links between background and attitudes. For him, "To leap from the knowledge of social background of national politicians to inferences about the power structure of society is quite dangerous. Even to proceed from such knowledge to judgments about . . . political behavior . . . can be treacherous." Robert Springborg, however, advances the thesis that "the knowledge of social background characteristics may be tantamount to knowing the entire array of an elite's political attitudes." See Springborg, "Social Background Analysis of Political Elite," unpublished manuscript, quoted in Lenczowski, *Political Elites in the Middle East,* p. 6.

34. Waterbury, *The Commander of the Faithful,* p. 82.

35. For instance, André Azoulay and Mohammed Kabbaj are the king's advisors in charge of economic matters. Both of them held positions in the second circle before moving into the first circle. Kabbaj held the commerce and finance porfolios before becoming a counselor.

36. Another symbolic change is the public appearances of Mohammed VI's wife. Some have interpreted his marrying a middle-class woman in March 2002 as another sign of his connection to the people.

37. Zartman, "King Hassan's New Morocco," pp. 24–25.

38. The Defense Ministry was downgraded to the National Defense

Administration, which is concerned with logistics and procurement. Hassan took on decisions concerning operational initiatives.

39. In October 2002 an "action committee of the free officers" sent an open letter to Mohammed asking him to eradicate corruption among high-ranking army officers. The communiqué called for the dismissal of seven generals, including Laanigari and Gen. Hosni Benslimane, head of the Gendarmerie. See Eileen Byrne, "Morocco, Unsettling Times," *Middle East International,* 8 November 2002, pp. 21–22. For the content of the letter, see www.wsahara.net/02/morarmopen.html (accessed on 18 December 2002).

40. His predecessor, Mohammed Alaoui Lamdeghri, had held the office for seventeen years.

41. Waterbury, *The Commander of the Faithful,* p. 87.

42. These appointments were made between August 1999 and October 2002.

43. For more details, see Tessler, "Morocco: Institutional Pluralism and Monarchical Dominance."

44. On the role of education in elite reproduction, see Vermeren, *Ecole, élite et Pouvoir: Maroc-Tunisie.*

45. Tessler, "Morocco's Next Political Generation."

46. "Senior officials" here refers to heads of public institutions, walis, and governors.

47. See Maghraoui, "Depoliticization in Morocco."

48. This section is based on a qualitative analysis of thirty-five interviews conducted with members of the PRE in September and October 2001 and July 2002. The sample included two ministers, senior officials appointed by King Mohammed to head prominent public institutions, the Speaker of the House of Representatives, leaders of political parties from the left, advisors of Prime Minister Youssoufi, leaders of influential NGOs, and influential members of the Islamist movement (PJD and al-'Adl wa-l-Ihsan). In terms of age, almost half of the interviewees were between thirty-four and forty-five years of age, while the rest were over forty-five. All of them had achieved higher degrees, in fields ranging from political science to economics to engineering. The majority of them had pursued their education in France. All of the interviewees were asked questions about their political itinerary, participation in the decisionmaking process, and perceptions of the process of change and the role they might play in it. The interviews were conducted in French. Only a few were recorded, reflecting the mistrust that some members of the PRE still have about expressing their views.

49. Interview, 27 September 2001, Rabat.

50. Interview, 23 September 2001, Casablanca.

51. Interview, 3 October 2001, Rabat.

52. Interview, 25 September 2001, Rabat.

53. See Maghraoui, "Political Authority in Crisis."

54. Interview, 28 September 2001, Rabat.

55. Interview, 11 October 2001, Rabat.

56. Some of the interviewees, despite the position and the power they hold, do not consider themselves part of the elite. Contrary to what has been emphasized by Waterbury, there is no common consciousness among members of the elite on belonging to an elite. Waterbury, *The Commander of the Faithful,* p. 123.

57. Interview, 12 October 2001, Rabat.

58. Interview, 28 September 2001, Rabat.

59. Interview, 25 September 2001, Rabat.

60. Interview, 9 October 2001, Rabat.

61. Interview, 30 July 2002, Rabat.

4

Syria:
Difficult Inheritance
Volker Perthes

In summer 2000 Syria experienced a quasi-monarchical change of leadership. Immediately after the death of Hafiz al-Asad, who had ruled the country since 1970, the late president's thirty-four-year-old son, Bashar, was installed as the new leader by the relevant state and party agencies. Their decision was then ratified in a public referendum. In July 2000 Bashar al-Asad officially assumed leadership of the highly centralized and authoritarian presidential system that had been shaped during his father's rule. The succession process was neither a break with the past nor the breakdown of the system that some observers had feared and others had hoped for, but rather a change at the top that had been prepared some time in advance to safeguard the stability of state and regime.

During the first three years of the "era Bashar," administrative and economic reform topped the agenda. Political reform remained limited. A wide-ranging personnel and generational change began concurrently within Syria's politically relevant elite. Bashar al-Asad needed the support and experience of the advisors he had inherited from his father, but the largely ossified regime elite needed renewal and rejuvenation to advocate and implement the reform agenda of the new president and to create a loyal base within the institutions of power—the bureaucracy, the Ba'th party, and the security apparatus.

In 2003 central figures from Hafiz al-Asad's policy team—often referred to as the old guard—still played an important role in Syrian government, although the exchange of political, administrative, and security personnel after the accession of Bashar al-Asad had been the most far-reaching in Syria in any comparable time span since 1970. This raises the issue of why, in spite of substantial changes within the PRE, policy shifts remained more limited than domestic and foreign observers had predicted. One frequently hears explanations pointing to intraelite conflicts, mostly emphasizing the influence of the old guard, which, as the argument goes, prevents Bashar al-Asad from pursuing a more ambitious reform program.[1] In a variation of this model, Patrick Seale, the veteran watcher of Syrian presidents and power politics, stresses the inability of the new president to effectively monopolize power.[2] Another explanation that supporters of Bashar al-Asad and others focus on is external factors, notably the Arab-Israeli conflict. This theory establishes a causal link between the peace process and the pace of domestic change, arguing that the ability of the regime to embark on substantive reforms decreased inasmuch as regional tensions increased months after Bashar al-Asad assumed power.

Lack of purpose, diffusion of power, and external constraints explain part of the difficulty in implementing reforms, as does bureaucratic politics. Beyond that, however, to understand the limited nature of reform and policy shifts in the first three years of Bashar al-Asad's regime, the character of elite change must be taken into consideration, notably the fact that the recomposition of the PRE has largely been a regime affair. Bashar al-Asad is a child of the Syrian political system in every sense of the word, and even the most reform-minded elements of his team, along with other members of the core elite, wanted in some ways to rejuvenate the regime but also to maintain what they had inherited, not undermine it. Considerable differences in worldview and style certainly existed between the people that Bashar al-Asad brought on or promoted and those members of the PRE who had been ensconced by his father. Their conflicts involved positions and policies as well as the speed and depth of reform. Regardless, the old and new elements of the Syrian leadership shared an interest in pursuing change in a gradual and controlled manner and also in maintaining control over transitions within elite circles. Consequently, the regime aborted early attempts by independent or opposition forces to gain positions of political relevance. The agenda of Syria's new elite, as well as its limits, were clearly reflected in the discourses that emerged along with and after the change at the top and in the ways the new leadership dealt with strategic issues.

Recomposition of the Politically Relevant Elite

When Bashar al-Asad stepped into the structures of the personalized presidential system that Hafiz al-Asad had established, no one expected him to immediately acquire the full scope of his father's hegemonic powers (although he assumed all his official posts). Before his inauguration as president, Bashar al-Asad had been promoted to lieutenant general and commander in chief of the armed forces and been elected general-secretary of the Ba'th party, the institution which, according to the 1973 constitution, "leads" state and society. The general-secretary of the Ba'th is also the president of the Progressive National Front (PNF), which, under the leadership of the Ba'th, integrates a number of smaller parties into the political system.

By 2003 Bashar al-Asad had clearly become the most important decisionmaker in the Syrian state, but he was not the source of all power. Other members of the leadership had obtained positions, influence, and legitimacy directly from the late president. Bashar al-Asad, in contrast, owed his position to the very regime at the top of which he had been placed. The new president did not make all important political decisions alone, and some decisions were apparently not ones he favored. A case in point was the decision that Syria would not attend the November 2000 Euro-Mediterranean conference of foreign ministers in Marseilles. The issue was reported to have been hotly contested among the Ba'th party's regional (Syrian) leadership.[3] While the president and some others wanted the foreign minister to attend the meeting, if only in order to avoid offending the French government and the European Union, the majority view, to which Bashar al-Asad eventually conceded, was that Syria should not participate in meetings that would include social events at which the Israeli foreign minister would be in attendance.[4]

Following the succession, certain members of the core elite wielded more influence over decisions of strategic importance than they would have under Hafiz al-Asad. The distribution of power within this elite, however, was by no means entrenched. It appeared initially that a collective leadership had coalesced that included but also constrained Bashar al-Asad. Gradually, within two years, however, the president asserted himself as Syria's primary decisionmaker, though not a hegemonic one, within a powerful core elite.

Bashar al-Asad's power derived from various sources. First, of course, he was the president, and the authoritarian structures of the regime provided that all lines of decisionmaking—including those bureaucratic and governmental as well as those within the military, security apparatuses, and the Ba'th party—flew through the president's office.[5] Bashar al-Asad also benefited from a dual legitimacy as the heir to his father and as a representative of the younger generation in a regime that had become gerontocratic in his father's last years. In addition, Bashar al-Asad possessed the advantage of knowledge vis-à-vis those representing the old regime elite. After the death of his older brother in 1994, Bashar al-Asad had built for himself the image of counselor to his father and, after some initial difficulties, a succession candidate who knew the world of new technologies and media—that is, someone who was up to date with the world, in contrast to most incumbent members of the regime elite. Doubtless, and again, in stark contrast to most of the members of the so-called old guard, Bashar al-Asad enjoyed broad popularity. Finally, he consolidated his power by systematically appointing trusted people to important positions, gradually increasing the number and the influence of members among the PRE who were loyal to him and committed to his agenda.

So who belonged to Syria's politically relevant elite some three years after the change at the top? Given that politics and political decisionmaking in Syria are not particularly transparent, a crystal clear picture cannot be drawn. On the basis of political systems analysis and the reputation of leading figures, however, plausible sketches can be made. One can safely assume that the core elite—members of the first, or inner, circle, where key domestic and foreign policy decisions are made—consisted of slightly more than a dozen people, among them some with official government positions, representatives of the security apparatus, and members of the president's family. Along with the president, this group included Vice President Abd al-Halim Khaddam (but not the second vice president, Zuheir Masharqa, who often represented the president at meetings of little importance but did not carry any political weight), the prime minister, foreign minister, defense minister, chief of military intelligence, and the deputy general-secretary of the Ba'th party leadership. Muhammad Makhlouf, the president's uncle, was generally considered to belong to the group but did not occupy a political or military position. Rather, he ruled a vast business empire and a network of cronies that Syrians generally referred to as the Mafia. He had considerable direct influence over economic and financial policies as well as over individual government officials.

These elite members owed their positions and influence to the late president. There were others, however, who only entered the inner circle with or under Bashar al-Asad. Among those were the president's younger brother, Mahir, and his brother-in-law, the former an officer in the palace guard, the latter a high-ranking officer in military intelligence. The interior minister, the head of General Intelligence (the Mukhabarat), the head of the General Intelligence domestic affairs department, and one or two other government ministers known to be close advisors to the president beyond their particular portfolios could also most probably be considered part of the core elite.

Other members of the cabinet and other advisors to the president should generally be counted among the second PRE circle. They did not make strategic decisions. Within the field of their portfolios, however, they were no doubt influential. Members of the second circle also included leading military and security officers, whose ranks Bashar al-Asad shuffled after his rise to power. Within the first one-and-a-half years, he appointed a new chief of staff and new heads of all but one intelligence agency.

Less influential elite members, with indirect influence over strategic decisions, agenda setting, and discourses—the third, or outer, circle according to the analytical model used here—included assistant ministers, provincial governors, the heads of Ba'th party provincial branches, as well as a couple of other high functionaries directly appointed by the president. Some independent personalities tried to enter this circle, but failed.

Bashar al-Asad's First Government

In December 2001 Bashar al-Asad appointed his first cabinet. The outgoing government, formed in March 2000, shortly before the death of Hafiz al-Asad, had also carried the fingerprints of the then-president's son, with some of Bashar al-Asad's people having been appointed to lesser posts. That cabinet, which remained in office for only one-and-a-half years, a rather short period compared to previous Syrian cabinets, was generally regarded as transitional, bridging the eras of Hafiz and Bashar al-Asad. Only six members of the new cabinet appointed in December 2001 had been in their respective positions before the March 2000 shuffle. Among them were Mustafa Tlass—one of the most trusted and long-serving companions of the late president, defense minister since 1971, and engineer of the succession process—and Foreign Minister Farouk al-Sharaa, who had occupied his office since 1984. These veterans who also stayed on in Bashar al-Asad's second government, formed in summer 2003, commanded experience with which the young president could hardly dispense. In contrast, most of the new appointees belonged to a younger generation and brought with them other qualifications, namely the knowledge needed to embark on technological and economic reform and promote Syrian integration into the world economy. The government thus reflected to a degree the conflicting agendas within Syria's new leadership.

Bashar al-Asad apparently made some compromise appointments, but the cabinet nonetheless illustrated his priorities and those of the new era—noticeably, while some persons changed, the profile of the cabinet he appointed in summer 2003 was very similar to his first. The direction was particularly apparent in regard to ministries dealing with economic policy issues, technology, and training and education. People sometimes referred to them and some of their aides as "Bashar's technocrats," and they were perceived as a team of reformers. Some in the group, namely the tourism minister and the then minister of higher education, had been close political advisors to Bashar al-Asad even before his assumption of the presidency. These appointees demonstrated an orientation toward technical modernization and, as it were, opening up to the world. The ministers of economy, finance, industry, communication, education, higher education, tourism, and agriculture held European or U.S. university degrees, most either in engineering or in economics. Most of them also held doctoral degrees from France, Britain, or the United States, and almost all are professionals with experience working abroad: the new economy and foreign trade minister had been a long-time World Bank official; the finance minister had once served as the World Bank's Arab executive director; the agriculture minister, the education minister, and the industry minister had worked as consultants for UN organizations. Several members of the reform team were "independents," meaning that they did not belong to the Ba'th party or any of the smaller PNF parties. Three of the reform team members, however, were or had been leading members of the formally nongovernmental Syrian Computer Society (SCS), over which Bashar al-Asad had presided until his ascent to the presidency and through which he had built his image as a modernizer. Bashar al-Asad had held no other official position before the death of his father. Several members of the SCS served as advisors to Bashar al-Asad after he became president or were appointed to leading administrative positions, such as the mayor of Damascus who became a minister of state in the 2003 cabinet.

Beyond their comparatively modern qualifications, most of the new recruits to the cabinet and the wider PRE were regarded as relatively "clean." Fighting corruption had been part of Bashar al-Asad's image before his accession. This sat well with international observers, who regarded corruption as a major obstacle to investment in Syria, and with the general public, but it also created exaggerated expectations. Any serious campaign to root out graft and extortion by governors, ministers, security officers, and other people connected to the regime would face resistance from parts of the core elite, including members of the president's family. Regardless, Bashar al-Asad's efforts to clean up the cabinet reflected a serious attempt to change the professional and moral profile of the regime and its personnel.

Although some of the people closest to the new president had worked with him in the SCS, the composition of the new cabinet revealed the continuing importance of three more established recruitment pools for elite positions: the security apparatus, the Ba'th party (though less so than in previous decades), and the state and public sector bureaucracies. Syria's fifteen provincial governorships have been among the most important posts in the state bureaucracy from which candidates for higher government or security positions are chosen. A governor (*muhafiz*) has great responsibility and must enjoy the president's confidence. The president appoints all governors, who thus represent the head of state and, together with the chiefs of local Ba'th party branches and intelligence services, oversee security and the political arena. Muhammad Mustafa Miru, for example, had been a governor for twenty years in different provinces before he was appointed prime minister in 2000. Deputy prime minister for services Naji al-Utri, who succeeded Miru as prime minister in 2003 after a short spell as speaker of the parliament (Majlis al-Sha'b), had been a governor of Homs; and the chief of the National Security Office, formally a Ba'th party position, not a government post, had been governor of Hama. Other ministers had directed large public sector companies or had moved up the career ladder of the government bureaucracy. This would generally qualify them to head service ministries, such as the ministries of construction or irrigation but, like the technocrats from the reform team, not to hold a security portfolio. The new interior minister, in contrast, formerly headed General Intelligence.

As a rule, provincial governors, cabinet members with security-related portfolios, and officials high in the security apparatus are card-carrying members of the Ba'th party. The same is not a precondition for a minister in charge of an economic dossier or other service portfolios. Some ministers, however, might owe their posts entirely to their party function. Generally, an accumulation of functions in different institutions with some role in political decisionmaking—for instance, being a government minister and a member of the Ba'th party's regional command—would increase the influence that a member of the political elite wielded. The prime minister, his deputies, the foreign and defense ministers, as well as the speaker of the parliament tend to belong to the twenty-one-member Ba'th party leadership.

Politicians and Bureaucrats

It is noteworthy that the cabinets appointed in 2001 and 2003 did not include businesspeople or politicians in the Weberian sense—that is, individuals who live for, rather than from, politics. Rather, ministers tended to be technocrats in the broadest terms, party functionaries, or both. The transitional 2000 cabinet had included one businessman—the first one in thirty years—an independent deputy whose appointment was interpreted as a nod toward private capital. He was not reappointed to the 2001 cabinet.

It would be incorrect to assume that there were no politicians, let alone no politics, in Syria. Since 1990 one-third of the seats in the parliament have been reserved for "independent" candidates, who run on individual tickets rather than as members of the Ba'th and PNF lists. The seats that the Ba'th and its smaller allies claim for themselves were not open for competition; the independent slots, however, were.[6] The main purpose for this arrangement was to integrate unrepresented groups into official state structures, particularly the business community, whose expertise and economic contribution were increasingly needed. Aside from a few intellectuals and a group of tribal leaders, most of the independent deputies have indeed been entrepreneurs or self-employed professionals.

In practice, the parliament, with its built-in Ba'th majority, acts in a consultative capacity at best, in addition to rubber-stamping decisions made in other places. Significantly, parliament did not become a source of recruitment for administrative or political leadership personnel. Most independent deputies, therefore, have remained outside the circles of political relevance, much the same as their Ba'thist colleagues without cabinet or party leadership positions. Notable exceptions were some independent deputies who tried to use their positions as platforms from which to influence public debate and to contribute to political agenda setting. Numbering no more than a handful, they were mainly businessmen, such as Ihsan Sanqar, a moderately conservative entrepreneur who won seats in the 1990 and 1994 elections, and Riad Sayf, a self-made industrialist with leftist leanings who was elected to the assembly in 1994 and 1998.

Sayf openly criticized the government, outlined alternatives to its economic and financial policies in his speeches before parliament, and distributed his statements—as other independent deputies did—among his friends and supporters. With the accession of Bashar al-Asad, he tried to establish the foundation of a possible opposition party, and he demanded, in parliament and in semipublic gatherings, that the Ba'th party's monopoly on power be broken.[7] Such daring behavior must be seen in the context of the so-called Damascus Spring, the general atmosphere of political opening, freer debate, and high expectations during the first six or so months of the Bashar era. By spring 2001, however, the political season had turned to autumn. During that following summer, Sayf and a number of other dissidents were arrested and indicted on such charges as trying to "change the constitution by illegal means" and spreading "false or exaggerated news." They were sentenced to up to ten years in prison.

While in parliament, Sayf had become a relevant figure in Syria's political life. He did not have a say in strategic decisions, but he was able to influence public opinion and force certain items onto the political agenda, placing him in the third circle of influence. His and the other dissidents' arrests and trials were a clear signal that the regime was not (yet) ready to tolerate efforts by independent groups or individuals to promote themselves, through parliament or extraparliamentary activities, into the politically relevant elite. Rather, the process of elite change would remain in the hands of those in the inner circle.

The regime's management of change within the PRE involved replacing some personnel in government and regime institutions, bringing to the fore a younger generation. The rate of exchange, as it were, was indeed substantial: Over two years, starting with the new cabinet in March 2000 and continuing through the cabinet shuffle of December 2001, forty-two of fifty-seven officeholders in the first and second circles of the politically relevant elite were replaced by newcomers.[8] The nature of the change included neopatrimonial aspects in that it enabled the president to build his own network of loyalists within the relevant institutions. Most of the newly appointed individuals, however, also represented what could be called an image of better governance. The personnel changes complemented structural and organizational reforms that were intended to strengthen government structures vis-à-vis other centers of power, and they in effect widened the PRE.

Among other measures he instated, Asad directed cabinet ministers to define and broaden the responsibilities of assistant ministers and to appoint advisory staff with clear job descriptions. After the 2001 cabinet shuffle, ministers could independently choose assistant ministers, whereas before these appointments had been the prerogative of the Ba'th party leadership. Such measures strengthened the authority of the ministers and the cabinet at large, as did allowing ministers to make decisions on investment and expenditures up to a certain amount, rather than submitting such plans to the prime minister. These changes in administration reduced the role of the party leadership, as a body, in day-to-day government affairs. The appointment of a high-ranking intelligence officer as interior minister can also be interpreted as an attempt to strengthen the government rather than as a power grab by the Mukhabarat. The aim was, it seems, to make the Interior Ministry the main institution responsible for domestic security and thus to somewhat curtail the relative independence of the various and often competing intelligence services.

All governors, almost all provincial party bosses, and the larger part of Ba'th party executives in the provinces were replaced within the first two years of Bashar al-Asad's tenure. All the new appointments came from the top, issued through presidential decrees or by the Ba'th party's regional leadership. Also, for the first time in more than thirty years, elections were held at the lower levels of the party structure. Members of the local branches were allowed to elect from within their ranks twice as many candidates for branch leadership positions as there were slots; the party leadership would then select half of this group to lead the branches. The leadership reserved the option to appoint those candidates who received the largest number of votes, and in most early cases did so. The new system for elections encouraged younger party members, who identified with the new president and his modernizing agenda, and brought new blood into the sclerotic veins of the party.

The sequence of personnel changes is of interest. Editors in chief of the state-owned media were the first positions to which the new president directly appointed new people. Provincial party leaders and governors came next. After the formation of the December 2001 cabinet, Bashar al-Asad replaced several leading figures in the security apparatus. A reasonable interpretation of this sequence is that Bashar al-Asad wanted to establish a firm, loyal base in the third and second circles of influence, thereby weakening alternative clientelist networks before he set about replacing personnel in sensitive political and security positions. A number of the dismissed editors as well as staff members in the presidential office were appointed ambassadors, an indication perhaps of the rather limited value Syria's leadership places on the country's diplomatic service.

Rejuvenation of the state and party apparatuses was a priority of the new leadership not only as a means of securing loyalty, but also as a component of administrative reform. When Bashar al-Asad succeeded his father, there was a widespread feeling that many of the old generation dominating the echelons of the bureaucracy and the party would have to go. In many institutions, leading cadres had stayed past their usefulness; the president of the student union, in office for fifteen years only to be promoted to a cabinet post directly thereafter, was but one example. As the president made clear in his inaugural address, new qualifications and skills were in order. Complaints about *biruqratiyya*—shorthand for red tape, incompetence, and lack of a work ethic—in the state administration and public sector were legion. Such problems would only be partially solved by retraining cadres already in place. A number of functionaries in their fifties and sixties would likely be unable to adjust to the new requirements in computer and language skills. Many cadres on the job were also thought to be highly resistant to reform.[9] The career paths of younger people had often been blocked.

In March 2002 Bashar al-Asad decreed that all civil servants over the age of sixty would be retired. The decision would affect some 80,000 employees, allow younger cadres to be promoted, and offer opportunities for new workers.[10] Some exceptions to forced retirement proved necessary, because so little had been done to train younger workers for leadership positions.

Party members in their thirties and forties in lower and middle functionary positions tended to view the process of change at the higher levels of party and state in generational—rather than ideological—terms. Members of this group comprised a generation seeking its share of power and positions, but not a change of the system. Such mid-level functionaries, who could not be counted within the PRE but certainly aspired to entering it, would for example complain that except for the president himself, there were no representatives of the "generation Bashar" in the party leadership and that the older generation continued to dominate it. They scoffed at the functionaries manning nongovernmental organizations close to the regime: "Did your realize," one of them asked, "that none of the leaders of the Popular Committee for the Support of the Intifada is under sixty?"[11] Asked about the differences between their generation and the outgoing generation, members of the new one defined themselves as more "objective" and more knowledgeable of the modern world. The younger functionaries certainly hoped that the new leadership would proceed with personnel changes, thereby increasing their chances of moving into higher or more powerful positions. This did not, however, indicate that the new generation necessarily had an alternative agenda to that of their predecessors or those they sought to replace.

Modernization or Reform?
Political Agendas and Strategic Issues

Not only did many of the newcomers to the PRE possess qualifications considered necessary for setting Syria on the course of reform and modernization, more than a few also favored a more discursive and transparent style of governance than had governments and party leaders of the past. New cabinet ministers began publicly addressing sensitive topics, such as high unemployment and financial losses in the public industrial sector.[12] In mid-2002, while presenting an economic reform program, the then deputy prime minister openly acknowledged that Syria's oil production would decline, and would not, in the midterm, be sufficient to finance necessary development programs.[13] Previously, the topic of faltering oil income had been taboo. The economy and foreign trade minister once even spoke of "ongoing resistance" to the government's economic reform program,[14] a statement that brought intraelite controversies into the public domain.

In substance, differences within the cabinet and the core elite went beyond personnel and positions and into the realm of policy change and structural reform. Personnel changes, of course, can reflect policy shifts and realignment of balances among regime institutions. For Syria, in addition to the upgrading of cabinet ministers, consider the gradual loss of power by the General Federation of Trade Unions. In the 1970s the unions had become one of the regime's main instruments of power—a corporatist mass organization designed to restrain the public sector workforce, not to advocate for working-class interests.[15] Izz al-Din Nasir, union president from 1977 to 2000, was long considered one of the strongest barons of the regime and a candidate for prime minister. The strength of the unions, however, began to fade during the 1990s in the course of a cautious economic opening and the growing importance of private business to the national economy. Nasir lost his position in the party leadership at the 2000 Ba'th congress. Thereafter, no one any longer mentioned his name, or that of any other union functionary, as a potential prime ministerial candidate.

Interestingly enough, in the months preceding the cabinet shuffles of 2001 and 2003, the names of a number of businesspeople, including one or two wealthy expatriates, were traded at the rumor bourse. The government remained, however, in the hands of loyal Ba'thists and bureaucrats. Discussion about potential candidates for higher office from among the business world, however, underlined the growing capital of Syria's private sector and its representatives. A number of younger businessmen were,

indeed, counted among the "Friends of Bashar," and not a few local businesspeople patently demonstrated their support for the new regime in order
to position themselves for future cabinet positions. They steered clear of
the Ba'th, which they considered a stronghold of the defenders of etatism.
As the government worked on a business-friendly image, and independent
technocrats moved into ministerial positions of greater relevance, regime-
friendly entrepreneurs could safely assume that their chances at political
participation would increase with time.

When discussing domestic political developments after the accession
of Bashar al-Asad, Syrians often allude to a more or less open antagonism
between the old guard and the new guard. Although these two categories
reflect something of a generational conflict, they do not necessarily capture
the essence of the political differences among the political elite. As some
newcomers adopted old thinking, and some of those who obtained their
positions under Hafiz al-Asad held rather modern views, it might be more
appropriate to speak of two tendencies that cross generational boundaries.
Within the elite there was a modernizing, technocratic tendency, represented by the president and his reform team, and an ideologically conservative,
hard-line tendency with strongholds in the Ba'th party leadership, the
bureaucracy, and parts of the security apparatus. There also was a liberal,
reformist tendency. From the beginning of the era Bashar, however, it was
positioned outside the core elite and remained largely marginalized. This
tendency mainly comprised some independent deputies and intellectuals,
including a few whom Bashar al-Asad had brought with him or had
appointed to relevant positions. The appointees would define themselves as
supporters of the president, who they thought would eventually set Syria on
a path toward democracy. The independent deputies and intellectuals, in
contrast, had doubts about the young president's democratic leanings. They
preferred to see themselves as a "loyal" opposition: They did not openly
question the president's legitimacy, and they accepted the rules of the
game, but they do not hide their desire to ultimately seek a democratic
transformation of the system.

The dynamics between these tendencies in the first years of the new
president's rule can be characterized as follows: The liberal, reformist tendency was encouraged by the succession from Hafiz to Bashar al-Asad,
because its members saw themselves as natural partners of the modernizers.
Under the influence of the conservatives, however, and in the context of
heightened regional tensions—the second Palestinian intifada began only
two months after Bashar al-Asad's inauguration—the modernizers gradually shifted from more liberal to more authoritarian notions of modernization.
Changes in the official discourse reflected this development, particularly in
the state-controlled media. Perhaps the clearest expression of this reorientation is the gradual replacement of the slogan "Reform and Renewal"

(*al-islah wa-l-tajdid*)—which had been introduced after the succession—by the more modest "Modernization and Development" (*al-tahdith wa-l-tatwir*). In addition to the actual policies enacted by the new power holders, public discourse offers clues about the differences among that elite concerning strategic policy issues—the reform of the economy, the Arab-Israeli conflict, and the opening of the political system—and about their common agenda.

The Economy: Enhanced Gradualism

The transition from Hafiz to Bashar al-Asad redefined national priorities in a way that critics had often demanded. Under the late president, economic policy issues were considered secondary matters. Under his successor, economic policies—generally those capable of strengthening Syria's economic competitiveness—were considered strategically important.

At the time of Bashar al-Asad's accession, the economy was without a doubt in bad shape. Economic reform measures and new oil finds had increased growth somewhat in the early 1990s, but in the second half of the decade annual growth hovered between a 1.5 percent decline and a 2.5 percent increase. Not even the latter figure was sufficient to keep pace with Syria's population growth of close to 3 percent. Per capita gross domestic product stagnated around $1,000 in the first half of the 1990s and decreased to about $800 in the second half of the decade.[16]

At the same time, social disparities grew and the number of poor increased. Unemployment was becoming a problem the government could no longer ignore: Some 250,000 Syrians entered the job market annually, but the state sector—which employed around one-fourth of the workforce—could not absorb more than 20,000 of them, the private sector perhaps some 60,000. Consequently, unemployment rose sharply. Lacking an investment climate that could attract foreign business and retain local capital, Syria remained largely dependent on its oil sector, which was responsible for some two-thirds of exports and up to 50 percent of state income. Oil exports were, however, set to decline in the midterm, because of increased local consumption and limited reserves, and the overstaffed and largely inefficient public industrial sector remained a burden on the treasury.[17]

In his inauguration speech, the new president declared economic reform and modernization the government's highest priorities, leaving no doubt in guarded but clear enough words that economic policies and performance under his father's rule had not exactly been satisfactory.[18] Bashar al-Asad's reform-minded technocrats would echo his sentiments, stressing, for instance, that Syria had been late in learning the lessons of global economic change and would now need to reform its economic policy, modernize the industrial base, and improve training and administration.[19]

Hafiz al-Asad had instituted limited economic reform in the late 1980s and early 1990s, the most important step being an investment statute (Law 10 of 1991) offering tax holidays and other incentives for Syrian, expatriate, and foreign investments of a certain size. Thereafter, other measures aimed at structural adjustment and liberalization were still discussed, but in practice the process stalled. Bashar al-Asad's efforts basically began where that earlier process had left off.

In rather quick succession, a series of laws and decrees were passed that in one way or another aimed at opening up the Syrian economy, encouraging private business, and modernizing administrative structures. A banking law allowed, for the first time since the nationalizations of 1963, the establishment of private banks. Other laws introduced financial banking secrecy and reorganized the Central Bank so that it could oversee private banking. It took a while to enact the necessary regulations, but in the spring of 2003, the first licenses were issued for one Jordanian and two Lebanese banks to establish businesses in Syria. New regulations made it possible for the state to contract foreign companies to manage public sector companies. Customs duties on imports for local manufacturing were drastically cut, and import regulations and restrictions on foreign currency transactions were eased and eventually abolished. Private commercial radio stations became legal. More important, a new law allowed the establishment of private universities; and a privately run "virtual university" began offering its services through the Internet in summer 2002.

Within months of the succession, the government established a committee on economic reform under the chairmanship of Muhammad Husein, an economics professor and a new member of the Ba'th party leadership who would become deputy prime minister in 2001 and minister of finance in 2003. Committee members represented a broad spectrum of academic experts, including economic liberals and leftist critics of the government.[20] The committee presented its still unpublished report to the president in spring 2001. Differences remained regarding the necessary scope of reform, pitting the more market-oriented members of the government and the broader elite against the more conservative elements who wanted the state to retain as much control over the economy as possible. There was little disagreement, however, that without a return to economic growth, Syria would not be able to cope with the problem of unemployment, which members of the new elite viewed with greater urgency than did the governments of Hafiz al-Asad.[21] Consensus prevailed that for the private sector to grow it must be given more space. Also uncontroversial was concern about administrative reform, not least in the public sector, education, and technical modernization.

For the president's reform team, technical modernization was centrally, and symbolically, about increasing computer literacy and the spread of

Internet connectivity. Syria's one subscriber per thousand people ranked extremely low, even by regional standards. The new government therefore embarked on the gradual introduction of computer training in schools, local production of affordable PCs, and plans to increase the number of Internet subscribers to at least 5 percent of the population. Regulations to allow Internet cafés, previously unlicensed, to obtain a license, were introduced; connection charges that were effectively prohibitive to the large majority were lowered. It appeared that the technocrats, because they had the full support of the president on this matter, were able to overcome objections of the security establishment, which hitherto had controlled the spread of communications technology.

The issue of privatization and the prospect of an association agreement with the European Union revealed some of the differences within the PRE over the course of economic policy reform. Both issues triggered internal debates, and both were eventually decided upon, in principle, within the inner circle. The EU was, and remains, Syria's most important trading partner. Negotiations on an association agreement in the context of the Barcelona process, or Euro-Mediterranean Partnership,[22] had commenced in 1998, focusing on free trade and aid. The goal was to improve market access for Syrian products on the European market, but also to force Syria to lower and eventually scrap tariff barriers on European imports. Syria would receive European technical and financial assistance to aid structural adjustment, particularly concerning institutional reform, training, and private sector exports. Under the Barcelona process, this type of agreement usually contains human rights and democracy clauses, which, although not necessarily taken seriously by signatories on either side,[23] were seen by many Arab leaders as an attempt to interfere in their domestic affairs, a view certainly held by the Syrian leadership.

Views differed within the Syrian elite about the desirability of an agreement with the EU. Critics argued that Syria would not benefit from mutual trade liberalization and should not do anything hasty. The then new finance minister, in an article published shortly before his appointment, emphasized any agreement's potential negative effects on existing industries and generally asserted that the Euro-Mediterranean Partnership would be detrimental to intra-Arab efforts at economic unification.[24] Meanwhile, members of the reform team were generally in favor of an agreement, considering it the safest way to guide Syria toward globalization and adapt its economy to international standards. While losses could be expected in the short term, an economic opening and reform of the domestic administrative and industrial structures would eventually prove beneficial and, anyway, were unavoidable. Why not, therefore, accept European assistance along the path?[25]

Despite reservations about the potential for European interference in domestic politics, the new regime elite decided to speed up negotiations. Their decision was clearly reflected in the public discourse: Rather than highlighting an agreement's potential harm to domestic industry, members of the elite, as well as the state-run media, focused on the positive effects of association with the EU. Some members of the government also introduced into the semiofficial discourse the concept of competition with neighboring countries—all of which had been faster in concluding respective negotiations with the EU—and stressed urgency in moving forward.[26] This was not only done in communications directed at the external environment. In an interview with the daily *al-Thaura,* for instance, the assistant minister of economy spoke of the "positive pressures" for productivity and competition and the increased investor interest that an association agreement would generate.[27] Other officials, such as then Industry Minister 'Isam Za'im, an ideologically more left-leaning member of the reform team whose political thinking reflected the ideas of the *dependencia* (dependency-theory) school, stressed that Syria, because of its special, independent path, did not have to take lessons from anybody, certainly not from the EU, the World Bank, or the IMF. Reform, modernization, and rehabilitation of the industrial sector, however, were urgent, and an association agreement would provide "millions of euros" in aid for that purpose. Syria should therefore prepare the ground for successful negotiations.[28]

The political leadership decided to adopt in essence a gradualist approach to economic reform. In contrast to earlier periods, however, reform was openly defined as a goal. It would be introduced piecemeal so as not to upset domestic balances, or, as one advisor of the president stated, "We'll go as fast as the people and the establishments can absorb change."[29]

The privatization issue, as it clearly had the potential to affect powerful vested interests, was even more contentious. The state sector, despite generating losses, continued to be an important instrument for patronage networks, mobilization, and political control. It also offered ample opportunities for illegal enrichment.[30] A decision in support of privatization would have had symbolic significance, announcing as it were, a clear break with Ba'th party ideology and antagonizing a substantial number of functionaries among the party and trade union ranks. Layoffs and the specter of social unrest were the main arguments used by members of the government opposed to privatization measures. They also claimed that the public sector was necessary for "strategic and security" reasons: As long as Syria faced potential Israeli aggression, the state must be able to secure basic goods, which in turn meant the need for a state-run industrial sector.[31]

Some young mid-level leaders of the Ba'th were not particularly opposed to the idea of privatization, and individual ministers evidently came to favor dissolving parts of the state sector. After internal debate, however, the core leadership decided against any privatization measures at the time. Public sector reform would be promoted; but no state firms would be dismantled or sold.[32] Government ministers who held other views no longer discussed the topic in public, demonstrating the limits of influence that technocrats in the second circle wield on such strategic decisions. In an interview in April 2002 with the London-based *al-Hayat*, which is widely read in Syria, the economy and foreign trade minister said that "he had the sense" that the privatization issue was "not being considered" for the time being. Would it be revisited?, the interviewer asked. The minister said he did not know. On a slightly different topic, when asked whether Syrian expatriates would be more likely to return and invest in the country if there were also political reforms, the minister made clear that he was "not a politician."[33] Obviously, such issues were the domain of the core elite.

Domestic Politics: Defining the Red Lines

As noted, the accession of Bashar al-Asad had raised expectations inside and outside Syria of substantive political opening and change. Much of Syrians' hopes were pegged to the new president's inaugural speech: While warning that Syria would not "apply the democracy of others," Bashar al-Asad nevertheless emphasized accountability, the rule of law, "constructive criticism," and "democratic thinking," the last of which, he said, was based "on the principle of accepting the opinion of the other."[34] A couple of steps taken within the first months after the change at the top also pointed toward political liberalization: Political prisoners were released; the military prison of Mezze was closed; and the notorious Tadmur prison was emptied. The state press allowed space for critics of government policy. The Progressive National Front parties were, for the first time, permitted to issue and publicly distribute party newspapers. Talk circulated in government circles about a party law that would broaden the scope for legal political activity. More important was the tolerant attitude that the regime initially displayed toward the so-called civil society movement, composed of individuals and groups who openly campaigned for political freedoms and democratic reform.

In September 2000 ninety-nine Syrian intellectuals signed an open letter to the president, demanding an end to the state of emergency (in place since 1962) as well as, among other things, the introduction of political pluralism and freedom of expression. Some of the signatories were politely invited to the offices of the domestic intelligence services, but no one was harassed or harmed. While uncertainty remained in terms of the regime's limits, as one of the outspoken prodemocracy activists put it, the "complex of fear" that had silenced Syrian society in the decades before had effectively been broken. Syrians and foreign observers began to speak of the "Damascus Spring." Political salons and clubs, organized by independent deputies or intellectuals and by tolerated opposition politicians, sprung up in the capital and in other cities, providing space for public debate.[35] An intensive debate among Syrian intellectuals also flourished in the Lebanese press.[36] Even members of the Ba'th attended salons, particularly those held by independent MP Riad Sayf or the Nasserite Jamal al-Atasi Forum. They did so in part to observe, but also to defend the party line. Younger Ba'thists attended because they shared the craving for more pluralism and openness. The so-called Basic Document of the Committees to Revive Civil Society, a manifesto by Syrian intellectuals distributed in January 2001, repeated the grievances of the earlier open letter but was more precise in demanding more space for civil society activities and passage of a democratic election law.[37] Also in January, Riad Sayf announced the creation of a liberal democratic party. In these heady months, dissenters were able to influence, if not determine, the course of public debate. In summer 2001, for example, critical discussion in parliament and heated debates between government supporters and critics at a public event ensued following public allegations by Sayf that the allocation of mobile phone licenses—one of which had been obtained by a company under the control of the Makhlouf family—had involved massive corruption.

The Ba'thist leadership was not, however, prepared to give up or share its power. In February 2001 the regime elite took off its velvet gloves and embarked on a political offensive clearly aimed at regaining its dominance over public discourse. Repressive moves against the dissident challengers followed. Vice President Khaddam, addressing university professors, warned that the intellectuals targeted were spreading ideas that threatened national unity. Was it, he asked, the breakdown of order and the civil war that followed Algeria's political opening that the intellectuals wanted to emulate?[38] Several officials spoke of the "red lines" that the intellectuals had crossed. In a March 2001 interview, Bashar al-Asad made it clear that national unity, the Ba'th party, the armed forces, and the "path of the late leader Hafiz al-Asad" were not up for discussion.[39] The Ba'thist leadership also accused the intellectuals of being "hateful," ignoring the Arab-Israeli struggle, denigrating the achievements of the Ba'th, and wanting to lead Syria back to the period of foreign occupation or military coups, this last argument an incredible statement from the mouth of Ba'thist leaders. Never too shy to speak his mind, Defense Minister Tlass warned, "We will not accept that anybody takes the power from us, because it comes from the barrel of the gun, and we are its masters."[40]

The president, who had initially been in favor of a more liberal approach to the civil society movement and other forms of dissent, apparently became increasingly annoyed by public demands for political reform, eventually siding with the hardliners. The authorities prohibited the activities of most of the salons. Sayf, who insisted that as a deputy he did not need authorization for meetings at his home, and stepped up his criticism of the government and of high-level corruption, was plainly warned about continuing his activities. Parliament lifted his immunity, and in August 2001 another deputy who had begun to attack the intelligence apparatus in strong public statements was arrested. In September, after holding a public meeting in his house, Sayf was arrested along with eight of his friends, among them economist Arif Dalila, who had a long record of speaking out against corruption and mismanagement. A few days prior, Riad Turk, a veteran communist leader who had spent seventeen years in jail under Hafiz al-Asad, was taken in after calling the late president a "dictator" on al-Jazeera. As noted above, all were subsequently put on trial and convicted.[41] The Damascus Spring had come to an end.

The regime elite clearly lacked consensus on the degree of openness and political reform desired or needed. Machinations involving the editor in chief of *al-Thaura* illustrate how internal differences over personnel, corporate influence, and the political overlapped. Shortly after taking office, Bashar al-Asad appointed Mahmoud Salamah to head *al-Thaura:* A left-leaning Arab nationalist and a former independent deputy and former public sector manager, Salamah had previously advised the president on economic issues. His editorship displeased the Ba'th party establishment: Salamah was not a Ba'thist, so his appointment threatened the party's monopoly over such politically important positions. Salamah then opened the paper to debates on issues that the civil society movement raised—such as civil society, liberalization, political change—gave room to authors who wanted to promote such debates, and covered lively parts of parliamentary discussions that had been omitted from the reports by the official news agency. The paper did not cross any red lines, as its criticism remained confined to a critique of policies, not of the regime as such. Loyalty to the president and the cult of personality were maintained. Still, *al-Thaura* became the most interesting of Syria's three national dailies. When the government tightened the screws on the salons, Salamah wrote an editorial asserting that the Damascus Spring—a concept abhorred by conservatives in the first place—was only now about to start: "National consensus . . . cannot be achieved in a society of parrots or by means of unilateral official discourse. It is achieved through political, economic, and cultural pluralism."[42] Salamah came under increasing pressure from the information minister, a hardliner in the new guard who eventually sacked him. Salamah's dismissal was seen as a sign, wrote Michel Kilo, one of the speakers of the civil society movement, that the Ba'thist leadership would not actually accept outsiders in leading positions, but would either co-opt them or exclude them. The process of change, he argued, had "started out so weak

that it could not protect its few supporters in the party and in government."[43]

By this time, the hardliners in the regime elite had been strengthened
by the military escalation of the Israeli-Palestinian conflict that ensued
after the election of Ariel Sharon as Israel's prime minister. The opposition-
ists, one member of Asad's reform team explained, simply did not understand "geopolitics." How could one expect that the president would allow
himself to be pressured by a couple of intellectuals while Sharon was at the
gates? Viewed from some analytical distance, regional tension might not, in
the end, have been the motive for the crackdown and the reversal of the
political opening, but it certainly helped convince the reformers that it was
time to close ranks with the more conservative elements within the party
leadership and security apparatus.

Rhetoric and Realpolitik: The Regional Policy Challenge

The Arab-Israeli conflict has indeed been an important variable for domestic Syrian developments in the past, not least in the building of a strong
security state,[44] and it remains the primary frame of reference for Syria's
external relations in general, dominating, among other things, relations
with Lebanon and with the United States. The oscillations of the conflict
have some bearing on the weight that individual members within the PRE
can command, and they certainly bear on elite discourse.

Bilateral Syrian-Israeli talks had come to another halt only months
before Bashar al-Asad assumed office. He and his team made clear that
they were prepared to restart the process once an Israeli government
accepted the principle of full withdrawal from Syrian territory in exchange
for full peace. An apparent change in approach to the peace process and to
regional policies in general was the new leadership's linkage of these policies to domestic, particularly economic, issues. Thus, while Bashar al-Asad
more than once uttered doubts that the Israelis were "ripe for peace," he
also expressed the conviction that Syria needed to end the conflict in order
to pursue his modernization agenda: "We have to work for peace in order to
advance the process of modernization."[45]

With the election of Sharon, however, peace talk moved into the background of Syrian public discourse. Instead, stark hard-line rhetoric dominated, with the president contributing his share. Apparently, the regime
elite did not care whether this discourse pleased the United States, Europe,
or Israel. Rather, there was a domestic and wider Arab populist element to
this theater—a conscious attempt, it seems, to enhance Bashar al-Asad's
popularity among the younger generations in Syria and in other Arab countries. Members of the broader regime elite wanted the president to present
himself as a young and outspoken leader who represented the interests of

all Arabs and dared to say what other leaders would not.[46] Bashar al-Asad struck a responsive chord among Syrians, Jordanians, and Palestinians alike when he spoke of the Israelis as being worse than the Nazis and of a "holocaust" committed against the Palestinians, as well as when he provocatively asked his colleagues at an Arab summit what exactly would have to happen before they would sever their diplomatic relations with Israel. If a thousand Palestinian martyrs weren't enough, "What about half a million? Or genocide? Or nuclear bombs on Arab capitals?"[47]

At the same time, the leadership left no doubt that Syria would join other Arab states in pragmatic policy approaches to the conflict. Consequently, Syria supported the Saudi peace initiative that was adopted at the Beirut summit in March 2002. Bashar al-Asad also expressed his conviction that peace would come "sooner or later,"[48] and he certainly wished for, to quote one of his aides, an "effective and constructive" U.S. engagement to achieve regional peace.[49]

Another new development in Syria's regional policies was its far-reaching rapprochement with Iraq. A cautious détente had begun under Hafiz al-Asad. After Bashar al-Asad's accession, relations deepened and included more frequent exchanges of political delegations and, notably, a substantial increase in trade; Syria became the most important supply route for unofficial (outside UN control) Iraqi imports. This partial reorientation of Syria's Iraq policy derived from two motives. First, cooperation with Iraq potentially involved enormous economic benefits, of which the new leadership team was very much aware. Of particular importance were discounted Iraqi oil deliveries. Syrian profits from this deal in 2001 and 2002 were estimated at up to $1.3 billion annually, a sum equivalent to some 15 percent of the state budget. Since many of the imports that Iraq financed from this deal were of Syrian origin or imported through Syria, the country's private sector also benefited considerably. Second, Bashar al-Asad and some of the younger people around him were apparently convinced that Iraq constituted Syria's "strategic depth." While this was a somewhat antiquated geopolitical concept, it fitted well with the Arab nationalist beliefs of many people within the party and among the public. Also, cooperation with Iraq became altogether popular for political reasons.[50]

Syria, thus, became the main supporter of Iraq in the phase that led to, and during, the 2003 Iraq War. The Syrian leadership clearly miscalculated the ability of the Iraqi regime to withstand the U.S.-led invasion. After the war, as a result of both its Iraq policies and its refusal to withdraw support for militant Palestinian organizations, Syria came under intense U.S. pressure—including threats of diplomatic and economic sanctions, and not excluding the threat of military action. Reconstituting a workable relationship with Washington, whose assistance in any settlement of its conflict with Israel, its primary foreign policy concern, Syria would eventually need, became an urgent necessity, but was not easily to be reached.[51]

Foreign policy remained chiefly the product of a group of people who had served Asad's father, namely, Vice President Abd al-Halim Khaddam, Foreign Minister Farouk Sharaa, and a handful of veteran diplomats. There was a dearth of young operatives in this field, particularly with international experience and knowledge of the world. A couple of young talents that Bashar al-Asad brought along from the Syrian Computer Society were occasionally used for missions abroad, but they generally remained in the economic policy arena. The lack of diplomatic cadres was mainly because the foreign service had been heavily politicized under Hafiz al-Asad; recruitment and promotion, with notable exceptions, depended on loyalty rather than diplomatic skills. Consequently, the Foreign Ministry made it clear that the 2002 decree on the retirement of civil servants over sixty could not be applied in its quarters.[52] As in other ministries, the success of *any* policy will to a great extent depend on the state's capacity to train and retrain personnel, a goal that ranked high on Bashar al-Asad's agenda for change.

The Limits of Change

Two and a half years into the era Bashar, the change in personnel within Syria's politically relevant elite had indeed been far greater than personnel shuffles in the fifteen or so years prior. The change in personnel complemented the young president's somewhat new style and agenda, which was clearly reflected in the discourse of his new appointees. Members of the new leadership were generally more aware than were their predecessors of Syria's economic and social challenges and more concerned about the economy and the country's place in a globalized regional and international environment. They were also more populist in their foreign policy rhetoric, but at the same time pragmatic in practice. Popular expectations of political opening or democratization had been nurtured by the president's inaugural speech, but they were largely disappointed. The newcomers were clearly of the opinion that, as one of them put it, "political pluralism and economic pluralism are not synonymous."[53] Economic reform and liberalization, in other words, would not be accompanied by an equivalent political opening. Little wonder that the "Chinese model" was often invoked in official and public political discussions.

Although members of Bashar al-Asad's team of reformers were not inimical to democracy as a concept, its implementation was certainly not a priority. They ultimately settled on a somewhat elitist approach built on classical arguments from modernization theory: In any country, so the logic went, only a small percentage of the people can actually influence decisions; democracy is premature as long as people are poor or lack education. In Syria's case, they said, it was necessary to let Bashar al-Asad and his team work to modernize the country. This meant improving the education system, advancing technical modernization and training, creating an economic opening, undertaking administrative reform, and strengthening state institutions. Political opening would come later, if things went well. Thus the president and his associates eventually cast their lot with the hardliners when the issue arose of how to deal with challenges from outside the regime elite.

In the terminology of transition theory, Bashar al-Asad and his modernizing reformers are liberalizers seeking a controlled opening of the authoritarian system without changing the underlying power structure. The result, quite often and as happened in Syria, is a return to repression. With no domestic resistance, and no threatening pressure in regard to domestic policy developments—U.S. and EU representatives limited their reaction to the clampdown on the civil society movement to cautious expressions of regret—there was little that would have convinced the elite to think twice about their actions.

The limits on policy change derive from the fact that the reproduction of the politically relevant elite was very much engineered from the inner circle. The regime elite chose its own successors; would-be climbers into elite circles needed the active consent of those already there. Those who tried to catapult themselves into political relevance through independent political activities or organizations were warned to respect the red lines—a concept that allows the possibility of being able to walk those lines or broaden them in the future. People who chose not to heed the regime's advice were reminded of the methods of the authoritarian state. Those who were co-opted into the elite were not keen to share their newly gained spoils with those who would challenge them in democratic competition.

Still, members of the new elite were not simply younger versions of those who had surrounded Hafiz al-Asad. These elites were no longer mainly the sons of the rural middle classes, the politics of which Hanna Batatu has so aptly described.[54] Rather, in terms of class, the newcomers to the politically relevant elite hailed from the state bureaucracy and the urban middle classes. Bourgeois elements remained excluded from positions of political relevance, but they may attain some in the future. Some businesspeople were clearly positioning themselves for that possibility. The co-opted membership of the elite, particularly on the reform team, included quite a number of urban Sunni upper-middle-class elements.

Although they were wary that far-reaching reforms, privatization in particular, could undermine social stability, the discourse of newer members of the PRE was not egalitarian. Neither did they emphasize the defense of the revolution, as their older colleagues were prone to do. Rather, they saw themselves as defending the state and its institutions, including the authoritarian constitution of 1973 that they inherited. Liberal contestants were accused of trying to return Syria to the 1950s, an era of instability. Members of the new elite were prepared to make the state more efficient—to enable them to confront economic and social challenges and to improve governance—but they then decided to proscribe competition that might force them into political compromises with contestants. In that sense, Syria's political elite remained exclusive.

Although a confessionalist reading of Syrian politics—emphasizing divisions between the Sunni majority and other sects, and the privileged position of the Alawi minority—has long been the dominant, if contested, trend in Syrian studies,[55] this approach has lost most of its analytical power in regard to the elite that emerged in the era Bashar. Certainly, Bashar al-Asad was an Alawi, and many relevant positions, particularly in the security apparatus, continued to be controlled by Alawis and even by members of his family. Also, confessional and regional loyalties persisted and were used to stabilize patronage networks. There were, however, a growing number of networks that transcended such "primordial" ties, the Syrian Computer Society being the most prominent example. Syria's politically relevant elite has evolved as a self-reproducing and narrow elite, but not an ethnic one.

It is noteworthy that even the chastised dissidents did not try to play on confessional divisions or highlight confessionalism. Rather, they emphasized divisions between the old guard and the new guard and between an authoritarian regime on the one hand and civil society on the other. Even the exiled leadership of the banned Muslim Brotherhood no longer denounced the regime as Alawi, instead focusing on such issues as the lack of democracy, rule of law, and citizenship.[56]

The new regime elite has certainly sought to stabilize the system as it was. Most likely, though, some of the political and economic elements needed to thoroughly do so will remain lacking. In the short term, the expected decrease in oil income and alternative rents, such as cheap oil from Iraq, might force the leadership to rely more on Syria's human capital and thus encourage it to open up somewhat more, even allowing contesting elites onto the political playing field. For example, it might consider giving a somewhat greater role to parliament and to parliamentarians, following the Egyptian model, as it has already done to some extent in its economic reform policies. This would not involve revolutionary change, but would create a more pluralist, politically relevant elite inclusive of hitherto poorly represented social groups, not least the business community.

One should not exclude the possibility that new political contestants might emerge, maybe from among students or religious quarters, particularly if the economic situation continues to deteriorate and chances for younger people to find their place are further reduced. Generational struggles inside the Ba'th party and inside the third and second circles of the politically relevant elite are to be expected. The leadership will, according to one of the president's younger advisors, continue to improve the "quality of people" in the parliament, the party, and other institutions, replacing cadres from the previous era with people who have the necessary qualifications to promote and implement reforms.[57] Indeed, Bashar al-Asad and his friends have not given up on their modernization agenda. After their initial preparedness to embark on a more inclusive route, however, they veered onto an authoritarian path, one that will likely discourage many of those who Syria will need to actually implement any serious reform program.

Notes

1. For example, see "Syria: Cabinet and Corruption," *Middle East International,* 11 January 2002, pp. 17f; Sherine Bahaa, "A Question of Time," *al-Ahram Weekly,* 14–20 June 2001.

2. Oral communication, June 2002, Geneva.

3. In Syria and Iraq, there exist respective "national leaderships" of the Ba'th party that claim to be pan-Arab. The leadership in each state is called the "regional leadership" (*al-qiyada al-qutriyya*).

4. "It is illogical that . . . the Israeli foreign minister is having dinner with us while the people are being killed in Palestine," explained Foreign Minister Farouk al-Sharaa on Syrian radio, 15 November 2000 (BBC, Summary of World Broadcasts).

5. On Syria's regime structures, see Perthes, *The Political Economy of Syria,* pp. 133–202; on political decisionmaking, see ibid., pp. 203–240.

6. For more detail, see Perthes, "Syria's Parliamentary Elections." The practice of "reserving" some one-third of the seats for independent candidates meant that about two-thirds of the seats remained reserved for the Ba'th party and its allies. The Ba'th would always command more than 50 percent of the seats.

7. Riad Sayf, member of the People's Assembly, Mudakhala hawl mahsru' muwazanat 2001 (Speech on the 2001 draft budget), mimeographed typescript, 7 November 2000.

8. These numbers are limited to the holders of official positions—the president and vice presidents, other members of the Ba'th party leadership, cabinet members, and the five top positions in the army and intelligence services. It does not include the entire first and second circles of influence.

9. Ibrahim Hamidi, "Damascus Looks to Rejuvenate State Institutions," *Daily Star,* 16 April 2002.

10. *Syria Report,* 4 March 2002 and 7 March 2002.

11. This and all other quotations are based on interviews held in Damascus in 2001 and 2002 unless otherwise noted.

12. See, for example, Industry Minister 'Isam Za'im's interview in *Tishrin,* 9 January 2002.

13. See *al-Hayat,* 1 July 2002.

14. See *Syria Report,* 9 April 2002.

15. See Perthes, *The Political Economy of Syria,* pp. 173–180.

16. All figures are based on the World Bank's World Development Indicators Database, April 2002.

17. For details, see Perthes, *Scenarios for Syria;* Oxford Business Group, *Emerging Syria, 2002.*

18. For an English version of Bashar al-Asad's inaugural speech, see *Syria Times,* 18 July 2000.

19. See, for instance, the Za'im interview in *Tishrin,* 9 January 2002.

20. Most of the people appointed to the eighteen-member committee who were not already in official positions were considered likely candidates for one or were attempting to position themselves for a ministerial or other government job.

21. See, for instance, Marzuq, "Al-Batala wa-l-faqr fi Suriya." Marzuq is an economist who was seen as close to Bashar al-Asad. He also coordinated, clearly with the consent of the political leadership, the so-called National Committee to Boycott American Goods in Syria.

22. The process, which started with the Barcelona conference in 1995, primarily aims to establish a Euro-Mediterranean free trade zone and to enhance common security in the Mediterranean. Its membership includes the EU states, Algeria, Cyprus, Egypt, Israel, Jordan, Lebanon, Malta, Morocco, the Palestinian Authority, Syria, Tunisia, and Turkey. By 2002 all of the non-EU countries except Syria had concluded association agreements with the European Union.

23. See, among others, Youngs, "The European Union and Democracy"; Reinhardt, "Civil Society Co-operation."

24. See al-Atrash, "Hawl al-tawahhud al-iqtisadi al-'Arabi wa-l-sharaka al-Urubiyya," pp. 87–90.

25. For an overview on this debate, see Abdel Nour, "Syrian Views of an Association Agreement."

26. See, for example, Economy and Foreign Trade Minister Ghassan al-Rifa'i, interview in Oxford Business Group, *Emerging Syria 2002,* pp. 36f.

27. Quoted in *Syria Report,* 16 January 2002. See also "In'ikasat al-sharaka al-Urubiyya 'ala al-zira'a" (Impacts of the European partnership on agriculture), *Tishrin,* 15 January 2002.

28. Interview with Industry Minister Za'im, *al-Hayat,* 1 September 2002.

29. *Jane's Foreign Report,* 20 December 2001.

30. This is not to say that market economies do not allow for corruption. Privatization certainly does, as demonstrated in many Eastern European countries. A large public sector—with books that lack transparency and whose losses are automatically borne by the state—is certainly conducive to illegal private appropriations of public funds. In Syria, this has been highlighted by corruption cases publicized in the context of an anticorruption campaign that Bashar al-Asad began before he became president. The sums involved were spectacular. In December 2001 a former deputy prime minister and a former transport minister, both originally economics professors, along with a third person, were sentenced to jail and ordered to repay $276 million, plus interest, to Syrian Airlines for fraud committed during the acquisition of aircraft.

31. Industry Minister Za'im as quoted in *al-Hayat,* 19 November 2001.

32. Author interviews. See also Industry Minister Za'im's interviews in *Tishrin,* 9 January 2002, and *al-Hayat,* 1 September 2002.

33. Economy and Foreign Trade Minister Ghassan al-Rifa'i, *al-Hayat,* 25 April 2002.

34. *Syria Times,* 18 July 2000.

35. The discourses and the main events of this period are well documented in Tayyara, "Al-Muthaqqafun al-Suriyun," and Droz-Vincent, "Syrie."

36. See particularly the editorial page of *al-Nahar* during summer 2000 and the special issue of *al-Adab*, March–April 2001.

37. The document, also called the "Manifesto of the 1,000," was published in *al-Hayat*, 12 January 2001.

38. Khaddam's February 2001 speech is reproduced in *al-Hayat*, 10 July 2001.

39. See *al-Hayat*, 15 April 2001.

40. Interview, *al-Majalla*, 6–12 May 2001. Tlass continued, "We came up with various military moves, and we paid with our blood for the power. And those, unfortunately, previously used to work on the line that America wants. Now they woke up and returned to their path."

41. See, for example, "Syria: More Trials," *Middle East International*, 17 May 2002. Turk was pardoned in November 2002, ironically on the occasion of the anniversary of Hafiz al-Asad's assumption of power. This was not, however, a sign of political relaxation. In December 2002 the Damascus correspondent of *al-Hayat*, Ibrahim Hamidi, was arrested and held for five months on the charge of spreading false news.

42. *Al-Thaura*, 3 March 2001 (BBC, Summary of World Broadcasts, 6 March 2001).

43. From *al-Nahar* (Beirut), as quoted in *Mideast Mirror*, 31 May 2001.

44. See Perthes, "Si vis stabilitatem, para bellum."

45. "Nous devons travailler à la paix pour faire avancer le processus de modernisation." Interview, *Le Figaro*, 23 June 2001 (author's translation).

46. See, for example, Bouthaina Shaaban, "Thalath asbab li-najah ziyarat Bashar al-Asad ila Fransa" (Three reasons for the success of Bashar al-Asad's visit to France), *al-Hayat*, 4 July 2001. Shaaban, who had worked as interpreter for Hafiz as well as for Bashar al-Asad, exemplified members of the president's reform team: A professor of English and a writer who had published abroad, she was made a member of the Ba'th party's central committee in 2000, appointed the director of press and information in the Foreign Ministry in 2002, and minister of expatriate affairs in 2003.

47. See Asad's speech at the 2002 Beirut Arab summit in *al-Hayat*, 28 March 2002.

48. Interview, *Le Figaro*, 23 June 2001.

49. Bouthaina Shaaban, letter to the editor, *International Herald Tribune*, 18 July 2002.

50. The political elite as well as its intellectual loyalists shared a generally pro-Iraqi outlook, particularly in view of an expected U.S. attack on Iraq. See, for instance, 'Imad Fawzi Shuaibi, "Suriya wa-l-Iraq: min qadam al-muharramat ila 'adwa al-'aqlaniyya" (Syria and Iraq: From gnawing at the taboos to the virus of rationality), *al-Hayat*, 4 November 2002.

51. See, in more detail, Perthes, "Syria Under Bashar al-Asad: Modernisation and the Limits of Change," *Adelphi Paper* (London: IISS), forthcoming 2004.

52. See Hamidi, "Damascus Looks to Rejuvenate."

53. Industry Minister Za'im, quoted in *Financial Times*, 15 May 2001.

54. Batatu, *Syria's Peasantry.*

55. See, with critical distance to purely confessionalist analyses of Syria's "power elite," van Dam, *The Struggle for Power in Syria*, particularly pp. 118–135.

56. See the Muslim Brotherhood, "Draft National Covenant of Honor," reproduced in *al-Hayat*, 4 May 2001. See also Wa'il Mirza, "Suriya wa-l-Islamiyun wa-l-taghyir: Muhaddidat manhajiyya wa-madakhil ila al-tafkir" (Syria, the Islamists,

and change: Methodological factors and starting points for thought), *al-Hayat,* 6 February 2001.

57. Thus, among other things, the Ba'th party required its candidates for the March 2003 parliamentary elections to have at least a secondary school certificate if they qualified as a "peasant" or "worker," and at least a bachelor's for all other categories (ArabNews.com, 18 January 2003). The turnover in the parliamentary elections of 2003 was impressive: although voters' choices were limited—it was certain that the lists of the Progressive National Front would take 167 out of 250 seats, leaving only 83 seats for independent candidates—178 of the 250 members of the legislature were new members (*al-Hayat,* 10 March 2003).

Part 2

Succession Looms

5

Egypt:
Succession Politics
Gamal Abdelnasser

In the second half of the twentieth century, Egypt experienced two thorough elite changes. Following defeat in the 1948 Arab-Israeli war, a socialist-military elite abolished Egypt's monarchy in the Free Officers Revolution of July 1952. Anwar Sadat, with his historic 1977 visit to the Knesset, made possible by the October 1973 war, once again reoriented politics and economics. Subsequently a pro-U.S., pro–Camp David, and pro-capitalist new elite replaced its predecessors. In effect, the two regional wars (1948 and 1973) shaped the common experiences of two generations (the so-called July generation and the October generation), the military pattern of elite replacement in Egypt, and the legitimacy of leaders from both generations, which was built first of all on military exploits.[1]

The October generation under Hosni Mubarak has built its legitimacy on three pillars: the rapprochement with Arab and Muslim states after the shock of the bilateral peace treaty with Israel; the return of Taba in 1989, the last piece of Egyptian territory held by Israel since 1967; and the geopolitical rent stemming from Egypt's peace treaty with Israel in 1979 and, more recently, from the participation in the U.S.-led coalition against Iraq during the 1991 Gulf War. This last element prevented the collapse of the Egyptian economy and allowed the government to invest in infrastructure and basic utilities.

Now the October generation is starting to retire. The president, his prime advisors, the key ministers, the speakers of both houses of parliament, the leaders of the political parties, the leading trade unionists, the heads of the national press, and the leading intellectual figures have all reached their seventies. The question of who will emerge within the core elite and who will replace the October generation is evidently urgent. It is possible to outline more than one scenario since any future development in the Middle East is highly dependent on regional war or peace, as will be shown below.

117

This chapter starts with the assumption that elite change in Egypt is not only a result of rejuvenation but also of structural decisions made by the core elite in order to recruit new young cadres. The prevailing image of a rigid and immobile political elite firmly entrenched in the apparatus of an authoritarian state conceals the efforts and the mobility of this new generation as they strive to become political power players. The largest national institutions—the military, trade unions, and political parties—systematically began to build up their cadres in the 1990s and have provided structures for social mobility. It is from these ranks that the new PRE is rising.[2] Three strategic issues are likely to be on their agenda: Egypt's foreign policy orientation, political and economic reforms, and the distribution of wealth.

The main question here is: Why do particular sociopolitical groups and persons move at certain points in time into strategically important positions and become members of the PRE while others do not? The aim of this chapter is to show patterns of elite dynamics either by circulation or replacement. Following is a map of the PRE composition as of 2002, which is an outcome of PRE mobility during the 1990s. The National Democratic Party (NDP) will subsequently be used in order to demonstrate the role such a large institution plays within the process of educating and recruiting young elite cadres. Furthermore, businessmen and women will be singled out as two groups that have gained influence on political decisionmaking from 1998 to 2002. Finally, the issue of presidential succession in Egypt is treated at length because the void surrounding this issue illustrates in a nutshell the dilemma of elite change in general.[3] Aspects of legitimacy and rule consolidation are stressed because future composition will depend on which group is able to secure wider public consent. The conclusion centers around four possible scenarios of elite change: one violent and unrealistic, one pessimistic, one optimistic, and a medium scenario, which is regarded as the most plausible. The author consciously chose a positive scenario for the final outlook based on a number of recent domestic developments that signal an opportunity to break away from military rule and to give leeway to a civilian-dominated PRE with a civilian president at its center. But with regional tension rising in Israel, Palestine, and Iraq, more confrontative scenarios might materialize as well. The transition to a wholly civil state in Egypt would require the continuation of the peace process with Israel. Only then might the military involvement in politics dissolve further.

Mapping Egypt's Politically Relevant Elite in 2002

Although the political system in Egypt is highly centralized, with most powers resting in the hands of the president, it does not mean that one man surrounded by a few advisors makes the political decisions alone. Middle Eastern countries tend to be portrayed as "highly personalized" states in which the leader, whether a king or president, has supreme authority. Contrary to this assumption, Egypt's internal and external policies are influenced by an array of people from state institutions and civil society. One can thus speak of a quantitatively large politically relevant elite, as well as a small, etatist elite.[4]

Two approaches are used for identifying elite members: First, the reputational approach is employed to see which actors have what kind of importance and backing as individuals. Significance is attributed to rumors, jokes, *hikayat* (stories), and so on, as background for this analysis. Second, an institutional approach concentrates on the formal position of elite members. Six main elite groups were singled out according to the three-circle PRE definition.[5] The first circle of elites comprises two groups, namely politicians of the ruling party and state technocrats[6] (see Figure 5.1). In the second circle, the two most influential groups are businessmen and trade unionists as well as members of parliament. The third circle includes the judges of the Supreme Constitutional Court and influential NGO activists as two new emerging groups. A group is understood here as a number of people of the same generation and same social background, with a common profession, historical experiences, and ideological outlook. Within every group the hierarchy is marked by different ranks. "Rank" is not meant here in the actual military sense but to denote those in an institution or a social group who have gained the highest prestige and merit. Out of each group the author chose a top representative as the ideal type for his group, but not in order to highlight an individual biography. "Elite change" is regarded here as a transfer of power from one rank to another, between groups, within circles, and between circles.

The president is at the center of two main groups in the first circle. On the one hand, he appoints the first ranks of the state technocrats, the military men, the diplomats, and the administration. On the other hand, he is also the chairman of the NDP, which holds 85.5 percent of the seats in the People's Assembly. The president is obviously the connection point between technocrats and politicians. The so-called government of technocrats denotes the weight of this group vis-à-vis the politicians in the cabinet. The official representatives of the two groups are the closest advisors for the president. On the technocratic side, there are Osama al-Baz, prime advisor for external affairs; Ahmed Mahar, foreign minister; Hussein Tantawi, minister of defense and military production; Omar Suleiman, intelligence chief, who is referred to as the "secret minister"; Habib al-Adly, minister of interior; and Atef Ebeid, prime minister. On the politician side, there are Safwat Sherif, NDP general secretary and minister of information, and Kamal al-Shazli, NDP vice-general secretary.

Figure 5.1   Egypt's Politically Relevant Elite, 2002

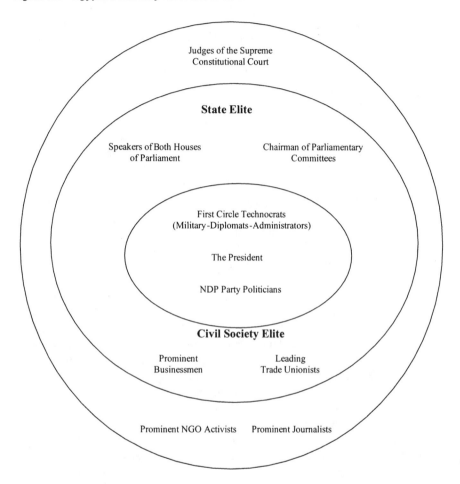

Although military and security officers and diplomats do not have the active or passive right to vote, and therefore do not participate in formal politics, they highly influence strategic decisionmaking. Some observers argue that the role of the military in Egyptian politics is diminishing, but it does not mean that its members are being excluded from the first PRE circle.[7] The possibility of terrorist attacks has strengthened the political weight of the security apparatus.[8] But demilitarization is still the underlying matrix for politics today: "Whereas the military supplied one-third of the ministerial elite and filled 40 percent of ministerial positions under Nasser, in Sadat's post-1973 'infitah government,' military representation dropped to about 10 percent, and it remained limited under Mubarak."[9]

Infitah, the Arabic term for *opening,* refers to Sadat's "open door" policies toward the West.

Diplomats have gained in importance in the first PRE circle during the Mubarak era. Under Amr Musa the Foreign Ministry developed into an entity that regarded itself not only as a state organ for implementing decisions, but also as an institution that makes decisions. Its importance rose with the seeming (initial) success of the Oslo and Barcelona processes. As Waterbury points out "the Ministry of Foreign Affairs appears to be the most hybrid public agency in Egypt, drawing its experts from the faculties of political science, intelligence, the military, and other parts of the administration."[10]

In the first circle, a transfer of power is under way from the military to civilian politicians. Depending on the external situation—that is, whether there is regional war or peace—the military has more or less influence, respectively, on political decisions than civilians. Another condition determining elite change in the first circle is linked to the decreasing or increasing influence of technocrats vis-à-vis politicians. An examination of the interplay between external (war versus peace) and internal (technocrats versus politicians) factors is essential to determining who among particular groups of elites is "in" and who is "out," though it is always a combination of both factors that decides whether a specific person is fit to move into a strategically important post.

Most members of the inner PRE circle are in their sixties or early seventies. They were deeply marked by the experiences of the 1973 October war and the peace process following the Camp David Accords. For the last thirty years they have operated as a nearly congruent "working team." The oldest minister in the cabinet is the seventy-six-year-old minister of justice, Mamduh 'Atiya. The youngest minister is Youssef Boutros Ghali, who is forty-six. According to al-Gauwadi, in 2001 the average age of the ministers was sixty-two, while that of the governors was fifty-two.[11] In terms of age there is no generational gap within the elite. The members of the second and third ranks who are in their fifties and forties are the emergent elites. They have been heavily influenced by the Islamicization of politics and society that took hold in the early 1980s and by the events leading to the Oslo agreement as well as its demise. The second and third military ranks did not participate in the October war or, for that matter, in any war against Israel. Such historical contexts are factors in the cohesion of these groups and could well be depicted as a third dimension of our model.

In general, members of parliament are in the second circle. The 2000 parliamentary elections resulted in remarkable mobility. More than two-thirds of incumbent parliamentarians were replaced: 329 MPs lost their seats, and 277 members were elected for the first time. Only one hundred out of the NDP's 444 nominated candidates were younger than forty-two.

The main conflict in the parliament is not between the ruling party and the marginal opposition (14.5 percent of the seats) but within the NDP. The most influential currents are the business lobby, representing the private sector, and the trade unions, representing the public sector. Among the seventeen chairmen of parliamentary committees there are four trade unionists and four businessmen. Among the twenty-one members of the NDP general secretariat, there are as well four trade unionists and four businessmen. Both lobbies exert pressure over the distribution of wealth in society; they demand a settlement of the constitutional quota regarding workers and peasants and a reform of the labor law. But trade unionists are losing ground to the business lobby.

With a workforce of around 18 million people, the president of the Egyptian Trade Union Federation (ETUF) is representing large segments of society and is, therefore, in the second circle. The ETUF is an umbrella organization, dating back to 1957, representing twenty-three unions with some 4.5 million members. Regular elections have been held at all levels of the organization. In its 1996 elections, the members selected 25,000 functionaries from among 145,000 candidates. Sixty-five percent of the functionaries were newly elected. Sayyed Rashid has headed the ETUF since 1991 and is also speaker of the People's Assembly. In the early 1970s, a process was begun to de-link the single party and the trade unions. In the mid-1980s the minister of labor ceased also being the ETUF president.

In the 1990s judges of the Supreme Constitutional Court, well-known journalists, and prominent NGO activists moved into the third PRE circle as important opinionmakers. The Supreme Constitutional Court's (SCC) rulings to dissolve the parliament of 1984 and 1987 and its landmark ruling in 2000 to put the parliamentary elections under full judicial supervision reflect the rising importance of the judges. As indicative were the rulings allowing radical Islamists to be tried before military courts and declaring privatization constitutional.[12] The judiciary has recently not hesitated to issue judgments at odds with the interests of the presidency and the NDP-dominated government. In addition, the SCC judiciary hold some of the best-paid positions among the state elite.

Journalists have also influenced political decisionmaking in Egypt. The debate on Islamic morality in society and the politically sensitive issue of a consumer boycott against U.S. and Israeli products in summer 2002, for example, were stirred up by Mustafa Bakri, the editor in chief of the weekly *al-Usbuaa*. Bakri demonstrated how the government can still be publicly cornered when it comes to relations with Israel twenty years after the signing of the peace treaty.

Nongovernmental organizations (NGOs) have brought together a younger age group and have grown in influence since the 1990s. A campaign by feminist NGOs for a change of the family status law is one example of how such a group can successfully influence the political agenda.[13] NGO leaders from the Gamaa Islamiyya and the more moderate Muslim Brotherhood must also be included in the PRE since their influence on politics in Egypt has been considerable.

Shifts of power are under way between all three circles. Judges of the SCC gained strength at the expense of parliamentarians. Certain NGO opinionmakers have obtained more weight than the traditional political parties. Prominent businessmen are moving into the center of power at the expense of trade unionists.

Circulation Patterns Among the PRE

As Singh points out "intraregime rivalries in Egypt have not equated with significant elite fissures as understood by comparative theorists of regime change. Egypt has experienced its share of perhaps unavoidable elite 'power games.' Examples include Nasser's rift with Chief of Staff Amr, Sadat's struggle to consolidate power after Nasser, and Mubarak's conflict with Field Marshal Abd al-Halim Abu Ghazzala. Yet the pattern of regime politics to the present day has not reflected the expectations of current theory, where crisis-induced, public elite fissures produce increased collective action and strategic behaviour."[14]

Patterns of PRE circulation are partly tied to external developments. On the one hand they are connected to relations with Israel and on the other hand to relations with the United States and the EU. Since the signing of the Camp David Accords, the general secretary of the NDP has always been pronormalization in regard to relations with Israel. This was true of Mustafa Khalil under Sadat and of Youssef Wali, minister of agriculture under Mubarak.[15] At the 2002 NDP congress, Safwat Sherif, the minister of information who has very good relations with Arab leaders, replaced Wali. At the time of Wali's replacement, Israel had launched a military offensive against the Palestinian Authority and reoccupied Palestinian-administered territories. This reflects one pattern of elite change, namely, where one stands vis-à-vis Israel.

The so-called technocrats, best exemplified by Atef Ebeid, former minister for public sector affairs (and later prime minister), primarily received an education in their field of specialization. Their appointments follow a pattern of bringing in people with a European education in times of increasing negotiations with the United States and bringing in people trained in the United States when negotiations with Europe are paramount. For instance, Atef Sidqi was prime minister from 1985 to 1996, a time of intense negotiations with the United States, the World Bank, and the IMF. He had graduated in 1958 from the University of Paris. His successor, Kamal al-Ganzuri, had graduated in 1967 with a Ph.D. from the University of Michigan and was appointed prime minister in 1996 after serving as minister of planning under Sidqi during the start of the Barcelona process and increased negotiations with the European Union. Prime Minister Ebeid was brought on in 1999, when efforts intensified to sign the Barcelona agreement and implement it. Ebeid had graduated from the University of Illinois, and as former minister of public sector affairs, he was regarded as a man of action—not of planning—and a proponent for liberalization of the public sector.

This pattern of appointments is meant to secure the loyalty of the staff. Behind such logic lies the widespread fear that people who have lived abroad or who hold dual citizenship will sympathize with the other side too much when a firm stand is needed during negotiations or they will be torn between the two sides in times of conflict or even war. A foreign education is still not accepted at the core of power; one need look no further than Mubarak and Musa for confirmation.[16] The loyalty of an MP with dual citizenship is similarly suspect, as was seen in the 2000 parliamentary elections, when legal objections were raised about the "Egyptianness" of several MPs. Furthermore, high-ranking army officers, judges, and diplomats are (according to internal regulations) not allowed to marry foreign women.

Recruitment Center: The NDP

Elections and political parties in the Arab world have not been viewed as instruments for cadre building or recruiting new leaders, but this is not necessarily the reality.[17] Since the war on Iraq, talk of the NDP as a possible force for elite rejuvenation and even democratization is coming back. "The country's elites (in government and in opposition) appear to have realised the importance of effectively incorporating Egypt's youth."[18]

Currently there are seventeen legally recognized parties, the most recent being founded in 2000. Five parties and one movement—the Muslim Brotherhood—are represented in the 2000–2005 People's Assembly.[19] The five parties are the NDP, the Liberal Party (al-Ahrar), the New Wafd, the National Progressive Unionist Party (al-Tagammu'a), and the Nasserite Party. The Muslim Brothers are likely the most politically relevant. As the party of the president, the NDP is enormously privileged and has never won an election with less than 80 percent of all votes.

Today the NDP's Central Bureau includes representatives of the modern industrial sectors, including information technologies, steel, and electronics. If a prominent businessman, for example, Ahmad Izz, rises in the ranks of the NDP, he simultaneously moves closer to the center of power. To a certain extent, the NDP general secretariat can be used as a gauge of elite movement and elite composition. In this case, Izz's path reflects the increasing importance of the business community in Egyptian politics. The Central Bureau also includes trade unionists from the textile and chemical industries, and from construction, as well as a representative of peasants with less than 10 *feddan*.[20] Another group within the Central Bureau are those ministers who are more politicians than technocrats, such as those heading the ministries of information, education, trade, tourism, and youth. These ministers were educated in the West or attended schools with a Western curriculum—as is the case with Minister of Foreign Trade and MP Youssef Boutros Ghali—or their appointment was the outcome of a long party career.

Elections have contributed slightly to changes in political personnel and to elevation into the politically relevant elite. Even if one regards the NDP as atrophied, it is still the party that has trained or will train part of the next political generation. Youth secretariats of parties, trade unions, professional syndicates, and NGOs actively direct programs for training young cadres. Hosni Mubarak's son, Gamal Mubarak, founded the Future Generation Foundation, an NGO aimed at assisting youth. At the political level, youth secretariats from political groups, and women's, peasants', and workers' organizations are the cornerstones of the political parties, especially of the NDP. The most important issue in the 2000 parliamentary election campaign was the high unemployment rate among university graduates.

Rotation of power among the competing political parties is not on the agenda in the near future. If it did become a reality, some reform by amendment of the constitution would likely be necessary, because the current constitution gives the president the power to form the government irrespective of a party's share of seats in the People's Assembly. The power of Egypt's government is centered in the presidency, not in its political parties. The beginning of a process to separate state and party may, however, have been foreshadowed during the NDP's eighth general congress in September 2002.[21] Before the congress, party members voted for 120,000 representatives, which resulted in the replacement of 70 percent of incumbent delegates.[22] At the congress, 10 percent of the delegates were women, and 60 percent of those present were considered "youth."[23] Mubarak's speech to the delegates centered on the issues of generational change and the introduction of young leadership. Four events at the meeting should be noted: Mubarak was confirmed as president of the party, but his son Gamal stood and voiced the demand of the delegates that in the next election for the party president, delegates be allowed to choose from among several candidates; it was decided that the congress would convene annually in order to vote on a fourth of the delegates and assess party accomplishments and goals; it was demanded that the NDP no longer be the "party of the government" but that the government become "the government of the party" (*hizb al-hukuma* versus *hukumat al-hizb*), hinting at a revision of the relationship between the state and the NDP; and, as noted above, General Secretary Wali was replaced by Safwat Sherif. Also notable was Gamal Mubarak's appointment as head of the new policies secretariat.[24]

Changing Sociopolitical PRE Profiles

The Business Community

In the mid-1980s, about a decade after the start of economic liberalization, the first echelon of Egyptian businessmen (and some businesswomen) began to enter politics. A decade later, with the beginning of privatization, their involvement in politics increased. Generally speaking, they replaced those personalities in parliament who had established themselves in the public sector.

In two non-Islamist scenarios for the future of Egypt, John Waterbury regards private sector representatives as an "increasingly important source for leadership."[25] What was still a potential scenario for Waterbury in his 1999 account crystallized in the 2000 parliamentary elections: Businessmen were running for election or founding newspapers in order to influence politics; one example is Rami Lakakh, who founded the *Cairo Post.* Businessmen won twenty-five seats in the 2000 elections. About 50 percent of them (twelve seats) were under the umbrella of the ruling NDP, three ran for the liberal Wafd Party, and ten were independents. These businessmen represented about 40 percent of the total seats won by independents. The popular movements, such as those on the left and the Muslim Brotherhood, did not nominate anyone from the business community. Furthermore fifty-two small entrepreneurs were elected. All three Copts who won parliamentary seats in 2000 were businessmen or economists.[26]

The business lobby is still not consolidated to a degree that would allow it to heavily influence politics. Amira el-Azhary Sonbol argues that some of its members, namely those merchants (*tujjar*) associated with international corporations, have more influence than others,[27] which would puts them in the second circle of PRE. Together, businessmen and small entrepreneurs doubled their seats in the 2000 elections. The remainder in the private sector is, according to Sonbol, those entrepreneurs who own small factories or workshops and who offer services mainly in the informal sector. They are not part of any elite circle, but they have amassed considerable wealth and therefore regard the current division of political power with some skepticism. It is the contention here that this stratum is clearly a middle class, standing between the elite and the masses: "They do not have the power to stop the exactions of the *khassa* (elites), but their wealth [gives] them the leverage to rise beyond the *amma*. Because the khassa needs them for the jobs they provide, the import-substitution products they produce, and the taxes they pay, they have considerable leverage."[28]

Women

Basic conditions are gradually changing in order to let more women participate and rise in the political decisionmaking process, even though to a much lesser degree. A parliamentary quota of thirty-five seats for women was introduced during the 1979–1984 term as part of a package of laws for improving the status of women initiated by former first lady Jihan Sadat. The Supreme Constitutional Court, under pressure from opposition social and political circles, reflecting, among other things, the growing influence of the Islamist movement, declared this measure unconstitutional. In 2000 the status of women surfaced as a major topic of political reform with the promulgation of Law No. 1/2000, which amended the personal status law and for the first time granted women the right to seek a divorce without specifying reasons before the court (*khul' a*).

Passage of the law had to overcome serious obstacles, including strong opposition in elite circles and among the public at large. The NDP opposed the law, which opened a split between the mufti (against) and the Shaykh al-Azhar (in favor). The clerical dispute was settled when al-Azhar's Islamic Research Academy voted to overrule the mufti in a step previously unheard of. The Shaykh al-Azhar even went to the parliament to convince skeptical MPs in a televised session on the new law's legality from an orthodox point of view. Resistance was fierce and included arguments that the law threatened family structures and thus society, not just the fate of some individuals.[29] Still the government insisted on pressing for the law. One of the noteworthy demands at the September 2002 NDP congress was the promotion of women as judges, since traditionally they have never occupied this post in Egypt. This was followed in January 2003 by the appointment of the prominent female lawyer Tehani el-Jebali to the Supreme Constitutional Court.

The 2000 election marked the first time that the Muslim Brotherhood put forth a female candidate for parliament in the Alexandria Raml district. But Jihan al-Halafawy's political ascendance was hindered by irregularities and intimidation of voters in by-elections held two years after she had won a majority in the first round. Only seven women currently sit in parliament, and they all belong to the NDP. But the fact that they were elected from poor urban and semiurban areas is of significance.

Moreover, women increasingly occupy important posts within diplomacy: "In 1999 seventeen Egyptian women ambassadors held the top positions in Egyptian embassies and consulates in such places as New York,

South Africa, Australia, San Francisco, Frankfurt, and Paris. The Egyptian Foreign Service has altogether 812 women working in the diplomatic service constituting 16.5 percent; twenty-four hold the title of ambassadors."[30]

Out of the twenty-three sector trade union secretaries, one is headed by a woman, Aisha Abdel-Hadi (Trade Union of Chemical Workers). Aisha Abdel-Hadi gradually moved into the second PRE circle when she was appointed to the Consultative Council (*majlis ash-shura*) and into the first PRE circle when she became a member of the NDP's Political Bureau.

Change at the Top and Presidential Succession

Mubarak is a typical product of the October generation. Born in 1928 in a peasant family of the delta, he received his education through the army and became part of a new military generation who planned and carried out the 1973 war under Anwar Sadat. Two years later he was nominated for vice president at the age of forty-seven to replace Hussein ash-Shafa'ei, one of the last members of the July generation in the core elite. In 1981 Mubarak became president as unexpectedly as Sadat had. He is now in his fourth presidential term.[31] The theme of the last presidential referendum, for the 1999–2005 term, was "Allegiance for all his life" (*al-bay a mad al hayat*).

Mubarak walked on very thin ice during the period that witnessed the Israeli invasion of Lebanon in 1982 and heightened tensions throughout the region. While accepting the Camp David Accords and benefiting from U.S. aid, he returned Egypt to the Arab fold, including returning the Arab League headquarters to Cairo in 1990. Mubarak has maintained Egypt's close ties to the United States while also championing strategic interests that run counter to U.S. concerns in the region (for example, in regard to relations with Libya, Iraq, and Iran). He reached a compromise between those PRE members who supported normalization of ties with Israel and those that opposed it. What helped Mubarak to maintain balance was the fact that he had never visited Israel.[32] In 1989 Taba, the last strip of Egyptian territory under Israeli occupation, was returned. In line with Sadat's pragmatic "land for peace" approach, Mubarak installed a lasting cold peace although still today most segments of Egyptian society are against normalization with Israel.

Mubarak opened a dialogue with civil society and allowed limited inclusion of its representatives in the political decisionmaking process. In February 1982 he brought his economic staff together with left-leaning economists for a conference that focused on adjusting infitah policies. A change in the election law replaced individual candidacies with party lists, which allowed the Muslim Brotherhood representation in the parliament in 1984 and 1987. That the Brotherhood's representatives voted in 1987 in favor of nominating Mubarak for a second presidential term demonstrates the success of Mubarak's balancing act. A recent compromise with the Islamists and the beginning of the release of thousands of Islamist prisoners in the summer of 2003 is the latest pillar on which Mubarak builds his long-lasting regime. Re-integrating this segment of society is a major condition for setting the stage for the presidential succession. Here, the International Crisis Group (ICG) noticed a shift in the fault-line of Egyptian politics. "Islamists have stated their willingness to put their more controversial societal projects to one side in order to ally with the secular opposition on two dominant themes: democracy and sovereignty, by which they mean the effective independence from the United States that intellectuals and activists perceive to be at growing risk."[33]

The Void

Since Egypt's transformation from kingdom to republic, the country has not experienced such a mystery as exists around the question of succession today. After 1952 it became automatic for the vice president to ascend to the presidency, bringing with him his personal entourage, following the death of his predecessor. This secured a smooth transfer of power to the new president. Mubarak, however, has not appointed a vice president.[34] This is somewhat surprising if one takes into consideration the periods of internal instability during his presidency resulting from the rise of violent Islamist groups, regional conflicts, and several assassination attempts against Mubarak and some of his ministers. The fact that no deputy was nominated, even after these unsuccessful attempts and open threats, has raised questions among the Egyptian people about the apparent succession void.[35]

Mubarak's answer to questions about who will succeed him has always been that he does not want to impose someone on the Egyptian people and that the constitution and state institutions will guarantee a smooth and legal transfer of power if need be. The constitution provides that the speaker of parliament in the first place, or the president of the Supreme Constitutional Court in the second place, would replace the president if the need arises— under the condition that they do not intend to stand as a candidate for the presidency themselves. One of them will technically rule until the parliament approves a successor. Mubarak's legalistic answer touched upon the issue of his deputy but clearly avoided the specific question of succession.

Fathers and Sons

Public discussion about who will follow Hosni Mubarak increased after the death of Syrian president Hafiz al-Asad (1930–2000), with the Egyptian opposition press openly comparing the Syrian case with the Egyptian and asking whether Gamal Mubarak would succeed his father as Bashar al-Asad had succeeded his.[36] The Syrian scenario sparked a general debate on hereditary successions in Arab republics as well as kingdoms. It made certain Arab intellectuals, among them Saad Eddin Ibrahim, wary that more Arab states (e.g., Egypt, Iraq, Libya, and Yemen) would act along the same lines.[37] The oppositional newspaper *al-Wafd* voiced the same concern. What appeared to underline their view was Gamal Mubarak's increasingly political role since the mid-1990s, when he became the spokesman for Egypt on the Egyptian-U.S. Presidents Council.[38] In 1999 the press reported that Gamal Mubarak was interested in founding a new political party called al-Mustaqbal (the Future), which would represent business interests—the party, however, did not materialize. That same year he became involved in youth issues and founded the Future Generation Foundation, which is working in the areas of housing for young people, training for graduates, and political awareness. He officially devoted himself to "preparing today a second and third generation of administrative and technical leaders for the challenges of the future" and stressed that "the door is open for young people, NGOs and political parties to engage in political activity."[39] In February 2000 Hosni Mubarak shuffled the NDP's Political Bureau. These changes reflect the effort to include highly respected and popular figures in the party's top decisionmaking organs who are not regarded as party bloc heads and to include more Copts.[40] They also demonstrate the increasing influence of the private sector. Furthermore, Gamal Mubarak was appointed to the general secretariat.

After the 2000 parliamentary elections, in which Gamal Mubarak did not run as a candidate despite rumors that he would, he was appointed one of four commission members responsible for party reform and officially charged with bringing young Egyptians into the party. Cadre building and rejuvenation of the party as well as the parliament started gradually in the 1990s and has produced some well-qualified second and third rank politicians.[41] Gamal Mubarak's activities in this arena may be seen as an attempt to establish his own political credentials and a minimum of legitimacy. But "the meteoric promotion of Bashar Asad to the rank of Field Marshal in the Syrian army cannot be repeated in Egypt," as Feldner rightly pointed out.[42] Moreover the Egyptian case will not automatically happen analogous to the Syrian case for several reasons: Asad implicitly installed his sons, beginning in the early 1990s, whereas Mubarak several times clearly and openly has excluded the handing over of power to his son. Gamal Mubarak has echoed this line more than once.[43] A majority of the Syrian PRE and public opinion arguably supported the succession of Bashar, but in Egypt the majority of the PRE and the general public do not subscribe to the idea that Gamal Mubarak should succeed his father. They argue that the state of the law is more advanced in Egypt than in Syria and that civil society is strong enough to resist this model. In Syria, Bashar Asad also had the backing of powerful members of the Asad family and Alawi leaders in the security apparatus. Gamal Mubarak does not have similar support.

Despite Egyptian opposition to the Syrian model, there are supporters of Gamal Mubarak—such as Yassin Serageddin, brother of the founder of the New Wafd, and Wahid Abd al-Magid, editor in chief of the *al-Ahram Strategic Report*—who have two arguments at hand. First, they assert, Gamal Mubarak has a real chance at the presidency if the only alternative is a military man. Second, they argue, he should not succeed just because he is the president's son, but at the same time he should also not be discouraged from pursuing the office because of his family name.[44]

What is regarded as a failure, cowardliness, or as an attempt to install Gamal Mubarak by many observers, might well be interpreted as a conscious strategy: It gives Mubarak the leeway to keep the path open for a civilian successor for the first time since the declaration of the republic.[45]

Understanding the Void

The people used below for "understanding" this apparent succession void are only meant as ideal types exemplifying different options. Although there is no vice president, there has always been a "number two" strongman: Abd al-Halim Abu Ghazzala, defense minister and advisor to the president from 1981 to 1993, and Amr Musa, foreign minister from 1991 to 2001 and currently secretary general of the Arab League, may be regarded as such. Gamal Mubarak needs to be added to this list as a member of the NDP's general secretariat since 2000, even if we cannot call him a "second strong man." He, as well as the other two, have been subject at one time or another to the public debate centering around the succession.[46] These three men offer clues for interpreting the current situation in respect to succession and thereby determining Egypt's future PRE. They are representative of three important institutions in Egypt: the Defense Ministry, the Foreign Ministry, and the next generation in the NDP. As noted, two institutions— the military and the foreign service—are officially exempt from politics. In reality, however, they play decisive roles in influencing Egypt's political agenda. Furthermore, both are channels for the promotion of future elites as is the NDP. The role of the party is often disputed,[47] but it must be included because of the weight of parliamentary members, 85.5 percent of whom belong to the NDP and will nominate the next president at the end of the current term.

Abu Ghazzala, Musa, and Gamal Mubarak also symbolize three different periods in recent history: from the assassination of Sadat to the Oslo agreement (1981–1993); the collapse of the Oslo agreement (1993–2001);

and the reform of Egypt's democratic experiment from within, starting with the first parliamentary elections under judicial supervision in 2000. During the first period, Abu Ghazzala served as defense minister, until 1989, when Taba was returned; he left his post as senior advisor to the president in 1993, when the Oslo agreement was signed. As a military man, Abu Ghazzala was considered to be the number two strongman as long as Egyptian territory was under Israeli occupation. With Oslo, however, the military's importance declined, and the diplomatic nationalist emerged. With it appeared Amr Musa as a potential successor to Mubarak.[48] Musa stayed in office from 1991 until the collapse of Oslo in 2001. Egypt's negotiations with the European Union from 1995 to 2001 were carried out under Musa's auspices and were connected to the unfolding of a peace process in the region. Among other goals, the Barcelona process was designed to establish ties between the Israeli and Arab markets and to integrate Israel into the region. An agreement was eventually signed by Foreign Minister Ahmed Mahar, a retired diplomat, shortly after Musa left office. Much speculation surrounded who would replace Musa at foreign affairs as was also the case following Abu Ghazzala's departure from defense. In both instances Mubarak chose "outsiders": Youssef Sabri Abu Taleb, mayor of Cairo, became defense minister in 1989, and Mahar succeeded Musa in 2001.[49] Mahar had been nominated by Mubarak as ambassador to the United States in 1992. He belongs to Mubarak's peace process generation and served Sadat at Camp David as security advisor. There have been few accounts of the internal workings at the Defense Ministry and the Foreign Ministry, but it is possible to identify divisions in both of them. The former involved cooperation with the multinational forces during the Gulf War,[50] and the latter concerned relations with Israel after the breakdown of the Oslo process. Mubarak thus found it necessary to bring in personnel who could moderate between the respective factions. This explains his surprising choices and the correlation between the number two strongman and regional developments, especially in regard to Israel.

These three key figures are also representatives of three different ideological currents: (1) Abu Ghazzala, a military-Islamist; (2) Musa, a diplomatic-nationalist; and (3) Gamal Mubarak with his civil-liberal tendency (see Table 5.1). The 1980s were dominated by the rise of the Islamist movement within formal politics—as members of parliament and as elected representatives of professional associations—whereas the 1990s saw a violent clampdown, putting the professional associations under pressure, destroying the so-called State of Imbaba (one of the poorest quarters of Cairo), and putting thousands of Islamist activists in prison. One might say that the 1980s were a time of military-Islamist outlook until the complete implementation of the Camp David Accords, whereas the 1990s were char-

Table 5.1   Three Options for Presidential Succession

	Option 1	Option 2	Option 3
Political circumstances	Conflict/War Internal crises	Cold peace/Cold war Economic stability	Peace Economic development
Strategic priorities	Liberation of national territory	Political and economic infrastructure development	Economic and political liberalization
Source of PRE	Military and security services	Civilian state institutions (e.g., foreign ministry)	Multiple political parties
Ideological outlook	Islamist-nationalist	Nationalist-liberal	Liberal-global
Ideal type	Abu Ghazzala	Amr Musa	Gamal Mubarak

acterized by the rise of nationalism and Egyptian diplomacy once again. The recent return of the Islamists to politics parallels the collapse of the Oslo process.

Four Scenarios for Elite Change

Adding a violent overthrow to the three options for presidential succession, four scenarios for change within the politically relevant elite need to be considered. The violent/pessimistic scenario results from an escalation of the Israeli-Palestinian conflict and the U.S. war on terrorism. It assumes that relations between Egypt and Israel will devolve to their status before Camp David. The danger here is not only the demise of the Oslo process, but the possibility that the region as a whole will be thrown back thirty years. Whereas nationalist ideologies—Zionism and pan-Arabism—have driven politics in the region in the twentieth century, a political roadblock by the religious and nationalist elements in Israel could lead to a similar military-religious response on the Arab side. A military elite adhering to a populist, isolationist Islamist outlook could come to power. Egypt would be governed by someone capable of presenting himself as a "heroic figure" in the ideological mold of Khalid Islambouli, Sadat's assassin. The face of such a government would be the Muslim Brotherhood. The compromise between the radical wing of the Brothers in prison and the parliamentary wing would read as follows: First, the external enemy must be defeated.[51] If the violent Islamist current becomes dominant, its first step will in all probability be to reverse the established U.S.-European-Egyptian platform in favor of strengthening ties with other Muslim countries, especially in Asia. But a violent scenario is not considered particularly realistic here for two reasons: First, the Muslim Brotherhood entered the political game in the 1990s and has already changed its slogan from "Islam is the solution," which they adopted in the 1980s, to "Respect for the constitution" in the 1990s. Secondly, the assassination of Rabin and the subsequent stalemate in the peace process prompted the radical Islamist currents to orient themselves toward the "external enemy" rather than their own governments, which culminated in the September 11 attacks.[52]

A second, more moderate but still Islamist scenario, is the ascendance of the Islamic awakening generation. The upcoming generation was mostly born in the 1950s and emerged at the end of the 1970s as leaders in the students' movement parallel to the Islamic revolution in Iran. Today they occupy important positions in many professional syndicates (especially the bar association, and the unions of journalists, medical doctors, or engineers) and manage the affairs of powerful NGOs. In 2000 they returned to parliament as independent candidates, tripling their seats. Their agenda is to a large degree procapitalist, but against what they call "Westernization" in the political and sociocultural sense. Their discourse, in addition to being Islamist, is populist and antiliberal. Their historical imprints are the Oslo process until its breakdown and the Islamicization of state and society. Their rise would be comparable to that of the Justice and Development Party in Turkey.

In the third scenario elites that advocate political and economic liberalism move into central posts within the next ten years. One could expect the appearance of a number of new parties with varied interests. The liberal agenda would take up the demands that are currently being voiced by the whole array of political opposition, including the Muslim Brotherhood. Their presidential candidate would open a dialogue between the various political currents, with debate centering on the legal framework of governmental and nongovernmental politics. But this requires opposition unity. It is difficult to make statements about the military's position in this scenario. Today's incumbents are the former classmates of Khalid Islambouli, but they have also profited from the peace and stability of the last twenty years. The state of emergency would be lifted and the rule of law enforced.

The fourth and most plausible option reflects a compromise between the different ideological trends within the upcoming generation, that is, a liberal-nationalist current. In this scenario the Brotherhood would be recognized as a political party and act as a conservative-religious restraint for the regime. There are personalities on both sides of the scale who represent moderate versions and who have well-educated young personnel ready to move into politically relevant elite positions.

Outlook

The next presidential referendum is scheduled for October 2005. Another term in office for Mubarak is constitutionally possible, but less plausible given his age and the debate about succession. If Mubarak leaves in 2005, this will be a significant event in that it would be almost the first time that an Arab leader left office alive without a coup d'état. It will be necessary to bring up the issue of consecutive presidential terms again and to amend the constitution in order to have direct, multicandidate elections for the presidency. The most important task of the next president is to manage the debate about constitutional reform.

A charismatic personality such as Amr Musa is an intermediary between the October generation and the younger generation. In terms of ideological outlook he could temper the moderate Islamists and the liberals. Known for his pan-Arab views, Musa is currently serving as General Secretary of the Arab League, which he brought back as a political broker. He can well figure as a crosspoint between Arab and Muslim countries, as well as between European and U.S. interests. What was regarded as a weakening of Musa's position as a result of Mubarak's fear of his strong foreign minister might well be regarded as a strength should he arise again at an appropriate moment in time. Musa is regarded as a brilliant and charismatic personality. There have already been signs of "Musa Mania" in Egypt.[53] Recent rumors[54] that Musa is being marginalized within the NDP only confirm his potential because historically someone who has been controversial and not favored within the party has succeeded the president. Sadat and Mubarak were the lowest common denominators the two wings of the NDP could agree on. This pattern of elite replacement is why Egypt currently faces a void.

Notes

The author thanks Bettina Dennerlein and Sonja Hegasy from the Centre for Modern Oriental Studies in Berlin for their comments.

1. In the 1948–1949 war of Palestine, Gamal Abdel Nasser and Zakariyya Mohieddin, who would later become Nasser's vice president, had gained prestige in the famous siege of Falujah. In the 1973 war Hosni Mubarak was a career air force officer.

2. This chapter is based on three field trips to Egypt in 2001 and 2002. The author interviewed up-coming members of the ruling NDP, rising businessmen, a leading female trade unionist, and former members of the military who are today active in private businesses or in private research institutions. Interviews with active military members are forbidden. Therefore the author relied on accounts of ex-military men as well as upon published personal comments by high-ranking military officials. Several interviewees asked not to be directly quoted or mentioned by name.

3. Talk of a successor to Mubarak had been taboo until January 2003, when Egyptian political commentator Muhammad Hasanayn Haykal raised the issue on state-owned television. *International Herald Tribune*, 9 January 2003.

4. Many members of the PRE are not connected to the cabinet or do not hold state positions. But intellectuals and members of the business community, university professors, student leaders, journalists, and others have at times influenced the political agenda or stimulated public debate to a degree that state institutions were forced to react.

5. On the three-circle model of politically relevant elites, see the introduction in this volume by Volker Perthes.

6. A technocrat is someone who realizes his or her political ambition through a professional field. A politician is someone who lives either for or from politics or both. Compared to the politician the technocrat does not abandon his or her original profession. It is clear that this definition is different from defining a technocrat as someone who has no political ambitions or does not live for politics. Instead of judging one's conscience and visible ambitions, the author prefers to define someone according to his or her position. Any other approach is as idealistic as to say somebody is not an artist because he lives from art.

7. Muhammad Abdul Aziz and Youssef Hussein assert that the military's role in determining Mubarak's successor cannot be neglected even if its influence in the decisionmaking process is decreasing. See Abdul Aziz and Hussein, "The President, the Son, and the Military"; also see Zohny, "Toward an Apolitical Role for the Egyptian Military"; Sonbol, *New Mamluks.*

8. Its numerical strength has been estimated at up to 1 percent of the population. See Sonbol, *New Mamluks,* or Abdul Aziz and Hussein, "The President, the Son, and the Military."

9. See www.1upinfo.com/country-guide-study/egypt/egypt128.html. The last time Mubarak wore a military uniform in public was the day of Sadat's assassination.

10. Waterbury, "Whence Will Come Egypt's Future Leadership?" p. 21. In 2001 the state secretary for international cooperation was transferred from the Ministry of Planning to the Foreign Ministry, which gave the latter even more weight.

11. al-Gauwadi, *The Egyptian Political Elite.*

12. Regarding the latter, opponents of the court's decision argued that the constitution prescribes a socialist economy in which the public sector leads the way.

13. Muslim women may now initiate a divorce proceeding without cause if they forgo almost all financial rights. One-and-a-half million women—which translates into more than 10 percent of all Egyptian families—have cases pending in a family court. Two-thirds of these are petitions for divorce. Coptic women have not yet obtained such a right. For a more detailed evaluation of the effects of the new law, see Mariz Tadros, "What Price for Freedom?" *al-Ahram Weekly,* 7–13 March 2002.

14. Singh, "Precluding Transition Politics," p. 17.

15. Wali's ministry benefited greatly from scientific and technological exchanges with the Israeli Agriculture Ministry. For an in-depth discussion of Wali's position in the party, his difficult relations with rural Egypt, and the media campaign and trial against him, see Gamal Abdelnasser and Nathalie Bernard-Maugiron, "Pouvoir de la censure ou censure du pouvoir? L'affaire Youssef Wali contre al-Sha'b," *Egypte Monde Arabe,* no. 3 (2000).

16. Mubarak spent only one year abroad at the Soviet General Staff Academy.

17. Until 2000, the general election code had assigned the supervision of voting committees to officials from the governmental administration and public sector units. It was always suspected that these officials were biased or yielded to directives from the administration to falsify election results by using voting cards of citizens who had not gone to the polls. After the Supreme Constitutional Court issued a judgment in 2000 stating that it was unconstitutional to allow persons other than members of the judicial authority to chair the polls, the election code was amended.

18. International Crisis Group, "The Challenge of Political Reform: Egypt After the Iraq War," *Middle East Briefing*, Cairo/Brussels, 30 September 2003, p. 2.

19. With seventeen seats they are the strongest oppositional faction in the parliament today.

20. One hectar equals 2.25 feddan.

21. The debate about whether Egypt is indeed liberalizing is ongoing among Middle East experts. Whereas Eberhard Kienle (*A Grand Delusion*, 2001) talks of "deliberalization," the International Institute for Strategic Studies sees "change in stability." "Egypt has moved unsteadily toward the political and economic liberalisation Mubarak seemed to promise when he took office in 1981. The pressures of Egypt's growing population, the entrenched interests of the massive bureaucracy and security services, and Mubarak's instinctive caution have ensured that forward movement is so slow as to appear retrograde." International Institute for Strategic Studies, "Mapping Egypt's Future," p. 2.

22. There are no accurate figures about NDP membership. They vary between 2 million and 4.6 million members. See Steve Negus, "Party Reform?" *Middle East International*, 12 July 2002. The number here reflects those members who have assumed active posts within the party.

23. *Al-Hayat*, 11 September 2002.

24. See "Egyptian Leader's Son Named Head of Policies in Ruling Party," MENA, 17 September 2002.

25. Waterbury, "Whence Will Come Egypt's Future Leadership?" p. 22.

26. The victorious Coptic NDP candidate was Economy and Foreign Trade Minister Youssef Boutros Ghali, a member of one of the oldest Coptic families involved in political life. For information about the Boutros Ghali family, see Goldschmidt, "The Butrus Ghali Family." The second Coptic businessman is Mounir Fakhri Abdelnour, general secretary of the Wafd Party, and the third is Rami Lakakh, a prominent businessman who acquired Egyptian citizenship—he is of Lebanese origin—and ran as an independent candidate. The High Administrative Court later stripped him of his parliamentary seat on the basis of his dual nationality.

27. Sonbol, *New Mamluks*, p. 200.

28. Ibid.

29. The televised parliamentary discussions in December 1999 were spectacular, with MPs yelling at one another, asking if from now on they were supposed to wake up in the morning and not find their wife next to them?

30. Sonbol, *New Mamluks*, p. 188.

31. According to the constitution, presidential terms are for six years. In 1980 Anwar Sadat changed a provision limiting the presidency to two successive terms. He justified this amendment, which he did not live long enough to benefit from, by the need to stabilize the executive during a period of transformation.

32. Mubarak's only visit to Israel was in 1995 to attend the funeral of Yitzhak Rabin.

33. International Crisis Group, "The Challenge of Political Reform," p. 2.

34. During the union with Syria, Nasser appointed five vice presidents.

35. We can safely assume though that there is a secret emergency plan for succession within the core elite.

36. For a detailed account of the positions of the Egyptian press, see Feldner, "Will Egypt Follow Syria's Precedent?" Samer Shehata points out that father-to-son successions are not characteristic of Arab political culture:

> With the succession of Bashar al-Assad in Syria and speculation that similar father-to-son transitions will take place in Iraq, Libya, Yemen, and Egypt, some journalists have already implied that dynastic succession is a product of Arab political culture. The claim might soon be made explicit in academic guise and could easily be deployed as another variant of the 'Middle East exceptionalism thesis.' . . . The relationship between father-to-son succession and 'Arab political culture,' however, is spurious for a number reasons. First, it is simply empirically false. Father-to-son successions have more often occurred in non-Arab contexts: in North Korea, the Democratic Republic of the Congo, Nicaragua, and Haiti. Rather than being the product of an essentially 'Arab political culture,' the phenomenon is more likely specific to a particular type of authoritarianism—centralisation of power in the person of the leader, a small ruling elite, the lack of institutionalised power centres outside the leader, a cult-of-personality, and long serving rulers who have been able to eliminate potential rivals.

Shehata, "Political Succession in Egypt," p. 112.

37. In its July 2000 issue the Saudi journal *al-Majalla* spread the term *jumlukiyya* (translates as "republicarchy"), which was invented by Saad Eddin Ibrahim. The unconstitutional "inthronization" of the sons in the republics is a sensitive issue.

38. The Egyptian-U.S. Presidents Council is a federation of Egyptian and American businessmen with the purpose of promoting investment in Egypt and advising the government on economic issues.

39. *Al-Ahram Weekly*, 11–17 May 2000.

40. Like Economy Minister Youssef Boutros Ghali, Environment Minister Nadia Makram Ebeid, the two businessmen Ibrahim Kamel and Ahmad Izz, or Youth Minister Ali Eddin Hillal Dessouki. Dessouki became minister for youth in 1999 and is a rising figure within the new PRE, despite Muhammad Abdul Aziz and Youssef Hussein's slightly polemical assessment that Dessouki is "a not very youthful fifty-five year old," *The President, the Son, and the Military*, p. 81. The author regards Dessouki as one of the personalities who can rejuvenate the NDP and promote the necessary cadre-building.

41. See Abdelnasser, "Political Change in Egypt."

42. Feldner, "Does Gamal Mubarak Have a Chance?"

43. See among others, James Drummond and Roula Khalaf, "Mubarak's Son Rules Out Succession," *Financial Times*, 24 April 2001.

44. See Feldner, "Does Gamal Mubarak Have a Chance?" For further secondary literature see, e.g., Jonathan Schanzer, "Gamal Mubarak: Successor Story in Egypt." *Policy Watch*, no. 669, Washington Institute for Near East Policy, 17 October 2002.

45. A popular Egyptian joke tells the story of Mubarak who wanders amongst

his people and asks everyone if they know him but nobody recognizes him. Only in the end does he meet someone who tells him: "Yes, I know who you are and I know the one before you and the one after you." An astonished Mubarak asks what he means and is told that before him was Sadat and before Sadat it was Nasser and after him it will be Ghamra (which is the Metro station following the one named after the three presidents).

46. According to the ICG, an independent MP filed a question to the government in June 2003 in order to clarify the consitutional status of Gamal Mubarak. This was followed by a lawsuit filed one month later against Hosni Mubarak for violating the constitution, which "requires, not merely authorises, him to designate a vice president." International Crisis Group, "The Challenge of Political Reform," p. 16.

47. Waterbury, "Whence Will Come Egypt's Future Leadership?"

48. Born in 1936, Amr Musa studied law in Cairo, and in 1958 began his career as a civil servant in the Egyptian Foreign Ministry. He became ambassador to India in 1967, ambassador to the United Nations in 1990, and foreign minister from 1991 to 2001. His tenure as foreign minister covered the Oslo process and the Egyptian negotiations with the European Union in the framework of the Barcelona process.

49. Ten people were considered possible successors to Amr Musa. Among them, Mahar was at the very end of the list. Confusion and speculation over Musa's replacement led to the erroneous announcement on television that Ali Mahar, Ahmad's younger brother and ambassador to France, had been appointed foreign minister rather than Ahmad.

50. A split became visible when Gen. Ahmed Bilal was recalled by Mubarak before the war started because of differences of opinion with the Saudi generals. In his place, Salah Halabi, head of the presidential guard, took command of the Egyptian troops. There are accounts of celebratory fire among the 40,000 Egyptian soldiers when Iraqi rockets were fired onto Israel. Halabi was later promoted to general.

51. On understanding the future of the Islamist project, see al-Zayat, *Aiman az-Zawahiri.*

52. See al-Zayat, Op. cit.

53. In 2000, with the start of the al-Aqsa intifada, "I Love Amr Musa and I Hate Israel," by Shaaban Abdel Rahim, became a popular song in Egypt, confirming the widespread image that Musa had acquired a much stronger standing when it came to Israeli policies than had Mubarak.

54. Rising NDP member, interview, 4 January 2003.

6

Saudi Arabia:
Dynamism Uncovered

Iris Glosemeyer

Unlike in Jordan and Morocco, where changes on the leadership level resulted in further elite change "from above,"[1] the Saudi core elite steered, rather than imposed, elite change. In a rather subtle manner it sought to take advantage of changes within and among different segments of the politically relevant elite. The analysis here concentrates on these elite segments, locating them in a model comprised of three concentric circles of influence.[2]

In 2003 the same members of the royal family had monopolized the first circle for two decades. The second circle of influence exhibited some diversity, including members of the royal family, the religious elite, and at times a few professionals. In contrast, the third circle, which comprises those who do not rule but influence the decisionmaking process indirectly by advice, lobbying, or nuisance power, was heterogeneous and dynamic. Its members represented the royal family, the religious elite, the tribal elite, the business elite, professionals, and challenging *ulama* (Islamic scholars). Sometimes competing with each other and sometimes forming alliances, these actors were either heading toward the second circle or about to lose their political influence completely.[3]

Two questions are raised by the dynamics of elite change in Saudi Arabia. First, how did the core elite manage to keep its position while the wider circles of the elite changed in terms of age, educational, social, and regional background, and attitude, and, second, how did these changes affect Saudi Arabia's political system? The answers involve the degree of political influence, the type of political capital, and the kind of institutions that actors have at their disposal. Moreover, socioeconomic developments as well as policies of outside actors beyond the control of the politically relevant elite influence their agendas and their political capital.[4]

Actors: Capital, Position, and Institutional Representation

During the first thirty years of the twentieth century, Abd al-Aziz Al Saud—commonly known as Ibn Saud—deployed tribal and religious forces to conquer and unite the different regions that comprise the Kingdom of Saudi Arabia. He strove to establish an absolute monarchy based on personalized patrimonial rule. Trying to overcome the country's religious and cultural heterogeneity, Ibn Saud and his sons employed Wahhabi teachings as a unifying ideology and developed a sophisticated marriage strategy with tribal and religious elites.[5] Thus, until the 1950s, in Saudi Arabia there were three groups of politically relevant actors, bound by mutual dependence and intermarriage: the Al Saud family and the religious and tribal elites, who prevailed over the few challengers emerging from among their ranks.[6] With the advent of measurable oil revenues in the 1950s, the Al Saud gained the means to develop the country and to fulfill the material demands of the population. The second generation of Saudis thus grew up in a rentier state per se. Although Saudi Arabia was to remain a rentier state for the foreseeable future, the third generation, Saudi young adults born in the 1970s and 1980s, grew up in an atmosphere of declining oil income.[7]

In the early 2000s, the royal Al Saud family still relied on material wealth, access to oil revenues, personal networks, and its size and degree of internal cohesion to maintain its influence. A small number of the royal family had pocketed the first circle and headed influential ministries.[8] Others occupied positions in the second and third circles and were appointed ministers with minor portfolios, deputy or assistant ministers, governors, and members of the Royal Family Council.[9]

The religious elite, the most influential ulama, was largely recruited from the same families for generations. They were represented in the second and third circles, and at times some of their members aspired to enter the core elite. The religious elite possessed traditional legitimacy and the means to defend or undermine the policies of the royal family, because the Saudi state was to a large extent legitimized by an eighteenth-century coalition between the Al Saud and the religious elite. Though only the head of the Saudi state had the right to call to (holy) war, he had to be accepted by the religious elite. In short, their main capital was their capacity to shape public opinion and to mobilize mass support. Efforts to integrate the ulama into the state apparatus led to the establishment of several institutions in the 1970s. Among them was the Council of Senior Ulama, established by King Faysal in 1971.[10] It comprised about twenty illustrious scholars, mainly from the Najd region, where the Wahhabi teachings originated.[11] Chaired by the grand mufti and regarded as the kingdom's highest religious authority, its fatwas had a nearly legislative effect.[12] Members of the religious elite were, however, divided into those who more or less supported the policies of the core elite and those who challenged it. Moreover, new actors emerged in the early 1990s from among ulama outside the religious elite. The most distinctive element among these challengers was a group of young scholars who became known as the Awakening Shaikhs.[13]

With the Al Saud and the religious elite having secured their positions, the tribal elite could be considered the losers of the game. While their intra- and intertribal social status may not have changed, they refrained from public debates and failed to build their own formal civilian institutions, unlike most other segments of the politically relevant elite. Tribal identities and tribal autonomy always presented a challenge to the Al Saud, who lack a tribal base. Thus, efforts at settling nomadic tribes and replacing tribal identity with a religious ideology were part of the Al Saud's strategy toward tribal leaders. The majority of Saudis became urbanized within a few decades, and in the early 2000s nearly 90 percent of the population lived in urban areas.[14] Accordingly, tribal traditions had merged with other ways of life, and "nomadic warriors"—the tribal elite's political capital— had literally disappeared. Thus, although the tribal elite still influenced the political attitudes of the large number of Saudis who were of tribal origin, their political influence depended mainly on the importance of the Saudi Arabian National Guard (SANG). Recruited from among the tribes, the SANG served as the counterweight to the regular army and the basis of support for the SANG commander, Crown Prince Abdallah. Moreover, the tribal elite ran the risk of losing their clients to the growing number of princes, many of whom were linked to the tribal elite by maternal descent and had established their own patronage systems. The nature of the rentier state turned many members of the tribal elite into clients of the core elite and undermined their positions in the second and third circles.

Winners had emerged from outside of the traditional societal elites. The business elite was on the verge of moving from the third to the second circle of influence using its money, its networks, and the chambers of commerce. In August 1999 the core elite announced a thirteen-member Supreme Economic Council (SEC) in order "to achieve coherence and integration between the actions of government machinery and special establishments for economic activity." The SEC was chaired by Crown Prince Abdallah and Prince Sultan and stocked with heads and representatives of concerned ministries and agencies, thus providing the business elite with additional opportunities to access the core elite. It was also equipped with a consultative body representing the economic elite.[15]

The professionals, another segment with increasing influence in the decisionmaking process, had only relatively recently been provided a platform—the Consultative Council (CC). While their networks developed slowly, their numbers were growing, and their skills were becoming more and more relevant. Under certain conditions one might see larger numbers of them moving from the third to the second circle, where they would be actively involved in decisionmaking on issues of national relevance.

A decade after the Awakening Shaikhs had entered the political scene in 1991, an interesting but fragile coalition of intellectuals emerged. Led by some of the Awakening Shaikhs, it included businesspeople and professionals. In terms of capital, they resembled the religious elite, but in contrast they were hesitant to reach out to the general population. However, new media enabled them to act as spoilers of the decisionmaking process without being represented in state institutions or being dependent on personal access to the core elite.

Repercussions of Elite Change on the Political System

While the core elite fended off direct interference in their affairs from outside, external factors and domestic socioeconomic changes impacted the composition of the politically relevant elite as well as the development of the political system. When in 1953 the Council of Ministers was established, it comprised members of the royal family as well as technocrats, some of them from abroad. After the integration of the ulama into the state apparatus in the 1970s, no further progress was made in developing the Saudi political system until 1992. While the politically relevant elite experienced a number of changes, this was not reflected in the political system. Rather, Saudi rulers kept insisting that Saudi Arabia's constitution was the Quran and the Sunna.[16] Only in March 1992 did King Fahd introduce a quasi-constitution, the Basic Law of Government. He simultaneously handed down two other essential laws to supplement the Basic Law: the Consultative Council Law and the Law of the Provinces. For the first time it was formally established that the king, who was also the prime minister, had the right to appoint all decisionmakers on the national and regional levels. The Consultative Council, an institution that had been demanded by different segments of the politically relevant elite, became the platform of the professionals, a particularly dynamic elite segment. The council's composition revealed the core elite's skills in managing changes within the politically relevant elite.

In 1999 the ruling elite further formalized the political system by limiting to four years each term of office for ministers, governors, and members of the Council of Senior Ulama.[17] The measure gave more power to the king, as the terms are renewable by him. The term limits did not, however, produce any measurable rejuvenation. In the early 2000s the younger generations were hardly discernible among the politically relevant elite. While nearly half of the roughly 15 million Saudi nationals were between the ages of fifteen and forty-nine, and less than 10 percent were fifty years old or older,[18] the male half of the latter group dominated the politically relevant elite almost exclusively.

Factors of Change, Strategic Issues, and Subjects of Debate

Slow but steady socioeconomic changes, particularly demographic changes, were among the factors determining the direction and the speed of elite change in Saudi Arabia. Other factors were midterm challenges arising from developments in the world economy, the information revolution, the end of the Cold War, and U.S. policy toward the Middle East. Yet other factors were unexpected events—such as the Iraqi invasion of Kuwait in August 1990 and the attacks on the United States on 11 September 2001— that accelerated the speed of ongoing developments or changed their direction without allowing the core elite time to adjust their strategies.

These factors raised strategic issues that had to be dealt with, such as the redistribution of wealth and power, the modernization of society (often expressed in the discussion on women's rights), and the direction of foreign policy. Most of these issues were already on the table in the 1980s, but the information policies of the core elite inhibited public debate about them. After Iraq occupied Kuwait, the Saudi public discovered that it could not rely solely on the state-run media because it published the news with a forty-eight-hour delay. Caught by surprise, the core elite proved unable to react immediately, that is, without internal consultation. Consequently, the Saudi populace increasingly sought information elsewhere. No matter how hard the government, supported by senior ulama, tried to prohibit satellite TV and control the Internet, new media, and thus information, became more and more accessible, especially to the younger generation. In particular, the news and TV shows on al-Jazeera inspired regular afternoon discussions among Saudi intellectuals. When strategic issues became the subject of public debate in 2001 and 2002, the (albeit limited) new freedom of the national media contrasted sharply with the core elite's information policy of a decade earlier. This reflected a strategy that acknowledged the new reality—information could no longer be controlled. New media broke the bounds of geographic constraints that had allowed control over its distribution.

Several of the above-mentioned issues were seized upon for public debate: A general consensus existed about the necessity of economic reform. Of course, the issue of the distribution of wealth and power was not publicly discussed, although it simmered and sometimes surfaced. Rather, the educational system and relations with the United States became the bones of contention between different segments of the politically relevant elite. Both issues were strongly affected by unexpected events.

Education

Efforts to raise education levels among the Saudi population had resulted in an enormous increase in the number of male and female university graduates of two generations. Since the 1960s tens of thousands of second-generation Saudis had received educations abroad, particularly in the United States. In the mid-1980s declining oil revenues and a sufficient number of qualified university teachers in nonreligious subjects—many of them the product of the first wave of Saudis educated abroad—led the government to have the majority of the third generation of Saudis educated at home, where the ulama ensured that they received a sufficient amount of religious instruction intended to make them devout Muslims and subjects.[19] When the public Saudi universities reached capacity by the late 1990s, the government approved privatization of the educational sector, including the establishment of private universities. These measures represented opportunities for the economic elite, who had more interest in the production of a qualified labor force than in the spread of religious education. Thus, the education of the next generation of Saudi students, the fourth generation, was again to differ from that of the preceding generations. This development inevitably challenged the religious elite, who fiercely protected their prerogatives in the educational system.

Thirty-two thousand university students—more than half of them female—graduated in 2000.[20] Less than 10 percent of these third-generation Saudis earned diplomas in economy, management, or engineering, whereas nearly 50 percent graduated in the humanities and another 15 percent in Islamic studies.[21] Such figures encouraged the economic elite to criticize the education system. The debate grew when it became known that fifteen of the nineteen September-11 hijackers were Saudi nationals, and the Western press accused the Saudi curricula of churning out Islamist militants.[22] The government's initial reaction was total denial of any link between the hijackers and the kingdom; discussion of the Saudi curricula outside the kingdom was seen as infringing on Saudi national sovereignty.

In March 2002, however, domestic public discourse about the educational system reached an unprecedented level after fifteen schoolgirls died in a school fire in Mecca that month. For decades the religious elite had kept girls' education under its direct control. Thus, it was held responsible for the girls' deaths, which were attributed to bad maintenance and alleged interference by members of the religious police, who were under the supervision of the religious elite. Within days, they lost their exclusive control over girls' education, not least because of extensive domestic media coverage of events. Subsequently, however, at least two editors in chief lost their positions. These moves were obviously meant to appease the religious elite[23] who took advantage of their weekly visits to Crown Prince Abdallah,

Second Deputy Prime Minister Prince Sultan, and Interior Minister Nayif to lobby for their cause. In autumn 2002, for example, after "driving . . . there in their Cadillacs and Chevrolets," they blocked the introduction of English lessons in primary schools. Teachers and books had already been procured.[24]

Relations with the United States

To understand the constraints under which the Saudi core elite acted, it has to be considered that Saudi Arabia, which possesses one-fourth of the world's known oil reserves, is extremely vulnerable to outside attack. Most of its vast territory is uninhabitable; by 2003, several long-standing border problems had only recently been settled, and the process of national integration had not yet been completed. In particular, the Shi'a minority in the oil-rich Eastern Province was being discriminated against, while the populations of other regions had maintained both their distinctiveness and, frequently, their resentment toward the rulers and their allies from the central region, the Najd.

King Ibn Saud (who died in 1953) had chosen the United States to be the kingdom's protecting power, so changes in the attitudes of the U.S. government toward Saudi Arabia considerably affected the kingdom's security. While the United States and Saudi Arabia jointly fought communism during the decades-long Cold War, it was Saudi Arabia (among other Arab states) that was left to take care of the Saudi "Arab Afghans," who fought the Soviet occupation in Afghanistan and began returning home in the late 1980s flush with success. Shifting their attention from the Soviet Union to the United States, some of these highly motivated young men found support among ulama who wanted to minimize Western interference in "Saudi affairs." This coalition challenged the core elite in the early 1990s, enraged by the deployment of nearly 500,000 U.S. troops to Saudi Arabia after Iraq had invaded Kuwait.

After September 11 the U.S. media began scrutinizing and roundly criticizing the U.S.-Saudi relationship and the European media followed suit. These attacks surprised the core elite, who had considered such criticism of Saudi Arabia unthinkable, because the kingdom had acted as a reliable swing producer of petroleum for decades, keeping oil prices stable, not least to the benefit of the industrialized world. It soon became clear that the United States—now freed of the need to consider a Soviet attack against the energy resources of the Gulf—had decided to reassess its policies toward Saudi Arabia, including the possibility of taking actions that threatened the integrity of the Saudi state.[25]

After a period of silence, the Saudi government launched a "charm offensive," hiring public relations companies for advice on improving the kingdom's image, inviting Western journalists to Saudi Arabia, and sending delegations of princes, businesspeople, academics, and officials (including women) abroad to defend Islam, Saudi Arabia, and Saudi policies. Even members of the religious elite, concerned about their image at home and in the West, traveled abroad to explain themselves.

As in the early 1990s, Saudi relations with the United States once again became the subject of domestic debate. A number of events made support of U.S. decisions even more questionable in the eyes of the Saudi public: Western accusations painting Saudi Arabia as an exporter of radical ideologies, the Israeli reoccupation of Palestinian-controlled territories, the war against the Taliban and al-Qaida forces in Afghanistan that killed and injured thousands of civilians without leading to the capture of Osama bin Laden, and preparations by the United States to invade Iraq. Unlike in 1990 and 1991, the public could now view and debate opposing interpretations of events presented by Western and Arab satellite TV, national media, and preachers at mosques. In autumn 2002, strategic issues such as economic and political reforms—including reform of the educational sector, which had dominated public debate into summer 2002—were washed away.

The Politically Relevant Elite: Changes Within the Segments

Not only the balance of power between the different segments of the PRE was in a state of flux. Changes within the segments indicated an increasing degree of dynamism.

The Al Saud: Formalizing Leadership

The Saudi royal family is a special case among the segments of the politically relevant elite, as by 2003 some of its members headed all key ministries and had monopolized the core elite for decades. In addition to challenges originating from outside the family, it had to cope with internal competition and ossification of the core elite while the family as a whole had grown into the thousands.

Incumbent Core Elite: Competition and Cohesion

When King Khalid (1975–1982) failed to monopolize power, those princes who had occupied influential posts under King Faysal (1964–1975) could reinforce their positions.[26] Thus, in 2003 most members of the core elite were princes of the first generation who had secured their offices and the associated political capital—money, prestige, networks, military and secret service capacities—in the 1960s and 1970s. They managed to sustain a workable cohesion, for example through intermarriage, which established informal channels, in spite of internal competition.[27] One of the two main camps within the family consisted of Hazza bint Al Sudairi's seven sons, commonly referred to as the Sudairi brothers. Six of them controlled the budget, major parts of the military, and the security apparatus and were thus members of the core elite. Apart from King Fahd (born in 1921), the most prominent of these brothers were Prince Sultan (born in 1924), defense and aviation minister since 1962, second deputy prime minister since 1982, and next in line for succession (after Crown Prince Abdallah); Prince Nayif (born in 1933), interior minister since 1975; and Prince Salman (born in 1936), governor of Riyadh since 1962.[28]

The second main camp consisted of a group of princes said to center on Crown Prince Abdallah (born in 1923), the only son of al-Fahda Al Rashid. In 1963 he became commander of the Saudi Arabian National Guard whose members were recruited from among the tribes. The guard counterbalanced the regular military forces under the command of Prince Sultan. Abdallah was appointed crown prince in 1982 and became de facto ruler when King Fahd's health deteriorated in 1995. Trying to balance the influence of the Sudairi brothers, several sons of the late King Faysal were thought to side with Abdallah on matters relating to the distribution of power within the royal family. Also, less influential first-generation princes appeared to have offered Abdallah their cooperation and were rewarded with high-ranking positions. This occasionally led to arrangements in which members of the different branches controlled each other.

While several princes of the Sudairi branch were either perceived as uncritically pro-American or as biased in favor of particular groups, Crown Prince Abdallah was the perfect choice for a national figurehead in times of rising political awareness, economic restructuring, and regional instability. Abdallah's image was that of an authentic reformer and, in contrast to many other princes, he had personal integrity beyond a doubt. His stance toward the United States was much more critical, and his support for the Palestinians was much more explicit than King Fahd's. This secured the sympathy of those parts of the population who criticized the United States for its policies in the Middle East. His peace initiative of February 2002, however, was not met with public enthusiasm. Meanwhile, members of the Sudairi branch maintained excellent relations with the U.S. administration, which was essential to guaranteeing Saudi Arabia's security.

Even though this looked like a perfect division of labor among the core elite members, some observers concluded that something of a stalemate between the two camps affected decisionmaking. Moreover, Abdallah's position was regarded as weak in comparison to the Sudairi brothers. Support from outside the royal family, particularly from the religious elite, was essential to counterbalancing their weight. That the crown prince enjoyed the sympathy of members of the opposition-in-exile, who were known for their harsh criticism of the Sudairi branch, gave rise to suspicions that they might have been on his payroll.[29] In fact, they supported Abdallah to counter the Sudairi brothers. In their view, "the Ministry of the Interior [headed by Prince Nayif] runs the country"—an inconvenient situation for any opposition.[30]

Growth Without Rejuvenation: Problems and Techniques

Apart from risks arising from internal competition, the royal family had to develop strategies to deal with two other challenges: the lack of rejuvenation within the core elite and the growing size of the family.

The core elite was hampered by horizontal succession, which since the death of Ibn Saud in 1953 and the appointment of his son Saud provided for a brother, instead of a son, to succeed the king. More than thirty brothers were eligible for the throne in 1953, and half a century later the crown prince was only two years younger than the ailing king. As a by-product of the rules of succession, no core elite member was willing to give up his position in favor of a younger family member, because the eldest surviving brother could be the one to pass on the throne to his sons. Thus, Saudi Arabia turned into a gerontocracy, and the upcoming generation change was to affect the majority of the core elite, not just the prime decisionmaker.

Even when offices were redistributed, rejuvenation was neglected. At the end of August 2001 Turki bin Faysal, a second-generation prince (born in 1945), resigned as chief of General Intelligence and thereafter devoted his energy toward representing Saudi Arabia abroad. In January 2003 he became ambassador to the United Kingdom, a move that reflected the growing interest in upgrading Saudi-European relations. Instead of a member of a younger generation, Prince Nawaf (born in 1933) was appointed new chief of General Intelligence. Like Turki, Nawaf was considered a close ally of the crown prince. However, he was a first-generation prince from among the former "Free Princes," who challenged the core elite with demands for political liberalization in the 1950s and 1960s. Prince Nawaf's appointment did not affect the balance of power within the royal family, as King Fahd's son Saud (born in 1950), deputy chief of General Intelligence since 1985, remained in place.

When King Fahd announced the Basic Law of Government in 1992, he addressed the succession problem and widened the group of candidates for succession by including the younger generations, hinting at the possibility of a future vertical succession. Thereupon the succession question attracted a lot of international attention, but its discussion remained taboo in Saudi Arabia. Although factors like "seniority, maternal descent, and availability of full brothers"[31] determined the chances of a candidate, qualification and the degree of acceptance by other members of the politically relevant elite were equally important. This was demonstrated when Crown Prince Faysal replaced King Saud in 1964 and when several princes were excluded from the succession of King Faysal in 1975 and King Khalid in 1982.

The core elite members were obviously prepared to pass on their positions to their surviving sons, by 2003 mainly in their fifties and sixties. Their promotions were overdue, which worked in favor of the religious elite, because the older first-generation princes would not even consider terminating the alliance between the religious elite and the Al Saud. The members of the core elite received a traditional education at home during the first half of the twentieth century, when the Saudi ulama had a monopoly on education, and their support for the Al Saud was essential. In contrast to their fathers, most princes of the second generation received their higher education in Great Britain and the United States and had been trained on the job afterward in second-circle positions.[32] The longevity of their fathers, however, excluded these sons from the core elite; by 2003 several first-generation princes had survived their sons.

While the core elite defended their position to the extreme, the royal family, including cadet branches,[33] had grown into the thousands. Its extravagances made it vulnerable to public criticism, especially in times of economic stress or regional instability. Eight years after the promulgation of the Basic Law of Government, another step toward formalizing internal procedures within this ever-growing family was taken when the Royal Family Council (RFC), representing the major branches of the family, was established in June 2000. In contrast to previous informal councils, this institution comprised only eighteen members, was chaired by the crown prince, and had bylaws limiting the mandate of its members to four years. Its regulations thus bore a slight resemblance to those of an upper chamber of parliament, indicating that Saudi Arabia could be heading toward some kind of constitutional monarchy in the long run. While the first RFC did not show many signs of activity, its mere composition—three genealogically distinguishable groups—revealed the internal policies and the strategy of the core elite toward the rest of the family.[34]

The first of the three groups comprised five first-generation princes who were members of the first or the second circle and well known for their sometimes contradictory opinions on the political future of the country. Sultan and Salman represented the Sudairi brothers, while Abdallah, Badr, and Talal represented other branches. Unlike the other four princes, Talal had not occupied an influential position for decades. As leader of the

Free Princes, which also included Badr, he had fallen out of favor. However, by now Talal was one of the ten oldest surviving princes of the first generation and seemed to have regained at least some of his political position. He had not given up his political demands, which were backed by his son Walid, one of the world's richest businessmen, whose economic strategies could be influencing the Saudi privatization process. Talal's membership could thus indicate a change in the attitudes of the core elite per se, perhaps an acknowledgment of the need for a more liberal domestic policy. These five first-generation princes were supplemented by a second group comprising four second-generation princes, some of whom occupied positions in the second circle and whose fathers were kings of Saudi Arabia, that is, they were the (likely) successors of their fathers as representatives of the respective family branch.[35]

That the third group, or the other half of the RFC members, represented collateral branches of the royal family or princes whose fathers were excluded from the succession indicated that the core elite formally reconfirmed this group's right to have a say in family affairs, although they were ousted from the core elite (and the second circle) decades ago. Thus, the significance of the Royal Family Council lies in its function as a formal regulator of family affairs and as an instrument for safeguarding internal cohesion.

In summary, the core elite had not experienced a change of personnel since the 1980s, but the internal balance of power had shifted since King Fahd's health deteriorated in the mid-1990s. Moreover, the core elite adjusted its strategies to defend the status quo within the family while reacting to internal and external demands for liberalization: Informal structures were formalized, and more liberal princes were promoted. Different branches balanced and constrained each other, aware that internal strife and lack of cohesion could endanger the survival of the family. Other segments of the politically relevant elite, however, could play the two main factions of the core elite against each other.

Religious Elite: The Traditional Intellectuals

The influence of the religious elite on public opinion gave its members the capacity to legitimize, or delegitimize, the rule of the Al Saud. Weekly meetings with members of the core elite provided the basis for their direct influence in the decisionmaking process. By simply not attending their weekly meetings with the crown prince—and thus threatening to withdraw their support—the religious elite blocked decisions.[36] The religious elite controlled major parts of the judicial system and had a veto power, especially with regard to the educational system. Most important, it could play off members of the core elite against each other because its approval was needed in matters of succession since King Saud was deposed in 1964.[37] Thus collective leadership served them better than a strong prime decision-maker. In October 2002, while public debate revolved around the question "Who is next after Iraq [to be bombed by the United States]?" the religious elite blocked the reform of primary school curricula by manipulating Abdallah and Sultan.[38] Nevertheless, after September 11 the senior ulama lost ground, as the core elite refused to leave religion solely in their hands. By taking the initiative with the charm offensive and condemning those who abuse Islam and damage its image abroad,[39] the core elite reinforced their image as defenders of the faith.

The ulama were far from a homogeneous group. They could be divided into senior scholars—born in the 1930s or earlier—who either supported the core elite or who challenged it, at least on certain matters. The most prominent among these were the late Abd al-Aziz bin Baz (d. 1999) and the late Shaikh Hamud al-'Uqla' al-Shu'aibi (d. 2002), both of whom taught many current scholars. Bin Baz initially supported the Awakening Shaikhs in 1991, and Shu'aibi branded the core elite "infidels," and thus illegitimate rulers, for siding with the United States in its war against Afghanistan in 2001.[40] Among these men's younger colleagues were some who fought against a "Zionist-Christian coalition" and others who tried to reconcile the prevalent Islamic school of thought with their changing society.

Challengers and aspirants.   Higher positions among the ulama were occupied by scholars not only senior in knowledge but also in age. Elite rejuvenation was particularly slow, which alienated younger ulama. When the core elite's inability to protect the country became obvious in 1990, and the Council of Senior Ulama issued a fatwa legitimizing the use of U.S. troops, the Awakening Shaikhs, born in the 1950s, came up with their own agenda—thus challenging the core elite and those parts of the religious elite who legitimized the core elite's policies.[41] The Awakening Shaikhs had the support of a number of senior scholars, among them some members of the Council of Senior Ulama, not least because they shared an interest in increasing the political influence of the ulama.

The Awakening Shaikhs and their allies submitted a petition to the king in February 1991, followed by a more detailed catalogue of demands in July 1992. The authors wanted more political influence and good governance and accountability, which they asserted would be achieved through the proper application of *shari'a*, thereby enabling Saudi Arabia to shed its dependence on the United States. As the "official rules" allowed the ulama to advise the Saudi rulers, their suggestions were legitimate and could not be ignored. Unintentionally these young ulama increased the capital of the incumbent religious elite, because the core elite needed the latter's cooperation to cope with the challengers.

The emergence of challenging ulama was not unprecedented; the core elite and the religious elite had been challenged by similar groups several times in the history of the modern Saudi state. In the 1920s Ibn Saud's religiously trained militia, the Ikhwan, rebelled, and in 1979, Juhaiman al-'Utaibi and his followers occupied the Grand Mosque in Mecca. Unlike previous groups of challengers, however, the Awakening Shaikhs did not resort to violence but to e-mail and fax machines before presenting their demands as recommendations to the king. Publishing their demands in the Arab press, however, made them vulnerable because it violated the rules of the game. The core elite was thus justified in forcing bin Baz, who had initially supported the Awakening Shaikhs, and the Council of Senior Ulama to denounce them.

Apparently, the core elite paid a price for the support of the incumbent religious elite, for example by giving them a free hand to spread Wahhabi teachings and by appointing bin Baz grand mufti, a position that had been vacant for more than twenty years. Simultaneously, the core elite made perfectly clear where they drew the line: In November 1992 the seven members of the Council of Senior Ulama who were said to have refused to distance themselves from the activities of the challengers resigned from their offices and ten new (though not necessarily younger) scholars replaced them.[42] A similar situation occurred in late 2001, when Crown Prince Abdallah felt the need to call upon the ulama to refrain from stirring up radicalism.[43] Shaikh Abdallah Al Turki, a member of the Council of Senior Ulama, head of the Muslim World League, and former religious guidance minister, seized what he perceived to be an opportunity and declared that the ulama saw themselves as equal partners in power (that is, members of the core elite). In response, Prince Turki bin Faysal, former head of General Intelligence, and Prince Talal bin Abd al-Aziz, member of the Royal Family Council, made use of the national media to explain that a scholar's role is to advise the ruler, not to rule himself.[44]

Succeeding the grandfathers: Supervised natural elite rejuvenation. In the decade after the Awakening Shaikhs had entered the political scene, several members of the Council of Senior Ulama passed away. When four new members were appointed in 2001,[45] none of them was a member of the Awakening Shaikhs. Nevertheless, the core elite promoted a change from the first to the second generation within the Council of Senior Ulama, as two examples illustrate.

Saudi Arabia's most influential contemporary scholar, Abd al-Aziz bin Baz, was born in Riyadh around 1910. He taught many of the younger Saudi ulama, and his influence reached beyond Saudi borders. That he lost his eyesight at an early age gave him additional points as a religious scholar. In the early 1990s his support for the core elite's decision to ask for international military deployments was as essential as his cooperation in denouncing the challenging ulama. In return for his cooperation, Abd al-Aziz bin Baz was appointed grand mufti in 1993. When he died in December 1999, his deputy, Abd al-Aziz Al al-Shaikh, was appointed grand mufti. More than thirty years younger than bin Baz, an offspring of Saudi Arabia's most famous scholarly (Najdi) family, and blind like his predecessor, Abd al-Aziz Al al-Shaikh had the potential to challenge the core elite. But, unlike other scholars, he did not demand equal decisionmaking power from the king; rather, his statements were very much in accordance with the policies of the core elite. That the senior ulama could not increase their influence since the end of the 1990s is at least partly due to the personnel change in the office of the grand mufti.

The biographies of two other members of the Council of Senior Ulama who were also appointed chairmen of the Consultative Council shed even more light on the core elite's recruitment strategy. Shaikh Muhammad bin Jubair was a renowned scholar who had occupied influential posts before he became the first chairman of the CC, a position he held until his death in January 2002. Born in a small Najdi town in the mid-1920s, he graduated in Islamic law from the Umm al-Qura University in Mecca in 1953 and made a career in the judiciary.[46] His successor, Shaikh Salih bin Humaid, also originating from the Najd region, earned his Ph.D. in the same subject from the same university, but was some twenty-five years younger. In contrast to bin Jubair, bin Humaid had a career as a professor and then a dean of Umm al-Qura University. He became imam and preacher at the Grand Mosque of Mecca and a member of the first and second CC. In 2001 bin Humaid became one of the highest-ranking ulama in Saudi Arabia when he was appointed head of the Presidency for the Affairs of the two Holy Mosques and a member of the Council of Senior Ulama, as had his father twenty years earlier. Like his predecessor, the second CC chairman was rather open-minded and liberal, trying to reconcile Islamic rulings with Saudi reality.[47]

With the appointment of bin Humaid as chairman of the Consultative Council, the Saudi core elite again proved their skillfulness in domestic affairs: As a member of the younger generation (by Saudi standards) who appeared to be an open-minded conservative (again, by Saudi standards), his appointment did not provoke those who want an opening of Saudi society and the political system. Because of his social and regional background, his career in theology, and his religious status, he fulfilled the same criteria as his predecessor; even the Najdi conservatives had little reason to criticize his appointment. The recruitment strategy of the core elite showed that they favored moderate second-generation scholars who either abstained from politics or pursued their agendas without challenging the core elite or inciting other relevant actors.

Business Elite: New Generations for New Tasks

In a rentier state like Saudi Arabia, the private sector depends to a large extent on the distribution of rents through government contracts. However, economic and demographic developments increased the influence of the business community, thus turning the relationship between core elite and business elite into mutual dependency. The Saudi population doubled between 1980 and 2000, but oil revenues did not keep pace.[48] While the public sector was hampered by (domestic) debt amounting to 100 percent of gross domestic product in the early 2000s, Saudi private capital abroad was believed to be around $1 trillion.[49] Repatriation of some of these monies promised to be a driving force in privatization initiatives and an instrument for creating new job opportunities for young Saudis.[50]

Already in the late 1990s the government had launched two economic programs: One aimed at privatization of such state-owned enterprises as electricity and telephone companies and even parts of the energy sector.[51] The other initiative, a "Saudization" program, whose conception dated back to the 1980s, was supposed to create jobs for young Saudis by reducing the number of expatriates, who make up one-third of the kingdom's roughly 20 million residents. Neither program was as successful as had been hoped, and the basic problems—budget deficits and youth unemployment—remained unresolved.

When the core elite called on the private sector to engage in the national economy, the business elite responded with demands for reform of the educational system, which was not producing a sufficient number of qualified workers. It was not the first time that the business community had made demands of the core elite. In the 1990s a number of businessmen had joined the authors of open letters to King Fahd, asking that action be taken against corruption and that more political participation be allowed, that is, access for them to the second circle of decisionmakers.[52]

Politically relevant actors of diverse social backgrounds made up the particularly well-organized business community. The most famous among them was one of the world's richest businessman, Walid bin Talal. Born in the mid-1950s, he was the grandson of King Abd al-Aziz Al Saud and of the first postindependence prime minister of Lebanon, Riyad al-Sulh. Like his father, Prince Talal, who was born to an Armenian Lebanese mother, Walid was famous for his outspoken liberal views. Although his non-Saudi maternal descent hardly qualified him for a first-circle position (according to the current Saudi social system), Walid used his wealth to make his political views known abroad and at home. He offered $10 million to New York City after it was attacked on September 11, but because he linked the attacks to the situation in the Palestinian territories, his donation was refused. The story was reported in the international media, which not only made the issue a subject of debate, but also propelled Walid into the limelight. When Crown Prince Abdallah called for donations as Ramadan gifts for poor Saudis in November 2002, Walid answered by offering to build 10,000 homes for the needy.[53] One could only assume that his gift came with a number of suggestions concerning the Saudi political system.

Although Walid might have qualified for the second circle of influence, the story is different for businessmen not belonging to the royal family, to one of the prestigious tribes, or to the scholarly families. Big merchants, some of whom have married their daughters to members of the royal family, always had informal access to the core elite and indirectly influenced economic policies. Moreover, in contrast to all other members of the politically relevant elite, they began to formally organize themselves half a century ago. Businessmen without social prestige or a sufficient amount of money could not influence the decisionmaking process on their own.[54] The Saudi chambers of commerce and industry, however, could. While they originally functioned as an intermediary between the private sector and the government, their members were represented on the Supreme Economic Council as well as the Consultative Council in the early 2000s and draft laws were sent to the chambers for comments. Not the least in their own interest, the economic elite took an active part in the charm offensive after September 11. However, their aspiration of becoming actively involved in the decisionmaking process, that is, entry into the second circle, did not materialize.[55]

Nevertheless, the chambers of commerce underwent extensive elite rejuvenation, resulting in increasingly outspoken political demands. This was best illustrated by the Jidda chapter. For decades, the male and female members of the first and probably most active Saudi chamber of commerce elected two-thirds of their board members.[56] This, however, did not guarantee a continual rejuvenation of the board, as one former chairman served for thirty years. In the early 1990s, several groups of young businessmen began coordinating their election campaigns and announced their own chamber policies. In the course of three rather tough elections, they gradually replaced the older generation of board members. In the early 2000s the board members were either young or middle aged, that is, between thirty and sixty years old, with the majority being in their forties.[57] Similar processes were ongoing in other chambers, and the competition among candidates was fierce.[58]

These new board members differed from their predecessors not only in terms of generation, but also in attitudes, which resulted in more open debates and more transparent policies. In the absence of older board members demanding the respect of the "youth," discussions became more lively and effective. This did not, however, mean that the older generation had lost its influence completely. In informal gatherings they could still count on the younger generations to listen to their opinions.

Technocrats, Professionals, and Islamist Reformers: New Actors, New Demands

Among Saudis who received Western (or Western-style) educations, three subtypes of modern actors are distinguishable: technocrats, professionals, and Islamist reformers. The core elite had been hiring technical-oriented experts, or technocrats, since the 1930s, when the first advisors were recruited from abroad and several ministries, among them the Oil Ministry, were given to them to oversee. Efforts to improve the education level of Saudi citizens led to the emergence of the professionals, who did not necessarily come from traditional elite backgrounds. In the 1970s this group was considered the "new middle class" and later the "new elites."[59] Some of them organized and voiced demands for more political participation in a letter to the king in December 1990, shortly before the challenging ulama published their demands.[60] Both groups were asking, among other things, for the establishment of a consultative council and judicial reform based on Islamic law.[61] Enactment of the Basic Law of Government and establishment of the CC were the core elite's eventual response to the demands voiced by the "liberals"—mainly professionals and businessmen—and by the "conservatives"—mainly ulama, but also Islamist reformers (without formal religious educations), as well as businessmen.

Both groups, in their requests for reform, reached out to the public, thus crossing a red line. A 1992 liberal-supported protest in favor of women driving provoked the "conservatives" to the utmost extent. They turned to the core elite, and finally Grand Mufti bin Baz issued a fatwa stating that women were not allowed to drive.[62] Shortly thereafter, however, the conservatives went too far in their attempt to raise public support for their demands by, for example, distributing taped sermons. In 1994 some of the Awakening Shaikhs were jailed and not released until 1999. Among them was Shaikh Salman al-Auda, a Najdi scholar born in the 1950s whose arrest was accompanied by a demonstration of his supporters in Buraida. He was released under the "secure mutual understanding of what [his] future circumstances would be" and thereafter refrained from public preaching and lecturing.[63] Thus, when the Consultative Council was inaugurated in 1993, the core elite chose its members almost exclusively from among the more moderate professionals. Only in 1997 did they appoint an Islamist reformer, of the third generation, who had signed the 1992 memorandum to the king. After his appointment, he withdrew from an opposition group, that is, he was effectively co-opted.[64]

It would be inaccurate to assume that a modern education necessarily leads to the formation of a liberal and Western-oriented grouping ready to balance the influence of religious activists. Although most professionals wished to reform (but not abolish) the political system, and would have appreciated rejuvenation among the core elite,[65] some turned into religious challengers or even revolutionaries who did not play by the rules: Osama bin Laden, the self-declared leader of a "Jihad against Crusaders and Zionists," was a civil engineer.[66] Others who called themselves Islamist reformers, for example, Muhammad al-Mas'ari and Sa'd al-Faqih, were medical doctors, engineers, and lawyers, but not the product of the formal higher religious educational system. This third type of modern actor is a hybrid, possessing the same skills and thus similar political capital as the professional, but simultaneously sharing some characteristics of the religious elite, such as the ability to mobilize public support. Islamist reformers established the Committee for the Defense of Legitimate Rights (CDLR) in 1993 and were arrested. Some of them emigrated to London and reestablished the CDLR, which later split and lost many of its activists and financial supporters to the Movement for Islamic Reform in Arabia (MIRA).[67] Led by Sa'd al-Faqih, a surgeon who, unlike Osama bin Laden, did not claim to be a religious scholar, MIRA fiercely denounced the royal family and communicated its interpretation of the situation in Saudi Arabia to Western journalists, researchers, and officials.

The Consultative Council: Professional Platform and Core Elite Tool

No other segment of the politically relevant elite could strengthen its position as much as the professionals, although few of them had entered elite circles as individual actors.[68] The size of this group and its growing importance require a closer look at the Consultative Council, an institution almost exclusively dominated by politically oriented but moderate professionals.[69] The CC's structure, procedures, functions, and even the biographies of its members were published. The topics it discussed were covered by the media, although the sessions were usually not public and there were no plans to allow television coverage of meetings. The procedure of *shura* (consultation) had thus become more transparent than it once was, a step further in the formalization of decisionmaking and the institutionalization of policymaking in Saudi Arabia.

The CC functioned as an advisory body to the government and the king. Its members were selected by the king for four years, and with each term at least half of its members were to be newly appointed. The continuous growth of the CC, however, allowed the majority of members from previous councils to keep their positions. The expansion of the CC from sixty to ninety members in 1997 and to 120 in 2001 indicated the royal family's intent to broaden the basis of its support. It also illustrated that the core elite's strategy of dealing with the growing number of highly qualified Saudi nationals who might challenge the family's political and social position was one of appeasement and co-optation. Furthermore, the establishment of the CC exemplifies the core elite's strategy toward second and third-circle elites, as the council supplemented and even had the potential to inherit the function of legitimizing the core elite's policies, heretofore held by the Council of Senior Ulama, thus reducing the core elite's dependence on the religious elite. That the council's presidency was reserved for the ulama could be seen as a kind of compensation.

Although the CC finally gained membership in the International Parliamentary Union, there were several characteristics that distinguished the CC from a parliament; two in particular were that its members were appointed and its functions were limited to consultation. It could not control the budget or promulgate laws, withdraw confidence from the government, or elect members of the executive.[70] Women were not appointed to the council, but allowed to observe sessions. Moreover, they were consulted on matters considered to be of concern to them. Discussions within the CC improved the flow of information from bottom to top and kept the core elite informed about the concerns of potential challengers. Hence, the core elite was enabled to influence public discourse through the CC in addition to the state-run media and newspapers owned by members of the royal family.

A brief look at some biographic data shows that CC members represented the generation born in the 1950s.[71] They remembered well the days of King Faysal and Egyptian president Gamal Abdel Nasser.[72] In 2001 only seven members were under forty years of age, whereas two-thirds of members were at least fifty. Most of them finished their educations during the 1970s and 1980s, which meant that more recent knowledge was scarcely represented. Nevertheless, their education level was outstanding: Between 55 percent and 65 percent of members of the three councils between 1993 and 2001 held Ph.D.s, almost exclusively from universities abroad. Only a few members received their doctorates from Muhammad bin Saud Islamic University in Riyadh or Umm al-Qura University in Mecca, where they were taught by Saudi ulama.

The occupational background of CC members was congruent with the type of education they received: Members with careers in the education sector and the state bureaucracy were represented far more than were members of the military, the private sector, or the religious establishment. Several members were appointed as ambassadors or ministers before, during, or after their CC terms, and some of them saw the CC as being equally important as the government.[73]

Belonging to a societal elite did not guarantee political influence and was not a precondition for being appointed to the CC—but it helped. The offspring of many influential families were appointed: several members came from major mercantile or famous ulama families, while the council's presidency was reserved for the ulama. Although many members were of tribal origin and some hailed from shaikhly families, none of them was a tribal shaikh. However, not all the families who played prominent roles in the history of the kingdom were represented on the CC, and the descendants of Ibn Saud were excluded.

The CC was officially not meant to function as an institution of regional representation. It could, however, still serve the goal of national integration. All regions that were merged into the Saudi kingdom in the first half of the twentieth century were represented in the CC, albeit not according to the size of their population; the central region was overrepresented in all three councils. Improved Saudi-Iranian relations and the 1993 agreement between King Fahd and representatives of the Shi'a community, who had been excluded from politically relevant positions, were immediately reflected in the continuous appointment of Shi'a members. One of them, who joined the CC in 1993, left it during his second term of office when he was appointed Saudi ambassador to Iran. It was the first time that a member of the Shi'a minority from the Eastern Province had received such a highly visible official position abroad and indicated a changing attitude toward religious minorities.

Although the number of CC members was increased, the functions of the council were not. In times of domestic and international tension, however, the CC could raise its profile. During the Saudi charm offensive after September 11, several CC members joined the delegations sent abroad or participated in international conferences. In October 2001, two months before his nephew Prince Walid bin Talal raised the issue of CC members being elected,[74] Crown Prince Abdallah expressed his hope that the CC would gain more "duties," as he put it.[75] He also later called for more public participation in Arab politics in an initiative presented at the Arab summit in early 2003.[76] This was a notable change in strategy, and maybe even in attitude, because originally Abdallah did not favor the establishment of a consultative council.[77] After the end of the Cold War, the exaggerated fear of leftist and revolutionary movements and regimes that the Saudi leadership inherited from the 1960s and 1970s[78] seemed to have given way to the understanding that the political system had to adapt to the changed circumstances. Thus, the introduction of the CC in itself indicated a change in the strategies of at least some members of the core elite.

In November 2002 the CC chairman, Shaikh Salih bin Humaid, suggested giving more power to the council in a special session attended by Second Deputy Prime Minister Prince Sultan.[79] The chairman did not, however, suggest the election of members. The lack of clients that many CC members suffered from made elections a double-edged sword as the electorate could replace the professionals with tribal leaders and other traditional social elites.[80]

The Timid Winners: A Fragile Intellectual Coalition

Although various actors' general conceptions of state and society varied, their means and political demands overlapped considerably in the early 1990s, when liberals as well as conservatives issued open letters to the king. Many of the groups' complaints were similar and could to a large extent be subsumed under a demand for more political participation (at least for the respective authors), less corruption, and more system efficiency (especially in the judiciary), in short, good governance. In retrospect, one of the authors (a businessman) of the liberal petition could just as well have signed the conservative one. In spite of the results that were eventually achieved, he was disappointed by the reaction of the royal family, which initially tried to assuage the petitioners. He remembered: "They invited us: come visit, talk to us every week, drink and eat and leave. They killed it [the demands for reform]. . . . [In comparison to the conservative petition issued a few months later] I feel ashamed: we were like beggars."[81]

Although Saudi political activists who chose to go into exile were vocal, not much was heard from those inside the kingdom, no matter the political persuasion, until 2001. After September 11 and in the atmosphere of the imminent U.S. military attack on Iraq, some of the Awakening Shaikhs who had been released from jail began presenting their views, this time in the international arena. Shaikh Safar al-Hawali published an open letter to President George W. Bush in October 2001 comparing the United States with the (pagan) Roman Empire.[82] A few months later he was cooperating with other Awakening Shaikhs and liberal intellectuals from different parts of the country, thereby for the first time overcoming regional and political cleavages. Only the members of the Shi'a minority in the eastern part of the country were excluded from this new alliance,[83] when, led by Shaikh Salman al-Auda,[84] Saudi male and female intellectuals of different social backgrounds and sometimes opposing political attitudes replied through the Internet to open letters published by American intellectuals in spring and autumn 2002.[85] They, however, refrained from issuing open letters to their own government until they had extended their network to other states of the Arabian Peninsula. On 21 November 2002 they published an open letter in *al-Hayat* (owned by Prince Khalid bin Sultan) in cooperation with well-known scholars, including Qatar-based Egyptian Shaikh Yusuf al-Qaradawi, who has shows on al-Jazeera, and a number of notorious Yemeni and Kuwaiti activists. Motivated by an imminent U.S. attack on Iraq, the signatories this time addressed their governments and societies, asking them to "reconcile" on the basis of shari'a and defend Islam and the Muslim world. They challenged the core elite and the incumbent ulama with their message: wrapped in among accusations of an imperialist conspiracy of Zionists and right-wing Christian lobbyists; the wording bore some resemblance to statements by al-Qaida members as well as to the rhetoric of nationalist liberation movements. It seemed, however, that the coalition was already on the verge of breaking apart, as several moderates, for example, the CC members who had signed earlier letters, withdrew their support.

Meanwhile, external demands for political change in Saudi Arabia—the most vocal coming from the U.S. government—and Crown Prince Abdallah's plan for reform announced on 12 January 2003 encouraged the hesitating liberals. On 21 January 2003, a group of 104 Saudi intellectuals, several of whom had signed earlier letters, petitioned Abdallah and thirteen other princes, among them Sultan, Nayif, Talal, and Nawaf. This time, members of the Shi'a minority were allowed to sign on, and Shaikh Salman al-Auda and his followers abstained. Abdallah reacted immediately by inviting the petitioners to come see him the next day. Much like King Fahd in the early 1990s, he promised his support and assured his guests that their demands coincided with his plans.[86]

None of the letters or the petition was published by Saudi domestic newspapers, and when *al-Hayat* reprinted a reply by U.S. intellectuals on 23 October 2002, the issue was banned in Saudi Arabia.[87] Those activists who had used audiotapes and fax machines in the early 1990s, however, proved adept at adapting to the Internet and satellites. With the open letters and the list of signatories available on different websites, one could assume that they reached young audiences in Saudi Arabia.[88] New actors had discovered an untapped political capital and a space uncontrolled by the core elite. These discoveries could result in future coalitions based on attitudes and programs rather than on status and heredity.

Conclusion

Elite change in Saudi Arabia did not result from a change in leadership of the country, but was largely a by-product of outside events and socioeconomic trends. Despite these changes, the core elite remained in control without rejuvenation and skillfully manipulated different segments of the politically relevant elite by assuaging, co-opting, and sometimes jailing potential challengers.

Overall, the second and third circles of influence became more heterogeneous during the 1990s, and most elite segments improved their ability to organize and coordinate activities. The religious elite defended its second-circle position, the challenging ulama remained in an unstable position in the third circle, the business elite moved closer to the second circle, and the professionals firmly established themselves in the third circle via institutions (rather than as individuals). Finally, a rather inclusive but fragile coalition of intellectuals emerged across several elite segments. It will take a comprehensive change of attitudes among the Najdi ulama to accept the Shi'a minority and to embark on a path of elite unification.

External factors did not affect the composition of the core elite, but they did affect its internal balance of power and influence its strategies. The core elite embarked on further formalization in regard to family matters and the decisionmaking process, and thus increased transparency to a limited extent. They adjusted their recruitment patterns and their strategies toward the national media and thus continued to control the path and the speed of system change.

The distribution of power between the two major factions within the core elite sustains inertia within this group, which sometimes works to the advantage of other elite segments. It also inhibits the core elite's efforts in active policymaking and modernization of the political system. Saudi Arabia's political system is an absolute monarchy only at first glance; in fact, the prime decisionmaker cannot make decisions without the approval of other members of the core elite and tolerance of those decisions by the second circle. In reaction to demands from the third circle some steps toward reform of the political system were taken in the early 1990s, but their scope was limited. However, subsequent changes in the balance of power within the politically relevant elite are likely to be reflected in future institutional changes, for instance, in increased functions of the CC.

The attitude of the core elite toward economic and political liberalization (or adjustment of the political system) became more benevolent, and the red line in this arena became wider. Challengers did not fully exploit this situation to push for changes in the political system. Unlike the challenging ulama, liberal challengers moved only tentatively. There are several reasons for the core elite's change in strategy and decision to grant its challengers a comparatively wide berth after September 11. First, it was not possible or advisable to ignore public discontent, especially when voiced by ulama. Second, compared to extremists or revolutionaries such as Osama bin Laden, who declared the Saudi government "un-Islamic" and thus illegitimate, the challenging ulama (merely) called for a reform of the system. Their means were nonviolent, many were ready to cooperate, and some were ready to be co-opted. Third, the challenging ulama attracted followers from among people who did not respect the religious elite and who would otherwise have supported the militants. Thus, for the core elite, the challenging ulama were the lesser evil.[89] Finally, a more liberal domestic policy, especially with regard to the liberals, promised to improve relations with the West, in particular with the United States. Thus, by early 2003 the future looked bright for professionals, moderate ulama, and the business elite.

Generation change was measurable in the second and third circles, but with the exception of the members of the economic elite, emerging elites in Saudi Arabia were in their fifties and not necessarily young. Elite change, especially in terms of personnel, was slow to the extent that whole generations were "disenfranchised" by their fathers and grandfathers.[90] The age structure of the population raised the issue of how to integrate politically aspiring young Saudis into the system or—from their point of view—what their political prospects were. It was telling that Saudi followers of Osama bin Laden seemed largely to be under forty years of age or, as Prince Nayif stated in an interview, were "boys between puberty and maturity."[91] This supported Prince Walid bin Talal's argument for a further opening of the political system in order to "contain them and make them part of the process."[92] But by 2004 only the "parent generation" had been integrated, while the "grandparents" were not yet willing to step down. There was no reason to doubt that Saudi Arabia would continue to be a rentier state. But as rents were unlikely to rise sufficiently to restore the situation of the early 1980s, the minimum that could be offered to younger generations was participation in some form of elections on the regional or the national level. That elections were not a concept alien to the Saudi politically relevant elite had been proven by the economic elite for decades. However, elections could bring the tribal elite back into the game and strengthen the position of the religious elite.

Notes

1. See Saloua Zerhouni's chapter on Morocco, as well as André Bank and Oliver Schlumberger's chapter on Jordan, both in this volume.
2. For a definition of politically relevant elite and the three-circle model applied here, see the introduction in this volume by Volker Perthes. To distinguish the different segments of the politically relevant elite, the basic criteria shall be their political capital. An individual might be a member of different segments simultaneously, but most elite segments are characterized by a specific political capital. Members of a segment thus employ different means to maintain or increase their degree of influence and may act collectively. Use of the concept of political capital has been inspired by Pierre Bourdieu's works. He distinguishes between the economic, cultural, social, and symbolic capital at the disposal of an actor who can use it in a particular field of action, like a player in a game. Furthermore, every player is bound by a set of rules typical of the field of action in which he is engaged, and players are divided into challengers and defenders of the status quo. For an introduction to Bourdieu's social theory, see Schwingel, *Pierre Bourdieu*.
3. Given that many members of the politically relevant elite in Saudi Arabia occupy official positions in institutions and organizations of some importance or have organized otherwise, they were approached, albeit not exclusively, through those organizations representing a particular segment.
4. Conclusions are drawn from a set of data: quantitative data on members of institutions, qualitative data from interviews conducted with Saudis in Abha, Berlin, Jidda, London, Riyadh, and Washington, D.C., in 2001 and 2002, and biographies

of distinguished personalities. In the case of the tribal elite, which could have been approached through the Saudi Arabian National Guard, conclusions are not backed by empirical data. The military elite had to be ignored completely because of unavailability of reliable information.

5. For a discussion of the marriage strategy of the Al Saud, see Al-Rasheed, *A History,* pp. 75–80, 219.

6. Wenner, "Saudi Arabia: Survival of Traditional Elites," p. 164.

7. Here, we refer to a three-generation ideal-type family developed by Mai Yamani. See Yamani, *Changed Identities.*

8. Only the Oil Ministry has been traditionally left to a "commoner," to counter the suspicion that the Al Saud are monopolizing the country's oil wealth and to avoid one member or branch of the family from having control of oil revenues.

9. This does not mean that every member of the royal family is politically relevant.

10. Simultaneously they headed others organizations and institutions (such as the Supreme Judicial Council, the Consultative Council, or the Muslim World League) or ministries (such as justice and religious guidance).

11. For the twenty ulama appointed to the council in 2001, see *al-'Adl,* issue 13 (Muharram 1422 [February 2001]).

12. Vogel, *Islamic Law,* pp. 93, 117.

13. Teitelbaum, *Holier Than Thou,* p. viii.

14. World Bank at: http://www.worldbank.org. For a comparison, see Wenner, "Saudi Arabia," p. 167.

15. The first sixteen-member consultative commission was said to be composed of key business leaders, twelve of whom held Ph.D.s. For details, see the website of the Saudi embassy in Washington, D.C.: www.saudiembassy.net.

16. This much-repeated credo—espoused whenever Saudi rulers were asked to draft a constitution for the kingdom—became the first article of the Basic Law of Government.

17. Interview with a member of the SAGIA delegation, Berlin, June 2002. See also the Saudi Arabian Information Resource (Ministry of Information) website: www.saudinf.com.

18. Data as published by the Kingdom of Saudi Arabia, Ministry of Planning: www.planning.gov.sa.

19. This applied mainly to less well-to-do families, because children of richer or more influential families continued to be sent abroad for higher education. For an overview of the educational system and the curricula, see, for example, Rugh, "Education."

20. Figures according to *Arab News* (online edition), www.arabnews.com, (accessed 14 November 2002).

21. Victor Kocher, "Überfremdeter Arbeitsmarkt Saudiarabiens," *Neue Züricher Zeitung,* 30 July 2002, p. 8.

22. See, for example, Thomas L. Friedman, "How Saudi Children Are Educated Is a World Class Concern," *International Herald Tribune,* 13 December 2001.

23. The editor in chief of *al-Watan* was immediately appointed advisor to the governor of Asir, Khalid bin Faysal, who also happened to be a principal shareholder of *al-Watan.* Interviews with editors of *al-Watan,* Abha, October 2002.

24. Interview, Jidda, 14 October 2002.

25. As during the 1973–1974 oil embargo (see Pollack, *Saudi Arabia and the United States*), in 2002 some U.S. politicians and political consultants considered

the option of forced regime change in Saudi Arabia and the separation of the Eastern Province from the kingdom.

26. Unless otherwise noted, this section is based on Kechichian, *Succession*.

27. Sultan's son Bandar, for example, was married to Saud bin Faysal's sister Haifa.

28. The other brothers are Abd al-Rahman (born in 1931), deputy minister of defense since 1978; Turki (born in 1934), who left the political scene after a scandal in 1979; and Ahmad (born in 1940), deputy minister of the interior since 1978.

29. Kechichian, *Succession*, p. 111; al-Rasheed, *A History*, p. 180.

30. Interview with a representative of the Movement for Islamic Reform in Arabia, London, July 2001.

31. Kechichian, *Succession*, pp. 24ff.

32. Fahd's son Muhammad was appointed governor of the Eastern Province in 1985. Sultan's son Khalid, who led Saudi forces during the 1991 Gulf War, was appointed assistant minister of defense in 2001. Nayif's son Muhammad became assistant minister of interior in 1999. Abdallah's third son, Abd al-Aziz, was appointed consultant to his father's court in 2001. Abdallah's second son, Mit'ab, held a position that made him the likely successor to his father as commander of the SANG.

33. The members of these branches, or collateral lines, are not descendants of Ibn Saud, but of his male relatives.

34. For the list of members, see *al-Riyadh* (online edition), www.alriadh. com.sa (accessed 5 June 2000).

35. These are Mish'al bin Saud, Khalid bin Faysal, Bandar bin Khalid, and Muhammad bin Fahd.

36. Interview, Riyadh, 27 March 2002.

37. King Saud (1953–1964) went to Greece after influential family members and ulama, concerned about his excesses, had agreed to depose him. For the power struggle within the royal family see Yizraeli, *The Remaking of Saudi Arabia.*

38. Interviews, Jidda, October 2002.

39. See, for example, the letter Crown Prince Abdallah wrote to U.S. president George W. Bush, published on the Saudi Press Agency website: www.spa.gov.sa (accessed 12 September 2002).

40. See, for example, *Economist,* 13 October 2001, p. 43.

41. For the following, see Fandy, *Saudi Arabia and the Politics of Dissent;* Kechichian, *Succession,* pp. 107, 193ff; al-Rasheed, *A History,* pp. 168ff.

42. According to Abdallah, *al-'Ulama,* pp. 417ff, Abd al-Rahman Marzuqi (born 1926) and Nasir Al Rashid (born 1916) were among the appointed. This contradicts Dekmejian, "The Rise," p. 634, and Kechichian, *Succession,* p. 166, who state that the new scholars were younger and more progressive than their predecessors.

43. For details, see *Arab News* (online edition), 15 November 2001.

44. For a summary of this debate, which extended into 2002, see Jamal Khashoggi, "Saudi Religious Establishment Has Its Wings Clipped," *Daily Star* (online edition), www.dailystar.com.lb (accessed 29 June 2002).

45. For details, see *Arab News* (online edition), 30 May 2001.

46. For a biography, see *Arab News* (online edition), 25 January 2002. For more details, see al-Shubayli, *Bin Jubair.*

47. For a biography and an exemplary fatwa, see *al-Hayat,* 9 February 2002. For the appointment to the Council of Senior Ulama, see the Saudi Press Agency website: www.spa.gov.sa (accessed 29 May 2001).

48. According to the *Human Development Report 2002,* the per capita GDP

annual growth rate for 1975 to 2000 was –2.2. Per capita GDP in 2000 was $11,367. Available at: http://hdr.undp.org/reports.

49. *Arab News* (online edition), 8 May 2001.

50. In 1999 the unemployment rate for Saudi males between twenty and twenty-four years of age was officially estimated at 15.8 percent, while half of the population was younger than fifteen and had not yet entered the labor market. Saudi American Bank, "Saudi Arabia's Employment Profile," www.samba.com.sa (accessed 8 October 2002).

51. Efforts at privatization in the energy sector became known as the Saudi gas initiative.

52. Interview, Jidda, October 2002.

53. For details, see *Arab News* (online edition), 24 November 2002.

54. "Sufficient" was said to be more than $2 billion. Interview with a representative of the Jidda Chamber of Commerce, Jidda, 15 October 2002.

55. Interview with a board member of the Jidda Chamber of Commerce, Jidda, 16 October 2002.

56. The remaining one-third were appointed by the government. Membership in 2002 was approximately 30,000. Interviews, Jidda, October 2002. For the 2001 elections, see, *Arab News* (online edition), 30 October 2001.

57. Interviews with members of the board of the Jidda Chamber of Commerce, Jidda, October 2002.

58. For the Mecca Chamber of Commerce, see *Arab News* (online edition), 18 January 2001.

59. See, for example, Rugh, "Emergence of a New Middle Class"; Heller and Safran, *The New Middle Class and Regime Stability;* Abir, "The Consolidation of the Ruling Class and New Elites."

60. Commonly, the petitions are referred to as the "secular" and the "religious" petitions. Neither petition, however, was secular. For a detailed discussion of these terms, see al-Rasheed, *A History,* pp. 168ff.

61. For the text and signatories, see Kechichian, *Succession,* pp. 193ff.

62. Interview, Riyadh, 27 March 2002. Fandy, *Saudi Arabia and the Politics of Dissent,* p. 49; Teitelbaum, *Holier Than Thou,* p. 31.

63. Douglas Jehl, "A Nation Challenged: A Critic: After Prison, a Saudi Sheik Tempers His Words," *New York Times,* 27 December 2001.

64. Interview with a MIRA representative, London, July 2001.

65. Interviews with members of the Consultative Council, Riyadh, March 2002.

66. As Osama bin Laden was a rather transnational actor after his expulsion from Saudi Arabia in 1991, he is not considered here to be a member of the Saudi politically relevant elite in the early 2000s.

67. See Fandy, *Saudi Arabia and the Politics of Dissent;* Kechichian, *Succession;* Teitelbaum, *Holier Than Thou.*

68. One of the few rather young exceptions was Adil bin Jubair who, after working for Prince Bandar bin Sultan at the Saudi embassy in Washington, became advisor on foreign affairs to Crown Prince Abdallah and his spokesman in Washington.

69. Interviews with members of the Consultative Council, Riyadh, March 2002.

70. The criteria for being appointed to the CC were laid out in the "majlis al-shura law": a member should be a Saudi national by birth and descent, a competent person of acknowledged integrity, and no younger than thirty years of age. The

tasks of the CC included discussion of the general development plan and of the annual reports forwarded by governmental institutions, including the ministries. With the approval of the prime minister, that is, the king, the CC could summon ministers and propose draft laws. As it was also entitled to study laws, international treaties, and agreements, it dealt with all strategic issues. Its agenda was set by the king, but a sufficient number of CC members could suggest topics to the king for inclusion on the agenda. The CC formed specialized committees, and with the approval of the chairman, non–CC members could be consulted on matters. For an analysis of the 1997 council see Dekmejian, "Saudi Arabia's Consultative Council."

71. When the third majlis was appointed in May 2001, the members' average age was fifty-four. Figures are compiled from biographies published by the council.

72. Interviews with members of the Consultative Council, Riyadh, March 2002.

73. Ibid.

74. *International Herald Tribune,* 29 November 2001.

75. Saudi Press Agency website, www.spa.gov.sa (accessed 16 October 2001).

76. For the text of the "Initiative for Reforming the Arab Condition," see *Arab News* (online edition), 15 January 2003.

77. See Kechichian, *Succession,* p. 59.

78. Vassiliev, *The History,* p. 469.

79. *Arab News* (online edition), 11 November 2002; Rainer Hermann, "Reformen im Ramadan," *Frankfurter Allgemeine Zeitung,* 6 December 2002.

80. Members of the Consultative Council were not necessarily seen as representatives by the inhabitants of the regions of origin. Interviews with members of the Consultative Council, Riyadh, March 2002.

81. Interview, Jidda, 20 October 2002.

82. The Islamic Assembly of North America (IANA): http://ianaradionet.com/letter (accessed 21 November 2002).

83. Interviews, Jidda, October 2002.

84. For a biography, see Fandy, *Dissent,* pp. 89ff.

85. Most of this debate was documented at http://www.americanvalues.org.

86. For the demands and the signatories, see the Movement for Islamic Reform in Arabia (MIRA) website: www.miraserve.com.

87. Interviews, Jidda, October 2002.

88. See, for example, www.nationvoice.com.

89. See also Roula Khalaf, "Winds of Change," *Financial Times,* 11 February 2002, p. 16.

90. The author owes this most appropriate term to anthropologist Shelagh Weir.

91. *Der Spiegel,* 17 December 2001, p. 158.

92. *New York Times,* 28 November 2001.

Part 3

System Preservation and the Cooperation of New Elites

7

Algeria:
System Continuity Through Elite Change
Isabelle Werenfels

In contrast to many Arab countries, Algeria has not been ruled by the same leader for two or more decades. Nevertheless, it has been governed by the same forces since its independence from France in 1962. A small number of military leaders and party functionaries who emerged during the War of Independence erected a bureaucratic authoritarian system with the army as its backbone. For decades they monopolized the key positions in state institutions. New recruits came primarily from the pool of "old comrades." Loyalties and networks established during the war prevailed after independence, and different "clans" of revolutionaries as well as clans based on regional and other allegiances within the elite competed over rents, power, and posts. At times these elites reached uneasy informal arrangements (as during the era of Houari Boumedienne, 1965 to 1978), at other times they engaged in fierce struggles over distribution of these "spoils" (as during Chadli Bendjedid's reign in the 1980s).[1] This relative continuity in elites seemed to end with the political opening in 1989 that promised radical system and elite change.[2] The military's coup d'état in 1992—following the triumph of the Front Islamique du Salut (FIS) in the first round of Algeria's first pluralistic and free parliamentary elections—put an end to this process and reestablished the power of incumbent elites.

Ten years after the abrupt end of that democratic experiment, two developments within the Algerian elite were apparent: first, there had been a sharp increase in the number of individual and collective actors constituting the politically relevant elite, that is, those who exert influence on decisions concerning strategic issues of national relevance, such as market and education sector reforms and democratization; and second, old guard "revolutionaries" were being replaced by two younger generations in many elite segments. Domestic and international factors had driven these changes: the civil war, which broke out after the 1992 coup and led not only to the bloody repression, but also to the co-optation and fragmentation of the

173

Islamist opposition;[3] the army's attempt to give its authoritarian rule a constitutional and democratic façade through presidential elections (in 1995 and 1999) and parliamentary elections (in 1997 and 2002); and an International Monetary Fund structural adjustment program and debt rescheduling, both of which not only brought new actors onto the political stage but also opened for incumbent and emerging elites rent-seeking avenues beyond hydrocarbon-related revenues. Although political and economic liberalization affected only marginally the rules of domination, they were enough to allow for new and, in many cases, young actors with a wide spectrum of agendas to enter the political stage.

Algeria in the early 2000s, according to the criteria used in much of the transition literature, was not an unlikely candidate for a shift from an authoritarian to a (somewhat) democratic regime.[4] Cracks had been increasing in the regime, including splits among the elite. Softliners (reformers) had contested hardliners throughout the 1990s, and in the early 2000s freedom of expression was remarkable, and popular sentiment appeared to be in favor of democracy.[5] The constitution gave the president substantial power, but not enough to principally preclude democracy. Moreover, the regime had experienced economic shocks and external pressure for extensive economic liberalization. Yet, the military prevailed over the political, and democratic tendencies remained confined to small nuclei of activists throughout the 1990s.

This analysis shares the assumption of Michael Burton and John Higley that "political elite transformations are the fulcrums for fundamental political change"[6] and argues that any attempt to understand the stickiness of Algerian authoritarianism needs to focus on the dynamics and recruitment patterns within the Algerian PRE as well as on the ways in which the politically relevant elite were shaped and constrained by domestic, international, social, and economic forces. Earlier studies of Algerian elites,[7] while excellent in many respects, were strongly conditioned by the modernization paradigm. They tended to neglect the embeddedness of elites in specific "traditional" and "modern" social structures and in the Algerian rentier economy and, hence, largely ignored the resulting interests, constraints, and conflicts.

The approach here combines an actor-oriented microsociological analysis with a more structure- and macro-oriented analysis in order to shed light on three issues: the nature of the changes within the Algerian politically relevant elite in the decade after the coup d'état, the implications of these changes for the prospects of system change, and the factors external to the elites that played into the relationship between elite change and system change.[8] The main argument is the following: The changes and dynamics in the outer circles of the Algerian elite in the second half of the 1990s narrowed the core elite's margin of action. Also, in the early 2000s the core elite was less unified than it had been immediately following the 1992 coup. These phenomena, however, were system stabilizing rather than destabilizing for reasons linked to core elite strategies and structural factors:

• The divides and vertical networks within the PRE prevented broad coalition building by contesting elites. This fragmentation was not just a result of the linguistic, ethnic, and regional cleavages within Algerian society, but also of the core elite's successful management of these cleavages using a threefold strategy of repression, co-optation, and encouragement of excessive (and often fake) competition by creating parallel structures.

• Recruitment into the PRE was, with few exceptions, limited to social segments that had been represented in the PRE for decades. This largely resulted from two mechanisms of exclusion: the Arabization policy and the claim to historical legitimacy, not only by incumbent elites and their clients but also by their offspring.

• A generational change in the elite reinforced an elite type, the nationalist reformer, who advocated substantial economic and administrative reforms but not system change.[9] Representatives of this type, thus, were paralyzed by a dilemma: the reforms they proposed would undo the social, political, and economic structures that had produced their elite status.[10]

• Given the above factors, changes in the elite could translate into system change if they coincide with a number of external and internal factors that in the past have affected the Algerian system: economic shock, widespread popular uprisings, and the types of external pressures that accompany acceptance of international agreements. When change comes to Algeria, it is unlikely to be Western-style democracy: The rentier nature of the Algerian economy and the country's existing social structures (shaped as they are, partly by the current elites) might simply produce similar political elites and structures.

The Algerian Elite

Between 1962 and 1989, Algeria was ruled by elites from three state institutions: the party, the army, and the bureaucracy (or public administration). Elites with a revolutionary past *and* an army career were found in the party and the bureaucracy and tended to constitute the decisionmaking center.[11] With the army-instigated demise of Chadli in January 1992, the military component in the core elite became more obvious. Throughout the 1990s little more than a handful of generals (in office or retired) made all strategic decisions. They either chose the president from their ranks (Liamine Zeroual in 1994), designated someone belonging to the old revolutionary guard (Mohamed Boudiaf in 1992, Ali Kafi in 1992), or in elections put all their weight behind a candidate from within the army (Zeroual in 1995) or without (Abdelaziz Bouteflika in 1999). To conclude from this that the core elite, with the exception of changes in presidents, remained static in composition, distribution of individual power, or strategies since 1992 would, however, be wrong. There were three developments in these areas after the late 1990s: (1) the emergence of the president, respectively the presidency as a (somewhat) separate power center,[12] causing conflict among the core elite and gridlock in decisionmaking; (2) the complete replacement of one generation of the revolution by a younger generation of the revolution; and (3) the efforts by the army to convey the notion of a new strategy vis-à-vis politics.

The First Circle: The Core Elite,
Last Bastion of the Revolutionary Generation

In 1999, at the time of Bouteflika's election, Algeria's prime decisionmakers, or core elite—*les décideurs,* or *le pouvoir (réel)*[13]—were without exception generals: the head of the army's general command since 1993, Mohamed Lamari; the head of army intelligence since 1990, Mohamed "Tewfik" Mediene; the president's advisor for defense issues and unofficial spokesman of the generals, Mohamed Touati; and two retired generals, Larbi Belkheir and Khaled Nezzar, a former minister of defense. Belkheir was the strongman during Chadli's rule and in 2000 returned to the presidency as the powerful director of the presidential cabinet, an appointment putting him at the interface between the army and the presidency and one imposed on Bouteflika by the military. Finally, a number of other generals could also be considered to belong to the décideurs, notably Smail Lamari, the number two man in army intelligence since 1992, and commanders of the six military regions. With no clearly discernible *primus inter pares* (first among equals), decisions were taken in opaque, informal, and consensus-oriented processes, which were often lengthy because of diverging interests and struggles between factions.[14]

Virtually all of these generals belonged to the same generation. They were born in the late 1930s, received their secondary education in French, and in the mid-1950s embarked on careers in the French military but later deserted to the national liberation army.[15] After independence they received military training at prestigious institutions, such as the Ecole Supérieure de Guerre in Paris and the Frunze Military Academy in Moscow, and they continued to communicate primarily in French.[16] As of 1988 these revolutionaries began to push aside their "older brothers," those who had fought the revolution from the start, who had not received professional military training, and who had kept their "younger brothers" from moving into key positions for years. The younger brothers continued this practice by blocking *their* successors, here referred to as the second generation. Only in the late 1990s did the first officers who lacked "revolutionary legitimacy" receive promotions to the rank of general,[17] and only in 2002 did the first generals from the second generation become *général-major*.[18] While an overwhelming majority of the revolutionary generation had come from the east—Batna, Tebessa, Souk Ahras—and had promoted young officers according to regional affiliations, the second generation, though still the product of a slight regional bias, represented a wider regional spectrum.

With the ascendance of Bouteflika, a civilian with a long diplomatic career and excellent ties to the West and the Gulf states, the presidency began to emerge as a power center within the core elite. According to Mohamed Lamari, Bouteflika was "le choix le moins mauvais" (the least bad choice),[19] but was, nonetheless, the army's choice; the other six presidential candidates dropped out of the race because of unfair campaigning conditions. Though Bouteflika had been the army's candidate, he soon found himself in a tug-of-war with the general command, which, along with part of the Algerian political establishment, was wary of his own authoritarian ambitions. Conflicts erupted over strategic appointments, such as Bouteflika's nominee for defense minister, a row that after several months ended with the president conceding and instead keeping the portfolio himself (as his predecessors had done). In another conflict, over the nomination for secretary general of the Defense Ministry, Bouteflika prevailed.[20] Another major point of contention was the president's reconciliatory policy toward radical Islamists that was formalized in the Concorde Civile[21] and included a controversial amnesty for demobilized combatants. The principal reason for Bouteflika's emergence as a powerful and (somewhat) independent actor and a décideur was his foreign policy success, which relieved Algeria of the international isolation that developed during its civil war. Bouteflika concluded an association agreement with the European Union in 2001, and in the wake of September 11 he established close ties with the United States, based on the "war against terrorism," and managed to obtain weapons that the United States had withheld. The army thus found it difficult to dispose of him. Bouteflika's domestic record was, however, meager: vast economic and administrative reforms he had promised did not pass the stage of proposals. His power struggles with the generals and others with vested interests in these decisions were responsible in part for gridlock on the decisionmaking level.[22]

Rumors of conflicts between the top echelon of the army and Bouteflika (and much of his entourage) became so widespread that in summer 2002 Mohamed Lamari publicly denied the allegations and reiterated the president's decisionmaking power. A few weeks after Lamari's statement, however, General Nezzar belied the alleged harmony and accused

Bouteflika of having orchestrated a campaign (notably in the foreign media) against the generals. Such contradictory messages from décideurs pointed to conflicts not only between the president and the generals but also between factions within the army.

The points of contention were political—dealing with the uprisings in Kabylia and with the (legal and outlawed) Islamist parties—as well as economic: the ability to control the hydrocarbon sector, the generator of 97 percent of exports and 77 percent of state revenues in 2000.[23] To determine the destination of hydrocarbon rents had been a main, if not the main source of core elite power since Boumedienne. Economic reform thus threatened the vital interests of core elite members, who commanded patronage networks built on the allocation of privileges such as import and distribution licenses.[24] The involvement of current and retired military officers in the private and the informal sectors of the economy had been increasing since the 1980s and was indirectly encouraged by an early retirement regulation for civil servants. Not surprisingly, many members of the core elite, for example Belkheir and Mohamed Lamari, placed family members in privileged positions in the private sector and were reputed to have made fortunes. Conflicts with Bouteflika could also be seen in the light of economic struggles, with the president trying to privilege his clients, as seemed to have been the case with the allocation of the first private mobile phone license.[25]

After a decade of controlling the state, the army in 2002 went to great lengths to publicly distance itself from politics and to create a new, "clean" image for itself. In July 2002, for the first time in the history of independent Algeria the head of the general command, Mohamed Lamari, faced uncensored questions in a press conference that lasted several hours. While journalists covered wide-ranging issues—from Lamari's salary to the release of FIS leaders and alleged army involvement in massacres of civilians—the not-so-hidden agenda of the army was to play down its role in politics and to counter allegations that it had been involved in mass killings. The army admitted that it had called the shots on matters of national importance from 1992 to 1999—in its eyes, to "save the republic" from what it called "Islamist theocracy"—but insisted that its political involvement had stopped with the election of Bouteflika.[26]

An optimistic interpretation of these statements would suggest the development of a more transparent relationship and a stronger demarcation between the army and the executive, as is the case in Turkey. More likely, however, they were merely produced for the international community as part of an effort to better sell the politics of repression. In other words, the generals were not "going Turkish," but simply "pretending to go Turkish." A real retreat from politics, after all, would involve relinquishing influence over the hydrocarbon rent, an unlikely scenario. An increasingly virulent anti-Bouteflika campaign in the run-up to the 2004 presidential elections in privately owned Algerian newspapers, reputedly under the influence of certain generals and accusing the president of being in collusion with Islamists,[27] seemed an indication that the army was gearing up for the presidential race and, contrary to its claim, was not yet ready to retire from kingmaking. Either way, the army was reacting to the changing international climate: Human rights campaigns and Algeria's growing ties with the EU and NATO—Algeria joined the Mediterranean Dialog in 2000—contributed to these developments.

The Second Circle: Clients of the Core Elite

It would be incorrect to think that the décideurs were able to or wanted to (completely) monopolize decisionmaking. In economic issues the commerce minister, who headed the negotiations for World Trade Organization membership, and the energy and mines minister, who also oversaw the state's hydrocarbon empire, Sonatrach, had a say. Depending on the issue in question, a number of other people were being consulted—these included Ali Benflis who became prime minister in 2000, and in 2001 general secretary of the Front de Libération Nationale (FLN, the party that ruled Algeria as a single party for twenty-seven years), and who was a main reason for the FLN being the top vote getter in the 2002 elections.[28] Others with advisory power were the presidents of the two parliamentary chambers,[29] certain presidential advisors (most of whom come from the president's region),[30] party leaders, or high functionaries. However, in most cases these individuals were, at best, the clients of core elite patrons. Along with the core elite, they constituted the ruling elite. Since they had strong advisory power but limited or sectoral decisionmaking capacities, they belonged to the second, or middle, circle of elites rather than to the inner, or first, circle. The latter in 2002 consisted of less than a dozen people, among them no clearly discernible prime decisionmaker (see Figure 7.1).

The second circle of elites was primarily a pool of important core elite clients from various state institutions and the cabinet (the cabinet being the most important collective actor in the second circle), drawn as well from the public economic sector, the private sector, and from among regime-supporting civil society groups. In rare instances one also found contesting elites, such as opposition figures, leaders of the Kabyle protest movement, and so on in this circle; but their presence was usually only temporary, resulting from a passing political constellation during which they were able to mobilize public opinion to an extent that made them as influential as a minister, albeit in a different way. Some second-circle elites had high profiles and exercised official functions. Others, such as Bouteflika's closest advisors, a number of retired generals, and the country's most important

Figure 7.1   Segments of the Algerian Politically Relevant Elite

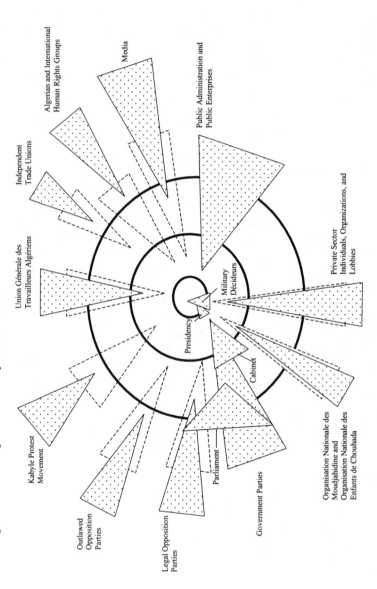

Notes: This figure shows dynamics within the PRE, indicating the range of movement of elite segments into and out of certain circles of influence, depending on political conjunctures. Members of the PRE are divided into three circles of influence. Actors in the first, or inner, circle have decisionmaking power on strategic issues; those in the second, or middle, circle have primarily advisory power on these issues; and those in the third, or outer circle, have either weak advisory power or, in most cases, veto or nuisance power. The triangles indicate the range of mobility. The influence of state institutions remains more constant than that of nonstate institutions and organizations. Leaders of the Kabyle protest movement, for instance, are at times outside the PRE, but at other times their activities allow them access to the third or even the second circles. This figure does not reflect the fact that members of one segment of the PRE (e.g., parliament) may also be members of other

	Political Socialization	Common Formative Experiences	Role Models	Family Background	Primary Language	Perception of Urgent Problems	Sector or Field
Neodinosaur	FLN and its satellites, regime-supporting NGOs	Death of Boumedienne, Islamist terrorism	Houari Boumedienne, Gamal Abdel Nasser	Revolutionary, *ulama*, nomenclature, tribal elites, local notables	French or Arabic	Unemployment, terrorism/security situation, national unity	Army, cabinet, parliament, public administration, FLN and its satellites
Nationalist Reformer	Regime-supporting NGOs, FLN and its satellites	1988 uprisings, return of Boudiaf, Islamist terrorism	Charles de Gaulle, Mohamed Boudiaf, Houari Boumedienne, Gandhi	Revolutionary, *ulama*, nomenclature, tribal, private sector elites, local notables	Mainly French but some Arabic	Economic reforms, terrorism/security situation	Army, cabinet, parliament, public administration, FLN and its satellites, private sector, NGOs
Islamist Reformer	Mosque, clandestine student movements, Islamic NGOs	1988 uprisings, democratic opening, 1992 coup, violence of the 1990s	Hassan al-Banna, Jamal al-Din al-Afghani, Nelson Mandela, Gandhi	Revolutionary, *ulama*, tribal, private sector elites, local, religious notables, and lesser privileged rural and urban	Arabic or French	Economic reforms, fight against corruption, national reconciliation, rule of law, democratization	Cabinet, parliament, public administration, private sector, religious charities, print media
Radical Democrat	(Clandestine) student movements; for Kabyles: family, high school, regime-critical NGOs	1980 Berber spring, 1988 uprisings, democratic opening, 1990 coup, civil war	Nelson Mandela, Olof Palme, Gandhi, Hocine Aït-Ahmed, Martin Luther King Jr., Che Guevara	Revolutionary, local notables, *marabout* families, and lesser privileged urban	French or Kabyle but some Arabic	Democratization, national reconciliation, rule of law, human rights, education sector reforms	Parliament, independent unions, print media, independent NGOs, Kabyle citizens' movement

Notes: This table shows the main elite types, or ideal types, born after 1960 and found among the Algerian PRE as of the second half of the 1990s. The balance of power among these types favors the nationalist reformer, with the neodinosaur a strong second. A fifth elite type, the rejectionist, is not included in this table because he is found in the PRE only temporarily. "Islamist terrorism," "violence of the 1990s," and "civil war" refer to the same events but reflect different perspectives on these events. While different ideal types may share perceptions of urgent problems, they differ regarding the means for solving these problems.

businesspeople, kept a low profile, acting behind the scenes. Virtually all of them had direct access to one or more décideurs and were able to influence decisions or give advice on matters of strategic interest, such as economic and education sector reforms and democratization. It was possible to discern at least five dynamics interacting in this circle:

• Its members had suffered a high degree of turnover. Algeria had eighteen governments between 1988 and 2002 (including major reshufflings), seven of them between 1998 and 2002 alone, a period that also produced four prime ministers.
• The older and younger brothers of the generation of the revolution were being replaced by the second generation (for example, Benflis) in virtually all elite segments, partly because of biological factors—the youngest members of the revolutionary generation were around sixty and approaching retirement in the late 1990s—but also as a result of a deliberate core elite strategy of rejuvenation.
• Private sector elites as well as elites with backgrounds in economics had gained influence, not least as a result of IMF-induced market reforms.
• Civil society elites were being co-opted into this circle.
• An increasing number of elites in the second circle could be described as nationalist reformers in the sense that they advocated substantial structural reforms in the economy and the administration with goals of efficiency, accountability, and the rule of law, but not a system change.

The second Benflis government, formed after the 2002 parliamentary elections, was a good example of these tendencies. It consisted of three parties: the FLN, the Rassemblement National Démocratique (RND, an FLN spin-off founded by core and second-circle elites in 1997), and the Mouvement de la Société pour la Paix (MSP, formerly Hamas, a moderate Islamist party co-opted into the government in 1994).[31] Roughly half of the government's thirty-nine ministers did not belong to a party, and the overwhelming majority could be described as technocrats; politicians in the Weberian sense remained rare. Most cabinet members came from the state bureaucracy, the public economic sector, the universities, or international organizations and institutions. One also found a civil society activist (for women's rights) and several members of the private sector. Entry into the circle for these people was paved by the Conseil Consultatif National and later by the Conseil National de Transition, the quasi-parliamentary bodies installed between 1992 and 1997 after the interruption of the elections and which included as wide a spectrum of regime-supporting groups as possible.

The Benflis government looked significantly different from governments of the early and mid-1990s: 50 percent of the ministers had never sat in a cabinet before; there were five women; only seven of the thirty-nine ministers belonged to the revolutionary generation (while in the early 1990s almost two-thirds had such a past); only one cabinet member came from an army background; and there had been an increasing tendency to recruit members from parliament. The recycling of political figures through cabinet posts, a decades-old practice, appeared to be in decline.

As to clientelist affiliations, ministers from the 2002 cabinet fell into four (partially overlapping) categories:[32] the president's men, the military's men, the prime minister's men and women, and people co-opted for the sake of social stability. The president's men tended to be the oldest ministers,[33] came from the west (in four cases from Nedroma),[34] were reform-oriented technocrats, sat in the more important ministries, and usually had (international) experience and high competence in their respective fields. In addition to "regional capital" and "capital of competence," several of these ministers also had "historical capital," that is, they had participated in the revolution and belonged to a network, such as the Ministère de l'Armement et des Liaisons Générales (MALG).[35] The prime minister's people tended to occupy less important ministries, came from the FLN, and reflected that party's new desirable profile: young, with university degrees (and, ideally, academic careers), and speaking the language of reform. Despite their relatively young age—most were in their forties—several of these ministers had historical capital qua inheritance, as children or relatives of prominent revolutionaries, martyrs, or *ulama* leaders.[36] Although a number of these ministers were elected to parliament in 2002, few had experience in party, local, or national politics. Many only joined the FLN or became active in it for the 2002 campaign; a lack of politicization appeared to have been an asset for upward mobility in this case. The military's men, roughly half a dozen ministers, had little in common except that they were reputed or confirmed to have *un parrain,* a godfather, in the first circle, in the army. Most of them occupied strategically important ministries, such as justice. Finally, there were the three ministers of the co-opted Islamist MSP. Without a godfather in the first circle, their influence was limited and, similar to some of the prime minister's men and women, they belonged to the third, or outer, circle of influence rather than the second circle.

Apart from the more powerful ministers, top cadres of the Union Générale des Travailleurs Algériens (UGTA), the powerful union under the single-party system, and top business elites also had clout in decisions on economic reforms. The UGTA was powerful both because it had access to the first circle, and because it had strong veto and nuisance power.[37] By rallying public opinion and political elites, it forced Bouteflika to shelve a new hydrocarbon bill that he had proposed.[38] Abdelmajid Sidi Said, the secretary general of the UGTA, and Omar Ramdane, president of the Forum des Chefs d'Entreprise (FCE), a lobby of more than sixty of the largest entrepreneurs, could not be ignored when it came to economic decisions. Both were invited to accompany the commerce minister to the fourth round of WTO membership negotiations in November 2002. The FCE also somewhat successfully advocated for regulations to weaken the Algerian import lobby and favor producers over traders. The import lobby, reputed to be close to certain army clans but not formally organized, for its part, fought to keep its privileges.[39] Finally, the wealthiest businessmen, usually with blood or familial ties to the army or politics, informally and individually tried to influence economic decisionmaking; a prominent example was Issad Rebrab, one of the country's biggest industrialists. Algeria's most prominent businessman, Rafik al-Khalifa, whose empire was on the verge of collapse in early 2003,[40] was unlikely to have wielded much political influence, as he was reputed to be a figurehead financed by generals or by Gulf countries (depending on the source of the allegation).

A further category of actors that could be part of the second circle was top cadres of state-sponsored but formally independent organizations, namely those that fell under the umbrella of the *famille révolutionnaire*[41] and could mobilize hundreds of thousands of Algerians in elections. This was true primarily of the Organisation Nationale des Moudjahidine (ONM), a veterans group whose secretary general in 2002 became minister of moudjahidine and who defended the material benefits and interests of veterans,[42] as well as the Organisation Nationale des Enfants de Chouhada (Children of Martyrs). The fact that these organizations were political instruments and had political weight was reflected in the state's allocation of funds to them: in the 2003 budget proposal the moudjahidine item was the fourth largest, receiving only one-third less than defense and more than higher education and the entire health sector. This situation also helped explain the apparently large number of *faux moudjahidine*—the number of officially acknowledged veterans rose from 24,000 in 1962 to 420,000 in 1999[43]—and the intense efforts to make hereditary the historical capital of veterans through organizations such as the Organisation Nationale des Enfants de Moudjahidine (Children of Veterans), founded in 1993. Being a cadre in one of these organizations or in an association of "victims of terrorism" was an excellent stepping stone for entering the politically relevant elite. The fictional and mythical famille révolutionnaire thus constituted what Olivier Roy calls a "modern *asabiyya*" (kinship-based solidarity).[44]

The Third Circle: The Subelites—Clients and Contesters

The third circle of the politically relevant elite was the most dynamic circle. The early 1990s, before the aborted elections, witnessed the mushrooming of the number of collective actors with indirect but substantial political influence through advising, lobbying, or possessing the power to effectively veto decisions or be a nuisance. Many of these actors managed to retain some of their influence beyond the coup. Furthermore, in the late 1990s new politically relevant actors emerged, for example, the Kabyle protest movement. This not only led to a sharp increase in the number of actors that were able to temporarily, as opposed to permanently, move into the third circle, but also led to a fragmentation of third-circle elites. Another tendency in this circle was the increasing dominance of young actors born after the revolution. These developments in the third circle, in conjunction with the recruitment and co-optation mechanisms used to sustain the second circle, were a primary reason for system continuity and relative stability in Algeria.

Two categories of actors informed this circle: clients and contesting elites. The clients had been "lifted" into the PRE by patrons from above, had good chances of moving into the second circle, and were found primarily in the RND and the FLN and its satellites (for example, in the Union Nationale de la Jeunesse Algérienne [UNJA], and the UGTA), in regime-friendly NGOs,[45] and in the two chambers of parliament. The Senate, or upper house, one-third of whose members were nominated by the president, could be seen as a parking lot for aging former top functionaries with historical capital or, for its younger members, a waiting room for entry into the executive or diplomatic corps. The lower chamber of parliament, the Assemblée Populaire Nationale (APN)—as of 1997 a multiparty chamber—while not a powerful institution in the constitutional sense, developed into a platform for controversial debates and agenda setting with the first-time appearance of two opposition parties[46] and three "semi-opposition" parties.

The APN, dominated by the RND in 1997, and by an absolute majority of the FLN in 2002, became a sphere of frequent elite turnover (more than 80 percent of 1997 MPs were not reelected in 2002) and of elite rejuvenation. In 1997, 11 percent belonged to the generation born after independence; in 2002 this number more than doubled, to 25 percent, and, conversely, the number of the revolutionary generation declined, from 16 percent to 5 percent. Both developments were engineered by party leaders. In 2002, moreover, a phenomenon previously witnessed in most Arab countries reached Algeria: the entry into politics of private sector elites. At the end of the single-party era in 1989, only 1 to 2 percent of MPs had a private sector background; in 2002 this figure had climbed to 10 percent. Finally, many of the regime-supporting MPs formed a clientelist link between local and national levels, between mass organizations (for example, the ONM, the victims of terrorism, the scouts) and between the first and second-circle elites who used these organizations and numerous smaller NGOs to broaden the power base of the regime. Hachemaoui pertinently termed such MPs *entrepreneurs de la médiation clientélaire* (entrepreneurs of clientelist mediation).[47]

The contesting elites, who wanted to alter or completely change the political system, comprised two large groups: Islamists and leftists. Although most contesting elites had imposed themselves or had been pushed into the PRE from below by such social forces as the Kabyle protest movement, their co-optation and movement into the second circle was not uncommon, as evidenced by the fortunes of some MSP and UGTA cadres and some media elites. As a result of their elevation, their positions softened, and they lost popular appeal because of their cooperation with the regime, as happened to the MSP. Though the MSP only received minor ministries, it could still be said to have obtained a certain veto power, because the government needed an Islamist party fig leaf to claim legitimacy through pluralism.

The most powerful Islamist actor was arguably the opposition Mouvement pour la Réforme Nationale (MRN, or al-Islah, which split from al-Nahda in 1999). It was the third most influential political force within the formal political system and had attracted former FIS activists and voters. The power of Islah laid less in its agenda of social justice than in its ability to hamper reforms in the education sector and other areas by presenting such measures as an "occidentalization" of society, thus mobilizing conservative opinion. It had informal nuisance power but limited formal veto power, because it remained a minority in parliament and on many issues had no allies. The electoral power of other contesting Islamist forces—such as the outlawed FIS and moderate Islamist, or Arabo-nationalist, Wafa, headed by Ahmed Taleb Ibrahimi, Boumedienne's long-time minister and a former revolutionary—was hard to evaluate because these groups could not operate openly. Ibrahimi, the most hopeful opposition candidate in the 1999 presidential race, had been accused of trying to create an FIS successor organization even though WAFA was by no means more radical or more Islamist than Islah. The fact that it had not been legalized spoke of its potential electoral power and the fear it aroused among the core and second-circle elites.

The FIS elite were physically eliminated, imprisoned, or deprived of their political rights throughout the 1990s. Nevertheless, the party's number one and two, Abassi Madani and Ali Belhadj, who were supposed to be released from prison in July 2003, could not be ignored by the regime. The support of the FIS leadership for holding presidential elections in 1999 and for the Concorde Civile was crucial to incumbent elites, because it offered them broad legitimacy and allowed for the integration of parts of the FIS electorate into the formal political process. With some FIS elites and part of its electorate co-opted, and with persistent quarrels between and within the leadership in Algeria and in exile, it appeared unlikely that the party (even if legalized) would regain the influence it held in the early 1990s, when its leaders were about to move from the second to the first circle. Finally, the remaining armed Islamist groups, Groupement Islamique Armés (GIA) and Groupe Salafiste pour la Prédication et le Combat, were able to muster indirect influence on certain strategic decisions in that they provided justification for the army not lifting the state of emergency and keeping up its repression. The GIA, especially, through massacres, played into the hands of the army, which in turn led to persistent and plausible rumors of army infiltration of these groups.[48]

Elites on the political left—from members of political parties to the Kabyle protest movement and human rights activists—formed another important opposition force. Their organization, however, exemplified the problems hampering opposition forces from uniting and becoming a real force of change. The most important parties on the left, the Trotskyite Parti des Travailleurs (PT), led by Louisa Hanoune, and the social democratic and Berberophone Front des Forces Socialistes (FFS), led by Hocine Ait-Ahmed, one of the nine principal leaders of the revolution, had advocated regime and system change for decades from within and without the political system. Though both of these parties shared a goal of democratization and national reconciliation that includes the FIS, they had fallen out over tactical issues, such as whether to participate in elections. Moreover, the FFS, which had strong regional roots and historical legitimacy, lost part of its constituency to the Kabyle citizens movement, or Arouch, a protest movement born in April 2001 following the killing of a young Berber in a police station.[49]

The Kabyle movement was formally organized into several committees, the largest being the Coordination des Arouch, des Dairas et des Communes (CADC).[50] Its leadership represented a new force in the third circle of elites and at the same time contributed to the fragmentation of the more established contesting elites. This movement, although not homogeneous or well structured, was able to take credit for the state finally accepting the Berber language, Tamazight, as a national language in April 2002.[51] Moreover, it succeeded largely at preventing—not least through violent means—the holding of local and national elections in Kabilya in 2002. It also substantially weakened the Berber FFS and Rassemblement pour la Culture et la Démocratie (RCD), which was forced to leave government as a result of the uprisings. These parties, as well as the government, tried to repress, split, and control the movement; and several movement leaders were arrested in late 2002. The Arouch, however, remained adamant that without the fulfillment of their political and social demands as stated in the so-called Platform of El Kseur,[52] they would neither negotiate nor cooperate with state agencies. While such maximalist demands threatened to drive the Arouch into a political dead end, the movement was not likely to simply disappear, since it was, among other things, an expression of a generational conflict, deriving much of its strength from the increasing number of young Berbers, who were completely alienated from (national) political life.[53]

The fact that the government was not able to repress the Kabyle protest movement the way that it had repressed the FIS[54] could be attributed to the presence of two politically relevant actors with strong nuisance power: the nongovernmental Arabophone and Francophone press, which were remarkably, but not entirely, free,[55] and national and international human rights activists. The press reported not only every move against the Arouch, but continuously uncovered scandals involving core and second-circle elites. In 1998, for example, a press campaign pushed General Mohamed Betchine, a strong and utterly corrupt Zeroual man, to resign.[56] The private press's vigilance, moreover, contributed to preventing the wide-scale manipulation of elections. Human rights activists, for their part, developed a nuisance power that moved them into the second circle, that is, until the events of September 11 internationally "legitimized" the Algerian use of force against Islamists retrospectively. From the mid-1990s onward Algerian and foreign human rights activists contributed to the isolation of the Algerian core elite by raising the question "Qui tue qui?" (Who kills whom?) in the French press, insinuating that the army had committed atrocities in order to discredit the Islamists and to justify the regime's repressive policies. In 2001 complaints of torture forced General Nezzar to flee from France overnight. Moreover, in 2002 a French court after long hearings dismissed a lawsuit in which Nezzar had accused former army officer Habib Souaidia of defamation. The latter had—in the media as well as in a highly publicized book—blamed the décideurs for the systematic and willful perpetration of atrocities.[57]

In view of these pressures, the army's public relations campaign could also be seen as a response to the globalization of justice and the fear of a Milosevic-like fate for décideurs. Other regime counterstrategies included trying to split the media and human rights groups. Several editors, columnists, and caricaturists had been co-opted (sometimes into the second circle) and were being used to attack regime foes and for agenda setting, while also being given leeway to criticize the regime.[58] As for human rights activists, those from truly independent organizations continued to suffer from clampdowns, while several regime-backed organizations, defending the human rights of some people but not of others, sprung up.[59] What ultimately prevented most contesting elites in the third circle from becoming stronger was the wildly fluctuating nature of their influence, which depended on the national and international climate. After September 11, for instance, independent human rights activists for a while disappeared almost completely from the PRE.

Continuity Through Change

The above analysis has shown that dynamics within the Algerian politically relevant elite, particularly the increase in the number of actors in the second half of the 1990s, led to a substantially reduced range of action for the core elite. Members of the core elite, in an effort to broaden their power base and to institutionalize controllable valves, responded to popular pressure by liberalizing the political system, albeit selectively. This allowed for young and less powerful third-circle elites (or subelites) to emerge and to at times successfully press for certain concessions or block core elite strategies. Such actions were made possible not least by changes abroad, such as the end of the Eastern European socialist paradigm, which resulted among other things in transitions to market economies worldwide, globalization of justice, and international treaties—putting pressure on a core elite exhibiting increasing disunity in vision and strategy. The core elite fragmentation opened spaces in which contesting elites could act. The result of these developments, however, was not system reform or system instability but, on the contrary, system continuity. The increasing fragmentation of the PRE, the recruitment mechanisms into the politically relevant elite (for example, core elites co-opting nonpoliticized young elites), and the nature of the channels of social mobility (for example, clientelist networks based on regional, familial, and historical capital) preserved the existing political structures. Underlying this situation were components external to Algeria's elite: The elites' fragmentation reflected longstanding and deep divisions in Algerian society as a whole—the core elite "merely" managed these division successfully. Recruitment mechanisms and channels for upward mobility embodied the vertical, primordial (familial, tribal, regional), and modern (revolutionary, rentier) networks as well as the informal (personalized) modes of negotiation and exchange found throughout Algerian society. This explained why, despite a common "enemy," contesting elites only once—in 1995 in Rom in a mediation of the Sant'Egidio Catholic community—agreed on a common political platform of national reconciliation that included the FIS.[60]

The personalized networks and the modes of exchange resulted in part from the rentier character of the Algerian economy.[61] This aspect of the economy was a principal obstacle to elite transformation and system change, because it helped the core elite to finance a costly divide and conquer strategy, consisting of repression (for example, of the FIS), co-optation (for example, of the Islamist MSP), and encouragement of real and fake competition through the creation of parallel structures. A classic example of this last mechanism was the creation of new parties to weaken existing ones by having the newer parties espouse similar agendas and address similar electorates to those of the established parties. Cases in point were the Berberophone RCD (to oppose the Berberophone FFS) in 1989 and the RND (to oppose the FLN, temporarily in opposition) in 1997. Also, businesspeople, former politicians, and generals founded or supported a plethora of private Francophone daily newspapers. In 2002 these numbered more than a dozen and served to weaken the effect that any individual newspaper might have, thus rendering the (Francophone) press less threatening. Finally, of the 57,000 associations in 2002,[62] only a few were truly independent. Many were regime satellites (for example, the victims of terrorism associations) or instruments for distributing benefits to regime supporters, for weakening independent and opposition NGOs, and, last but not least, for integrating emerging young elites into the fold.[63] Examination of these young elites and the mechanisms of generational change in Algerian politics offered additional clues into why, despite the dynamic nature of the third elite circle, shifts in the second circle, and changes in the balance of power in the first circle, the Algerian system remained remarkably resistant to change.

Grandchildren of the Revolution

It seems superfluous, but it is nevertheless important to stress that a different generational experience produces a different "generation entelechy."[64] Obviously, a common experience does not lead to homogeneity among an entire generation, and elite rejuvenation does not necessarily mean wholesale changes in attitudes, strategies, or policies. What an actual generational change and an approach focusing on it offer are a chance to pinpoint areas of change. Equally important, they highlight continuity, for one must remain aware that focusing on elite transformations "risks underestimating the persistence and exaggerating the change."[65] By using common historical and common formal educational experiences to delineate different generations, it was possible to discern three generations among the Algerian politically relevant elite in the early 2000s: the revolutionary generation, the second generation (coming of age after independence), and the third generation (born around or after independence). The elites of the revolutionary generation, whether opposition or regime elites, were marked by the war of independence, by the rivalries and rifts the war generated among Algerians, and by what Mohammed Harbi terms an "esprit de secret, de suspicion et de rivalité" (a spirit of secrecy, of suspicion, and of rivalry).[66]

The second generation, born between the mid-1940s and the late 1950s, had memories of the war but had also been significantly marked by an era of hope: the euphoria of independence and "the golden years of Boumedienne" involving state building, ambitious industrialization projects, and high oil prices. It had enjoyed generous state scholarships to France, Eastern Europe, the Arabic- and English-speaking worlds;[67] job opportunities had been abundant and social mobility fairly high. The educational system—although geared toward mass education and slowly beginning to be Arabized—had still featured private schools and "showed an imbalance in favor of those whose families already [held] wealth, status and power."[68] Nevertheless, upward mobility had been widespread in this generation: The step-by-step Arabization of the official sphere turned command of Modern Standard Arabic, rarely found in the revolutionary generation, into an asset during the 1970s and opened channels for ambitious young people with non-Francophone rural or less privileged backgrounds. Among the institutions producing elites were technical and engineering schools, the École Nationale d'Administration, the Faculté de Droit in Algiers, and the army academies. Networks based on familial, regional, and revolutionary affiliations as well as mass organizations, such as the UGTA, the UNJA, and the Union Nationale des Femmes Algériennes (UNFA), were channels of upward mobility. These FLN satellites helped form an etatist, socialist, collectivist, and nationalist identity. This "ideology of the state," together with the opportunities offered to the second generation, had inspired a sentiment among this generation that they could never give back to the state what it had given to them. Hence, it was not surprising that the second generation of elites had turned out to be obedient rather than rebellious and had remained in the shadow of its heroic fathers, particularly of one strong man: Boumedienne. Hardly any representatives of this generation had ascended to key positions in the FLN or the administration until the early 1990s, none made it to the top echelons of the army until the late 1990s, and none occupied the presidency.

The main socializing experiences of the third generation of elites were, in contrast, a chain of primarily discouraging or violent developments: the economic decline during the Chadli years that accelerated socioeconomic problems; the bloodily repressed riots of 1988 that led to three short years of democratic opening, accompanied by the euphoria of a political spring but also increased social tensions linked to the ascendance of the Islamist FIS; the military coup after the FIS election victory; the assassination of President Boudiaf, who had represented a ray of hope;[69] the outbreak of the civil war; and, throughout the 1990s, rampant unemployment, low social mobility, and the emigration of more than 400,000 Algerians with higher diplomas.[70] This elite generation, moreover, suffered from a decline in the school system, which had been completely (but poorly) Arabized by the early 1980s (with the exception of the natural sciences at the university level) and produced what many Algerians refer to as "illiterates in two languages." With state scholarships to foreign countries becoming scarce, this generation of elites was educated almost exclusively in Algeria, mainly at the Sciences Po and the Faculté de Droit of Algiers University. Army elites constituted the sole exception: they continued to be sent abroad for training. At military academies, English was pushed as of the mid-1980s. In terms of elite training and international exposure, the army was, therefore, far ahead of the civilian sector.

While this third generation of elites was (not yet) found in the first circle, and while its members were only slowly moving into cabinet positions—two in 2002—they had in the army attained the rank of colonel and were increasingly found in ever-higher positions in the general command. They were also moving into top positions in the private and public economic sectors, in the state administration, and in parties. More than half of the top cadres of the FFS in 2002 were born after the revolution, and even the FLN's *bureau politique*, the eternal stronghold of the so-called dinosaurs, had one member under forty years of age. The executives of the Islamist parties from their beginnings included members of the third generation, adding a generational component to the confrontation between the regime and the Islamists. With the regime excluding the younger generations from power, the FIS in the early 1990s became the primary forum for their political voice. It appeared that the Arouch, at least for the Kabyles, took on this function in the early 2000s.

The most striking common feature of the third generation of elites was the fact that it had been recruited almost exclusively from certain privileged layers of society, in many cases from within the PRE: from well-known revolutionary families[71] or from the larger (and largely imaginary) *famille révolutionnaire*, from the nomenklatura (administrative and FLN cadres and military elites), locally important families (including postrevolutionary "notables," such as local party functionaries), families of religious notables (*ulama* and religious brotherhoods), prominent tribes, and the private sector. Remarkable still was that almost none of the core elite's offspring could be found in top positions in state institutions. Most of them were educated abroad (in France, the United States, or Britain) and either stayed there or returned and went into the private sector. A few were found in the army, but not (yet) in its top echelons.

A principal reason for "elite reproduction" was the Arabization of the school system, which hampered the social mobility of Algerians who did not grow up in a privileged French-speaking household, in a Francophone urban milieu, or attend schools in France. The army's general command as well as the cabinet communicated primarily in French. Ministers, generals, and directors of enterprises made it clear that French was a prerequisite for promotions into the upper spheres of the Algerian system. Even in Islamist parties, mastering French seemed, judging from the high number of top cadres that spoke it beautifully, a plus for one's career, even if party leaders refused to speak it publicly for ideological reasons. To a limited extent, the only space open to actors from backgrounds other than those above were independent unions,[72] independent NGOs, the Arabophone press, and

Islamist parties. Thus, as Pierre Bourdieu notes, the educational system contributed to reproducing the existing order.[73]

A second reason for the reproduction of the current elite and for existing social hierarchies was the monopolization of historical legitimacy by incumbent elites. A link, no matter how remote, to the fictitious famille révolutionnaire was a key asset for entering the PRE. It was no coincidence that when Leila Boutlilis, one of the female members in the second Benflis cabinet, was presented to the media, her being an offspring of a famous "martyr" was mentioned more prominently as a merit than her being a well-known professor of cardiology. Historical legitimacy as a criterion for recruitment thus experienced a renaissance. According to John Entelis, it had become less important in the late 1970s;[74] in the wake of the regime's fight against Islamism in the 1990s, however, historical legitimacy regained importance and was extended to organizations fighting terrorism. The fact that the PRE, despite its still strong egalitarian and populist rhetoric, recruited mainly from within and from the same privileged societal segments, did not, however, preclude newly recruited young elites from developing attitudes that differed from their older predecessors.

The Faces of the Young Elite

As Mannheim stresses, an "actual generation," composed of those with common historical experiences, is divided into "differentiated, antagonistic generation units" because common historical experiences are dealt with in different ways.[75] In the Algerian case, the domestic and foreign media have tended to reduce these units to binary categories, such as *éradicateurs/réconciliateurs* (eradicators/reconcilers) or Arabophone/Francophone or Arabophone/Franco-Berberophone or Islamist/democratic, and so on. Such dualities, usually relying on one variable only—for example, language or attitude toward Islamists—have overlooked complex crosscutting of political, ethnic, linguistic, and regional cleavages and neglected additional dimensions, such as outlooks on economic reforms. Their explanatory power for elite change as well as for system change has been limited. The inclusion of a wider spectrum of variables[76] allows for the construction of five different "ideal types" in the third generation: the neodinosaur, the nationalist reformer, the Islamist reformer, the radical democrat, and the rejectionist (see Table 7.1.).[77] The balance of power in the third generation favored the nationalist reformer, while in the second generation the dinosaur prevailed.

The neodinosaur—found in the army, cabinet, and parliament, as well as in public administration, and often an FLN, or in some cases, an RND member—was the most reform averse of the ideal types. He had been socialized in a family belonging to the nomenklatura or in organizations such as the UNJA that have also functioned as channels for upward mobility.[78] He was a populist nationalist in the tradition of Boumediennists and saw himself as the true inheritor of the revolutionaries. His motto was *continuité* (continuity), and his political program was to slow reforms in the administrative, education, and economic sectors on the one hand while demanding state programs to alleviate socioeconomic misery on the other. Democracy was seen as having arrived with the demise of the single-party system in 1997; it now only needed some consolidation.

The rejectionist was the opposite of the neodinosaur. His principal goal was a change of what he viewed as a completely corrupt and murderous regime and elite. He was not interested in reforms, rejected negotiations, and was ready to flirt with violence to achieve his goals, arguing that (violent) uprisings, rather than negotiations, had been the motor of change in the Algerian past. In the 1990s he was found primarily among the more radical FIS cadres, whose visions of post-FLN Algeria revolved around an Islamic social order and the Islamic values of the revolution that were betrayed after independence. As of 2001, the most influential rejectionists were leaders of the Berber protest movement. They saw themselves as revolutionaries in the tradition of a Che Guevara or Algerians such as Abane Ramdane, who had been killed by revolutionaries who later took over the state. At the same time, paradoxically, the leaders of the protest movement, in accordance with dominant sociocultural practices, excluded women almost completely and included a revitalized concept of an archaic organizational structure, the Arouch, in their movement. Few rejectionists were found in the PRE, and they had no chance of advancing in the existing system because they refused co-optation.

The radical democrat—found in small numbers in parliament but mainly in independent unions, NGOs, and newspapers and in the FFS, PT, and occasionally RCD—was also rooting for regime change, but through nonviolent means and often from within the system. He tended to be Berberophone or Francophone and his goal was a secular, social democratic system that allowed space for the FIS. For him, too, the revolutionaries—with the exception of figures such as Ait-Ahmed—betrayed the main goal of the revolution: the establishment of a democracy. His main concerns were democratization, human rights, a functioning judiciary, and a fairer distribution of state resources. He was, hence, blocking some reforms (for example, privatization) while pushing other (political, educational, and administrative) reforms. In contrast to the neodinosaur, he was neither a functionary nor a bureaucrat but a true politician in the Weberian sense. His upward mobility, however, was usually limited to the third circle of elites.

The Islamist reformer—found in the MSP, to some extent in the Islah, in the cabinet and parliament, and the Arabophone press—was usually an Arabophone and could also be described as a democrat. He shared many of the concerns of the radical democrat—rule of law, human rights, the fight against corruption—except his vision of society was shaped more by Islamic than by universalist values; yet he tolerated other political and social visions. He blamed the postrevolutionary elite for having betrayed the Arab-Islamic pillars of the revolution and for having subscribed to authoritarian, socialist, and Francophone values instead. Like the conservative neodinosaur, he opposed education sector reforms—namely, the early introduction of French—but advocated a market economy, transparency, and accountability. He, too, tended to be a politician in the Weberian sense, and his influence could reach into the second circle by agreeing to limited deals with the regime and by utilizing his nuisance power.

The nationalist reformer—found in the FLN and the RND, in government, parliament, the public administration, the public and private economic sectors, and many NGOs—exemplified why the Algerian system remained virtually unchanged, despite much talk of reforms. He had one foot in politics (parliament), one foot in business, and at the same time was a cadre in a (large) NGO. While his background was similar to that of the neodinosaur, he differed in outlook and behavior. He communicated openly and critically about the country's problems and was convinced that substantial structural reforms in the administration, the economy, the judiciary, and the educational system were the only way out of the political, social, and economic crisis that Algeria had suffered for more than a decade. Political reforms, however, were not a priority, and he had internalized the modernization paradigm in that he saw economic and social development as a prerequisite for democracy. The nationalist reformer viewed economic and administrative reforms as means to ease tensions and satisfy interest groups in order to postpone or avoid political concessions and prevent system change.[79]

With nationalist reformers from the third and the second generation moving into key positions (in most ministries and, arguably, the presidency), why were the economic, administrative, and education sector reforms advocated by them not implemented? The answer is found not only in the opposition of groups with vested interests (for example, importers in the case of privatization) or with different visions of society (for example, Islamists in the case of education reforms based on universalist values), but because the reforms were slowed by the nationalist reformer himself: The reforms he advocated, namely transparency, accountability, and the rule of law (eventually leading to strong state institutions), would have undermined the very structures (of informal networks based on primordial ties and personalized relations) that "made" him. He thus was likely to make choices that did not threaten these structures. In other words, attitudes were not primarily what guided his decisions, rather it was the personalized and clientelist relations with individual elites that shaped and constrained him.

The personal trajectory of a third generation nationalist reformer illustrates this point.

X was a private sector consultant from a family in western Algeria with links to the ulama (and thus had historical legitimacy). In high school he dated a general's daughter, was introduced to several décideurs, and began doing (vaguely defined) "favors" for them. In 2002, he advised several ministers informally, had close ties to the country's most important business leaders as well as to several generals, and was among those who advised the generals of the need to change the army's image. At the same time he mediated between international governmental, nongovernmental, and multilateral organizations and the Algerian ruling elite. His business relationships with Algerians were highly informal, and when called upon to solve a problem, he often succeeded with one phone call to a highly placed person. He openly talked about the importance of giving and taking in informal exchanges of favors that did not necessarily need to be of a material nature.[80] X's analysis of Algeria's problems and shortcomings in no way differed from those of the World Bank or foreign diplomats, and he organized workshops on corruption, transparency, accountability, and lobbying. Yet, X's activities were geared toward improving Algeria's image rather than toward real structural changes, and they were conditioned by his efforts to satisfy those who protected him rather than by advocacy for the reforms he deemed necessary. When Bouteflika was in good standing with the army, he publicly backed him; when the president fell from favor, he criticized him in the media, even though Bouteflika and his entourage were arguing for reforms that X thought important. As all nationalist reformers, X had great respect not necessarily for the décideurs, but for the army as an institution, which he perceived as functioning better and more according to merit than all other institutions.

X did not hold a formal political position and may have been unique in what he did professionally, but the way in which he operated within the system and subordinated his reformist agenda to the needs of negotiating and renegotiating his personal ties with various patrons did not differ much from the ways in which nationalist reformers in the second circle, including prime ministers, negotiated with core elites, except that the members of the second circle spoke about it less openly. X's example, moreover, showed that patron-client networks were highly dynamic and subject to constant negotiating and renegotiating.

Elite Change and System Transformation: The Impact of Sociocultural and Economic Factors

Patrick Chabal pointedly states about Africa that politics are not "functionally differentiated, or separated, from the sociocultural considerations which govern everyday life."[81] This also held true, even if to a lesser extent, for Algeria during the period examined, and is an issue completely overlooked by actor-oriented transition models that try to reach general (universal) conclusions about possible transition trajectories.[82] Even if an elite ideal type, such as the radical democrat, moved through a pact into the second or even the first circle and participated in decisionmaking, it remains questionable whether such movement would ultimately lead to democracy. For even in Algerian parties that had a Western-style democratic agenda, internal politics and personnel decisions remained guided by sociocultural and primordial considerations more than political ones. The FFS for instance was run by a charismatic patriarch, who, coming from a *marabout*[83] family, possessed religious capital and placed family members in strategic positions. No Algerian party leader allowed a strong rival to rise within his party. Dissent within parties, moreover, quickly led to schisms (for example, Islah from Nahda). If the charismatic leader disappeared or left the party, the party more or less vanished (as happened to Nahda after its leader, Djaballah, left the party and founded Islah). Even those political figures who saw themselves as the new revolutionaries or praised "modern" values of citizenship, such as the leaders of the Kabyle movement, had a discourse deeply shaped by sociocultural practices in that they spoke of the movement's *code d'honneur* (code of honor), thus resorting to a central concept of "traditional" Kabyle social organization.[84] Also, they excused the complete absence of women in the movement as in the "arouch's tradition."

What Harbi stated about the inner life of the FLN in 1954 still held for Algerian party politics five decades later: "What one finds here are relations of power and influence in which personal relations and family and regional ties fuse. It is less a matter of pure political relations than of community relations expressed in a modern language."[85] In Algerian politics, even in the early 2000s, one did not find figures such as Lebanese prime minister Rafik al-Hariri or former Polish presidential candidate Stanislaw Tyminski or former Estonian foreign minister Tom Ilves—men who had made their careers or their fortunes outside their country and could at least initially operate outside traditional social and economic networks. Ministers who earlier had an impressive career in international organizations—for example, Hamid Temmar, privatization minister, and Chakib Khalil, energy and mines minister—and a clear and radical reform vision were immediately initiated into "clans," in these cases, Bouteflika's, which made them targets of his foes and subject to his maneuvering and efforts to duck reforms.

In view of the importance of patronage networks and informal structures for the stability of formal political structures in Algeria, it can be argued that the nature of the country's economy was a prime reason for system continuity. The Algerian economy in the early 2000s remained one of rent distribution and informal exchange rather than of production: 97 percent of export revenues came from the hydrocarbon sector, imports offered a prime opportunity for quick and big money, and the informal economy (consisting also primarily of import and distribution) constituted up to 30 percent of the country's GDP.[86] The hydrocarbon rent allowed the ruling elite to sustain distribution networks[87] and to buy allegiances and loyalty from a substantial number of Algerians.[88] The hydrocarbon rent, moreover, helped to finance military repression of insurgencies, to "penetrate civil society" (as one young RND cadre and head of a large regime-founded NGO bluntly put it), and to alleviate the most potentially explosive social misery. Oil (or gas) thus could be said to have turned control of the state into a zero-sum struggle.[89] This raised the stakes for incumbents as well as for contesting elites and was not likely to allow for "a negotiated compromise under which actors agree to forgo or underutilize their capacity to harm each others' corporate autonomies or vital interests."[90]

Perspectives for Change

Analysis of the Algerian politically relevant elite in the decade after the 1992 coup d'état leads to the conclusion that dynamics and changes within it did not translate into policy shifts indicative of a system change. Instead, change guaranteed systemic continuity; the same patterns of domination persisted despite the surfacing of a number of actors with substantial veto and nuisance power, generational change giving rise to a young reform-oriented elite type, and increasing disunity within the core elite. Core elite strategies, recruitment policies, as well as structural factors external to these elites explained this dynamic.

First, changes among the elite linked to political and economic liberalization created a release, allowing contesting elites some influence and giving potentially frustrated young elites hope for long-awaited upward mobility through co-optation. Obviously, the ruling elite was not able to fully control the dynamics arising from its liberalization policies; the Berber movement, the press, and the Islamist Islah became stronger and more independent than (presumably) expected, but core elite policies largely succeeded in preventing the formation of a broad coalition of contesting elites by successfully playing on regional and tribal divides, historic rivalries, ethnic sentiments, linguistic rifts, and religious-secular divides in the PRE. Second, though generational changes within the PRE gave rise to young elites, the ruling elite only enabled a few unrepresented or underrepresented social segments and groups to enter. Most young members of the elite were the offspring of the nomenklatura and the privileged, a phenomenon that resulted from the Arabization policy as well as the monopolization of historical legitimacy by incumbent elites and the conversion of this legitimacy into an inheritable symbolic capital. Even though many of these young elites had a clear vision of the country's structural problems and a reform agenda, they were not willing to push such a program if it entailed jeopardizing the social and economic networks and clientelist structures of which they were a part. Finally, sociocultural practices, the hydrocarbon rent, and market reforms benefited the current ruling elites and their clients.[91] They allowed the highly personalized networks and blurred boundaries between the military, political, bureaucratic, and economic spheres as well as between formal and informal institutions to be sustained.

The situation, however, was not static. Constant struggles shifted the balance of power between factions within the PRE, and the elites were vulnerable to external influence and pressures. As discussed above, Algeria's joining NATO's Mediterranean Dialog and international human rights campaigns had an effect on elite strategies. In an era in which the United States considers outside intervention for regime change legitimate and in which the arm of international justice seems to reach into more and more areas of the world, Algerian core elites thus are likely to be forced to make more political concessions in the future. It can, moreover, be expected that pressures arising from the association agreement with the European Union and membership negotiations with the WTO will push Algeria's elites to implement the reforms nationalist reformers thought necessary but hesitated to push through because of resistance and fear of losing out—namely those involving transparency, accountability, rule of law, demonopolization of the economy, and protection of civil liberties. Most likely, substantial political and economic changes in the short and medium term will come about only if pressure coincides with further core elite disunity (leading to implosion), a fall in hydrocarbon revenues (making it difficult to maintain the distributive networks), and popular uprisings that extend beyond one region and shake the whole country.[92] In 1988, when oil prices and unrest came into play, the government decided to push ahead with reforms. A confluence of all the factors above, resulting in such a push in the future, is, however, unlikely.

Even when Algeria's system is shaken, it is questionable whether the outcome will be more democratic. The rentier structures, the fractionalized nature of Algerian society, the dominance of personalized vertical networks preventing the development of a horizontal (class) conscience, and the absence of strong state institutions that are insulated in a Weberian sense might perpetuate the current pattern of simply reproducing similar political elites and structures. Moreover, as long as most formal institutions work according to informal (personalized) rules and remain weak, and as long as civil unrest and low-level (Islamist) violence prevail, the army as the most cohesive and well structured institution will be able to present itself as the indispensable backbone of the state and use the prospect of internal disorder to justify its presence in state affairs.[93] It is, hence, likely that what may appear to be a transition from authoritarianism will merely lead from one variant of authoritarianism to another, and possibly a more competitive one.

Notes

I would like to thank Miriam R. Lowi and Oliver Schlumberger for important comments on earlier drafts of this chapter.

1. For an excellent analysis of the elite of the war and the early years of independence, see Quandt, *Revolution and Political Leadership;* for elites under Boumedienne, see Zartman, "Algeria: A Post-Revolutionary Elite"; under Boumedienne and Chadli, see Entelis, "Algeria: Technocratic Rule, Military Power." For general postindependence developments as well as elite struggles over competing projects, see also Hidouci, *Algérie: la libération inachevée.*

2. In October 1988 Algeria witnessed uprisings in many parts of the country. The army responded with a brutal crackdown, leaving hundreds dead. These events propelled Chadli and the reformers around him to push political reforms. In 1989 a new constitution was adopted in a referendum, ending single-party rule, permitting the formation of associations of a political nature, and allowing freedom of expression and of assembly. These reforms marked the beginning of a democratization process.

3. For an excellent account of the war, see Martinez, *La guerre civile.*

4. For example, O'Donnell et al., *Transitions from Authoritarian Rule;* Przeworski, *Democracy and the Market.*

5. Quandt, "Algeria's Uneasy Peace," p. 19.

6. Burton and Higley, "The Study of Political Elite Transformations," p. 182.

7. Quandt, *Revolution and Political Leadership;* Entelis, "Algeria: Technocratic Rule, Military Power"; Zartman, "Algeria: A Post-Revolutionary Elite."

8. The sources on which this analysis is based are three: (1) in-depth semistructured interviews conducted in Algeria in 2001 and 2002 with ninety-two members of the PRE, including retired generals, Prime Minister Ali Benflis, former prime ministers and current ministers, party leaders, MPs, administrative cadres, and party, union, business, media, and NGO representatives; (2) data on the career trajectories of individual elites from questionnaires handed out to interview partners and from the print media; and (3) analysis of decisionmaking processes based on data from interviews and print media on positions and strategies of key players vis-à-vis the strategic issues of economic reform, education sector reform, and democratization.

9. The term "system change" is used here in the sense of the transition literature, that is, it refers to the transition from one type of polity (authoritarianism) to a different type of polity (democracy). System reform, as used in this chapter, means adaptations within the existing system.

10. With no existing or accessible polling data on this generation, the primary bases for analysis were fifty-two interviews with elites born after 1960 that focused on socioeconomic and educational background, political socialization, career patterns, networks, positions on strategic issues, and perceptions of the country's biggest problems as well as solutions for these problems.

11. Zartman, "The Algerian Army in Politics"; Yefsah, "L'armée et le pouvoir en Algérie."

12. The presidency is used here as a collective, including not only the president but also his closest and most powerful advisors.

13. Since *le pouvoir* is also used to describe a system of domination, *les décideurs* shall be used here for the primary decisionmakers.

14. The choice of Bouteflika, for instance, entailed drawn out, heated negotiations among the decisionmakers.

15. For short biographies of many of the elites discussed in this chapter, see Cheurfi, "La classe politique algérienne."

16. Many of them were not literate in Arabic. General Mohamed Lamari, at his first press conference in July 2002, switched to French after half a sentence even when the questions asked were in Arabic.

17. While there were statutes governing retirement (*statut de retraite*) for army officers, the regulations did not apply to generals, who could stay in office as long as they wanted. Hence, widespread rumors seemed credible that a wave of frustrated colonels in their late forties and early fifties took early retirement in 2001 and 2002 because they saw no prospects for advancement.

18. General-major ranks above a general and is the second highest rank in Algeria. The highest is general of the army corps, a rank awarded only to Mohamed Lamari.

19. *Le Matin,* 14 December 2002.

20. The army said it objected to the president trying to build a network based on regional affiliations. Both candidates for defense came from the town of Nedroma in Tlemcen, the province from which Bouteflika's family hailed.

21. The Concorde Civile is a law ratified in a 1999 referendum. It foresaw a treaty with armed groups that put down their weapons and amnesty, probation, or mild punishment for members of these groups (depending on their individual actions).

22. A case in point is the privatization of state-owned industries, where intraelite struggles presented a major obstacle to this process. See Werenfels, "Obstacles to Privatization."

23. In April 2001 the brutal killing of a young Kabyle in a gendarmerie station in Kabylia sparked uprisings and riots in the entire region. More than one hundred Kabyle youth were shot dead by security forces. These events led to the emergence of a protest movement with coherent political demands. Demonstrations, riots, and sit-ins were still taking place in Kabylia as of early 2003.

24. Karabadji, "L'économie algérienne"; Tlemcani, *Etat, bazar et globalisation.*

25. *Le Matin,* 7 September 2002, and 14 December 2002.

26. Another part of the army's public relations campaign was an October 2002 international symposium on terrorism at which several generals for the first time talked publicly about the confrontations with the Islamists, trying to justify army policies.

27. See *Le Matin,* 22 December 2002.

28. Benflis's relations with the most politically relevant generals were reputed to be better than Bouteflika's relations with them, making Benflis a possible army candidate and Bouteflika competitor in the 2004 presidential race. This was rumored to have caused friction between Bouteflika and Benflis.

29. These were the Senate, installed in 1997, and the Assemblée Populaire Nationale.

30. Bouteflika surrounded himself with close to thirty advisors, most formally appointed, several, including his two brothers, brought in informally, with a majori-

ty coming from western Algeria. With the formally nominated advisors having status equal to that of ministers, it could be argued that Bouteflika formed a shadow cabinet, based on primordial (familial, tribal, or regional) ties and consisting of some of his advisors and some members of the official cabinet.

31. For more on the co-optation of MSP, see Hamladji, "Cooptation, Repression and an Authoritarian Regime's Survival."

32. Elite profiles and recruitment dynamics in the upper echelons of the public administration did not differ much from those in the government. The transition from the revolutionary generation to the second generation was ongoing, and recruitment similarly personalized. Historic, regional, and family capital as well as competence was also important.

33. There were also women—for example, Khalida Messaoudi, information and culture minister and government spokesperson—but they represented exceptions to the rule.

34. Nedroma has been producing national elites for decades (see Gilbert Grandguillaume, *Nédroma: l'évolution d'une médina*), but after the arrival of Bouteflika it was possible to speak of a powerful "Nedroma clan."

35. The MALG was the predecessor of the Sécurité Militaire and continued to constitute an important network. Of the roughly 500 "Malgache" alive in 2002, six were generals, three ministers, a number were ambassadors, and one was the powerful governor of Algiers.

36. L'association des Ulamas d'Algérie, a force during the early days of the independence struggle, lost political importance after independence but remained an important solidarity network. See M. Haddab, "Pour une approche structurale du champ des élites en Algérie" (unpublished paper, University of Algiers, 2000).

37. Nuisance power refers to the ability to be a thorn in the side of the core elite and thus influence certain of their decisions.

38. It involved allowing foreign companies to become majority stockholders in hydrocarbon exploitation, something hitherto reserved for the state company, Sonatrach.

39. The first draft of the proposed 2003 finance law heavily favored large importers.

40. See *Le Monde*, 1 March 2003 and 21 March 2003. This son of a former minister and Malgache moved within seven years from owner of a pharmacy to head of Algeria's largest business empire, which included a private bank and an airline. See *Le Nouvel Observateur*, 18 July 2002.

41. The term *famille révolutionnaire* was coined by Zeroual in the mid-1990s in an effort to rally all non-Islamist forces under an umbrella of nationalism and homage to the revolution.

42. Among these privileges were a yearly pension of between 92,000 DA ($1,196) and 620,000 DA ($8,065), a right to a duty-free car import, and, until the 1990s, the right to a taxi license.

43. *Le Quotidien d'Oran*, 20 April 2002.

44. Roy, "Patronage and Solidarity Groups."

45. Many of the large Algerian NGOs fell into what Sheila Carapico calls GO-NGOs, or government-organized NGOs. See Carapico, "NGOs, INGOs, GO-NGOs and DO-NGOs."

46. These parties, for instance, forced onto the agenda the sensitive issue of the missing (Islamists) of the civil war.

47. Hachemaoui, "La représentation politique en Algérie," presents an excellent analysis of what he terms "jeu social," that is, the logics of identification, solidarity ties, strategies, and modes of representation of actors.

48. See, for instance, François Gèze, "Algérie, la violence d'état reste aux commandes," *Politis,* 20 December 2001.

49. *Arouch* means "tribes" in Maghrebi Arabic and is used also to refer to specific traditional forms of social organization at the local level.

50. The CADC was an umbrella organization consisting of different local and regional committees, including revitalized (or reinvented) traditional village committees as well as newer urban neighborhood and administrative district committees.

51. Had the state refused to do so, it would have further reduced the ruling elites' legitimacy and raised (repression) costs for the state.

52. This platform, made public in June 2001, consisted of fifteen demands—some political, some economic, some cultural—which, if applied in their entirety, would have implied a change in the rules of domination.

53. Many young Berbers viewed someone like the thirty-something Belaid Abrika, one of the CADC's imprisoned leaders, as more capable at enunciating their socioeconomic and political discontent and championing their identity claims than such political players as the twice-as-old FFS leader Hocine Ait-Ahmed, who lived in Switzerland in exile and was considered to belong to the political establishment.

54. FIS's demands in some respects, such as those concerning the departure of incumbent elites and socioeconomic justice, were similar to those of the CADC.

55. Until the late 1990s journalists were killed (by whom is not always clear) and after that regularly harassed and jailed. Investigating embezzlement and links between business and terrorism, especially on the local level, was extremely dangerous (see *Liberté,* 23 July 2002). Also, there was indirect intervention in advertising by state enterprises. Moreover, many newspapers were "private" rather than "independent," because their owners had ties to décideurs, and each paper ran relentless campaigns against the foes of its patrons.

56. It is, however, highly unlikely that the press was acting entirely on its own. Rather, it was used by Betchine's foes to dispose of him.

57. Souaidia, *La sale guerre.* For a décideur's account of the violence in the 1990s and the court case, see Nezzar and Maarfia, *Un procès pour la vérite.*

58. This is obvious from long-term analysis of the media and was confirmed in interviews with journalists in this situation.

59. One example was the RND-backed Association Algérienne pour la Promotion de la Citoyenneté et les Droits de l'Homme (founded in 2002), which had no interest in defending Islamists.

60. The Algerian décideurs dismissed the mediation as outside intervention.

61. For a definition of rentier states and mechanisms of distribution, see Luciani, "Allocation vs. Production States."

62. *Le Matin,* 25 and 26 January 2002.

63. The increasing involvement of such international governmental and nongovernmental institutions as the National Democracy Institute (in Washington, D.C.) and German political foundations supporting regime and opposition forces tended to enforce rather than counter core elite policies and is worth being studied in depth.

64. Mannheim, *Essays on the Sociology of Knowledge,* p. 309.

65. Burton and Higley, "The Study of Political Elite Transformations."

66. Harbi, *Une vie debout,* p. 328. See also ibid., and Quandt, *Revolution and Political Leadership,* for political socialization, trajectories, and ideal types in the different (age) groups within what are here somewhat crudely referred to as the generation of the revolution and the older and younger brothers.

67. Because scholarships were given by various ministries as well as enter-

prises, such as Sonatrach, it was difficult to obtain absolute numbers. Entelis, "Technocratic Rule, Military Power," p. 104, speaks of 2,500 Algerian students in 1977–1978 at U.S. colleges alone, most of whom can be assumed to have had state scholarships.

68. Zartman, "Algeria: A Post-Revolutionary Elite," p. 279.

69. Boudiaf was killed by one of his security guards. An official inquiry concluded that the killer had acted alone on behalf of Islamists. Boudiaf's family claimed (and most Algerians believed) that he was killed by "the generals," among other things because of his inquiries into their corruption networks.

70. *Le Quotidien d'Oran*, 17 December 2002.

71. As Harbi, *Une vie debout*, and others have noted, many of the revolution's leaders came from privileged families, that is, social elites under colonialism.

72. Cadres of independent unions, for example, the Syndicat Autonome des Personnels de l'Administration Publique (SNAPAP), were only temporarily able to enter the politically relevant elite. Even though these unions were barred from certain sectors, including the state economic sector, and though the UGTA remained the government's prime and often sole interlocutor, their membership rolls and popular support continued to rise, and their young, dynamic cadres managed to put issues neglected by the UGTA and its organizations on the public agenda.

73. Bourdieu, *La réproduction.*

74. Entelis, "Algeria: Technocratic Rule, Military Power," p. 111.

75. Mannheim, *Essays on the Sociology of Knowledge*, pp. 305–312.

76. These included political socialization, perceptions of the country's problems, attitudes vis-à-vis the above-mentioned three strategic issues—market and education sector reforms as well as democratization—as well as economic, social, and cultural factors that shaped elite behavior.

77. Based on interviews with members of the PRE born after 1960.

78. By October 2002, of three members of the UNJA executive interviewed in April 2002, one was an advisor to a minister, one was president of the council for a large Algiers neighborhood, and one had managed to get reelected to parliament even though more than 80 percent of former MPs were not reelected.

79. Several nationalist reformers interviewed showed great respect for such authoritarian leaders as South Korea's Gen. Park Chung Hee and Tunisia's Zine al-Abidine Ben Ali, who managed to push through economic reforms and lead their countries to (relative) prosperity.

80. Hachemaoui, "La représentation politique en Algérie," offers an outstanding account of such giving and taking, based on a microanalysis of transactions between individual actors, party apparatuses, intermediaries, formal and informal, local and central authorities during election campaigns.

81. Chabal and Daloz, *Africa Works: Disorder as Political Instrument*, p. 148.

82. See ibid., note 4, and Higley and Gunther, *Elites and Democratic Consolidation.*

83. A marabout is a local religious leader to whom supernatural powers are ascribed.

84. For the centrality of the sentiment of honor in Kabyle social organization, see Bourdieu, "The Sentiment of Honour."

85. "On y trouve des rapports de pouvoir et d'influence où se mêlent relations personnelles, liens familiaux et régionaux. Il s'agit moins de rapports purement politiques que de rapports communautaires exprimés dans un langage moderne." Harbi, *Une vie debout*, p. 207.

86. *North Africa Journal*, 2 December 2002.

87. When these networks were in danger of collapsing because of low oil prices, IMF intervention and debt rescheduling in 1994 rescued the system and allowed continued distribution to regime-supporting segments of society.

88. According to "Algeria's Economy: The Vicious Circle of Oil and Violence," *ICG Africa Report,* October 2001, up to 800,000 Algerians were estimated to profit from patronage systems (though not all necessarily are linked to the oil rent). Algerian scholars and elites interviewed by this author, however, estimated these figures to be much higher.

89. M. R. Lowi, "Algeria, 1992–2002: Toward a Political Economy of Violence" (manuscript on file, 2002), convincingly argues that oil has raised the stakes of fighting between incumbent elites and Islamist insurgents and has thus contributed to prolonging the civil war.

90. O' Donnell, Schmitter, and Whitehead, eds. *Transitions from Authoritarian Rule,* pp. 37–38.

91. For ways in which market reforms have done this, see Werenfels, "Obstacles to Privatization."

92. Most members of the young elite seemed convinced that violence in the form of popular uprisings rather than negotiations would lead to system change.

93. Quandt, "Algeria's Uneasy Peace," p. 20.

8

Tunisia:
Economic Transformation and Political Restoration

Steffen Erdle

"President-for-Life" Habib Bourguiba's ouster by his prime minister, Zine El Abidine Ben Ali, on 7 November 1987 was Tunisia's first change at the helm of state since independence from France in 1956 and the abolition of the monarchy in 1957.[1] The putsch happened at a moment when the country appeared on the verge of collapse, staggering between a deep economic recession and quickly escalating conflicts that pitted Habib Bourguiba's increasingly paralyzed regime against Rachid Ghannouchi's increasingly assertive Islamic Tendency Movement (MTI). Finally, when it appeared that this crisis might bring down the entire system, members of the political elite under the leadership of Ben Ali decided to forestall a revolt from below by reforming the system from above—which necessitated the removal of Bourguiba. Consequently, the new rulers promised not only to restore law and order, but also to enhance public liberties and political participation commensurate with the country's relatively advanced social development and "political maturity."[2]

The ensuing years took a different turn: Ben Ali has not only successfully consolidated his newly acquired position, he has also substantially reconstructed the former Bourguibist system. After a liberal intermezzo of three years, he switched to a two-track strategy of repression and reform, reasserting state power while gradually opening up the Tunisian economy. At the same time, he began rejuvenating the regime's political personnel and reshuffling the underlying social coalition in a way that would allow him to replace useless elements and potential rivals by more qualified and reliable people. In doing so, he preserved the main political institutions, such as the hegemonic ruling party and the overpowering central state, but superimposed on them a full-fledged presidential *makhzan,* which also includes the different security services and important business representatives.[3]

Therefore, Ben Ali's "New Tunisia" provides an excellent example of the successful adaptation of an authoritarian system to a changed environment. This transformation process is characterized by three features: it has been selective (limited to the economic sphere and adjacent sectors); incremental (controlled at every stage by the regime authorities); and conservative (designed to maintain the system and the prerogatives of the rulers). Elite change has played a key role in the success of this strategy.

The aim of this chapter is to explain why elite change has not led to system change, why economic liberalization has not taken on a political dimension, and whether the outcomes are contradictory or complementary. To do so, it will focus on three main questions: (1) What is the actual relationship between Tunisia's political system, elite circulation patterns, and public policy choices? (2) Was it new challenges and new agendas that triggered elite change and pushed the current incumbents, or was it rather the other way round? (3) Was it some sort of "path dependency"—a specific institutional heritage and specific organizational structures, which have dominated both the input and the output side—that set "action corridors" no political actor could afford to ignore?

I will first summarize how the political system in general and the New Regime in particular have evolved, which parameters are guiding political action, and which factors have triggered elite change. Then, I will analyze how the politically relevant elites[4] have changed under Ben Ali, locating them in three circles: the first for the ruling elite, the second for executive and intermediary elites, and the third for implementing and contesting elites. Afterwards I will look at their specific attitudes vis-à-vis strategic questions, focusing on three fields: home affairs, external relations, and economic policies. Finally, I will put my findings in a broader context, trying to find out whether intraelite and state-society relations have also changed, what distinguishes the new order from the old regime, and how Ben Ali has managed to defuse the system crisis.

Setting the Stage: Tunisian Politics, 1956–2003

The Crisis of Bourguibism

After independence, Tunisia was ruled by an elite who had arisen from the national resistance movement dominated by the Neo-Destour Party ("constitution" in Arabic), founded in 1934 by Bourguiba himself. Most members of this elite shared background, upbringing, and outlook: most came from the emerging petty bourgeoisie of the eastern coastal provinces and had received a secular education in a Francophone environment. Upon coming to power, they quickly moved to exclude military and religious elites from political decisionmaking, while relegating labor and business elites to subordinate positions.[5]

This new elite would occupy the leading positions in all those organizations that were to play a key role in political life: The first was a strong state bureaucracy, already created under the Husaynid rulers in the nineteenth century and further strengthened during the French mandate between 1881–1956. The second was the all-encompassing ruling party, which, effectively monopolizing political power after 1956, would finally become the only party after 1963. The third were the *associations nationales*, corporatist organizations that were to co-opt the population along functional lines and provide support for government policies. The most important were the General Union of Tunisian Workers (UGTT); the Tunisian Union of Industrialists, Merchants, and Artisans (UTICA); the Tunisian Union of Farmers and Fishermen (UTAP); the National Union of Tunisian Women (UNFT); and the General Union of Tunisian Students (UGET).[6]

The outcome was a "party state–state party" complex in which the upper echelons of public administration would be filled with party members, while the leading bodies of the ruling party would be taken over by government representatives.[7] At the apex of this pyramid-like system sat President Bourguiba, who, being the head of state, chairman of the party, and commander in chief of the armed forces, would soon become the supreme decisionmaker and uncontested political arbiter.[8] Consequently, Habib Bourguiba once quipped to a journalist, "The system? What system? I am the system."[9]

However, the glaring failure of the collectivist experiment between 1961–1969 (the Neo-Destour Party was renamed the Destourian Socialist Party, or PSD, in 1964) was a severe blow for Habib Bourguiba. In fact, it was not only a key government strategy that had failed, but an entire regime type—the state elites' bold attempt to systematically and autonomously modernize and transform industrial production and social relations at large.

Bourguiba, however, managed to weather the crisis and maintain his position with the help of a two-track strategy. On the one hand, he switched to a mixed economy, combining central planning and market mechanisms. Although public companies would continue to occupy center stage, private operators were encouraged to assume a larger role. On the other hand, he streamlined the regime institutions, purging them of both liberals and leftists. He would later rely increasingly on techno-bureaucrats in central government—preferably recruited from his native province, the Sahel, and particularly from his home town Monastir.

However, this pyramid-shaped, top-heavy system was too insulated and inflexible to absorb a rapidly growing number of highly educated youths, and to accommodate the widely diverging interests of an increasingly complex society, both being direct results of the regime's economic and educational policies. In other words, it could neither produce growth

rates commensurate with demographic developments, nor provide participatory opportunities commensurate with political demands.

Even though it appears at first glance that the above-mentioned crisis
was triggered by an unfortunate combination of unfavorable circumstances—deteriorating exchange rates, plummeting oil prices, and several
bad harvests—a closer look reveals that it was caused by the fundamental
structural deficits and disruptive effects of a specific system type and
regime strategy: The "political contract" of the postindependence period
foresaw that the state would temporarily monopolize power in exchange for
public welfare and material opportunities for everyone. At some point
between the mid-1970s and mid-1980s, however, it became obvious that
only a small segment had really benefited from these arrangements, that the
large majority would further be excluded from social advancement, and—
worse—that the political framework would not allow this situation to be
rectified. In other words, the Bourguibist elites were no longer able to reconcile their emancipatory, inclusivist, meritocratic ideology with their
authoritarian, exclusivist, and particularistic governance.

The Evolution of the New Regime

The New Regime's life can be divided into three stages. The first, or liberal, phase, which lasted until 1989–1990, witnessed a careful opening of the
political system and a gradual overhauling of regime institutions. Exiles
were invited to return home, scores of detainees were released, and discredited institutions such as the State Security Court and the Public Prosecutor
were scrapped. The PSD was renamed the Constitutional Democratic Rally
(RCD), electing Ben Ali as its new leader; opposition parties were legalized, with the exception of those organized along religious, linguistic, ethnic, or regional lines or those that did not subscribe to "national accomplishments" and "human rights"; and the presidency-for-life was abolished,
with the head of state limited to no more than three consecutive terms of
five years each until the age of seventy.[10]

At the same time, the new rulers continued the economic restructuring
and structural adjustment agreement that their predecessors had signed in
1986 with the Bretton Woods institutions in exchange for financial assistance. It contained the usual policy package known as the "Washington
Consensus": stabilization of public spending, exchange rates, and balance-
of-payment-flows; liberalization of foreign trade; deregulation of market
controls; plus the start of a privatization program.

In November 1988 all of Tunisia's political forces, including the MTI,
came together to sign a national pact that was expected to consecrate the
ahd jadîd ("New Era" or "New Covenant") inaugurated by Ben Ali. It contained a detailed policy package, which covered everything from national

identity and home affairs to economic policy and external relations, and to which all political forces had to agree if they wanted to obtain legal status.[11]

The elections of 1989 marked the end of this honeymoon.[12] The MTI, after renaming itself the Renaissance Party (to comply with the new party law), was disappointed by the regime's refusal to grant it legal status, yet emboldened by the landslide victory of the Algerian Islamic Salvation Front (FIS). Unwilling to serve as the regime's fig leaf or to sacrifice its dream of an Islamic state, it openly defied the authorities, riding on anti-Western feelings following the Gulf War. After an Islamist attack on an RCD bureau, the New Regime decided to eliminate its only serious rival, sensing that it enjoyed complete impunity among Western governments at that time. After two years of massive repression, the Islamist movement had been duly knocked out of the political game; its organizations were dismantled, its followers silenced, and its leaders and activists either imprisoned or exiled.

The second, or repressive, phase, which lasted until 1994–1995, thus began with the reassertion of state power and the speeding up of economic restructuring. Having crushed the Islamist movement, Ben Ali began to target the secular opposition, including human rights activists or independent-minded journalists. The situation soon reached the point where any political dissent or independent activity was automatically perceived as a serious challenge and immediately answered with repressive measures.

At the same time, given the profound changes in the external context (such as the EU's eastward enlargement and the conclusion of the Uruguay Round), the new rulers began to transform the state-led, import-substitution economy into a market-driven, export-oriented economy.[13] The country's integration into the global economy, underlined by its accession to the World Trade Organization (WTO) and its participation in the Euro-Mediterranean Partnership (EMP), reached the point of no return when it concluded an association agreement with the European Union that is to lead to a bilateral free trade zone by 2010.[14]

The third, or ongoing, phase is mainly concerned with developing a politically sustainable order that will allow Ben Ali to integrate emerging social forces within the existing institutional arrangements without abandoning ultimate control of political power. The regime's preferred strategy is a state-controlled pluralism: On the one hand, it has granted "constructive" opposition forces disproportionate parliamentary representation (currently 20 percent of all popular assemblies), but on the other hand it has subjugated previously relatively free social spaces (such as mosques and universities) to close state control. Hence, although new opportunities for legal political action were opened at the regime level, old channels for effective political action were closed at the societal level.[15]

A landmark of this system reconfiguration was the successful "deconstruction" of the succession issue and the de facto return to life-long rule in May 2002. A public referendum that yielded the usual 99 percent "yes" votes abolished the constitutional restrictions that prohibited a fourth term for Ben Ali, while raising the maximum age to seventy-five.[16] From a legal point of view, Ben Ali will be able to rule at least until 2014.

Factors of Elite Change

First and foremost it is important to understand that as the only professional military person in an elite composed of civilian politicians and university graduates, Ben Ali had always been an outsider in the Bourguibist establishment.[17] He was not a party man but an army man, whose bases of support were in the Interior Ministry and the security apparatus. Hence, he could not be sure to find the necessary political backing and professional skills within the institutions he had inherited from Bourguiba. Hence, the first factor that triggered elite change was the need to replace the old guard, which was seen as potentially unreliable and discredited, with a new elite that would be sufficiently dependable and competent. They would need to be personally committed to fending off the "Bourguibist stalwarts" (who controlled the party and bureaucracy) and the Islamists (who dominated schools and universities), as well as sufficiently qualified to carry out structural adjustment measures and corresponding administrative reforms.

The second factor was the transformation of the Tunisian economy. Since the early 1970s the economy had been divided into four sectors: an offshore sector totally geared toward external markets and integrated into the world economy; an onshore sector largely protected from foreign competition and regulated by public bodies; a public sector comprised of most capital-intensive and technology-intensive endeavors; and a private sector primarily composed of family enterprises flourishing in some niche markets. This separation between the onshore and offshore sectors persists, as does the juxtaposition of the private and public sectors. Services and manufacturing industries, however, constitute today the backbone of the economy, while agriculture and extractive activities have lost importance. A diversified and vibrant business community has emerged over the past fifteen years that provides a growing share of badly needed employment and investment. At the same time, the state not only continues to have decisive input in Tunisia's economic life—accounting for about 60 percent of gross fixed investment—it has also preserved its former control of strategic sectors, such as the financial sector and public infrastructure. This means that there are a growing number of successful businessmen whom the state needs and courts as partners—while continuing to determine the rules of the game and the terms of the partnership.

The third factor was the expansion of the education system. Beginning in the early 1970s Tunisia's policy was to quickly expand public education by introducing Arabophone curricula at the secondary level, while maintaining Francophone elite schools at the university level. This mix of egalitarianism and elitism, however, systematically penalized young Arab speakers with a rural background, and thus introduced a hidden class and cultural bias in elite production. The New Regime has both continued and modified this policy: It has not only substantially increased public investment for education and research, but also systematically extended higher education to the (poor) interior provinces. Compared with the situation in the past, an ever-increasing number of young Tunisians are able to get a university diploma, which still is the condition sine qua non for elite status. At the same time, it has exacerbated the dual character of the education system, introducing the state elite schools at the high school level while establishing legal equality for private ventures. This means that in spite of enhanced educational access and improved literacy rates, the built-in dichotomy between Arabophone facilities for the rank-and-file and Francophone institutes for the chosen few has actually increased.

The New Faces of Tunisian Elites

How have these developments modified power relations and circulation patterns among the Tunisian PRE?[18] To illustrate, the PRE can be positioned in three concentric circles according to their respective influence on political decisions.[19] The first, or inner, circle is composed of the ruling elite—those people who occupy top or key positions in the state and party apparatuses. They have the last word on strategic issues of national relevance—that is, they alone have the power to make or veto decisions in any field. The second circle is made up of the main executive and intermediary elites—that is, the upper ranks of the state bureaucracy, the ruling party, and the public sector, as well as the leading figures in the national associations, the labor unions, and the business community. They play important roles in the implementation of public policy and the maintenance of political power. They may have a substantial influence on strategic decisions, though mostly concerning technical questions in their particular field. The third circle is composed of implementing elites—that is, the midlevel of the groups mentioned before—but also of contesting elites—to be found in independent NGOs and opposition parties. Although they have no chance of vetoing decisions or seizing power, they may nonetheless have an indirect impact through their "nuisance power." Moreover, they often reflect frictions and cleavages within society or the regime that would otherwise be invisible to outsiders, particularly foreigners.

The First Circle: The Ruling or Core Elite

Under the New Regime, real power gradually, but steadily, shifted from the formal political institutions in the capital to the rather informal structures around the president. Therefore, the core elite occupying the first circle is basically tantamount to the three strands of the presidential sphere: the "palace," the "lieutenants," and the "entourage." The palace is Ben Ali's two-tiered personal apparatus in the suburb of Cartage that comprises administrative services, comparable to a normal ministry and concerned with day-to-day tasks, and a small group of political advisors, composed mostly of former ministers and senior officials, but also close friends and family members. In fact, the palace has grown so much in size and power that it has become the country's actual government and an unrivaled power center.

The lieutenants are Ben Ali's personal nominees first and foremost in the "power ministries" (in particular, home affairs, foreign affairs, social affairs, international cooperation, and other economy-related portfolios) and the RCD Politburo (currently sixteen members). Particularly the security apparatus (*mukhabarat* in Arabic), which is made up of various competing secret services, has virtually become a "state within the state," employing 150,000 to 200,000 people and supporting up to 10 percent of the country's population.

The entourage includes all those people related to or affiliated with the president and his wife, essentially hailing from five clans: the brothers and sisters of Ben Ali himself; the brothers and sisters of his second wife, Leila Trabelsi; and the families married to his three daughters—the Chiboubs, Mabrouks, and Zarrouks. This is only the tip of the iceberg, however, since all persons that have managed to marry into these clans are also considered presidential relatives—for example Hedi Djilani, UTICA president and the father-in-law of Hassan Trabelsi, the eldest brother of Leila Trabelsi.

The first circle thus comprises the leading representatives of central government who control all subordinate or attached bodies at the national and regional levels, as well as a small number of powerful families who do not need formal positions to exert substantial influence. Core elite status accordingly consists of two different dimensions: one that is accessible to all political elites and one that is reserved for family members. Participants hedge their bets not only by accumulating positions in various sectors of the political system (for instance, many cabinet members also preside over party structures), but also by employing traditional means of social advancement (for example, prominent politicians marrying into business clans and vice versa). The final outcome is an intertwined elite held together not only by political or institutional affiliations, but also by interpersonal and primordial ties.[20]

Because of limited resources and numerous candidates, Ben Ali relies on a politically tried-and-true method that maximizes the possibilities of rewarding followers and minimizes the danger of breeding rivals: the "musical chairs" approach. Through regular cabinet shuffles and party congresses, the ruling elite (and the political elites at large) continuously circles the regime core, usually without being in too long, but also without being out forever. Normally, first-circle members are at some point detailed to an embassy abroad, an international organization, or a public enterprise, while particularly promising second-circle elements are selected from among party members and state officials. The outcome of this process is a replenishable pool from which regime-level command positions are filled.[21]

All in all, Ben Ali has both continued and modified recruitment practices of the old regime. He has completed the replacement of politicians with technocrats (a process that started in the 1970s), that is, people who are able to offer the necessary professional experiences or technical skills rather than representing specific political agendas or social groups. In doing so, he has given preference to outsiders and newcomers, that is, people who had been underrepresented in or excluded from decisionmaking during Bourguiba's rule. This means the members of the postindependence generation, who occupied middle management positions in the late Bourguibist period; women, whom Bourguiba and his collaborators saw as legally equal but not politically employable; and people from the interior provinces, who were distrusted and despised by Sahelis and Tunisois alike.[22]

Within the core elite, three profiles stand out: security experts, economic experts, and administrative experts. The first type is represented by Abdallah Kallel, a well-known regime hardliner and since 2001 Ben Ali's security advisor (and the RCD's treasurer); and Ali Chaouch, Kallel's successor at the Interior Ministry and since 2001 the secretary-general of the ruling party. The second type is exemplified by Mohamed Ghannouchi, the main architect of the economic reforms and since 1999 Ben Ali's prime minister; and Mohamed Nouri Jouini, formerly Ben Ali's economic advisor and since 2002 the person responsible for economic development and international cooperation. Among the administrative experts, one finds trained lawyers and university professors, including Abdelaziz Ben Dhia, since 1999 Ben Ali's special advisor and thus the regime's de facto number two, and Abdelwahhab Abdallah, since 1987 Ben Ali's spokesman and formerly Bourguiba's information minister.

This new elite of apolitical technocrats and social upstarts offer Ben Ali two distinct advantages. They have the qualifications necessary to execute the presidential directives and consolidate the regime's power, while lacking a power base that would enable them to lead a political life of their own, let alone challenge the head of state. They are a "dream team" whose members are as dependable as they are disposable.

The Second Circle: Executive and Intermediary Elites

Under Ben Ali, "Tunis," that is, the ruling party and ministerial bureaucracy, has clearly lost ground to "Cartage," that is, the palace and the presidency. While the government has been pruned into an implementing organ exercising tangible influence mostly on "technical matters," the RCD has become a presidential party dedicated to an individual rather than to an ideology. Whereas cabinet members and party bosses were major power brokers and well-known public figures during the Bourguiba era, they are now little more than amplifiers and implementers of decisions made elsewhere. The main loser has been the prime minister, who, instead of acting as the official crown prince, has been downgraded to a mere government coordinator.[23]

Although the state administration continues to employ a sizable percentage of the working population, only a small part of it can claim elite status. These are mostly members of central government, the upper echelons of the ministerial bureaucracy, and the leading ranks of regional administration. Among cabinet members, one often finds the same profiles as in the first circle, a clear indication of Ben Ali's efforts to groom a shadow elite that may become the next generation of the New Regime. In particular, the cabinet shuffles since January 2001 have brought in a new generation of highly qualified but completely unknown technocrats who hold the less important portfolios or who sit in junior ministerial positions.[24]

As a general rule, all civil servants have to pass a public exam called the *concours*. Given the elitist nature of the education system, the large majority of successful candidates are graduates either from the state's administrative academy (École Nationale d'Administration, ENA) or from a *grande école* (mainly the engineering schools). However, it seems that a thin line separates professional appointments from political appointments. The former, which concern most positions in the state bureaucracy, are filled through these public competitions, which means that, as a general rule, having a university diploma and being a party member is sufficient to make an applicant competitive. In contrast, the latter, which begin above the position of director, are filled through ministerial decrees, which means that a long record of RCD membership and close ties to the core elite are essential.[25]

Although the ruling party claims almost two million adherents, or onefifth of the total population, only a chosen few of its members belong to the second circle. These include the leading ranks of the party's central bureaucracy, the 236 members of the Central Committee, and the secretaries-general of the coordination committees at the regional level. According to party accounts, recruitment campaigns have focused on three groups: the young, women, and academics. This is reflected in the socioprofessional makeup of the current Central Committee: 90 percent have a university diploma, 20 percent are women, 65 percent are under the age of fifty-five.

The recruitment pattern that Ben Ali has adopted for the RCD allows him to strike a balance between assuring control from above while allowing input from below. He appoints the upper ranks of the party headquarter and roughly one-third of the Central Committee (with cabinet members, provincial governors, and the heads of the national associations being ex officio members). The other Central Committee members are elected every five years by the party congress, whereas the regional party secretaries are selected by Politburo members from among local candidates.

In any case, it is striking that both the state bureaucracy and the ruling party have been eager to set up their own in-house elite schools from which they recruit for their respective upper and middle management. Among them, the most important are the ENA and the RCD's Académie Politique, whose main task is to spot and train "high potentials" among the young generation, to provide them with modern leadership skills, and to arouse in them the necessary esprit de corps.

In spite of liberalization, the public sector continues to play a leading role as a producer, an employer, an investor, and a manager. Hence, most extractive companies remain in state hands, as do strategic economic assets such as public infrastructure providers and key financial institutions. Major power shifts, however, have taken place within the overall institutional context. "Facilitators," export and investment-promoting agencies, have gained ground over "regulators," purely administrative or redistributive bodies. Generally speaking, the public sector continues to serve as a cash cow and a parking lot for regime elites insofar as all executive positions are still staffed by top politicians and senior officials.

Although Ben Ali has succeeded in firmly reasserting his authority over the ruling party and state bureaucracy, he still cannot do without their support. The ruling party, with its eight thousand branches, is still the main link between the ruling elite and Tunisian society. Compared to it, other representative bodies such as the National Assembly and the national organizations are only of secondary importance. Although its importance in decisionmaking and strategic planning has waned, its centrality in providing "political education" and ensuring social co-optation has grown. By the same token, the public sector, with its almost one million employees, remains the primary channel for upward mobility for ordinary citizens. In fact, the current trend among the Tunisian bourgeoisie to reorient themselves or their children toward a business career appears to involve only those who possess the necessary amounts of physical or social capital.

The economic opening of the past decade and the ensuing transformation of Tunisian society at large have also affected the social allies of the ruling elite. The private sector has been considerably strengthened vis-à-vis the labor unions in regard to political leverage and social prestige. At the same time, the power relations have not only changed between both camps, but also within them. New forces within the business community, such as the manufacturing industry, export companies, and consulting firms, have increasingly sidelined traditional components of the regime coalition, such as small firms, merchants, and artisans.[26]

Although business in general has gained, however, it is only a small number of industrial groups that really matter. Each of them is simultaneously involved in numerous activities across the economic spectrum and is run by a single family, usually with close ties to the ruling elite. Even though most of them had emerged before 1987, a few newcomers, mainly from the presidential entourage, have joined their ranks under the New Regime.

This industrial bourgeoisie has become a major pillar of the New Regime and the main winner in economic liberalization. It not only effectively controls the economy's most profitable sectors, but has also practically pocketed UTICA's leading bodies. This is evidenced by the fall 2001 elections for UTICA's national council, which witnessed a spectacular breakthrough of these so-called captains.

Today, two organizations claim to represent the private sector: UTICA, which is generally seen as a state body and is run by Hedi Djilani, a wealthy textile manufacturer and a presidential relative; and the newly created Institut Arabe des Chefs d'Entreprise (IACE), which is open only to large companies and is led by Chakib Nouira, the son of former prime minister Hedi Nouira and CEO of the main private bank BIAT.

On the contrary, the labor unions have been severely affected by the changing international environment and the new government policies. Since public sector employees traditionally comprise their social base, the twin processes of globalization and privatization have continuously undermined their position both vis-à-vis the regime and the population at large. This "stagrosion"—stagnation and erosion—at the leadership and membership levels is evident in that the UGTT's leading bodies continue to be governed by the old-school "labor bosses," who mostly belong to the two postindependence generations, come from the southeastern provinces, and have a background in the public sector.

Particularly under Ismail Sahbani's leadership (1988–2000), the once-powerful labor unions effectively became a regime satellite, with the effect that debate was controlled or suppressed and critics silenced or expelled.

Since his fall from power in 2000—he had described himself as the regime's "No. 2" and was rumored to nurture political ambitions—the headquarter has lost part of its power. In the first democratic elections ever held by an official regime institution, some opponents have made their way back into the executive committee, while a third movement is struggling for a democratic renewal outside the official structures. Hence, although most old leaders have finally been able to weather this crisis, the current heated debates among union activists about whether to return to politics or even side with the opposition show that the outcome of this process is far from certain.

Generally, UTICA differs from the UGTT insofar as it has managed to renew and reinvent itself, that is, to attract a new generation of private entrepreneurs and to transform itself into an influential actor in the reform process. Its success is not only due to a radically different context, but also to direct regime intervention. Although both Djilani and Sahbani were the president's lieutenants in their respective organizations, their missions were quite different: Whereas the former was supposed to reconstruct UTICA, to instill a corporate identity in the private sector, and to assist the public authorities in the country's economic overhaul, the latter was tasked with deconstructing the UGTT, purging it of opponents of the regime and keeping workers out of politics.[27]

It is obvious, however, that organized lobbies in general and the private sector in particular have neither dared nor bothered to become real players in political life (let alone a counterweight to regime authorities). Although businessmen have adopted a more self-conscious, proactive attitude and exert more influence "upstream" (in decisionmaking) and "downstream" (in policy implementation), they still fall short of the traditional "red lines," such as questioning the regime's strategic decisions or political monopoly. "The regime," writes Eva Bellin, "is not willing to permit the translation of economic clout into contestatory power. Yet, economic power does confer some political influence for private sector entrepreneurs, but only in the sense of winning them access to state elites. Successful entrepreneurs may consult with the regime, even criticize regime policies, but only *doucement* [softly] and *entre amis* [among friends]. The moment criticism is expressed as a public challenge the state perceives this as a test of force and brings all its strength to bear to quash it."[28]

The Third Circle: Implementing and Contesting Elites

Implementing elites comprise the second and third tiers of the above-mentioned organizations. They include the middle echelons of the state bureaucracy and ruling party, most members of the national assemblies and professional associations, and leading figures in the media and propaganda apparatus. They are mainly tasked with carrying out the instructions of their superiors, whom they influence to a very limited extent and only in very indirect ways.

Contesting elites are those people who refuse to join regime institutions or who choose to oppose regime policies. In Tunisia, they are traditionally composed of "outsiders" or "dropouts," that is, all those who have lost ideological conflicts at the regime level or distributive conflicts at the societal level. These "losers" would either go on to set up their own parties—as did Ahmad Ben Salah's Popular Unity Movement (MUP) on the far left, and Ahmad Mestiri's Democratic Socialist Movement (MDS) in the social-democratic mainstream—or fall back on existing social organizations, mainly UGET and UGTT, with the aim of turning them into a weapon against the regime. Since 1987 they have split into those who have organized as formal political parties and those who have preferred to act within more informal arrangements.[29]

Opposition parties basically comprise two camps: those who enjoy official status and parliamentary quotas—such as the cooperative branch of the MDS, the Popular Unity Party (PUP), and the Renewal Movement (the latter two collaborative offsprings of the MUP and the Tunisian Communist Party [PCT]), as well as the Unionist Democratic Union and the Social Liberal Party (creations of the regime itself); and those who continue to be outlawed and persecuted, such as Rachid Ghannouchi's MTI, Hamma Hammami's Communist Party of Tunisian Workers (POCT), and Moncef Marzouki's Republican Congress. Somewhere in between are Ahmed Nejib Chebbi's Progressive Democratic Party and Mustapha Ben Jaafar's Democratic Forum for Work and Liberty, which have both received recognition but are not represented in parliament, probably because they are perceived as still being too critical.

At this stage, the *illegal* opposition has lost most of its political clout; they have either been forced to operate exclusively from Europe or to proceed with extreme caution within Tunisia. At the same time, the *legal* parties have lost most of their popular support; they have shrunk to primarily intellectual audiences of the few big cities and sometimes of the capital alone. In fact, some of them are so entrenched in the political system that they have become comparable to the "bloc parties" in some communist systems. The outcome has been paradoxical: for the first time, there is an opposition that is legally recognized and institutionally represented, but at the same time it has much less latitude and leverage than it did under Bourguiba. Since legal opposition parties can currently no longer be considered effective political players, once again organized social lobbies have become the regime's main adversaries.

Civil society also consists of two camps: those that deal exclusively with one-dimensional, mostly nonpolitical (charitable, cultural, sports, etc.)

activities, such as the national organizations and most recently founded nongovernmental organizations; and those that work on general activities, including political issues such as the Tunisian League for Human Rights (LTDH), the National Council for Liberty in Tunisia, and the Tunisian Association of Democratic Women.

The overwhelming majority belongs to the first category. They have either been created or co-opted from above, charged with taking over certain state tasks or skimming off foreign development assistance, which means they are either pure state subsidiaries or have parastatal functions. Only a tiny minority belongs to the second category. They continue to be impeded or oppressed, mostly dating back to Bourguiba's time or the early days of the New Regime, an indicator that they represent the "real" civil society and verge on being political proto parties.

A new segment that falls somewhere in-between the above groupings is small-scale political entrepreneurs. Good examples for this category are Rachid Driss, founder of the Tunisian Association for International Studies; Abdeljelil Temimi, founder of the Temimi Foundation for Historical Studies; Taieb Zahar, director of the bilingual magazine *Réalités/Haqâ'iq;* and Hachemi Hamdi, director of the London-based television channel al-Mustaqilla. Although they have highly diverse social backgrounds and political outlooks (some being basically inclined toward the regime, others rather opposed to it), they have one thing in common: They have used new technologies (such as the Internet and satellite television) or their own "social capital" (consisting of prestige, in the case of a notable family like the Temimis, and connections, in the case of a former ambassador like Driss) to carve out a niche for themselves where they might have a relatively free discussion on political questions that are normally considered sensitive or taboo.

Another group whose position is somewhat unclear are former notable families. These families—such as the Ben Achours, the Charfis, and the Zghals, to name but a few—which dominated religious institutions and cultural life in the pre-Bourguibist era, have produced a considerable number of critical intellectuals and regime opponents since 1956 and particularly since 1987. It seems that they were never able to stomach the authoritarianism of the Bourguibist regime and their marginalization by the Sahelian newcomers. Thus, many of them continue do to what they had done before—maintain a critical distance from the political leaders or enter into open conflict with them.

It should not be assumed, however, that the political opposition and the civil society are entirely powerless. In fact, they have managed on a number of occasions to put the regime on the defensive, and even make it backtrack on some decisions. These results, however, were not achieved because of their organizational resources or mass support, but rather because of their mobilization of outside support. The most effective strategy has been attention-grabbing events, such as hunger strikes that are reported by the Western media. That people resort to these kinds of actions illustrates not only the degree to which the system is closed and the opposition is marginalized, but also the degree to which the regime is concerned with its international image and dependent on foreign financial inflows.

The Political Agendas of Tunisian Elites

Have PRE political attitudes and interaction patterns also changed? This can be determined by examining their positions on a few strategic issues. In the realm of home affairs, how do they view the basic identity of the body politic and the main rules of the political game? In regard to external relations, how do they envisage Tunisia's position within its regional context as well as its future relations with the European Union? In terms of economic policy, where should the boundaries be drawn between the state and the market, and how should the costs and benefits of liberalization be distributed?

Home Affairs

The first years of the New Regime were overshadowed by a tug-of-war over the polity's cultural parameters that pitted the Islamist movement against the secularist establishment. However, the regime's decision to keep "Islam out of politics" ruled out the slightest possibility of regime change or genuine competition in political life. After that, the new rulers pursued several strategies vis-à-vis the Islamists that went beyond the simple use of force. On the one hand, they sought to buy off moderate elements, particularly among religious scholars and "progressive Islamists," by acting on some of their demands, such as Arabizing public administration and secondary education and enhancing the place of Islam in the state-run media and the school curricula. On the other hand, they struggled to drain the MTI's social and intellectual wells by targeting state support at vulnerable groups and promoting a modernist understanding of Islamic concepts. In fact, the kind of Islam that they attempt to promote is moderate, tolerant, apolitical, and cosmopolitan, compatible not only with the regime's participation in the Barcelona process but also with Tunisia's opening toward the global market.[30]

At the same time, the new leaders have modified their concept of the state as well as the relations it entertained with society. As before, "their" state resembles a *pater familias,* responsible for political guidance and social tutelage, while the party represents the "school of the nation," serving as the common platform of all truthful citizens as well as the training ground of all would-be leaders. In their eyes, the elites organized in the state-party complex not only have the right to guide and shape society but even have a duty to do so. This requires cooperation between the state and the party whereby the former provides the instruments and the latter the ideology. Unlike the PSD under Bourguiba, however, the RCD should be a mirror rather than a vanguard of society; therefore, it should continue to advance society, but refrain from disrupting it.

Since the elimination of the Islamists and the consolidation of the regime, however, the original promises of the new rulers—liberty and democracy—have resurfaced. The regime elite have responded in two ways. First, they have tried to reproduce the corporatist system in the political sphere, by creating political reserves for the "loyal opposition." Their role (or, as the regime puts it, their "duty") is to integrate those currents into the system that remain outside the reach of the RCD. However, even though they concede that other parties have the right to exist, it is obvious that only one party has the right to rule.

Second, they have tried to capture the democracy, human rights, and good governance discourse by developing their own reading of these concepts: On the one hand, they promote a comprehensive interpretation— insisting that collective and social rights are as important as individual and civic rights—that allows them to counterbalance shortcomings in the political arena with accomplishments in the social realm. On the other hand, they pursue an incrementalist approach—in principle, people are politically "mature" but in practice they need further "preparation"—that allows them to deflect recurring criticism of their political demeanor without making any binding commitments on their side.[31] As Ben Ali has put it,

> We are convinced that the success of any approach depends on its respect for the specific nature of each society. Accordingly, we have built our approach on a comprehensive and integrated notion of human rights, in which civil and political rights are interwoven with social, economic and cultural rights. In other words, we have rejected the uneven treatment of the different aspects of human rights. All the aspects of human rights are equally important and all of them complement each other. Our effort is therefore focused on guaranteeing the rights to employment, food, education, healthcare, social security, child and family protection, and support for vulnerable categories in society, as much as it is focused on guaranteeing freedom of expression, and freedom from discrimination.[32]

Hence, the priority of the regime is clearly stabilization and modernization, not liberalization and democratization.[33] Admittedly, they do allow for a certain degree of prior consultation and popular participation in decisionmaking, but not open contestation of public policies or real competition for political power. Similarly, they claim not only to act as a motor that is able to steer the country toward modernity, but also as a protector that will cushion the impact of globalization. It shows that Ben Ali is still determined to uphold key elements of the Bourguibist state, particularly the mix of developmentalism and welfarism.[34]

As a result, both business and labor tiptoe around the regime when talking about politics. Both sides do defend their interests and push their agendas vis-à-vis the state authorities and their respective counterparts (with more or less vigor and success), but neither seeks to empower Tunisian society as a whole or to change the basic rules of the game. For instance, although businessmen have increasingly become active and influential in politics, they do not try to generalize (let alone institutionalize) their achievements. The few instances in which they address political questions mainly concern minor administrative modifications (less red tape and bureaucratic interference) rather than fundamental democratic advances (effective power for elected officials and independent courts).

On the contrary, the contesting elites appear to be crippled by the crisis of socialism and Arabism and divided over whom to support in the clash between the regime and the Islamists. After a period of confusion and apathy, they have chosen to focus on issues that represent the smallest common denominator among themselves and that would allow them to broaden their power base, such as a separation between the RCD and the state, an independent judiciary, access to the media, more seats in parliament, the liberation of prisoners, and so on.

Acknowledging the failure of the cooperative approach, and feeling the growing anger of the Tunisian "street," the political opposition in late 2000 began reorganizing and reorienting itself. This has led a number of opposition groups, from among the political parties and civil society, from the far left to the Islamist tendencies, to join forces in a "democratic pole." At the same time, regime opponents and independent candidates have scored clear victories in all genuine elections since late 2000 (FTDH, UGTT, lawyers, etc.). This means that for the first time since the mid-1980s, antiregime sentiment has reached the outer fringes of the regime coalition and the disgruntled components of the middle classes.

Thus, absent a substantial consensus and sophisticated programs, the objective of democratization has become the rallying point for contesting elites. Moreover, the "d-word" offers another advantage: it allows them to reach out to the West and to the Islamists at the same time. Evidence suggests that this is more than a change in tactics; it is a change in strategy.[35] In fact, there seems to be growing anxiety within Tunisian society that the regime institutions will not be able to absorb the profound disruptions caused by free trade and prevent a social explosion leading to another system crisis. Many of their representatives point out that Ben Ali may be about to miss the last chance for a peaceful settlement, making the same mistake as his illustrious predecessor.

Foreign Affairs

Under the old regime, the Tunisian PRE had been able to agree on what the country's foreign policy should look like: obtaining guarantees against external threats and securing access to financial resources without compromising national independence or state power. Given Tunisia's limited military means and its close economic ties with the West in general and Europe in particular, this spelled diversifying external relations as much as possible without jeopardizing privileged relations with Paris and Washington.

Upon coming to power, however, Ben Ali's regime had to face a dramatically changed environment, particularly with regard to Tunisia's weakened position after the EU's southward expansion and the profound political crises of the entire Maghreb region. As a consequence, the new rulers departed from some concepts that had guided foreign policy since national independence: They made clear that they would be more willing to cooperate with their Arab neighbors and to adhere to international regimes, thus de facto abandoning the policy of neutrality and autonomy that their predecessors had pursued for decades.[36] Thus, in 1988 Tunisia launched the Arab Maghreb Union (UMA) with Algeria, Morocco, Libya, and Mauritania, which aimed at creating a common market among the member states while at the same time enhancing their bargaining position vis-à-vis the European Community. Finally, in 1990 it entered the General Agreement on Tariffs and Trade (GATT), a move that highlighted the shift away from a closed etatist economy and toward an open market economy.

In the early 1990s gridlock in the UMA and the acceleration of globalization led the ruling elite to shift its political focus from the intraregional (Arab-Maghreb) level to the interregional (Euro-Mediterranean) level. It should be noted, however, that although they have agreed to enter the global economy, as evidenced through their accession to the WTO and association with the EU, they still prefer to do so through regional blocs, which are supposed to offer a certain degree of complementarity in the industrial policies of participants and protection from the destructive effects of globalization.[37]

At the same time, the ruling elite continues to cling to a rather orthodox understanding of international relations. To them, state security is tantamount to national security, given that in the world of sovereign nation-states and "dog-eat-dog" policies, power prevails over reason and the North dictates the terms; in other words, in a world haunted by anarchy and injustice, only the state can guarantee the integrity and survival of the people. Such a reading offers two advantages: It allows Tunisia's rulers to demand foreign intervention against "Israeli aggression" (the Palestine conflict not being an internal affair), while rejecting similar moves directed against Arab countries (for instance, Libya and Iraq).[38]

Since the state should be the sole interlocutor of other states, and the main interface to the outside world, the regime has always resisted support for civil society by foreign actors and has only reluctantly accepted the insertion of "political conditionality" in the Euromed accords. This concept of the state is also very handy insofar as it allows the Tunisian leaders to rebuff rival claims from the outside (for example, by the European Union and international organizations) as well as from the inside (for example, by political Islam and civil society). Their stubborn and mostly successful resistance to international and particularly European pressures (such as the IMF's demands of reducing social spending or the EU's attempts at sidelining regime authorities) proves that they will concede an intensification of cooperation only if it does not affect the bases of their power.

This approach can best be seen within the Euro-Mediterranean Partnership, where the new rulers are simultaneously pursuing a maximalist and a minimalist agenda. On the one hand, they try to promote a comprehensive security concept that also includes nonmilitary, "soft" issues, such as racism, fundamentalism, and terrorism, while on the other hand, they struggle to exclude particularly sensitive areas, such as culture, governance, and sovereignty. In general, their criticism of European policies can be subsumed under three points: financial assistance through the EU's MEDA program is insufficient; agriculture and services (including freedom of movement) should be included in the EMP; and social and cultural affairs should be given more attention.

At least in public, the regime allies have more or less accepted these choices—business more, the unions less. Although UTICA fully supports the EMP, it is obvious that the private sector is deeply divided over this issue, with export-oriented big companies being pitted against import-competing small and medium manufacturing enterprises (SMEs). Even though the UGTT has not gone further than saying that the EMP needs to be amended, and the social dimension strengthened, conversations with unionists reveal that they harbor a deep distrust of the entire Euromed project. At the same time, however, both sides are fully aware that the EMP is the best deal for their country; it offers the most promising and least painful way for Tunisian enterprises to log into global economic networks and prop up their limited growth potential.

The political opposition and civil society groups seem to have comparable misgivings about Tunisia's stepped-up integration into international regimes and the EU's growing presence in the Arab world. In a way, they see themselves caught between two contradictory concerns: on the one hand, they are clearly interested in gaining new funding opportunities and political protection from the EU; on the other hand, they have largely preserved the nationalist sensitivities and etatist mentality of the ancient regime. A way out of this dilemma is to support the project as such while requesting amendments, for example, more attention for the "human dimension" and more cooperation with civil society. Still, it is obvious that a clear majority of the contesting elites is profoundly suspicious of, if not outright hostile toward, a Euromed free-trade zone.

The September 11 attacks presented the regime authorities with a mixed bag of unexpected opportunities and potential pitfalls. On the one hand, the so-called war on terror has helped the regime leaders to reassert carte blanche in home affairs and to renew their "special relationship" with the Western world. On the other hand, Tunisia's attractiveness to investors and tourists was severely damaged by the attacks, and any talk of regime change or "democratic dominoes" is particularly unwelcome in Cartage. The position of the opposition, however, for once is unambiguous. Although they strongly criticize "U.S. imperialism" and EU "security paranoia," they are fully aware that the attacks have strengthened their adversaries "to the point that soon the key date for the Tunisian regime will no longer be 7 November, but . . . 11 September."[39]

Economic Policy

Since independence, economic questions have been the main battleground for the Tunisian PRE. Even the *infitah* (opening) initiated in the early 1970s was only a shaky compromise between the antagonistic agendas of socialists and liberals. Given the paradigmatic changes in economic policy under the New Regime, this bone of contention has basically been buried. Since the late 1980s, the official line is that economic growth should be achieved through market mechanisms instead of state planning and that private business rather than the public sector should act as the driving force.[40] Thanks to this development strategy largely modeled on the "Asian Tiger" countries, the Tunisian economy has continuously registered annual growth rates of over 5 percent throughout the past decade, placing it well above the regional average of the Middle East and North Africa region (MENA).

In practical politics, however, regime authorities have clearly endeavored to accommodate different agendas. They concede that the state should withdraw from undue interference in market decisions, especially from direct participation in industrial production. At the same time, however, they stress the need for the state to maintain the social equilibrium and continue to control strategic economic sectors such as energy, transport, communication, and eventually banking. Hence, preserving social peace and preventing mass layoffs receive priority, even at the cost of reduced economic growth and lost investment opportunities.

This last point can also be inferred from the sluggish privatization process, whose effects have so far hardly touched upon the financial sector and public infrastructure and whose application to the education system and health care is still being hotly debated. So far, the basic approach has been to keep the privatization process controllable and reversible, which means limiting it in time and scope and assuring that no public monopoly be replaced by a private one. It can also be gleaned from the much-needed reform of the social security systems, where the regime has avoided any move that might arouse popular discontent or affect its political patronage devices. Instead, the ruling elite has pursued a three-pronged approach to social security that offers the best cost-benefit ratio: social insurance schemes covering all citizens; direct financial assistance targeting poor families; and ad hoc, tailor-made state services dispensed from the president's budget.

The "depoliticization" or "privatization" of social conflicts has disciplined and divided the "social partners." Business is split into a state-tuned, antiliberalization group and a market-tuned, proliberalization group, the latter of which only represents a tiny minority of private entrepreneurs, albeit one controlling UTICA's leading bodies and the country's large industries. It seems that the latter group, often identical with export-oriented companies, is increasingly making use of public resources to prepare for the world market, while the former group, mostly tantamount to the import-competing companies, is devoting itself to lobbying political authorities and delaying the economic opening as much as possible in order to pocket transitory benefits and to prepare their "early retirement."

The unions are also split into two camps: a dominant group that continues to pursue its traditional "no-no" line—that is, postponing further liberalization while protecting social accomplishments, such as a broadly defined public sector and a relatively rigid labor code; and a minority movement that is trying to switch to an offensive approach—which implies becoming actively engaged in the restructuring processes at company level and finding new adherents among underrepresented groups, such as young and female workers in the private and services sector. It is obvious that for both camps, however, the interests of their constituencies and bureaucracies have priority over those of the unemployed or newcomers.

The UGTT and UTICA, however, both seem increasingly unable to integrate the growing conflicts among their respective constituencies, a problem that is made worse by their monolithic makeup and co-opted leaderships. Meanwhile, contesting elites, who mostly come from bourgeois and intellectual backgrounds and grew up infused with Marxist or pan-Arab ideologies, seem either not to care for economic issues or are unable to table credible proposals, while the Islamist activists, who have traditionally taken up the cause of social justice and spoken on behalf of the petty bourgeoisie, have been refused a voice in politics. It is obvious that labor unionists and regime opponents still cherish their traditional beliefs of protectionism and statism and have only grudgingly accepted the new context of liberalization and globalization. An alliance between them could be dangerous to the regime, especially if they were to be joined by large numbers of small entrepreneurs, merchants, and artisans, who tend to form the social base of political Islam and will be the main victims of free trade.

Between Technocratic Government and Patrimonial Rule

Elite change under Ben Ali has had a vertical dimension (the rise of new groups within existing organizations) and a horizontal dimension (the entry of new groups into the political process). The main winners have been those groups who were able to provide the necessary financial resources or technical competencies for the new rulers to implement economic reforms and maintain the political system. These were the techno-bureaucrats in public administration, members of the security apparatus, representatives of big business, and the ruling families around Ben Ali.

It should be noted, however, that the New Regime has also reproduced long-established patterns of social interaction and elite circulation. First, the central state continues to do what it has been doing since the nineteenth century—mastermind, orchestrate, and implement the course, pace, and scope of change in society. Second, access to the core elite continues to be restricted to members of the political elite, which demonstrates that the patterns of political recruitment are hardly affected by changes in economic policy. In fact, state-society relations continue to flow from the top down: neither the former's composition nor its preferences necessarily reflect those of the latter.[41]

Therefore, it may be argued that the "System Ben Ali" skillfully combines technocratic government and neopatrimonial rule, but on a much larger scale and in a more sophisticated manner than his predecessor.[42] On the one hand, one is faced with formally democratic institutions (parliaments, parties, elections), but without the necessary legal underpinnings (freedom of information, expression, and association). Since the unity between state and party continues, and the regime still controls the levers of power, the admission of opposition parties and their representation in popular assemblies are ineffective. On the other hand, one must distinguish between formal state bodies that seem to work with reasonable efficiency and according to bureaucratic principles and an overarching presidential *makhzan* that monopolizes ultimate political control and determines the decisionmaking process according to its own logic and its own interests. The existence of both vertical and horizontal loyalties, associated with the French state model and local political culture, account for the specificity and stability of this system.

Bourguiba maintained his power by preventing the institutionalization of politics, Ben Ali by achieving the neutralization of politics. Bourguiba had to resort to divide-and-rule policies vis-à-vis other political actors to prevent the emergence of counter-powers. He undermined the workings of institutions and fanned up conflicts among elites, forcing them to seek his arbitrage to overcome a gridlock of the system.

On the contrary, Ben Ali has managed to achieve the submission of the political elites by attaching key power resources—force (the security services), money (wealthy families), and knowledge (the palace technocrats)—to the presidential *makhzan*. This way, he not only reduced his dependency on state institutions, degrading them to mere implementers of his policy decisions.

These changes at the level of elites and institutions interact with other changes with regard to the modes of governance and registers of legitimacy.[43] In fact, while reconstructing the regime and consolidating his power, Ben Ali has followed a two-pronged, intensive and extensive, approach that counterbalances the aforementioned state-controlled transformation of the economic and adjacent sectors with an ad hoc outsourcing of some particularly difficult or lucrative tasks. This has not only allowed him to increase the available patronage resources, but also to distribute them in a new, sometimes more arbitrary, sometimes more equitable, manner. In this way, he has tried to trade off his undeniable socioeconomic accomplishments for his unfulfilled political promises. In other words, access to wealth and posts should make people forget about the lack of liberty and democracy. Mobilization of political support and diffusion of social conflicts should be achieved through an improved satisfaction of *customers* rather than an increased participation of *citizens*.

This way, Ben Ali has managed to redefine the social contract that keeps the ruling coalition together and links it to the different social strata. In fact, the new formula has allowed him to relieve himself to a certain extent of the onerous obligations and political restrictions imposed by the old-style clientelism (such as employment guarantees in the public sector, and financial subsidies for the urban bourgeoisie) and the main regime institutions (party and bureaucracy). In hindsight, it appears that the regime has passed through three stages: from being the administrator of social demands and modernization processes in the 1950s and 1960s, via being their arbiter in the 1970s and 1980s, to being their facilitator since the time of the "Change of 1987."

This leads us back to the questions asked at the beginning: Why has there not been more change, or, better said, why has there been this specific change? Why have the new rulers maintained the political system wherever possible and only modified it when absolutely necessary? Why have neither the private sector nor any other social force become a major player in political life? Why have both the political opposition and civil society been so easily and thoroughly sidelined? Five factors may help us to explain these results: the background of the ruling elite; the influence of class alliances; the fragmentation of Tunisian society; the logic of the political system; and the preferences of external actors.

First, the new rulers who moved to top positions after November 1987 represent the "Generation Bourguiba" and an "Elite Ben Ali." They are mostly middle-aged individuals who were born between 1935 and 1955, trained in the new institutions of the young republic, started a professional or political career in the 1970s and 1980s, and held middle-management positions by the time of the "Change." Thus, the fact that they spent their formative years under the old system but made decisive breakthroughs under the New Regime might explain not only their conservatism in political questions but also their loyalty to Ben Ali.[44]

Second, political elites are intrinsically intertwined with strategic social groups on institutional and informal levels. The New Regime elite that came to power after 1987 essentially represents the *génération de l'ouverture* (postindependence generation), which resulted from two social groups merging through education and marriage between the late 1950s and early 1970s: the old Tunisois families, who had dominated the beylical *makhzan* and religious life, and the new political rulers who came from the petty bourgeoisie of the Sahelian provinces.[45] This may also explain why there is no real corporate spirit among, and no real pressure from, private entrepreneurs and the Tunisian bourgeoisie at large. Not only are they aware of their own vulnerability and dependency, they are also content with their privileged access to decisionmakers and thus with their comparative advantages over potential competitors.

Third, the political system continues to discourage radical change. It does so through the overlapping of state and party, insofar as neither of them would be able to survive without the other; through the interdependence of power and wealth, insofar as a prominent position in the political apparatus gives privileged access to resource allocation; and through the accumulation and linkage of posts, insofar as all leading figures of the Tunisian PRE simultaneously hold key positions in various sectors. Hence, it is precisely the nonseparation and overintegration of institutions and elites that hamper the institutionalization of succession and the transition to democracy. In the case of Tunisia, all cards would be on the table, and no arbiter would be at hand to guarantee respect of the rules of the game and impose sanctions in case of a foul (as the army did in Turkey and the monarchy in Morocco).

Fourth, Tunisian society continues to be marked by several overlapping cleavages. A deep gap separates the coastline from the hinterland on the one hand, and the Arabic speakers from the French speakers on the other. While the coastal population has been increasingly exposed to European cultural life and integrated into trans-Mediterranean networks since the nineteenth century, the interior provinces have been more faithful to their traditional ways of life and have staunchly clung to their Arabo-Islamic heritage. It is this factor that has enabled the new rulers more than anything else to play the different opposition groups against one another and freshen up the original elite consensus of Bourguiba's epoch. In other words, it was the emergence of political Islam and the specter of an Algerian-style civil war that helped rally the urban, Westernized, Francophone bourgeoisie around Ben Ali's regime and convince the reform-minded middle classes to accept only limited technical changes.

Fifth, foreign actors have also contributed to the preservation of political authoritarianism. Particularly the European Union has rather prioritized stability over democracy along its southern flank (contrary to its stance vis-à-vis Eastern Europe), favored short-term material interests (such as market access and political stability) over long-term moral considerations (such as human rights and good governance), and channeled most of its assistance through state agencies (around 95 percent since the mid-1990s). As a consequence, the population increasingly perceives the regime as a bulwark against an unfettered global capitalism and as a router for foreign aid flows. Ultimately, both Western politicians and their Tunisian counterparts seem to conceive of political authoritarianism as a necessary means of pushing through structural adjustment and fending off eventual resistance either from within or from below.

All these factors help in understanding why the ruling elites have so far been able to absorb external shocks and digest social changes without being forced to open the political system and share political power. They also show that economic liberalization has so far strengthened rather than weakened political authoritarianism, and that the EMP has played a decisive role in this regard. Through economic liberalization, the New Regime has been able to renegotiate the political contract with Tunisian society and with its Western allies. To the inside, it has redefined the "grand project" that justifies its ongoing tutelage over ordinary citizens; to the outside, it has redefined the rentier status that guarantees it preferential access to foreign donors.

The Tunisian case may thus serve as a good example of how an authoritarian system can indeed survive an economic transformation, under two conditions: if it continues to monopolize the neuralgic spots of economic life and if it manages to control the financial exchanges with the external world. In other words, it must be able to place itself at the interface and act as a gatekeeper between public and private, inside and outside.[46]

Notes

1. Since the Tunisian constitution stipulated that the prime minister was to succeed a president who was physically or mentally unable to perform his duties, Ben Ali assembled several doctors, who confirmed Bourguiba's "incapacity." For this reason, Ben Ali's coup has often been called a "constitutional" or "medical" coup.

2. Declaration of 7 November 1987, Agence Tunisienne de Communication Extérieure, Tunis.

3. The term *makhzan* (literally "storeroom" or "warehouse") denotes the entire web of political institutions, social alliances, and interpersonal relationships that is coalescing around the Moroccan monarchy. It epitomizes the interlinkage and overlap of formal and informal institutions, and of political and economic power, around a prime decisionmaker (e.g., a king or president) that has become the defining feature of political life in the Arab world.

4. See the introductory chapter by Volker Perthes in this volume.

5. On the political system and contemporary history, see Brown et al., *Tunisia;* Moore, *Politics in North Africa;* Camau, *Pouvoir et Institutions au Maghreb;* Entelis, *Comparative Politics of North Africa;* Perkins, *Tunisia;* Camau, ed, *La Tunisie au présent;* Zartman, ed., *The Political Economy of Reform;* Zartman and Habib, eds., *Polity and Society in Contemporary North Africa;* Entelis, ed., *Islam, Democracy, and the State;* Murphy, *Economic and Political Change.* On the political elites and their social context, see Hermassi, *Leadership and National Development;* Stone, "Tunisia: A Single Party System"; Laarif-Beatrix, *Edification étatique et environnement culturel;* Charfi, *Les ministres de Bourguiba;* Vermeren, *Ecole, élite et pouvoir.*

6. Even though they were all either created or controlled by the political leadership, some of them, such as the UGTT and UGET, were able to maintain part of their autonomy and influence, while others, such as the UTAP and UNFT, were nothing more than vassals and instruments of the regime.

7. In fact, it is this complex that is referred to by Tunisians as the *pouvoir* or *sulta* ("power" in French and Arabic respectively), and that shall be translated as *regime* in this book.

8. Among others, he had the right to nominate governments, dissolve parliament, make or veto laws, and appoint or dismiss key officials (such as ministers, governors, judges, and the heads of the army and the police).

9. Quoted by Moore in Brown et al., *Tunisia,* p. 41.

10. The new constitution stipulated that the national assembly's president instead of the prime minister would stand in should the head of state die. However, he would only be charged with organizing the elections for the presidency *but barred from participating in them.*

11. *Pacte National,* Agence Tunisienne de Communication Extérieure, Tunis.

12. Thanks to the ongoing validity of the electoral code (single-list, first-past-the-post system), the RCD garnered all the seats in parliament with about 80 percent of the votes. Even though the MTI had to present itself on "independent lists," it managed to get 15 percent of the votes, and even 25 percent in the cities, more than the rest of the opposition together.

13. The trigger was thus exogenous: Since the WTO outlawed preferential treatment among member states, the 1976 accord that granted Tunisian industry duty-free access to the European Community had to be renegotiated.

14. The stakes are substantial: Tunisian entrepreneurs will be offered unhin-

dered access to some 600 million consumers, while the EU promises to provide financial and technical assistance for economic and social reforms. The Tunisian state, however, will forfeit substantial revenues from customs duties (up to 20 percent of the annual budget), and a large number of private companies (current estimates are about 30 percent) are likely to disappear.

15. This democratic facade also caters to the EU association agreement, which made "democracy, human rights and the rule of law" an essential precondition for the agreement's validity.

16. In exchange, Ben Ali offered to establish a second chamber modeled on the Moroccan case and to admit opposition candidates to the 2004 presidential elections.

17. Born in 1936 into a humble family of Hammam Soussis, he joined the army at the age of fifteen. In 1964 he was appointed director of military security, and in 1977 he was promoted to director-general of national security. After what was considered his inadequate handling of the "Gafsa affair" of late 1980—in which an armed group, presumably trained by Libya, took the southern town of Gafsa and held it for several hours against the police—he was sent as an ambassador to Poland, where he witnessed the triumph of the Solidarity movement over the communists and the subsequent restoration of political order by the armed forces. The 1984 "bread revolt" brought him back as the head of the mukhabarat, and the ensuing escalation of the struggle between the regime and the Islamists paved his way to the top. In April 1986 he took over the Interior Ministry, and in October 1987 he became the undisputed number two of the regime, being appointed prime minister and secretary-general of the ruling party.

18. In this chapter, "political elites" denotes the leading echelons of the ruling party and the state bureaucracy. "Regime elites" has a broader meaning, which includes the leading figures of the regime's main social allies too (for example, the national associations and the business community).

19. For more on the three-circle concept, see the introduction to this volume by Volker Perthes, "Politics and Elite Change in the Arab World."

20. So far, Ben Ali has tried to keep his familial and political spheres separate. Only rarely do family members receive official positions, and even less seldom political ones. Because of the lack of data about the entourage and the mukhabarat, this chapter focuses on the party and the government.

21. Tunisian embassies resemble a "who's who" of former core elite members. Tahar Sioud in Brussels, Faiza Kefi in Paris, Mohamed Jegham in Rome, Fethi Merdassi in Berlin, and Neziha Ben Yedder in Beirut held key posts until recently. Contrary to other Arab countries, Tunisian diplomatic posts are not political graveyards, but parking lots and sometimes career springboards.

22. Although the rule of Monastiris has not been replaced by the rule of Soussis, regional affiliations still play an important role in political life, as can be seen from the fact that since 1987 all three prime ministers and all Central Bank governors have come from (or near) Ben Ali's hometown.

23. Media broadcasts tend to underline this: either they show ministers from behind as they listen to the president, or they indicate their functions without mention of their names. This may explain why the majority of citizens neither know nor care about the composition of the government.

24. There are also many communicators (diplomats and journalists) and technologists (engineers and scientists) in the government, but they rarely occupy key posts or ascend to the first circle.

25. Attempts to circumvent the *concours* have always existed and some have

succeeded. The pronounced esprit de corps of Tunisian officials, and the essentially meritocratic outlook of the middle classes, however, tended to thwart most of them. It is thus mainly the institution of the *concours* that accounts for the considerable professionalism and social heterogeneity of the Tunisian administration.

26. For further reading, see Zghal, "Nouvelles orientations du syndicalisme Tunisien"; Bellin, *Stalled Democracy.*

27. This is not to say that the UGTT has become entirely irrelevant vis-à-vis the UTICA, as can be seen from the 2002 collective wage negotiations, in which the former clearly scored a victory over the latter with the support of the regime.

28. Bellin, "Civil Society," p. 144.

29. For further reading, see Bellin, "Civil Society"; Lamloum and Ravenel, eds., *La Tunisie de Ben Ali.*

30. For further reading on the regime's cultural and religious policies, see Sha'ban, *'Udat Hannabaal . . . aw Tajdid 'Ahd* [The Return of Hanibal . . . or the Renewal of an Era]; Beji, "La pédagogie des Lumières ou la réforme du système éducatif tunisien." For further reading on the Islamist movement, see Magnuson, "Islamic Reform"; Dunn, "The al-Nahda Movement."

31. Their standpoint is that everybody should have a say (right of consultation) and should have a share (right of solidarity), while making perfectly clear who is in charge and who will stay in charge of running the country. It is a revamped version of classical corporatism, in which society resembles a body: every organ has its place and its role, acting in perfect (organic) harmony and according to functional (noncompetitive) principles.

32. Interview, "Democracy Is the End Result of a Historical Process," *Middle East Insight,* 19 June 2000.

33. It seems that whenever there are disagreements among the elites, they do not follow ideological fault lines between left and right, hardliners and softliners, but rather entail power struggles and interest conflicts between "clans" and institutions. Examples are the current polemics about rampant corruption in the presidential entourage, which is actually a turf war between the establishment and newcomers, and the recurring friction between the security apparatus and economic reformers, which is basically about the appropriateness of state repression.

34. For further reading, see Camau, "D'une République à une autre"; Sadiki, "Bin Ali's Tunisia."

35. Whether to cooperate with the Islamists was an issue that earlier had divided the opposition. Today, however, most seem to agree that there is no chance of changing the political system or achieving social peace without them.

36. For further reading, see Cassarino, "The EU-Tunisian Association Agreement"; Murphy, "The Foreign Policy."

37. On a multilateral level, Tunisia is actively engaged in several (inter)regional schemes, such as the GAFTA (a free trade area among fourteen Arab states), the Eizenstat initiative (a free trade initiative between the United States and four Maghreb countries), and the Aghadir process (a free trade zone among the Arab signatories of Euromed association agreements), while on a bilateral level it increasingly focuses on "uncharted territories," mainly the Gulf countries, the Iberian Peninsula, and Northern Europe. These initiatives, however, are meant to be complements to the Euro-Mediterranean Partnership, not substitutes for it.

38. That they use the socioeconomic term "North" rather than its politicocultural equivalent, "West," is revealing in itself since it shows which factors constitute in their eyes the main driving forces and dividing lines in international relations. As Ben Ali put it, "I do not think that the future will be determined by conflicts

between civilizations or religions, especially not in the current context of globalization. I see future conflicts being determined by economic needs and development pressures. In certain regards, religious extremism was in fact a by-product of the Cold War, since it was nurtured as a means to fight communism." (Interview, "Democracy Is the End Result of a Historical Process," *Middle East Insight,* 19 June 2000.)

39. Khemmais Chammari, quoted in *Le Monde,* 10 November 2002, p. 4.

40. For further reading, see Boyan, *Forcing Freedom;* Dillman, "The Political Economy of Structural Adjustment"; Dillman, "Facing the Market"; Murphy, "Economic Reform and the State"; Murphy, "The State and the Private Sector"; Alexander, "Labour Code Reform."

41. This confirms Laarif-Beatrix's findings with regard to the late Bourguibist period. See Laarif-Beatrix, *Edification étaque et environnement culturel.*

42. Whereas Bourguiba had been a first among equals (at least at the beginning of his rule), Ben Ali's style is rather a "consultative unilateralism." The more he has consolidated his position, however, the more his accessibility has diminished. Moreover, who has influence, and to what degree, constantly shifts. He seems to be much more amenable to outside advice, when "secondary" (especially economic) decisions are concerned, than when "hard" (specifically security) matters are at issue.

43. For further reading, see Khiari and Lamloum. "Le Zaïm et l'Artisan."

44. Moreover, they are mostly people who had met Ben Ali during his earlier careers as security director and interior minister or joined him during the years following the November coup. This confirms Zartman's observation that the personal factor still is of crucial importance for elite socialization. See Zartman, *Political Elites,* p. 8.

45. See Vermeren, *Ecole, élite et pouvoir.*

46. So far, the regime has managed to prevent the internationalization and independence of private business and civil society. Foreign investors need a ministerial waiver to exceed the official ceiling of 49.99 percent of business capital, and NGOs need ministerial permission to receive financial support from a foreign donor or private source, both being granted only ad hoc upon formal application.

Part 4

Elite Change Under Domination

9

Lebanon:
Building Political Dynasties
Rola el-Husseini

Torn by civil war from 1975 to 1990, Lebanon has emerged as a relatively stable country as the result of the compromise between the warring elites set out in the 1989 Ta'if agreement. The accord, initiated by Saudi Arabia and other Arab countries under the auspices of the international community, modified the long-standing power-sharing formula between Lebanon's religious communities. Its implementation reaffirmed and strengthened Syrian tutelage over the country.[1]

Lebanon made the transition from anarchy to stability between 1989 and 2000. A modification of the composition of the politically relevant elite[2] in Lebanon also took place during this transitional period, with a rejuvenation and renewal of personnel in the main governing institutions.[3] The new members of the PRE came from various social, professional, or political backgrounds, indicating the entrance of groups previously not included. Postwar changes of personnel among the political elite and the new institutions created by Ta'if have not, however, affected the attitudes, behaviors, and perceptions of the PRE. Ta'if has only created new balances of power but has not changed the way the political system works.

Syria's role in Lebanon's affairs makes it a variable in any study of the Lebanese elite, as it influences not only the composition of the elite but also constrains political outcomes.[4] The postwar elite can be divided into three categories: (1) redefined elites, resulting from individuals repositioning themselves within the system during the 1990s; (2) conjunctural elites, resulting from changes in balances of power; and (3) the emerging elite, composed of young people positioning themselves on the fringes of the state institutions, poised to enter when the opportunity arises. These categories are heuristic devices, therefore permeability between them is to be expected.

In terms of the circles of influence model, the core elite are primarily the presidents of the republic, the Council of Ministers (the cabinet), and

239

the Chamber of Deputies (the parliament). The second circle is composed of cabinet members, influential political and communitarian leaders, and religious leaders. The third circle comprises mainly the members of parliament, advisors of political leaders, and the Christian opposition. It is possible to link the ideal-types presented with the circle model by arguing that the redefined elites are in the core and the second circle. Conjunctural elites are in the second and third circle. The emerging elite are clearly in the third circle, sometimes even on its fringes.

Among Lebanon's incumbent elites, it is possible to identify a few prototypes. As individuals are more important than political programs in Lebanon, biographical portraits of the incumbents illustrate the trajectories of their elite groups. Profiles of emerging elites reveal the routes Lebanon's future elite will likely take in entering the political system. Analysis of the political agendas and discourses[5] prevalent among members of the second and third circles of the PRE shed light on their attitudes and behaviors toward two issues of strategic and national importance—Syrian-Lebanese relations and the future of the political system. Incumbent elites' actions in regard to these issues guarantee their control of and eventually their children's monopoly of the political sphere.

Interelite Struggle and the Political System

Because prewar Lebanon is seen as a consociational democracy, one in which elites of different communities share power, study of its elite is crucial to understanding the way the country's political system works.[6] Consociationalism implies a pact between elites to regulate the sharing of power and to control political life. Consociationalism alone, however, cannot explain the change in Lebanon from a "disunified" war elite to a "consensually unified" postwar elite.[7] Lebanon's ruling elite today are unified around several strategic issues, such as the Syrian political and military presence in Lebanon, which they perceive as a guarantee of stability.[8] The threat of another breakdown of the political system is also a unifying issue for the Lebanese PRE.

Prewar Lebanon

The founding act of independent Lebanon is the National Pact of 1943, a gentlemen's agreement between the representatives of the main communities, namely the Maronites and the Sunnis. This unwritten pact, combined with the constitution promulgated in the 1920s, governed Lebanese political life until 1975. The pact resulted from negotiations between notables, the local leaders (*zu'ama*) of the Sunni and Maronite communities, and under the auspices of bankers and prominent merchants from the Greek Orthodox and Greek Catholic communities, thus making the contract consociational.[9]

Consociational societies were defined in the late 1960s by Arend Lijphart as those governed "by elite cartel designed to turn a democracy with a fragmented political culture into a stable democracy."[10] Lebanon experienced consociational democracy from its independence in 1943 until the outbreak of the civil war in 1975.[11]

The civil war represented the failure of the consociational model in Lebanon. The elites' inability to deal with socioeconomic and ideological challenges in addition to external interference—notably from the PLO—were the primary causes of the breakdown of the state. The endogamous nature of elite recruitment, in which modes of recruitment allowed continuity and reproduction of the same elite, created a representational gap between the elite and the masses. Elite recruitment involved a long-standing pattern: enrollment of the sons and brothers of notables, landlords, and *zu'ama* and exclusion of newly emerging groups in society. The inability of the elite to sustain their "grand coalition," defined by Lijphart as one of the conditions for consociational democracies, was another factor in the breakdown of the state. This inability was mainly because the consociational model could not handle external loads on the system in addition to the internal radicalization provoked by the post-1967 Arab-Israeli politics. On a sectarian level, the refusal of the Maronite elite to relinquish some of its prerogatives to other communities was one of the reasons that led to the collapse of the elite cartel and to the end of elite cooperation. Hence, during the civil war, the state broke down. In most of Lebanon's confessional groups, the war led to the emergence of a new leadership, "war elites," who had managed to create financial and political capital through their participation in the conflict. They were incorporated in the settlement of 1989, and some of them managed to reinvent themselves as politicians in postwar Lebanon.

The Ta'if Agreement

The Ta'if agreement modified the power-sharing formula in Lebanon. A change *in* regime, not a change *of* regime, took place, as consociationalism was not abandoned in favor of a deconfessionalized power-sharing formula. A constitutional amendment implemented in September 1990, however, changed the political system from one with strong presidential prerogatives to one in which the parliament held more powers. The new pact also extended prerogatives to the president of the Council of Ministers.[12] The sectarian distribution of positions, however, remained intact: the president of the republic was to be a Maronite, the president of the Council of

Ministers a Sunni Muslim, and the president (or Speaker) of the parliament a Shi'a Muslim.

As the presidency of the republic was traditionally held by a Maronite, the new system effectively meant the termination of Maronite hegemony in Lebanese politics. In contrast, the Shi'a gained more clout as the importance of the presidency of the parliament increased. Since the Second Republic was designed as a parliamentary republic, dissolution of the parliament by the president has become almost impossible. The term of the president of the parliament was extended from one year to four—the length of the legislature—which allows him more independence, authority, and freedom of action.[13] This new formula has effectively created three centers of power, which in Lebanese political jargon is called the Troika. It also allows for major political players representing less influential communities to have a say in decisionmaking through their appointment or the appointment of their clients as ministers.[14] In short, the demands of communities deemed politically disadvantaged were taken into consideration in the new political system. The number of parliamentarians was increased from ninety-nine to 128,[15] and seat distribution in the parliament was changed from a 6:5 ratio in favor of the Christians to 50:50 Muslim-Christian (which does not reflect actual demographics).[16]

Postwar Lebanon

In addition to the Ta'if agreement, the 1991 Treaty of Brotherhood and Cooperation and seventeen other treaties legitimize and institutionalize Syrian involvement in internal Lebanese affairs.[17] Syria thus became a major actor not only in elite formation but also in policymaking. As two observers note, "The Ta'if agreement . . . which ostensibly resolved sectarian conflict in Lebanon, has in reality transformed the postwar Lebanese entity into a Syrian satellite."[18]

Syria's influence on postwar elite formation is best seen in the selection of the president of the republic. Not only have all Lebanese presidents since 1976 been in one way or another approved by Syria, in recent years they have all been the "Syrian candidate" for the position. It is also apparent among one segment of the PRE, parliamentarians; a seat in the Chamber of Deputies is the first step toward membership in the political elite and is a training ground for future politicians and aspirants and recruits to executive branch positions.[19] New members entered the politically relevant elite through the executive's nomination in 1991 of forty MPs to replace representatives who had died during the civil war and to fill twenty-nine newly created seats. All those selected were close to Syria. The 1992 elections saw the return of twenty-nine out of forty of these nominees to parliament, the 1996 elections brought twenty-five of them back,[20] and in 2000 twenty-one of these fixtures in Lebanese political life were reelected. Elite circulation in 1992 was almost 83 percent, however 38 percent of these new MPs had had a family member in parliament. Circulation was high compared to the last prewar legislature of 1972 where it was on the order of 39 percent. Nevertheless, in 1992, the percentage of parliamentarians from political families was close to the 1972 percentage, which was 44.4 percent.[21] Every postwar election has involved gerrymandering; the electoral law has been changed three times to ensure that Syrian allies emerge as winners.[22]

Postwar Elite Configuration: Settlement, Convergence, and Co-optation

Although consociationalism aptly describes the Lebanese political system and pattern of governance, it fails to explain the interaction of political actors within the system. Their interaction involves agreement, exclusion and convergence, and finally division. Loosely using the concepts developed by John Higley and Michael Burton, these three movements can be labeled elite settlement, elite convergence, and co-optation. The effect is the consolidation of those elites in place in the system and the exclusion of challengers.[23]

The Ta'if accord exemplifies an elite settlement, which occurs when "previously disunified and warring elites suddenly and deliberately reorganize their relations by negotiating compromises on their most basic disagreements."[24] Such a settlement also involves "prior occurrence of a conflict in which all factions suffered heavy losses."[25] In the case of Lebanon, Ta'if allowed elite groups that had emerged as a consequence of the civil war to formally enter the political system. In elite settlements, not all elite groups involved in a conflict necessarily participate in its settlement; some may be alienated or marginalized by it. In Lebanon, the settlement of the civil war largely excluded Gen. Michel Aoun and his followers as well as the Lebanese Forces (LF), a Christian group. It can be argued that the Lebanese settlement shunned popular Christian representatives with war capital in favor of Syrian-supported Christians who parachuted into the parliament and the cabinet, especially after the largely boycotted elections of 1992 and 1996.

The gradual acceptance of the rules of the game by some Christian elites who had boycotted legislative elections in 1992 and 1996 and the participation of the Lebanese Forces in the municipal elections of 1998 support the view that from 1996 to 1998 Lebanon was undergoing elite convergence.[26] The perception among Christians that Ta'if had not been applied had created frustration and rejection of the status quo among their leadership. In 1992 Christian candidates and voters had largely boycotted the elections with the blessing of the Maronite patriarch, Mar Nasrallah

Butros Sfeir. The elections, held nonetheless, brought into parliament MPs who were not perceived as true representatives of the Christian population. By 1996 some Christian leaders seemed to have learned a lesson and began fighting "with the government's weapons," which signaled the beginning of convergence. Yet, the Christian leadership remained divided. The patriarch adopted this time a more nuanced position, leaving the people to their conscience. From Paris, exiled Christian leaders called once again for an electoral boycott. A group of Christian leaders in the country who did not necessarily agree with the government and its policies, however, decided to play within the rules of the game, acting as a competing elite.[27] Most members of this group were not elected.

The 2000 legislative elections brought further disintegration of the Christian opposition, with a continuation of convergence. In these elections, the Maronite patriarch's position was remarkable: he called for a unified Christian position toward elections, whether in favor of or against them. As a Lebanese observer points out, in 2000 and "contrary to previous elections, boycotting did not convince people of its efficacy as they now knew the difficulties faced by someone who does not follow the rules of political games."[28] By 2000 the Christian political establishment had come to understand the futility of their boycott and accepted the need to play according to the rules laid out by Syria and its Lebanese allies.

This elite convergence did not comprise all groups of the PRE. Challenging groups that were perceived as representatives of Christian popular opinion were targeted for co-optation by the incumbent elite. The latter adopted a policy of divide and conquer in 2000, and soon thereafter important challenging groups began splitting into factions, one agreeing to play by the rules and one preferring to remain outside the system, opposing it. Hence, the Lebanese Forces were permitted in January 2001 to hold a political conclave as a first step toward regaining their license to legally participate in politics. The LF had met with internal splits during its years outside the political arena. The government allowed them to convene because it supported the faction behind the organization. At the same time, the government banned an opposition LF faction from public or political activity.[29] It adopted the same policy toward the other major Christian party, the Kata'ib, or Phalange. Between 1990 and 2001, the Phalange had slipped into relative political obscurity, and by the late 1990s its local leadership had aligned itself with Syria. The return from exile of Amin Gemayel—the former president and the son of Phalange founder Pierre Gemayel—and his attempts to take back the party and its Christian following led to a swift response. In 2002 one of the Phalange leaders was co-opted, effectively splitting the party into one faction that sided with the government and its policies and an opposing faction, the so-called reform movement, headed by the traditional leadership of the party, that is, by the Gemayel family.

Through convergence and co-optation, the majority of contesting or challenging Christian elites were brought into the Syrian fold and the government. The only Christian party not targeted by the government was the Free Patriotic Movement (FPM) of the exiled Aoun. The reason for this is probably twofold: First, Aoun and the majority of his cadres are outside the country, and those inside have not conceded to the demands of the government. Second, rejection of the Syrian presence and interference in politics is at the heart of the FPM's rationale and gives it credibility and legitimacy in the eyes of its constituency.

As politics in Lebanon is elite politics, settlement, convergence, and co-optation allowed the shift from the fragmented war elite to a more consensually united postwar elite. The incumbent elite is now unified around the rules of the game and certain issues, including fear of system breakdown. This unity has permitted the transition from a broken political system to a rather stable consociational system.

Redefined Elites

Five groups in the political arena during the civil war were able to redefine and reposition themselves in the postwar period in ways that allowed them to officially enter the system through elections or appointment. These groups are former warlords "recycled" as politicians, religious rebels, Syria's clients, entrepreneurs, and military personnel.

Former Warlords

The peace settlement between the various warring elites included a general amnesty that allowed the former heads of the militias to enter the political arena. They were backed by Syria and managed to be elected as parliamentary representatives of their communities. These former warlords, however, especially those representing Christian communities, have since been slowly ousted from the political scene. By 2002 one had been jailed, a second sent into exile, and a third assassinated. Only two former warlords remain relevant: one is Walid Jumblat, who represents the Druze community and can be placed in the second circle of the PRE. However, Jumblat is also a notable, the heir of a dynasty that has for several centuries led the Druze. The second relevant former warlord is Nabih Berri, president of the parliament and a leading Shi'a. While Berri has for the past ten years been part of the core elite, the reasons for his rise to power are different from Jumblat's: he exemplifies the warlord backed by a foreign power. According to one of his political opponents, "Berri could not physically survive a single day had it not been for the protection of Syria."[30] As there is no longer war in

Lebanon, it can be safely assumed that being a former warlord is no longer a channel for elite formation in Lebanon.

No other politician who gained a coat of arms during the civil war is as remarkable as Nabih Berri. He hails from a modest southern family that emigrated to Sierra Leone, where he was born in 1938. He was sent to Lebanon for schooling, eventually receiving a law degree in 1963 from the Lebanese National University before going on to study for a year in France.[31]

Full of ambition, in the 1968 and 1972 elections, Berri tried to run on the list of then-parliament Speaker Kamel al-As'ad, but al-As'ad refused to back him. Berri turned against the Shi'a traditional leadership and aligned himself with Imam Musa al-Sadr's Harakat al-Mahrumin, the Movement of the Deprived. The Movement of the Deprived created a political wing, Amal, in 1975, and Berri became a member of its political bureau. In 1980 Berri sidelined the head of Amal and was elected president of the group's Command Council. He moved the organization closer to Syria, and Amal ultimately became Syria's main client in Lebanon. Berri thus received military equipment and training for his militia and, after the war, was rewarded by Syria for his loyalty. He was nominated to parliament in 1991 and elected in November 1992. With Syrian backing, Berri was soon voted president of the Chamber of Deputies. In 2000 he was reelected to lead the parliament for a third consecutive term.

Nabih Berri has created a wide clientelist network using the apparatus of the state; he has placed loyal men in all its organs, especially in such institutions as Télé Liban and Middle East Airlines, which can provide jobs for his sympathizers. The payrolls of state apparatuses are bloated with Shi'a personnel who owe their jobs to Berri. It is rumored that no Shi'a gets a position in the state without his approval.[32]

The Religious Rebels

The complexities and specificities of Lebanon's political system, based on loyalty to the clan or the confession, have marginalized political parties to the benefit of other structures. That is not to say, however, that political parties do not exist in Lebanon. They do, but they rarely have a coherent ideology, a goal, or even a structure. Hizballah is the exception. Hizballah is not a party structured around a person or a family, which makes it uncommon in Lebanese politics. According to a rising member of the Christian opposition, "The postwar political elite is money-oriented, willing to make concessions to Syria at varying degrees of servitude. The only exception is Hizballah, which has a logic of its own, an objective, and, most importantly, a model of society. This simply does not exist in any other formation."[33] Hizballah's leaders emerged on the political scene and gained capital as a result of the war and their resistance to the Israeli occupation of southern Lebanon. Secretary-General Sayyed Hassan Nasrallah, his deputy, and several high-profile MPs—religious rebels—are undoubtedly the most prominent among the newcomers to the Lebanese political scene.

In the 1980s Hizballah was a group set on creating an Islamic state in Lebanon based on the Iranian model. Hizballah shelved its demand for such a state (at least nominally) in the 1990s and agreed to play the political game. The party participated in the 1992 parliamentary elections, and eight of its candidates took seats. This milestone marks the start of the "Lebanonization" of Hizballah, that is, its incorporation into the political system. This process led eventually to the legitimization of Hizballah's armed resistance against Israel and Lebanese unification around the resistance until Israeli withdrawal from the south in 2000. Hizballah's members ran in the 1996 and 2000 legislative elections, taking seven and then eight seats. The relatively large number of Hizballah representatives and sympathizers in parliament demonstrates the party's importance.[34] Charisma is perhaps Hizballah's key form of political legitimacy. Hizballah MPs and their allies can be placed in the third circle of politically relevant elite.

Hassan Nasrallah was born in 1960 into a modest Shi'a family. Nothing in his background predestined his leadership of a major political party or his becoming a leading political figure on the Lebanese scene. At the age of fifteen, he joined Amal, which was at the time headed by Imam Musa al-Sadr. A year later, he left for the holy city of Najaf, in Iraq, to study theology. There he met Abbas Musawi, who was to become his lifelong friend, mentor, and predecessor as secretary-general of Hizballah. In 1982, after the Israeli invasion of Lebanon, Nasrallah and others split from Amal and founded a new party, Hizballah. Early on, Nasrallah was not part of the decisionmaking council of Hizballah, but he rose quickly in the ranks of the new party. In the late 1980s Musawi became secretary-general, but in 1992 the Israelis assassinated him. Nasrallah was elected as his successor in spite of his relative youth.

The mind behind the so-called Lebanonization of Hizballah and the creator of the "balance of terror" theory for dealing with Israel, Nasrallah is a charismatic leader in the Weberian sense of the term. His importance in the political sphere was consecrated internationally in June 2000 by a visit to Hizballah's offices by UN secretary-general Kofi Annan.

A calm, intelligent, pragmatic man, Nasrallah has also the reputation of being a humble one, especially compared to his political peers in Lebanon. Having risen in the ranks of a structured party with acumen, serenity, and charisma, Nasrallah is probably the sole member of the PRE not attempting to create a political dynasty. The party he heads does not operate that way.[35] It is difficult to place someone such as the secretary-general of Hizballah or his deputy within the circle model, but they certainly belong to the PRE, moving between the third and second circles of influence, depending on the issue at hand.

Syria's Clients

As almost all the groups in the Lebanese PRE pay allegiance to Syria in one way or another, one could argue that they are all Syria's clients. As defined here, however, "Syria's clients" consists of those members of the PRE who solely rely on Syria for their presence and influence in Lebanese politics. These actors have no constituency, nor do they possess the political, social, or economic capital to create one. They are found in all three circles of the PRE and belong to various confessions and political currents. They can be easily dismissed from Lebanese politics if they outgrow their usefulness. If they last in the political arena long enough, some might manage to develop political capital. They then use their position to build a political constituency through a mixture of terror, clientelism, and corruption.

The embodiment of a Syrian client is probably Michel Murr, a former interior minister and former vice president of the Council of Ministers, considered Lebanon's Fouché.[36] Murr was the strongman of the Second Republic, or the "superminister," as he has called himself. He was born in the town of Bteghrine in 1932 as the son of an entrepreneur from the Metn in Mount Lebanon. He studied at the University of Saint Joseph, Beirut, where he graduated with an engineering degree in 1955. Murr was by profession an engineer and entrepreneur before moving on to politics. His first political success came in 1968, when he was elected as an MP for the northern Metn region. He received his first ministerial portfolio in 1969, but a few years later, in 1972, he lost his parliamentary seat.

From the early 1970s until 1989, Murr disappeared from the forefront of Lebanese politics but remained politically active. In 1985 he endorsed the Syrian-brokered Tripartite Agreement as a way to end the civil war. When the agreement was broken, Murr had to flee the country, living in exile in Paris between 1986 and 1989.[37] His loyalty to Syria, however, was later rewarded. After the Ta'if agreement, Murr returned to Lebanon to become one of the pillars of the Second Republic, entering the first postwar cabinet as vice president of the Council of Ministers and defense minister. He kept the former position for ten years and also served as interior minister in various cabinets. He reentered parliament through the 1991 nominations and won in the highly contested 1992, 1996, and 2000 polls.

Over the course of a decade, Murr was able to create a power base resting on fear and corruption, as he controlled the majority of the state's security agencies, including the police. His position in the state and access to its agencies allowed him to co-opt people through jobs—significantly, placing loyal security agents in key positions in the administration and the judiciary.[38] Murr's positions thus permitted him to monitor everything and everyone in his constituency of the north Metn and impose his will.

In 2000, with the nomination of Rafiq Hariri as prime minister, Murr was circumvented during the formation of the cabinet in favor of his son Elias. Murr has already alluded that in the 2005 parliamentary elections, he will step aside in favor of his son. In his years in the core elite and with Syria's backing, Murr became a power with which to reckon. He has been outside the core elite since October 2000, but he has managed to elevate his son Elias and, with Syrian compliance, had tried to get his daughter Myrna into parliament in the 2002 by-elections. Indeed, Murr is proud to note that even though he did not inherit a political position from his father, he has managed to create a fledgling dynasty.[39]

The Entrepreneurs

The postwar period witnessed an increase in the importance of entrepreneurs on the political scene. These entrepreneurs—exemplified by former prime minister Rafiq Hariri—came with international experience, attitudes, and behavior different from those of traditional politicians. They have surrounded themselves with teams of experts educated in the West who advise them on issues ranging from politics and economics to the media and public relations. Their campaign style is also different. As they have no inherited constituency or social base, they have tended to create philanthropic foundations and extend wide-ranging favors in attempts to create a clientele and a network.

Rafiq Hariri, the "merchant prince,"[40] is perhaps the most renowned Lebanese political figure outside the country. During the past decade, he has managed to become an unavoidable player in Lebanese politics and the foremost representative of a new trend in politics—the importance of wealth.

Hariri was born the son of a Sunni farmer in 1944 in Saida, a small town in southern Lebanon. In 1965 he emigrated to Saudi Arabia, where he set up his first contracting firm in 1969. In 1977 his company built the Messara Hotel in record time in Ta'if. The job established his company's reputation for dependability, and in 1978 Hariri became the business partner of a Saudi prince. He was soon afterward granted Saudi citizenship, and by the early 1980s Hariri was one of the 100 richest men in the world.

Hariri had started his long road to the Lebanese premiership as early as 1982. After the Israeli invasion of that year, he put his resources, free of charge, at the disposal of the Lebanese government to clear rubble and repair roads in Beirut. In 1983 and 1984 Hariri participated in the peace conferences in Switzerland as the Saudi king's special envoy. While these early attempts at bringing peace to Lebanon did not bear fruit, they were important steppingstones in Hariri's road to power. The crowning of his attempts to enter politics came in 1989 when, as part of the Saudi delegation, he participated in the National Reconciliation Conference, held in Ta'if, Saudi Arabia.

As Hariri was not landed and had no constituency, he developed a network among the chief protagonists of the Lebanese civil war and ingratiated himself through his generosity. He also moved to create a constituency with the establishment of the Hariri Foundation, a nonprofit organization offering scholarships to young Lebanese of all confessional and political affiliations. Between 1979 and the early 1990s the Hariri Foundation distributed more than 32,000 scholarships.

In the 1980s Hariri established ties to the regime of Hafiz al-Asad, often mediating between Damascus and political players in Lebanon. In 1992 he was appointed prime minister, with Syria's blessings, and was reappointed three consecutive times. He had to resign in 1998 with the election of a new president. He refused to be reappointed and after a two-year period outside power, Hariri made his comeback as premier in 2000, after having won a landslide victory in a run for parliament.

In the 2000 legislative elections, Hariri presented himself from Beirut, his sister Bahia Hariri stood from Saida, and it was rumored that his son, who had married a woman from Tripoli, had planned to present himself in the north. The Syrians, however, forbade his son to run in Tripoli in order to protect the local Sunni chieftain, Omar Karameh. Bahia won a seat but has announced that she will not run again in 2005. Rafiq Hariri likely understands that the Syrians will never let him create a stronghold in Tripoli, so his son might run in Saida in 2005 instead. Hariri's aim, like other newcomers to the political arena, is to create a "political family."[41]

Military Personnel

In the course of its short history, Lebanon has had two presidents with military backgrounds: Fuad Shihab (1959–1964) and Emile Lahoud (1998–). The commander in chief of the armed forces, like the president, has always been a Maronite. Bearing in mind the history of other Arab states, one might wonder why Lebanese commanders—with the exception of Michel Aoun in 1989—have not attempted to seize the presidency by force of arms. The answer might lie in the fact that the army has never been an important actor in Lebanese politics. Under the First Republic, it was always small and weak; it was also divided along religious lines, with each brigade (roughly) representing a confessional group. Some army leaders had been offered the presidency in crucial moments of Lebanese history but rejected it.[42]

The ascendancy of Lahoud to the presidency in 1998 signaled an increase in military interference in Lebanese politics and a new phenomenon, military involvement in the judiciary. This militarization seems to come with Syria's blessings and with a tendency toward authoritarianism.[43] While this militarization is categorically denied by some military observers, who argue that the military has lost influence under Lahoud,[44] the evidence is to the contrary.

Lahoud's interjection of the army into the political arena and Michel Murr's use of the police and internal security forces in politics highlight the extent to which the military and security apparatuses have become forces in the past few years. In the words of the editor of a daily newspaper, "The army in Lebanon has almost become a new confession, one that needs to be taken into consideration in the national constellation."[45] One could therefore argue that Lebanon is moving toward the *mukhabarat* state paradigm that characterizes some neighboring regimes.

General Emile Lahoud, the eleventh president of Lebanon, was born in 1936 to a military family. After retiring from the army in 1959, General Jamil Lahoud was elected as an MP in 1960 and 1964. In 1966 he was appointed minister of labor and social affairs. Emile Lahoud would emulate his father's involvement in politics.

In 1956 Emile Lahoud joined the military academy as a marine cadet officer. He was promoted to commander of the First Fleet and spent considerable time training abroad. When his maternal cousin Gen. Jean Njeim was appointed commander of the armed forces in 1970, Lahoud was moved to an administrative position in the army, notwithstanding his naval background. He stayed in the army, mainly in administration, and steadily rose in its ranks.

In 1989, after the signing of the Ta'if agreement, Lahoud was appointed commander in chief of the army. It is said that he had connections to an influential Syrian army officer who recommended him for the job.[46] During his tenure as commander, Lahoud rebuilt the emasculated and destroyed army, expanding troop ranks from 20,000 to 70,000 and re-equipping it with the help of the United States. Lahoud is credited with having unified the army and for having attempted to stamp out sectarianism and regionalism from its ranks by creating mixed brigades and frequently rotating personnel throughout the country. Rejectionists abroad argue that this commitment to eliminate sectarianism is a smokescreen for Lahoud's ongoing attempts to "Syrianize the army," as officers are now more frequently sent to military academies in Syria than to traditional training facilities in the West.

Lahoud's ties to Syria led him to become its candidate for president in

1998. To pave the way, Syria pressured the parliament into amending Article 49 of the constitution, which prohibits high-ranking military officers from running for president within two years of leaving their post. In October 1998 parliament acted, allowing Lahoud to run for office; a month later he became president. Lahoud's presidency has brought interference in the political sphere by the military and increased Syrian involvement in political life. Like other Lebanese politicians, Lahoud is trying to use his presidency to establish roots in politics and create a political dynasty.

Thus far, he has appointed his brother Nasri as commissioner of the military court, and his twenty-five-year-old son, Emile Jr., a political novice, was elected to parliament in 2000. Emile Jr. ran on the list of Michel Murr, his sister's father-in-law. Emile Jr. did not accomplish much in his first two years as a parliamentarian. Whether he is reelected to the next legislature—on his way to becoming a fixture in parliamentary life—will not ultimately depend on his abilities as a politician but on his Syrian connections. In addition, should his father's term as president be extended anywhere from three to six years, as is rumored, Emile Lahoud Jr. will certainly be reelected to the 2005 legislature.

Conjunctural Elites

Some elite groups have gained or lost influence at certain conjunctures in postwar Lebanon. These groups are mainly composed of the notables and the clergy. In the case of the notables, the war saw their power eclipsed, but in the postwar period they regained influence, especially as war elites were sidelined. The clergy have always had a foot in political affairs, but they tend to be more involved at certain moments than at others, namely, when the political leadership of the community is weak or fragmented.

Notables

After the civil war, the Christian community experienced a resurgence of notability, as the warlords of the Christian militias were crushed and the alternative Christian leadership was exiled after Ta'if. In the 2000 legislative elections, Christian warlords backed by Syria suffered defeat by the young sons of the traditional political families. This rejuvenation of political families is likely the beginning of a trend in Lebanon, fueled by Christians' increasing dissatisfaction with their political representation since the signing of the Ta'if agreement.

In the early stages of the war, Christian notable families formed their own militias.[47] In the late 1980s these families were challenged by new leaders who emerged from within the militias. The downfall of the

Christian warlords started during inter-Christian fighting in 1989 and 1990 and continued throughout the 1990s, when they were excluded from the settlement of the conflict. This latter turn of events exacerbated the warlords' decline and aided in the political families' reassertion of their status as the legitimate representatives of the aspirations of the Christian population.[48]

There seems to be a regional dimension to the presence of notables in the political elite. For example, the percentage of Christian and Muslim MPs belonging to notable families in northern Lebanon is higher than in Beirut and the south. This is probably due to the fact that the north was less affected than other parts of the country by the civil war and has tended to retain, at least in its elite composition, the features of prewar Lebanon.[49] The perfect example of the new Christian notable who managed to replace his family in the political constellation is Pierre Gemayel.

Pierre Gemayel Jr. was elected in 2000 as a Maronite MP for the Metn region at the age of twenty-eight. As a political neophyte his election came as a surprise, especially as he managed to beat the government candidate. Gemayel ran as an independent and received around 35,000 votes, placing him second among the Maronite candidates in his district.

The involvement of the Gemayel family in Lebanese politics is relatively recent, dating back three generations, to the 1930s. The family, however, is intrinsically linked to the modern history of Lebanon, mainly as concerns the Maronite community. The grandfather and namesake of Pierre Gemayel in 1936 founded the Kata'ib, one of the main Christian players in postindependence Lebanon. The Kata'ib under the elder Pierre Gemayel had participated actively in the civil war but became irrelevant after the end of fighting.

Pierre Gemayel was born in 1972, studied law in Paris and Beirut, and worked in a legal firm in Beirut for a short span before taking over his father's legal practice. Then he ran for parliament in 2000. Trying to appeal to the constituency that elected him—a protest vote against the government candidate—he has joined the ranks of the opposition through his connections to the Qurnet Shahwan gathering.[50] He argues that Lebanon enjoys "a half-sovereignty and a half-independence"[51] and calls for redeployment and then the withdrawal of Syrian troops and for a containment of Syrian interference in Lebanese domestic affairs. He opposes Syrian-backed military actions by Hizballah in the contested Shebaa Farms, perceiving these operations as playing into the hands of Syria and as being counter to Lebanese interests.

With the help of his father, former president Amin Gemayel, Pierre tried to revive the defunct Kata'ib as a major player. His attempt, however, failed after the government split the party by co-opting one of its cadres. Now the Kata'ib has a pro-Syrian faction, headed by Karim Pakraduni,[52] and an anti-Syrian faction, controlled by the Gemayel family. Pierre Gemayel still appeals to a large Christian constituency as the scion of a traditional family that has represented the Maronite community since Lebanon's independence. He is a reminder of the days when the Maronites had real political power. He is also a member of the opposition, protesting Syrian involvement in Lebanon, trying to shake off Christian disenchantment, and attempting to increase Christians' political weight.

The Clergy

The clergy have always played a role in Lebanese public life because of the nature of allegiance in Lebanon and its political system. Citizenship has not really taken root in Lebanon. Commitment to the nation comes after loyalty to the family, the personal representative of one's interests, and the clerical leader of one's sect.

The clergy have a great say in the personal affairs of the people because Lebanon's Personal Status Law remains confessionalized. Religious leaders are opinionmakers, as they help shape public perceptions and influence agenda setting, even on secular issues. Also, the addition of Article 19 to the constitution in 1990 officially increased the role of the clergy in political life by establishing a constitutional council and allowing religious leaders to advise the council on such matters as personal status, religious practices, and education.[53]

Some religious leaders have a weight that cannot exclusively be explained by charisma or primordial ties or the religiosity of their flock. Their importance goes beyond their respective sects, touching the whole of Lebanon. In essence, their effect on the political scene is not that of a religious leader, but of a politician. The current Sunni mufti, Muhammad Qabbani, certainly does not have such weight, nor did the former Maronite patriarch Antoine Khreish in the 1980s. The presence of strong political leadership obstructs religious leadership and diminishes the latter's importance in politics. It is only when a conjuncture of events or situations creates a void in the political leadership in a community that sect leaders become politico-religious leaders, and by extension leaders of the community.

The Maronite community, for example, has a long history of the clergy interjecting itself into politics. The Maronite Church began gaining influence in the eighteenth century, and in the nineteenth century Maronite patriarchs assumed political leadership of the community, defining Maronite relations with other communities and speaking on behalf of the sect.[54] Their role abated with Lebanon's independence and the ascent of political leaders from the community. Today, however, Patriarch Mar Nasrallah Butros Sfeir has assumed a leadership role, acting as the spokesman of the Maronite sect, if not the entire Christian community. Sfeir is spearheading the movement for Syria's withdrawal and a cessation of its involvement in Lebanon.[55] It is remarkable that Sfeir had a minor role in late 1980s politics and appeared on the political scene as a major player in the 1990s. His rise was made possible by the disintegration of the Christian leadership on the eve of the Second Republic and the refusal of the Christian community as a whole to accept the Ta'if agreement and to play the political game.

Similarly, the role of the Sunni mufti as a representative of his religious community was slowly transformed into that of a political leader with the breakdown of the political system in 1975. The waning influence of the Sunni militias and the dissociation between Sunni leaders and their constituents led to an increase in the importance of the then-mufti, Hassan Khaled. His dive into politics, among other factors, led to his assassination in 1989.

The Second Republic brought with it peace and a redefined office of the prime minister. It also brought a new, strong contender for Sunni leadership, namely Rafiq Hariri. With Hariri acting as the voice of the Sunnis, the community needed no politico-religious representation. The choice of a new mufti took some time, as Hariri wanted to preclude a strong contender for Sunni sympathies. In the early 1990s, the importance of the mufti's office dwindled, as it was headed by the scholarly and not very charismatic interim mufti, Muhammad Qabbani. By the time Qabbani was officially installed in 1996, Hariri was well established and no longer feared competition from within the community, especially from a lackluster mufti whom he endorsed.

Emerging Elites

The 1990s saw the emergence of peace in Lebanon and by extension the return of electoral life. Lebanon had not held elections since 1972. With the first postwar elections that took place in 1992 a whole generation could exercise its right to vote for the first time.

Lebanese in their thirties and forties, who should have been the backbone of any new political elite, were excluded from political positions to the benefit of older elites, who commanded such resources as money, Syrian backing, or war legitimacy. Hence, a distinction is evident between emerging elites and young elite members who followed their fathers' footsteps into politics. These new young elite, mainly men,[56] have places in the current political constellation. They are, however, waiting in or on the fringes of the third circle of the PRE for the opportunity to officially enter the political system, assuming an elected or appointed position. Two obstacles block the entry of the youth to the elite: primordial links that create a clientelist system and the lack of official entrance channels. There are no schools for the formation of elites and real political parties where the young can slowly climb in the ranks and be recruited into the elite do not exist. Young people must therefore attract the attention of a powerful political player. By becoming his protégé, the young person will enter the political elite through nomination and rarely through elections. Sometimes, the political player will help the youth create a political constituency.

Four channels of entrance to the political elite are identifiable: affiliation with NGOs, mainly those dealing with human rights or good governance; positions in state administration; being the son of a powerful political actor; or belonging to the rejectionist group, choosing to remain outside the system and hoping some day to abolish it.[57] As ideal types, these newly emerging elites are the civil society activist, the technocrat, the heir, and the nationalist rebel.[58]

The Civil Society Activist

The civil society activist is in his thirties or early forties. He is part of the war generation, those who were politically socialized during the civil war. He has allied himself with a major pole of power, usually a communitarian pole, and thus entered the third circle. He is the son of an upper-middle-class family and sometimes has or had a relative in politics. He is a highly educated professional—usually a political scientist, economist, or lawyer—with impressive credentials from prestigious Western universities. He has tried his luck in legislative elections but was either trounced or was unable to muster the necessary funds for successfully campaigning or getting accepted on a list. It is too early to determine the attitude and discourse of this ideal type once he formally enters the system, but his present position, under the auspices of communitarian leaders, points toward his adopting the sectarian attitudes and behaviors of the present Lebanese political elite. He will probably not be able to enter the second circle, as the political leader he works with will not allow it.

The Technocrat

The technocrat belongs to the middle class. His parents are typically civil servants, and he has never had relatives in politics. He is also from the war generation, and for that reason was sent abroad to further his education. He studied finance or engineering and is the graduate of excellent universities in both the Francophone and Anglophone worlds. He has worked abroad for five to ten years, and in Lebanon marketed his skills as an expert at the start of the short economic boom in 1994. He is now in top management in the Lebanese public administration. He has placed himself under the protection of his community's leader, advising him on technical matters, and is thus in the third circle. He is as keen as the civil society activist to enter the political system as an elected or appointed official, but he is also aware that he can always leave the country if need be. He can easily find a job on the international job market.

The Heir

The heir is a son of an incumbent or a member of the present political elite. His age can vary between the mid-twenties and the mid-forties. He has studied business or management and has been prepared to succeed his father in his businesses (e.g. the sons of Hariri or Issam Fares) or through political posts (e.g. Emile Lahoud Jr. and Elias Murr). Good relations with regional or international actors have been cultivated: the heir can be a personal friend of the George Bush family (Issam Fares's son) or close to the Saudi royal family (the sons of Hariri). One should also not neglect the links of the heir with certain members of the Syrian elite. For example, the sons of Hussein el-Husseini, former Speaker of the house, were close to Basil al-Asad: photos of al-Assad are displayed in Hassan el-Husseini's office. The Hariri family had close personal and business relations with the family of the Syrian vice-president Abdel Halim Khaddam (the cellular phone company Liban Cell). This generation of heirs is starting to enter politics as we have seen in the nomination of Elias Murr to the ministry of interior in 2000.

The Nationalist Rebel

The nationalist rebel is generally in his twenties or early thirties. He is from the middle class or the lower middle class, probably a Christian and a sympathizer of the outlawed Lebanese Forces or the banned Free Patriotic Movement of the exiled General Aoun. He is a student at one of the Christian universities in the former Christian enclave. The nationalist rebel is politically active, participating in large-scale demonstrations against the regime. He is dissatisfied with the distribution of power in post-Ta'if Lebanon and disenchanted with Christian representation by the elite. He rejects Syrian-Lebanese relations in their present form and questions Lebanese sovereignty and independence under the present system.[59]

The nationalist rebel is part of a rejectionist group seeking to change the political system and the elite. He wants a Lebanon devoid of Syrian influence and thus an elite that is not subservient to Syria and is more representative of the aspirations of the people. If the regional situation changes and Syria's influence in Lebanon abates, the nationalist rebel will find himself in a unique position as a representative of a large segment of Lebanese society. In the more likely case of continued Syrian influence, at least for the foreseeable future, some of the more pliable individuals of this group will be co-opted and integrated into the second and third circles of the PRE.

Elite Agendas, Discourses, and Perceptions

Examination of PRE members' discourse is helpful in understanding their attitudes and behaviors.[60] To grasp how incumbent elites have been maintaining themselves in power and consolidating their hold on the system, one must look at the policies they have endorsed in regard to relations with Syria and changes in the political system. These policies, as presented here, are gleaned from the discourse of PRE members, revealing perceptions, attitudes, and sometimes conflicting agendas.

Syrian-Lebanese Relations

Syrian-Lebanese relations and the need for their reevaluation came to the fore in March and September 2000, largely because of a change in the regional constellation. Indeed, with the death of Hafiz al-Asad, the loosening of the Syrian grip on Lebanon, and Israeli withdrawal from the south, there was a change in the political discourse. Although Syria's armed presence and its intervention in Lebanese political affairs have been taboo subjects for discussion, they have now become part of a national public debate.

At first glance, there seem to be two distinctive agendas in the PRE concerning this issue: one anti-Syrian, seeking Syrian withdrawal from Lebanon and cessation of Syrian influence in Lebanese affairs, and one pro-Syrian, in favor of the status quo. Yet, contrary to what one might expect, there are no real differences among the discourses of the PRE on Syrian-Lebanese relations. A possible explanation is that the Syrian presence makes possible the control of the system by the present incumbents while the Aounists or the LF are excluded.

The majority of our interviewees agree that Syrian-Lebanese relations are not balanced and that there is a need for a readjustment. Although all concede the need for an "excellent" if not "special" relationship with Syria, they also agree that Syria interferes too much in Lebanese affairs. Some people close to the government, that is, in the third circle, think that Syrian involvement is sometimes justified, if not good for Lebanon, as it guarantees system stability.

The majority of those interviewed would like Syrian-Lebanese relations to be more of a partnership concentrating on economic relations, in addition to security and foreign affairs, because of the ongoing Arab-Israeli conflict. Indeed, even competing elites affirm that Lebanon's position internationally can only be strong if it continues to align itself with Syria.

Those who are more sympathetic to Syrian involvement in the PRE are usually men between fifty-five and sixty, socialized before the war, and mainly Sunni. They are nostalgic for Arabism and see Syria as the embodiment of this ideology that they adopted in their youth. Some of the younger generation, those socialized during the war, go so far as to say that the problem is "Syria should have allied itself with a more representative Lebanon," meaning that Syria's allies in parliament and the cabinet do not represent the Lebanese population.[61] This demand for better representation comes mainly from Christians who are unhappy with their MPs. It is also heard from sympathizers of Prime Minister Hariri who think his attempts at economic reforms are being blocked by Syria and its Lebanese partners, namely Hizballah and President Lahoud.

The withdrawal of Israeli forces from southern Lebanon in 2000 had created a schism in Lebanon regarding Hizballah and its operations. After the events of 11 September 2001, more voices—especially among the conjunctural and emerging elites—began crying out for less Syrian involvement, especially in Lebanese foreign affairs and dealings with Israel. They would like Lebanese support to end for Hizballah and its operations against Israel in Shebaa Farms (allegedly supported by Syria). These voices are rising as Hizballah has been placed on the U.S. and Canadian lists of terrorist organizations and is in danger of appearing on the European list as well. Indeed, they view government support for Hizballah's actions in the south as a liability for Lebanon when seeking assistance from donor countries and such institutions as the International Monetary Fund and the World Bank.

Future of the Political System

While most of the PRE members interviewed grant the need for a change of the Lebanese political system and talk openly of a future deconfessionalized system, they place it in a far away future, well after their time. They clearly recognize that the confessional system provides them and their children the opportunity to monopolize the political scene and that any change in the system will lead to a change in elites and the emergence of a new political elite. As the issue is part of the national discourse, they propose a set of steps to prepare the way for the eventual creation of a deconfessionalized political system. First, they argue for a restructuring of the judiciary and for its total dissociation from the executive. They also propose to reform the Personal Status Law to separate religion and state.

In general, they also argue for a more uniform electoral law, one not tailored before every election to bring Syria's cronies to power. The PRE members interviewed also maintain the need for the creation of new political parties—modern parties based on ideology and not on personal loyalties. As one interviewee asserted, "Confessionalism is a cover for clientelism and for a parochial mentality. We have to break this vicious circle." He added, "Change cannot come from within the system. It is civil society and the private sector that must push for change."[62]

Some even propose to follow up on the bicameral solution provided for in the Ta'if agreement, which recommends a nonconfessional parliament and a confessional Senate. The Senate would act as an advisory body, without legislative rights, and would concern itself with issues of an existential/*masiriya* nature (i.e., issues that impact the future of the state, in addition to issues of humanitarian importance). The idea was floated in October 2002 and gathered support among the Druze, who hoped to acquire the presidency of the Senate for themselves. The revived notion of a confessional Senate was, however, short-lived.

Although there is no generation gap concerning deconfessionalization of the political system, there seem to be divisions among the communities on the issue: While large confessions, such as the Shi'a, seem in favor of a deconfessionalized system in which parliamentary seats are not divided according to confessions, other smaller communities such as the Armenians vehemently oppose the idea.[63] One might expect the same reaction from the Druze. Both communities are aware that they would politically fade in the new system, as their political power and weight would be diminished in a nonconfessional Lebanon. Rejection of a deconfessionalized political system is also prevalent in the Christian community at large. The Christians, a demographic minority, are afraid of losing the privileges they have in the present system, in which they share power on an equal basis with the Muslims.

A provision for the deconfessionalization of the system was also in the National Pact of 1943, which established the postindependence political system. The provision was never acted upon, however, until the political system crumbled in 1975, as confessionalism implied that political representation would be monopolized by communitarian elites. In that sense, the present attitude of the elite vis-à-vis the deconfessionalization of the political system carries a strong impression of déjà vu.

Conclusion

The end of the civil war has allowed for a rejuvenation and renewal of the PRE in Lebanon. The parliamentary nominations that followed the Ta'if agreement and the 1992 elections brought new faces into the political elite, and the leaders of warring factions officially entered the political sphere.

The peace has also modified the composition of the PRE, and introduced new groups.

Change has not, however, been substantial in terms of elite attitudes and behavior. Whereas the prewar elite was made up of a coalition of landlords, notables, and professionals, the postwar elite largely consists of war elites, rich entrepreneurs, Syria's clients, and military personnel. The parallel between the two elite cartels is clear: the postwar incumbents try to emulate postindependence elites in their policies in an attempt to block the system. The civil war has allowed for more involvement by the clergy in the political sphere, and the Lahoud presidency has led to an interjection of the military and security apparatuses into political life.

By the end of 2003 the Lebanese system appeared closed to the entry of new elite groups, but some are slowly emerging. Their entrance into the political system through election or appointment depends on several variables—resources, connections, and so on—the most important being Syria. As one Christian MP from the opposition stated, "The political elite is made up of around 300 people under Syrian surveillance and in complete subservience to Syria's will. . . . The Syrians operate on several levels— social, political, and electoral—to eliminate any attempts of breaking through by new elites who think differently."[64]

Indeed Syria carries a lot of weight in the composition of the PRE, especially the core elite and members of the second circle, but its alliances sometimes shift rapidly and in unfathomable ways. As long as Syria has influence in Lebanon and as long as there is no change of the system, there will only be one of two forms of elite circulation: members of the elite are chosen from within the pool of incumbents and a number of would-be incumbents ready to be co-opted.[65] Circulation is then pure reshuffling, a kind of musical chairs. Alternatively, circulation is simply generational: when a member of the elite dies, his political capital passes on to the son or nephew who has been groomed for the role and has the right (mainly Syrian) connections.

The confessional representation model creates a political system that is not viable in the long run, as demonstrated in 1975. The current system still contains the seeds of its own destruction. A change of the system would doubtlessly lead to a change in elites, therefore the members of the PRE do not seem open to such a scenario. While generally accepting the prospect of a deconfessionalized political system, the prevailing discourse among the PRE sets it in the long-term, postponing it as long as possible and thus guaranteeing their continued dominance and that of their descendants over Lebanese politics, in what seems to be an emulation of prewar outlooks concerning this crucial issue.

Clientelism and corruption are rife, and the three heads of state are accused of contributing to this corruption. The policies that the government has tried to implement have been blocked on the political level because of squabbles among the incumbents. Lebanon's economic policies favor the privileged classes, which are enmeshed with the political elite, thereby also guaranteeing their own and their descendants' monopoly of the system.

Educated young people, who could act as a counterbalancing force, are disenchanted with their lack of economic prospects, corruption, and their inability to participate in the political process. They are leaving the country en masse, emigrating mainly to Canada and Australia.[66] This brain drain does not appear to trouble the government, which seems content with the hard currency remittances these immigrants send home. The departure of these potential contenders for power ensures the future of the political dynasties created by the elite.

The Iraq War and the U.S. military victory, however, have created a new dynamic in the Middle East. The United States appears willing to attempt to remodel the region through forced regime change. It looks as if Syria, and by extension Lebanon, are now on the U.S. radar. As Syria was granted quasi-tutelage over Lebanon in exchange for its siding with the multinational forces in the 1991 Gulf War, its perceived siding with Iraq in the 2003 war might lead to a termination of its influence in Lebanon. With the voting of the Syria Accountability Act in the U.S. Congress in October 2003, and rumors of President Bush's willingness to ratify the law, U.S. pressure on Syria to withdraw from Lebanon and curtail its interference in Lebanese affairs will probably have a direct impact on the political elite. It might also allow groups that are currently marginalized to enter the political system. This perceived pressure is already having an impact on Lebanese incumbents, who are starting to get on the defensive, while anti-Syrian activists such as members of Aoun's FPM are gaining hope.

Notes

1. Syria's decision to join the coalition in the 1990–1991 Gulf crisis and war led to international acceptance and indifference toward its role and policies in Lebanon. On the Saudi-sponsored Ta'if agreement, see Maila, *The Document of National Understanding;* idem, "L'Accord de Taef deux ans après" (The Ta'if Accord: An Evaluation); and al-Abed, *Lubnan wal Ta'if.*

2. For a definition of this concept and the circle model, see the introductory chapter by Volker Perthes in this volume.

3. Parliamentary turnover set a record in 1992: more than 80 percent of elected MPs were new. In the 1996 elections, the percentage fell to 35 percent. Bahout, "Les élites parlementaire libanaises de 1996," p. 29.

4. On Syria's role in Lebanon, see Abu Khalil, "Determinants and Characteristics of Syrian Policy in Lebanon."

5. This analysis is based on fieldwork conducted in Lebanon with members

of the PRE in September and October 2001, April and May 2002, and April and May 2003. The sample consists of semistructured interviews with fifty-three PRE members of the second and third circles.

6. For more information on prewar Lebanese elites, see Binder, *Politics in Lebanon;* Johnson, *Class and Client in Beirut;* Hudson, *The Precarious Republic;* and Harik, "Political Elite of Lebanon."

7. Disunified elites are those for whom "structural integration and value consensus are minimal . . . [where] factions disagree on the rules of political conduct and the worth of political institutions." Consensually unified elites are elite for whom "structural integration and value consensus are relatively inclusive. . . . All important elite factions share an underlying consensus about rules of the game and the worth of existing political institutions." Burton, Gunther, and Higley, "Introduction: Elite Transformations and Democratic Regimes," pp. 10–11.

8. The Syrian army has been present in Lebanon since 1976. In 2003 its troops were estimated at 20,000 to 30,000. In February 2003 they were redeployed for the third time in less than two years, supposedly in compliance with the Ta'if agreement, which had foreseen the total withdrawal of Syrian troops.

9. Hanf, *Coexistence in Wartime Lebanon*, p. 70.

10. Lijphart, "Typologies of Democratic Systems," pp. 3–44.

11. Hudson, "The Problem of Authoritative Power in Lebanese Politics," p. 227.

12. Sayegh, *Al-Nizam al-Lubnani fi thawabitihi wa tahawulatihi,* p. 44.

13. Mansour, *Al-Inqilab 'ala al-Ta'if,* pp. 45–46; Sayegh, *Al-Nizam al-Lubnani fi thawabitihi wa tahawulatihi,* p. 46.

14. Before the war, the Greek Orthodox community usually aligned with the Maronites. This changed after the war. The Druze community, relatively small in number, carries more political weight than groups with the same or similar demographics.

15. The number was set at 108 MPs in the Ta'if agreement, but it was changed in practice to 128 after Syria applied pressure to accommodate some of its clients.

16. There has been no census since 1932, but observers agree that Muslims are today the majority in Lebanon. The Central Intelligence Agency estimates that 70 percent of the population is Muslim and 30 percent is Christian. See the CIA website at http://www.cia.gov/cia/publications/factbook/geos/le.html#People (accessed 3 February 2003). The Lebanese ministry of interior has estimated the size of the main religious communities as follows: Shi'a 25 percent, Sunnis 23 percent, Druze 6 percent, Maronites 25 percent, Greek Catholic 6 percent, Greek Orthodox 10 percent, Armenian 4 percent. Cited in Figuie, *Le point sur le Liban,* p. 9.

17. These wide-ranging accords tie Lebanon to Syria in all fields: military, political, social, economic, educational, and cultural. For an understanding of how Syria legitimized and institutionalized its presence in Lebanon, see Thompson, "Will Syria Have to Withdraw from Lebanon?"

18. Khashan and Haddad, "The Coupling of the Syrian-Lebanese Peace Tracks: Beirut's Options," p. 206.

19. See Abdo Baaklini et al., *Legislative Politics in the Arab World,* pp. 92–93.

20. Bahout, "Les élites parlementaire libanaises de 1996," p. 30.

21. Farid al-Khazen, *Intikhabat Lubnan ma ba'da al-harb,* pp. 109–111.

22. For more on postwar elections in Lebanon, see al-Khazen and Salem, *Al-Intikhabat al-ula fi Lubnan ma ba'd al harb;* Salem and Abi Saab, *Al-Intikhabat al-niyabia wa azmat al-dimuqratiya fi Lubnan.*

23. Challenging elites are those individuals or groups who do not want to play by the rules of the game or are not allowed to play the game at all.

24. Higley and Gunther, eds., *Elites and Democratic Consolidation in Latin America and Southern Europe,* p. xi.

25. Burton, Gunther, and Higley, "Introduction: Elite Transformations and Democratic Regimes," p. 14.

26. "Elite convergence [starts] once successive electoral defeats convince major dissidents and hostile elites that to avoid permanent exclusion from office they must beat the newly formed dominant coalition at its own electoral game. This requires that they acknowledge the legitimacy of existing democratic institutions and promise adherence to democratic rules of the game." Ibid., p. 24.

27. Competitors do not necessarily accept the rules by which they agree to play.

28. Farid al-Khazen, *Intikhabat Lubnan ma ba'da al-harb,* pp. 224–225.

29. *Daily Star* (Beirut), 28 January 2002.

30. Interview, Beirut, 3 June 2002.

31. *Middle East Intelligence Bulletin,* http://www.meib.org/articles/0012_ldl.htm. This website, established by Lebanese rejectionist groups in the United States, posts portraits of several members of the Lebanese political elite. These must not always be accepted as fact, as they are biased.

32. Informal talk with a young Shi'a civil servant, Environment Ministry, Beirut, 26 September 2001.

33. Interview, Beirut, 16 October 2001. For a comprehensive study of Hizballah, see Norton, "Hizballah of Lebanon."

34. On average the pro-Hizballah parliamentarian bloc is composed of twelve MPs, but the number varies of course from legislature to legislature.

35. In 1996 his eighteen-year-old son, Hady Nasrallah, was killed in an operation against Israeli occupation. Nasrallah was offered the corpse in a swap, but he refused, insisting that the Israelis also return the bodies of other Hizballah operatives.

36. Joseph Fouché (1763–1820) was minister of police and later security chief under Napoleon. A manipulator with few equals, Fouché was the consummate survivor.

37. Saliby, *Za'amat wa 'A'ilat,* p. 43.

38. This was especially the case after a relative by marriage, Emile Lahoud, became president of Lebanon.

39. Saliby, *Za'amat wa 'A'ilat,* p. 43.

40. Denoeux and Springborg, "Hariri's Lebanon," p. 3.

41. These are families who represent their communities in politics for at least three generations.

42. Dupont, "La nouvelle armée libanaise," p. 3.

43. The president, nominated and voted on by parliament, enjoys the total trust of Damascus. In a 2001 report, Freedom House classifies Lebanon as an authoritarian regime, putting it in the same category as Syria. While this author does not agree with that classification, one cannot deny that freedom and democratic practices have become more restricted since the ascent of Lahoud to the presidency.

44. Interview with a retired general, Beirut, 2 May 2003.

45. Interview, 17 May 2002.

46. Middle East Intelligence Bulletin, www.meib.org/articles/0111_1d1.htm (accessed 18 November 2002).

47. The Gemayels developed the Kata'ib and later the Lebanese Forces. The Frangiehs formed the Marada. The Chamouns created the Numur.

48. Not all the warlords were excluded from the settlement—only those who did not side with Syria, namely Aoun and Samir Geagea of the LF. Elia Hobeika, another warlord, for example became a minister in postwar governments.

49. According to Joseph Bahout, notables constituted 41.6 percent of northern MPs in the 1996 legislature. Bahout does not give comparative figures for other Lebanese regions. Bahout, "Les élites parlementaire libanaises de 1996," p. 28. On the flexibility of families and their ability to adapt to changing circumstances, see Ziadé, "Tripoli: famille et politique," pp. 274–311.

50. This is a group of Christian dignitaries who on 1 May 2001 signed a document affirming the Maronite bishops' declaration advocating Syrian redeployment in preparation for complete withdrawal from Lebanon. Since that date they have been active as an opposition group, mainly from within the system. On the declaration, see note 55 below.

51. Undated speech, Kata'ib website, www.al-kataeb.org (accessed 16 October 2002).

52. In late 2002 and early 2003, Pakraduni visited Damascus several times to meet with President Bashar al-Asad and other Syrian leaders. In April 2003 he was appointed state minister for administrative reform in the newly formed government.

53. Ofeish, "Lebanon's Second Republic," p. 105.

54. For a history of the Maronite Church in Lebanon, see Harik, "Maronite Church and Political Change in Lebanon."

55. On 20 September 2000, the Council of Maronite Bishops issued a statement that not only broke the taboo against public criticism of Syria's role in the country but also challenged Syrian rule in Lebanon. As George Rabil points out, this "call could be interpreted as an attempt not only to take over the leadership of the Maronite community but also to try to rally around . . . a national opposition to Syria." Rabil, "The Maronites and Syrian Withdrawal," p. 36. Sfeir is on record as having described the entire Lebanese government as "a creature of Syria." Claudia Rosett, "Syria's Tightening Grip on Lebanon," *Wall Street Journal,* 5 February 2003.

56. The relative absence of women is not only apparent in the political elite at large but also in this emerging elite. Indeed, while women are highly represented in the judiciary, there have traditionally been no women in the executive; the few women in the legislative tend to be relatives of male politicians. Few women rise in the civil service to top positions, but steps were made in that direction in the 2001 administrative nominations. Unlike some other Arab countries, there are no places reserved for women in parliament or the administration. The absence of women from the political sphere when they are so present in the public sphere can only be explained by the patriarchal and highly personalized structure of Lebanese society.

57. The media is not a channel for upward mobility used by emerging elites and does not play an important role in elite formation or agenda setting. There are several competing privately owned daily newspapers and television stations. Although the media is relatively free when compared to that of other Arab countries, any impression of freedom of the press is quickly dispelled upon a closer look. Some newspapers are owned by politicians, while all private television stations belong to important political actors. Only one journalist, Gibran Tueini, the editor in chief and owner of *al-Nahar,* seems capable of setting agendas or altering discourses, as he did in March 2000 with the open letter to Bashar al-Asad, which led to the declaration of the Maronite bishops in September 2000 and can be said to have triggered the national discourse on Syrian-Lebanese relations.

58. These ideal types are based on interviews conducted in Lebanon between 2001 and 2003.

59. An estimate of the segment of the population this ideal type represents is difficult to give. However, the September 2003 by-elections show that this segment is a substantial one, at least in the Christian areas. The FPM candidate in the elections garnered only 3,000 votes less than the candidate backed by the government and major political actors.

60. This section is primarily based on fieldwork conducted in Lebanon with members of the PRE in September and October 2001, April and May 2002, and April, May, and June 2003. The sample consists of semistructured interviews with fifty-three PRE members of the second and third circles.

61. Interview, 8 May 2002.

62. Interview, 27 April 2002.

63. Interview with an Armenian MP, Beirut, 19 October 2001.

64. Interview, Beirut, 22 October 2001.

65. A change of the system implies doing away with the consociational formula and deconfessionalizing the political system.

66. Official Lebanese sources estimate the number of departures at 15,000 per month. See Nahla Chahal, "Etat et confessions: la formidable capacité d'intégration du système libanais," p. 131. While this figure is debatable and needs to be qualified, it is quite telling.

10

Palestinian Territories: From State Building to Crisis Management

Hans-Joachim Rabe

On the morning of 1 July 1994, a black Mercedes limousine crossed the Rafah border from Egypt into the Gaza Strip. Under the watchful eye of Israeli soldiers, and surrounded by Palestinian security officials, the car headed through a chanting crowd of people waving Palestinian flags. The driver stopped between a marching band to the right and a red carpet to the left. At 10:47, Yasser Arafat stepped out of the car, knelt, and kissed the ground, marking a new era in Palestinian elite politics.

Arafat's arrival triggered a transformation among Palestinian elites. The Oslo agreements, which he signed in September 1993 and September 1995 with Israeli prime minister Yitzhak Rabin, started a new race for power and authority within the Palestinian territories. The establishment of a Palestinian protostate and the new relationship between the Palestine Liberation Organization (PLO) and Israel shook the foundations of the political stratum of the Palestinian territories. Politically relevant elites regrouped along new lines and struggled for control over political institutions, economic assets, and sources of political legitimacy.

Palestinian elites have been, in a sense, like tigers in a bubble—internally strong and able to roar, flex their muscles, extend their claws, and strike. Were they, however, to extend their claws against anyone or anything outside their domain—against Israel in particular—the bubble would burst and they would fall.

The Oslo agreements created a new political and economic setting that initiated the formation of a new power elite in the West Bank and Gaza Strip under the central command of Arafat. This elite created and managed a centralized system of control on the domestic level until fall 2000, but it remained weak and dependent in the regional context. With the outbreak of the second intifada in September 2000, this elite came under mounting pressure from internal and external forces. As the escalating conflict with Israel led to a systematic disempowerment of Arafat and parts of his core

267

elite, alternative centers of power emerged within Palestinian society. In combination, these internal and external pressures started a reform process within the infant Palestinian protostate. As of early 2004, this process remained short of having produced ample results, as the Palestinian territories were sliding deeper into a political and economic crisis.

The Oslo Bubble

An intrinsic feature of Oslo became quickly and strikingly clear: the signatories had created the basis for a Palestinian entity that was to be internally strong but externally weak. In one sense it would be a politicoeconomic bubble in which Palestinian elites would interact and compete. Oslo created a structural and legal framework cementing Israeli superiority on the strategic level, with Israel, and to a lesser extent international donors, controlling the "taps" that the Palestinian Authority (PA) needed to govern effectively. Most significant, Israel controlled all of the borders around the Palestinian entity and the air space above it. At checkpoints, from watchtowers, and on patrols, the Israeli army kept a close eye on what and who was entering or leaving Palestinian territory. By the late 1990s the Gaza Strip had been sealed by a fence with five heavily guarded exit points, Israeli gunboats patrolled the coast, and fighter jets frequently crossed the skies. The West Bank, in contrast, had been split into zones of influence: Areas A, B, and C. The PA could act autonomously only in the eight major towns, or Area A. In Area B, which included most Palestinian villages and refugee camps, the Israeli army and Palestinian police shared authority. In Area C, which comprised about 70 percent of all West Bank territory, including settlements, water reservoirs, and agricultural lands, the Israeli military remained in full control. Critics have compared the map that emerged under this arrangement to Swiss cheese, jesting that Palestinian elites were trapped in the holes.

Israeli control over the movement of people, goods, and services in the Palestinian territories had profound economic effects. Israel blocked or opened economic lifelines to Palestinians according to its security demands or political considerations. Agricultural produce, raw materials, manufactured goods, workers, merchants, and managers were all subjected to closures and Israeli soldiers at checkpoints. Another key tap—import revenues from value added tax (VAT) and customs duties, which accounted for up to two-thirds of the PA budget—were to be collected by Israel and then transferred to the PA. These arrangements meant that from one day to the next, the Palestinian economy could be thrown into turmoil or largely put on hold depending on Israeli considerations.

The Oslo Accords stipulated the establishment of a "strong"

Palestinian police force, but restricted its power through the nature and the amount of weapons that it could possess. While Oslo allowed the PA to import only specific numbers and types of pistols, rifles, and riot-control vehicles, the Israeli army maintained its full range of modern military equipment. Oslo also laid out the primary task for the Palestinian police: The PA, Oslo reads, is to "act systematically against all expressions of violence and terror" and "to ensure the immediate, efficient and effective handling of any incident involving a threat or act of terrorism, violence or incitement."[1]

These arrangements established the parameters for the creation of a coercive entity on the domestic political level while keeping that entity weak and dependent within the regional context. Edward Said has argued that by signing Oslo "the PLO has transformed itself from a national liberation movement into a kind of small-town government."[2] The PA, however, held command over an extensive institutional infrastructure, initiated a massive recruitment process for its bureaucratic and coercive machinery, re-regulated the local economy, and wielded power potentially affecting some 2.5 million people. It was within and around this institutional setting that Palestinian elites regrouped and repositioned themselves after the signing of Oslo.

The Politics of Elite Change

Arafat's return and the arrangements he agreed to implement profoundly transformed the political landscape of the Palestinian territories. As the process of protostate building unfolded, conflicts arose between new and old elites over what that protostate should look like and who would dominate it. These disputes changed the Palestinian body politic, reshuffling the composition of elite circles and altering the dynamics within them. To be specific, Oslo triggered three processes that changed the structural political framework of Palestinian elite politics: the rearrangement of the Palestinian political stratum, the injection of an outside national leadership, and the rise of a potent Palestinian protostate.

The Altered Political Landscape

The political stratum regrouped into three major streams, drifting toward or away from the Oslo process and the institutions it produced. A mainstream nationalist camp came forward under the leadership of Yasser Arafat. This grouping was dominated by members of Fatah, the largest and most influential movement in Palestinian politics, and supported by politicians from such smaller secular factions such as the Palestinian People's Party (PPP) and the Palestinian Democratic Union (FIDA). Proponents of this stream supported the Oslo process, favored a negotiated settlement with Israel, recognized the legitimacy of the PA, and participated in state building. Opinion polls in September 1993 indicated that about half the Palestinian population supported factions belonging to this category.[3]

On the other end of the spectrum appeared a rejectionist, anti-Oslo front. Its supporters considered Oslo a sell-out of the Palestinian national movement, did not believe that negotiations would pave the way to Palestinian independence, and therefore boycotted participation in state building. This front comprised religious and secular streams, including among the secularists the leaders from the leftist-communist Democratic Front for the Liberation of Palestine (DFLP) and the Popular Front for the Liberation of Palestine (PFLP). These parties, according to polls conducted in September 1993, had the support of about 10 percent of the population, with the trend clearly pointing downwards.[4] More powerful were the religious activists from Hamas and Islamic Jihad, whose agendas openly called for armed struggle, the destruction of Israel, and the establishment of an Islamic state in historic Palestine. The religious groups could rely on support from about 20 percent of the Palestinian population.[5]

Situated between these two extremes was a loyal but increasingly critical opposition. Assembling within Fatah and independent political camps, this opposition supported the Oslo agreements and recognized the legitimacy of the PA, but it remained skeptical of how negotiations with Israel were being handled and the state-building process managed. This stream, particularly within Fatah, included a potentially powerful conglomerate of leaders and constituencies.

Courtesy of the Oslo agreements, the national PLO leadership formerly in exile and its cadres were injected into this arena of political allegiance. Around 14,000 "outsiders"—PLO functionaries and fighters—gradually arrived from Tunisia, Lebanon, Algeria, and other Arab countries. The modes of political socialization of inside activists and the outside PLO functionaries were very different. Resident politicians had been molded by their involvement in the first intifada, by occupation, active resistance, and life in refugee camps and Israeli jails. The prison experience in particular—which affected virtually the entire political stratum of inside activists—had created a sense of cohesion among these individuals and garnered them "street credentials" and political legitimacy. Access to the circle of inside leaders was in many instances a democratic process. In university student councils, from which many leaders emerged, activists had had to struggle for votes. In contrast, the outside leadership's political experience, at least after the PLO's expulsion from Lebanon in 1982, had been marked by diplomacy, negotiations, and office life in Amman, Damascus, or Tunis. As Khalil Shikaki argues, "This political elite, socialized in Arab countries, had been raised with an emphasis on national as opposed to democratic agendas: a quota system such as prevails in the PNC [Palestinian National Council] was the closest they had come to [democratic] practice."[6] Given these different political trajectories, a clash of interests and cultures between the inside and outside leadership seemed inevitable. Glen Robinson went so far as to argue that the outside leadership intended "to create a political process that was the antithesis of the politics of the new [inside] elite. [The] first job of the 'outside PLO' was to neutralize the 'inside PLO' in order to assert its own authority."[7] He had a point.

The primary means for achieving that goal was the construction of a powerful protostate under the auspices of Oslo. With up to twenty-five ministries, at least eight security services, approximately thirty public institutions, and around 100,000 employees, the Palestinian protostate developed into the biggest employer in the Palestinian territories and the controller of the lion's share of cash flow. While the PLO officially remained responsible for Palestinian politics on a national level, and the PA was supposed to be a subordinate local body, these formal arrangements were de facto turned upside down. For the PLO as an organization fell into a deep political sleep, while the protostate developed into the most powerful actor on the Palestinian political scene. People who held strategic positions within it were to become political "tigers" with extensive powers over people, cash, and guns.

Arafat: Political Solar Plexus

Protostate building in the Palestinian territories followed a pattern in terms of theory and practice. Political scientists would attach the label "neopatrimonial" to the emerging political system.[8]

At the center of this system sat Arafat, who controlled and directed the political process through a network of personal relations and informal control mechanisms. He manipulated decisionmaking, institution building, and elite formation in such a way and to such an extent that it is hard to overestimate his dominance of the Palestinian political system from 1994 to 2000. He occupied all top positions within the PLO and the PA. As chairman of the PLO, head of the PLO Executive Committee, and commander of the PLO's military organizations, Arafat was not only the prime decisionmaker, he had also become the symbol of the Palestinian revolution. In public opinion polls, he was always the most popular leader, often ten times more so than any other politician. Palestinians elected him to the presidency of the PA with an overwhelming majority, and he promptly appointed himself interior minister, a position that gave him command over all Palestinian police and security forces. In addition, he remained the leader of Fatah, the most powerful faction within the PA and the PLO.

By the stroke of a pen, Arafat could appoint, dismiss, promote, or demote personnel in senior political positions across a wide political spectrum. He played such a politically muscular role that by 1997 Haydar Abd al-Shafi, a prominent and critical member of the Palestinian parliament, had come to the conclusion that "it is really difficult to talk about political [elites] after Oslo. The sole decisionmaker has been Chairman Arafat. The rest of the political elite . . . expressed views. But the decisions were solely Arafat's."[9] To envision Arafat's position within elite circles would place him right in the middle of the first, or inner, circle.[10]

Arafat, however, could not rule solely on his own. Like any leader, he had to delegate powers and responsibilities, a fact that produced some extremely powerful figures in his immediate political orbit. These men, the core elite, were largely recruited from the returning PLO cadres. These returnees and the minority of insiders among them were generally senior members of Fatah, over fifty years of age, and with a history of working with Arafat. The core elite occupied the nerve centers of the rising regime but they nonetheless had to operate within a wider system of governance and had to struggle with popular and ambitious competitors.

The Center Circle: Core Elite Politics

Although the Oslo agreements remained vague on the specifics of regime type, the text painted a picture of a democratic process of general elections, separation of powers involving three branches of government, and the rule of law. Upon entering the West Bank and Gaza Strip, the PA stated that it would "enhance the concepts and principles of democracy and elections . . . maintain the preservation of citizens' rights, general freedoms, independence of the judiciary system, separation of powers and equality of opportunity."[11] Among the public, these principles were widely supported: more than 90 percent wanted fair elections, more than 80 percent favored a free press, and some 70 percent supported a multiparty system.[12]

Formal Democracy Versus Informal Control

In January 1996 formal democratic structures began to emerge as a parliament, the Palestinian Legislative Council (PLC), was elected. Although observers noted a number of irregularities in the run-up and the implementation of the elections, Palestinians from the West Bank, East Jerusalem, and Gaza were relatively free to choose their representatives. The religious and secular anti-Oslo front boycotted the elections, and only a few individual opposition members made their way into the new parliament. The elections confirmed Fatah's dominance, but critical elements within Fatah (the so-called Fatah independents), representatives from opposition parties, and independent politicians won around 40 percent of the seats. Of significance, more than two-thirds of council members came from the inside leadership.

The cabinets Arafat appointed were composed largely of these elected representatives—as by statute, he was obliged to do—and reflected the parliament's heterogeneity. All the cabinets had a relatively equal balance between insiders and outsiders, included members of parties other than Fatah, represented various regions and clans, and consisted to a considerable degree of technocrats with qualifications for their respective portfolios. Also notable was that each cabinet included outspoken critics of Arafat. From this perspective, the formal protostate elite reflected political pluralism and social heterogeneity.

Arafat, however, manipulated the cabinet in a way that its representative composition had little to do with de facto political control: to put it bluntly, he assigned the most powerful ministries to the Fatah returnees who had risen with him through the ranks of the PLO in Beirut and Tunis. Nabil Shaath, a long-serving member of Fatah's Central Committee, took over the Ministry of Planning and International Cooperation, the de facto foreign ministry, which played an important role in channeling funds from donors into development projects. Muhammad Nashashibi commanded the Ministry of Finance, thus wresting control over the collection of taxes. The largest ministries in terms of personnel, which offered their leaders potentially influential patronage networks, were equally staffed with returnees. Riad Za'noun headed the Ministry of Health, with about 5,000 people on its payroll.[13] Yasir Amr controlled the Ministry of Education, which employed some 19,000 people. In contrast, the smallest and least important ministries were given to insiders and non-Fatah cabinet members. Imad Faluji, a former Hamas spokesman, directed 163 employees in the Ministry of Youth and Sports. Bashir Barghouthi of the PPP gained control over a mere twenty-five employees at the Ministry of Industry.

Critical, non-Fatah cabinet members were further restricted, for directly beneath their ranks Arafat appointed loyalists as deputy ministers, assistant deputies, and director generals. Some of them allegedly received and transmitted orders via direct lines to Arafat, bypassing their superiors, sometimes overriding their objectives. These informal networks restricted decisionmaking powers of some ministers and blocked their ability to build independent patronage networks. With those ministers held at bay, only a select group of ministers moved into the inner circle of elites.

To reduce the influence of the cabinet as a corporate actor, Arafat refused to convene meetings only involving the ministerial elite. Rather, cabinet sessions were integrated into weekly meetings of a wider group of actors, generally referred to as the "Palestinian leadership." In addition to ministers, this group included heads of the security services, members of the negotiating teams, Arafat's presidential advisors, the Speaker of the parliament, and members of the PLO Executive Committee. Among this leadership of sixty or so, the ministers were outnumbered. Repeated attempts by cabinet ministers to hold separate meetings were squelched by Arafat.

Notably, this wider leadership was granted special privileges under the terms of Oslo, as the agreement divided Palestinian officials into three categories of so-called VIPs. Holders of VIP cards were to be allowed to pass Israeli checkpoints at times when non-VIP Palestinians remained confined to their respective localities. The Palestinian leadership comprised VIP 1, enjoying the widest possible freedom of movement, a strategic political asset given the territorial fragmentation of the self-rule areas and the frequency of Israeli closures. Within this group, the balance of power further shifted in favor of Fatah returnees: all presidential advisors, all security chiefs (except two), and most negotiators were senior members of Fatah who had returned to the Palestinian territories in the wake of Oslo.

Apart from the cabinet, only the PLO Executive Committee formed a heterogeneous elite within this leadership pool. By virtue of the organization's statutes, its members necessarily had to represent a wide political spectrum. As Shikaki pointed out, however, "members of the PLO Executive Committee [had] no resources [except] a vote. [They had] a role only in as much as they [were] either part of Arafat's office or members of the cabinet."[14] Membership of the PLO Executive Committee was thus no sufficient precondition for belonging to the first circle. It had to be backed up by other positions and resources.

Heads of the security services, in contrast, controlled a powerful infrastructure, commanding approximately 40,000 staff members, the equivalent of almost half of all PA employees and roughly 8 percent of the entire Palestinian workforce.[15] Estimates put the annual cost of these services at $720 million, a considerable chunk of the PA budget.[16] The most senior members of these services were Arafat-loyal returnees, with the prominent exceptions of the heads of the Preventive Security Services (PSS), Muhammad Dahlan in Gaza and Jibril Rajoub in the West Bank. As former intifada activists deported by Israel, they combined firsthand knowledge of the Palestinian resistance on the ground, an asset Arafat needed, with experience working with the PLO in Tunis. The security services operated in a legal void. Neither the PA nor the PLO had the power to monitor their activities. They remained accountable only to Arafat. Members of this group took prominent seats at the table of the inner circle.

Some of Arafat's presidential advisors, who became extremely powerful players, also belonged to the inner circle. The presidential office—with some 250 staff members and an annual budget of close to $100 million—

embodied the hub of Palestinian decisionmaking. For instance, Muhammad Rashid (Khalid Salam), Arafat's advisor on tax issues, came to play an important role in managing state-controlled companies, headed delegations to negotiate economic issues with Israel, and for all intents and purposes held more sway than Economy and Trade Minister Mahir al-Masri. Some individual advisors enjoyed, in many cases, more power than PA institutions. Azmi Shu'aibe, a member of the first cabinet, observed that one "result of the de-emphasis on institutions is that everything has to be referred to the office of the president, which means that anyone who works there, by virtue of his proximity to the president, is now more important than any minister. These are the ones who decide which dossiers are placed before him and who gets to see him. And seeing the president is necessary since projects and financial support must be approved by him rather than through normal institutional channels."[17]

Negotiators comprised another powerful group of the first circle. As the Palestinians' relationship with Israel was the most strategic topic on the national agenda, and would determine the extent of Palestinian sovereignty, the protostate's access to international markets, and the very legitimacy of the political regime, negotiators conducted their business extremely close to the center of strategic decisionmaking. There is little empirical data on the internal workings of the negotiating teams, which confirms the point that strategic decisionmaking was conducted within a closed circle. Like other core elite members, negotiators derived their political potency from occupying several positions simultaneously. People such as Shaath, who was a senior negotiator, "foreign minister," and member of the Fatah Central Committee, were accumulating strategic positions of power and thereby moving closer to the core elite center.

The Two Faces of the Core Elite

A select group of security chiefs, presidential advisors, senior negotiators, and ministers came to form a closed and influential core elite within Palestinian politics after the signing of the Oslo Accords. The internal dynamics of this group involved conflicts allowed, stirred, and moderated by Arafat. The rivalries within the core elite, an intrinsic feature of its inner workings, occurred on two levels: between different groups and within these groups.

The security services, for instance, intruded upon civilian institutions and their areas of operation. Ignoring court rulings, engaging in economic activities, and manipulating recruitment into the civil bureaucracy became quite common activities. Among such transgressions was "the blatant interference by several security and military government services in the affairs of the Customs Office, which caused the Ministry of Finance to lose its ability to control and safeguard the transfer of money into the treasury, causing waste and manipulation of public funds."[18]

Within the security establishment conflicts erupted over powers and responsibilities. For instance, in 1996 in the northern West Bank, members of Force 17, the presidential guard, and the PSS fought turf wars over political constituencies "with the [presidential guard] generally representing the concerns of Nablus' more established residents and [Jibril] Rajoub's operatives being stronger in the refugee camps, villages, and poorer quarters of Nablus."[19] Such developments revealed an essential characteristic of Arafat's neopatrimonial leadership style: By "allowing tensions to simmer between the various security forces [and other segments of the core elite] he fragments them and forestalls the coalescing of any alternative power centres."[20]

Constantly shuffling powers and responsibilities among those around him became another trademark of Arafat's leadership. He managed to keep the core elite unstable and in competition against one another by constantly moving individuals closer to the center or farther toward the periphery. As Shu'aibe observed, "If there [was] an important meeting with the Israelis, [Arafat] may send Saeb Erakat, or Nabil Shaath, or Yasir Abed Rabbo, or Abu Mazen. All of them [understood] that . . . this means that this man [chosen] is closer to the president. They understand because they are not a team; they are individual persons."[21] The ties of cooperation and dependency within the center circle linked individual members to Arafat rather than to each other. Arafat's core elite was thus two-faced: united toward its political environment but internally fragmented.

The Second- and Third-Circle Elites

The Palestinian protostate was built virtually from scratch. One locus of elite politics within this entity revolved around the production of second and third elite circles and active elite manipulation outside it.

Four processes have primarily governed the transformation of political elites outside the core: systematic disempowerment of the parliamentarian elite; installation of a powerful second stratum elite in administrative and coercive institutions; integration of critics into the lower ranks of the protostate; and the neutralization of political opponents outside the governing structures. The core elite's success in such power plays has varied.

Checks and Balances

No place exists for institutional checks and balances in neopatrimonial systems. As evidence, witness Arafat's largely successful efforts to disempower the emerging elite within the infant Palestinian parliament. Upon entering the political arena created by Oslo, the eighty-eight members of the PLC found themselves in a potentially hostile environment. With the powerful core elite already up and running for some eighteen months, and with the PLO officially responsible for Palestinian politics on the national level, PLC members were "eager to define the relationship between the Council and the PA in a way that [would ensure] their independence and authority."[22]

The most serious impediment to the PLC's ability to do its job was the absence of a Basic Law regulating its powers vis-à-vis those of the executive branch. Arafat repeatedly refused to sign any of the several drafts of the Basic Law that the council sent to his office. The fact that he finally signed it in 2002 was not an indication of success by the PLC, but the intervention of other factors, particularly pressure from external forces.

Without an established legal framework, the PLC had no legal ability to check executive power. Equally detrimental to its position was the fact that its internal procedures for setting agendas were controlled by the core elite. Speaker Ahmad Qurai (Abu Ala), a long-serving associate of Arafat, apparently often blocked controversial issues from making it onto the agenda. The PLC's statutes entitled him to do so. As one member of the council's Economics Committee complained, "Many issues we were supposed to discuss and take a decision upon, he tried to stop. Any issue that would [lead to] a dispute with the president, he [tried] to stop. . . . Many times, we went with him to see the president [where] he was supposed to speak. But *we* would speak and he would listen."[23]

PLC members did, however, attempt to assert their collective power vis-à-vis the executive branch of government. On some occasions, they succeeded in forcing action; they even managed a few votes of no confidence, usually involving allegations of corruption. At such moments Arafat intervened personally. By fall 1998 it had become common practice for Arafat to call meetings with Fatah representatives, the majority of PLC members, days before they were to cast their votes. During these sessions, according to one Fatah PLC member, "Arafat would tell them: 'We are in a very difficult situation. The U.S. is putting pressure on me, and Israel is putting pressure on me. Why do *you* want to put pressure on me as well?"[24] To many, this was a legitimate concern.

Those who acquiesced to Arafat's political "reasoning" often received material rewards. Council member Hatem Eid observed during various PLC sessions that "a number of council members came to the podium, one after the other, with papers for the president to sign. I cannot expect him to help me pay for my children's schooling [and] at the same time oppose his decisions or be part of an investigative committee. The fact that the majority of council members—or a good part of them—have tried to serve their personal interests has undoubtedly affected the performance of the council."[25] By convincing and rewarding the bloc of Fatah representatives, Arafat generally managed to keep the council under his control.

Before 2000, the PLC only once managed to pass a vote of no confidence. The topic was corruption, and the target was the ministerial elite, some of whose members had apparently used public positions for private gains. Those who withdrew confidence from the government formed a small majority and Arafat reacted curiously: He reshuffled the cabinet—but did not remove those ministers against whom the most serious accusations had been directed. Instead, he created ten new ministerial posts for PLC members.[26] That way, he drew a "critical mass" of opponents into the patronage networks of the core elite, neutralizing the PLC for some time to come.

As a corporate actor, the PLC thus remained weak. The influence of individual members depended upon their access to resources, such as posts within the core elite or positions within Fatah. PLC members without these resources found themselves excluded from the second and third circle of elites. More powerful actors within these circles emerged within the bureaucratic and security apparatuses of the protostate.

Bureaucracy and Security

The PA bureaucracy and its military wings were constructed and staffed anew in the wake of Oslo, from the most powerful minister to the least important office clerk and from the most influential security leader to the lowest-ranking traffic warden. By spring 1998 the protostate employed at least 48,000 civil servants and 38,000 police and security officers—the equivalent of roughly 17 percent of the Palestinian workforce.[27] In Gaza, the share of public sector employment topped more than 30 percent.[28]

The most striking feature of the public sector was its fragmentation, which was fostered by power struggles among the core elite over resources, staff, and patronage. In addition, public sector employees came from various regional, political, and professional backgrounds, as the PA hastened to integrate returnees and residents into its civil and coercive machinery. Political appointments were a major feature of the recruitment process. Scholars have noted a tendency "to employ and promote public servants on the basis of their political or sectarian affiliation" rather than based on their professional qualification and expertise.[29]

Strategically important within this larger apparatus were the VIP 2 cardholders, a group of about 150 people spread across the Palestinian territories and operating in civil and military institutions. These VIPs formed part of the second circle, enjoying a high degree of mobility, important positions in political management, and by virtue of being appointees, a high degree of proximity to the center.

In the civil ministries, political appointees formed a layer between ministers and their clientele. Although data is scarce, the available evidence suggests that returnees played a significant role within this layer, accounting for more than one-third of deputy ministers and occupying offices especially in those buildings where the minister was a resident. According to Shikaki, however, what was "most important, more than anything else, for a deputy minister or a director general [was] a direct line to Arafat—where you report to Arafat directly rather than through your minister, and where you receive orders from Arafat and his advisors directly rather than through your minister. [The minister] cannot fire the person appointed by Arafat. . . . He basically has to live with him."[30] This group acted as a counterweight to the power of ministers and formed an important part of the second circle of elites.

There is little data on other members of this second circle, although it almost certainly included second-rank officers in the security apparatuses, as there is no reason to believe that Arafat's neopatrimonial leadership did not equally restrain his security chiefs. In addition, but perhaps less important, heads of the some thirty public institutions, including those overseeing water and electricity, as well as local governors and mayors can also be assigned to the wider periphery of the second circle of elites, perhaps bordering on the third circle. The approximately 200 holders of VIP 3 cards who occupied positions within the middle and lower ranks of the protostate generally belong in the third circle.

Recruitment patterns in the second and third circles of the protostate structures drive home a further point: the establishment of a one-party Fatah-dominated system. Jamil Hilal has argued that "the Oslo Agreement has hurried, or has been manipulated to hasten, the Palestinian political system towards what looks like a one-party system generating a neopatrimonial-bureaucratic regime."[31] Membership in Fatah has thus evolved as a major precondition for recruitment into the networks of the core elite and the surrounding circles. It is difficult, however, to separate the VIP circles from the wider political and economic periphery. Azmi Bishara has pointed out that the new "elite consists of a few hundred people, but the circle connected to them, and who therefore benefit from the situation, number in the thousands. The group has a hierarchical structure, with several channels connecting them to Israel, from officials in the smallest ministry to those responsible for security, the economy, and civilian coordination. . . . Palestinian society has been neutralised and is resentful. Palestinians cannot travel, they cannot satisfy their daily needs without the services of this elite group. Palestinian society has been penetrated from the top down by its clientelist network."[32]

The neutralization Bishara refers to targeted a number of individual and corporate actors who had gained political and social power before the creation of the PA. They included, in particular, Fatah activists involved in the intifada who were viewed by the PA as serious threats to its power: They were partially armed, experienced in resisting authority, and had become a de facto political leadership on the ground.

Salim Tamari argued that some of these groups had become "extremely violent and uncontrollable [so that] the security apparatus [and] the Palestinian administration had to make one major decision: [Would] they control the armed elements by crushing them or by hugging them? It was a difficult decision, as some of them were very unruly. Arafat had to make a decision, and the decision was that they would be incorporated into the security apparatus."[33] The PA's strategy to include this element through its civil and military institutions worked for some time, managing to keep it at bay, but its members were carefully watching the core elite and remained ready to buck the command structure if need be. In a sense, they represented a "dormant elite," ready to take action and to penetrate elite circles controlled by Arafat.

The Anti-Oslo Front: Within Fatah and Without

The PA chose a largely exclusionary and, in part, suppressive route in dealing with armed and unarmed elements of the secular and religious opposition to the Oslo process. The basic strategy was to push them from the politically relevant domain.

The secular opposition was relatively easy to dismiss. The DFLP and the PFLP were the biggest losers in the Oslo process by virtue of their boycotting PA institutions and thus depriving themselves of government positions, patronage, and clout. Internal conflicts over how to deal with the new realities further weakened them. Their rejectionist stand and lack of an alternative political program reduced their popularity among Palestinians. As international donors stopped funding organizations in the anti-Oslo camp, their capacity to provide social support services drastically shrank. Shikaki argued that within the secular opposition, there was "no solid group that we could call elite. If you look at the [high-ranking] leadership in each group you find [that about] 80 percent have disappeared, either joining other factions, mainly Fatah, or the PA, went into their own private business, or left the organization altogether."[34]

In contrast to the secularists, religious activists—especially those within Hamas—remained influential actors, deriving political significance from their financial independence from the PA and Western donors, a clearly articulated Islamic political program, a network of charitable organizations, and considerable levels of popular support. While the PA co-opted and accommodated some religious leaders, it occasionally moved with force against those elements threatening the Oslo process, which was the basis of the PA's legitimacy. Following the first suicide bombings in West Jerusalem in February and March 1996 during the Israeli election campaign, the security services conducted an unprecedented sweep of arrests, raiding private homes, mosques, and universities, ultimately detaining some 900 suspected activists.[35] After a second wave of bombings in fall 1997, the PA arrested some 400 suspects, closed sixteen charitable societies run by religious organizations, took control of the money-generating Islamic *zakat* committees, and shut down the Hamas-affiliated newspaper *al-Risala*.[36] These measures weakened the religious corporate infrastructure on the ground and marginalized its political leadership. Religious actors, however, continued to have influence on strategic issues, because their bombings put negotiations on hold, triggered Israeli retaliation, and prevented the PA from delivering political results. These religious actors were thus fighting outside the governing protostate structures over influence on decisions made by the core elite.

Another serious opposition to the core elite's strategy of centralizing and dominating the political scene and its institutions came from within Fatah. While Fatah supplied the majority of public employees, and its members stood to benefit the most from the structure of the protostate, its popular leaders challenged the core elite's efforts to effectively turn the movement into a state party under the command of Arafat. The *tanzim*, an influential and armed wing within Fatah that was largely led by insiders, played a particularly important role in that respect.

Marwan Barghouthi, the political face of the tanzim, described this conflict as a struggle between a conservative, elite-oriented old guard of outsiders and a younger, more democratically oriented stream of inside activists.[37] The political strength of the inside leaders rested, above all, on their ability to mobilize Fatah supporters. Instrumental to such mobilization was the Fatah Higher Council (FHC), which was established in 1991 and developed into a political counterweight to the outside-dominated Fatah Central Committee and its members, such as Ahmad Qurai or Nabil Shaath.[38]

Notably, the FHC pushed successfully for a more democratic political process within the movement. According to Graham Usher, "Steered by Barghouthi, between 1994 and 1999, some 122 Fatah conferences were held in the West Bank, involving the participation of some 85,000 Fatah activists and resulting in the election of some 2,500 leaders. A similar process occurred in Gaza, but at a slower pace and with less participation."[39] Of significance, Arafat and members of the core elite were unable to stop this process despite repeated attempts to do so. As Barghouthi stated, "The [Fatah] Central Committee and Mr. Arafat attacked me and considered [elections] a big violation of the internal system of Fatah. There was a big clash about that. . . . They tried; we fought. [We had] a tradition of democracy in the prisons [and] people did not understand [why if] they had a right in prisons to elect [representatives] they [did not] have the right now under the new authority. So it was illogical not to have elections"[40]

Although the inside Fatah elite and its constituencies generally remained loyal to the PA, they became increasingly critical of the core elite's policies. Their critique was directed "especially against those 'outsider'-led security forces who showed a penchant for arresting, torturing and sometimes killing detained Fatah activists."[41] The stalled peace process and the fact that the core elite and those on its fringes were predominantly outsiders prompted further criticism.

Arafat and the core elite created an ambiguous relationship with critical inside Fatah leaders. On the one hand, the insiders' criticism and demands for popular participation did not fit into their neopatrimonial style of political management. On the other hand, the inside leadership represented a crucial link to the tens of thousands of Fatah cadres spread across the West Bank and Gaza. Salim Tamari has argued that inside Fatah leaders "irritated" Arafat "because they criticized. But he also wanted a tool which mobilizes the masses. . . . So Fatah became two parties. It became the party in power and attracted all kinds of opportunists who all of a sudden became Fatah in order to have a piece of the cake, and activists who felt they should continue the radical tradition of nationalism."[42]

The inside Fatah leadership, therefore, steadily moved from various positions inside and outside the protostate bureaucracy, inching closer to the center circle of elites. Its entree was its strong street presence as well as its acquisition of firearms and explosives, which gradually undermined the core elite's monopoly over the means of coercion. The tanzim leadership did not, however, enter the center circle until after the outbreak of the al-Aqsa intifada in September 2000. Rather, it remained largely quiet, yet watchful, as the core elite gradually slid toward a crisis of legitimacy. This crisis, which gradually emerged as the Oslo process unfolded, was to a large extent caused by the economic decline wrought by Oslo and by the controversial economic activities of PA officials.

The Economics of Elite Change

Once established in the Palestinian territories, Arafat and individuals around him moved quickly to reinforce their political power with economic clout. Their actions prompted the formation of a new economic elite that was closely connected to or was part of the regime's political elite. The economic changes accompanying the formation of this elite put the core elite in a precarious situation: The core's influence on the economy brought it leverage through patronage, but conversely the rapid and deep-rooted decline of the Palestinian economy threatened its legitimacy and that of the Oslo process, as living standards for Palestinians fell while poverty steadily rose.

Economic Dependence and Decline

Two structural elements governed socioeconomic development in the West Bank and Gaza Strip: a shift in Israeli economic policies vis-à-vis the Palestinian territories and the influx of donor money into the Palestinian self-rule areas. Together, these further polarized the Palestinian class structure. While large segments of the population slid down the economic ladder, the Palestinian protostate and its economic core elite gained disproportionate influence over issues affecting the infant Palestinian economy.

The Israeli government's contribution to Palestinian class polarization was its decisive turn from structural integration of the Palestinian economy in favor of separation from it. The key to understanding the resulting changes after Oslo is "closure." The United Nations has stressed that "to make sense of economic and social trends in the WBGS [West Bank and Gaza Strip] . . . it is essential to understand closure [as a] policy of distinct separation between the population of Israel and the WBGS."[43] Israeli-imposed closures varied in strength, duration, and impact, but the effects of the policy were, regardless, long term.

Closure affected all strata of Palestinian society and threw large segments of the population into economic turmoil. The private sector business elite that had emerged during the occupation suddenly faced long-term supply-side shocks. Because merchants and traders imported the vast majority of their products from Israel, closures blocked their access to goods, deprived them of business opportunities, and reduced their income. Between 1992 and 1996 the volume of imports from Israel to the Palestinian territories fell by almost one-third.[44] Manufacturers and subcontractors were equally hard hit, as they could neither obtain Israeli raw materials nor fulfill their contractual obligations toward Israeli companies. The United Nations notes that these developments "forced several firms to shut down operations completely while nearly all of them significantly reduced their level of output."[45]

The Palestinian workforce lost stable employment opportunities as a result of Israeli closures. In 1992, 38 percent of all Palestinian workers earned their income in Israel or in Israeli settlements. By 1996 this figure had temporarily fallen to around 5 percent.[46] Closures propelled large segments of these workers into temporary or permanent unemployment. When complete closures were enforced, unemployment levels reached up to 50 percent.[47] Such an unstable, risky, and hostile economic environment made foreign investors reluctant to invest. The number of private foreign investors willing to take a chance in the Palestinian territories fell continuously, reaching "negligible levels" by the end of 2000.[48]

The standard of living among Palestinians fell drastically, pushing significant segments of the population—especially the refugee communities in Gaza—close to or below the poverty line. The humanitarian situation reached alarming levels as early as March 1996, when the United Nations Relief and Works Agency registered the first "urgent calls for the Agency to undertake [increasing levels of] food distribution" in Gaza.[49]

Where resources are scarce, patronage thrives. The influx of international donor assistance, which started in the wake of Oslo and was partly channeled through PA institutions, only reinforced the core elite's political leverage. Martin Beck has argued that "the amounts granted to the PA might seem scarce if seen from an outside perspective. Given the structural weakness of the Palestinian economy, however, the PA is the group within the Palestinian system which holds the lion's share of the available resources."[50]

The structure of external funding had several effects. First, it financially oiled the protostate and its growing bureaucratic apparatus. As employment opportunities grew scarce throughout the Palestinian territories, the PA's power as a corporate employer swelled. Second, the PA's role in the distribution of donor aid gave the core elite influence over jobs and tenders in municipal and other projects. Reports of irregularities in the administration of these funds have been numerous and at times convincing. Third, the considerable imbalance between the monies collected through taxes and the monies flowing from external grants and loans put the protostate on the road to rentier politics. The Palestinian economy's dependence on Israel was now being joined by dependence on Western and Arab donors.

Politics over Economics

The core elite around Arafat, evidence suggests, viewed the Palestinian economy primarily as a political tool. As a former undersecretary in the Ministry of Economy and Trade confirmed, "In the initial phase, our economic planning [was] completely determined by political reasoning. We [had] to be professional from a political point of view; not from an economic point of view."[51] The PA's shaping of the domestic economy was apparently driven by one priority:

to get as much money as possible in order to keep [the] leadership moving without being dependent on Israel or donors. That was the priority. If you have a political battle, you have to be independent in your resources. This is how they have legitimized getting as much money as possible—cash, direct, immediate, not long-term, not medium-term, immediate—in order to sustain this leadership for the coming five years, no matter what the damages in the medium and long term would be.[52]

This goal pushed the core elite almost automatically into a conflict with the private sector over business opportunities, for these had become scarce. In Gaza, where the number of trucks allowed to enter and leave was restricted, economic trade opportunities became, in the true sense of the phrase, a zero-sum game. For one person's gain—getting a truck through—would be another person's loss, in having a truck wait. With Palestinian security services controlling the Palestinian side of the checkpoints, businesspeople from the PA or individuals connected to it enjoyed a clear advantage. Individuals from the private sector who lacked PA connections would often leave the competition empty handed. As Ghassan Khatib argued, "Whenever there [was] an opportunity to make money, it was given to PA-connected persons. . . . As a result, there [emerged] a new [elite] connected to the PA and protected by the security services."[53]

The PA moved quickly to establish monopolistic control over some strategic commodities. The number of monopolies created remains in dispute, with claims ranging from zero to twenty-seven. Evidence suggests, however, that at the least petrol, cigarettes, cement, and some other commodities were monopolized under the direct control of the PA, its security services, or people well connected to these institutions. This brought into existence new economic elites that moved within a sophisticated and clandestine system of informal control mechanisms.

The types of monopolies were many: There were monopolies in the classical sense, meaning that one company or dealer was officially allowed to import a given commodity; there were quasi-monopolies, meaning that certain commodities could be officially imported by anyone but were de facto controlled by the PA; there were "mother companies," working as conglomerates in different sectors, sometimes dominating sectors; finally, there were public shareholdings of private companies, though not always to the satisfaction of their managers. These practices overlapped in a complex network of companies and individuals connected to each other and to the top political leadership. The two most controversial companies within this system of monopolistic control were the Palestinian Company for Commercial Services (PCCS) in the West Bank and the al-Bahr Company in Gaza, whose activities came into focus during a PLC inquiry in the summer of 1997.

PCCS was founded in the spring of 1995 and developed into an influential economic octopus in the West Bank. It was headed by Arafat's advisor Muhammad Rashid (Khalid Salam) and, according to a member of the PLC's Economics Committee, "started with cement." He continued, "We have been told that President Arafat provided several million dollars to set up the company, which earned large amounts of money relatively quickly by monopolizing the trade in cement. The initial investments could be paid back and profit could be used to buy shares of other companies."[54] By 1998 PCCS had acquired shares in at least twenty-nine companies involved in a variety of enterprises, including agriculture, construction materials, telecommunications, investment, insurance, and banking. The acquisition of shares was conducted by request or by "persuasion." Another member of the PLC's Economics Committee stated, "People have complained to us that pressure had been put on them to sell 30 percent of their shares to the mother company. But [Khalid Salam] said he would only buy shares of companies that [requested him to do so], either because they were in financial need or because they thought working with the authority would bring them some advantage."[55]

The nature and the activities of the al-Bahr Company in the Gaza Strip revealed parallels to the PCCS mode of operation. Like core actors in the political arena, PCCS and al-Bahr operated in a legal void in the economic world. When asked about al-Bahr and PCCS by the PLC, the finance minister replied that they were private companies, and hence their profits would not be collected by his ministry. The deputy minister, when asked about their taxes, replied that they did not pay taxes because they were public.[56] This legally uncertain status made it extremely difficult to oversee their activities.

As one member of the investigative committee recalled, "We brought Khalid Salam [and others] in front of the council. When you bring those guys to the council most of them will tell you that they are not responsible [and] tell you 'We are working for the president.' But the problem with those guys is that nobody oversees what they are doing. They just go directly to the president and can [give] and take cash."[57]

Core Elite Economics

The establishment of informal economic activities in the Palestinian territories prompted the formation of a new economic elite circle around Arafat. Ehud Ya'ari argued that the "reins of the economy have been handed to Arafat's cronies, a small coalition of security men, some members of the top political echelon and a few middle level professionals who have been with him in Beirut. They control all the deals and the 'clip coupons' from them."[58] Connections to Israel, the primary supplier and conduit of goods, became an essential asset. Privileged movement, granted by VIP cards, aided the rise of this group.

The first circle of the economic core elite consisted of officials who managed companies and enforced monopolies. Such members of the economic elite epitomized the political core elite or even belonged to it—largely returnees or deportees who had worked with Arafat in exile and were members of or closely associated with Fatah. While each of them enjoyed a certain degree of autonomy, they nonetheless remained ultimately dependent on him.

Internal fragmentation characterized this economic elite, as it did its political counterpart. As the former undersecretary argued, "Chairman Arafat has a goal . . . money, immediate, fast. . . . So everybody [around him] can determine how to reach that goal. Some do it through monopolies, some through investment in industry, agriculture, or trade. So each person, minister, or instrument has tried to compete with the others by bringing in more money through different means."[59]

This inner economic circle interacted with a second, wider circle of PA employees and private businesspeople. Empirical data is sketchy, but reports indicate that control over economic benefits was in some instances "outsourced" to the private sector. People belonging to this privileged group can be viewed as part of the second, or middle, economic circle of elites. Interactions involving a wider, third, circle were fluid, because tendencies by PA officials to turn public posts into private gains were widespread.

What became evident was the correlation between political posts and access to scarce economic resources. This tendency stretched across the institutional spectrum of the PA. The PA's comptroller general, Khaled al-Qidweh, in his first report of May 1997, stated that some $323 million—the equivalent of about 40 percent of the PA's annual budget—had been misused or mismanaged by public employees.[60] The political arena had virtually become a launching pad for economic success and was turning a Marxist axiom on its head: It was not one's economic standing that determined one's political influence. Rather, the opposite held true: One's political connections determined one's economic success.

A Question of Legitimacy

While the core elite was relatively successful in establishing a centralized system of political rule backed by economic means, its members and the political system were gradually sliding toward a legitimacy crisis. The Oslo process and the way in which it was being managed could not produce the economic or political dividends promised to or expected by the Palestinians.

Leila Farsakh has argued that the major developments that "aggravated the economic woes" of Palestinians included "the deterioration of living standards, growing rather than diminishing dependence on Israel, fragmentation of Palestinian . . . economic unity and the installation of a Palestinian Authority more successful in redistributing government revenues to a few private interests than in spurring economic growth."[61] By 1998 the number of people living below the poverty line—those living on less than $2.10 a day—exceeded more than 35 percent in Gaza and about 15 percent in the West Bank.[62]

Frustration with economic deprivation coincided with frustration with the political system. By 1996, polls indicated that 60 percent of Palestinians believed that widespread favoritism existed in government agencies, and more than 55 percent said that they never received the services for which they had applied, while noting that the speed and the quality of services depended upon one's connections.[63] They found public participation in decisionmaking restricted, media self-censored, and in many cases the rule of law bluntly breached. Sara Roy has argued that this "perceived lack of choices led to alienation from the new system and a withdrawal from larger society."[64]

On the national level, Oslo's "products" had a "quality control" problem. In June 2000 slightly more than 35 percent of Palestinians trusted the methods of managing the negotiations, while more than half did not trust the methods applied by the leadership.[65] Israel still controlled some 60 percent of the West Bank, while its settlement policy continued unabated, with the number of settlers in the occupied territories having doubled between 1993 and 2000.[66] Negotiations on the final status issues—among them Jerusalem, refugees, and settlements—had produced no results, while attempts by Arafat, Israeli prime minister Ehud Barak, and U.S. president Bill Clinton at the Camp David summit in summer 2000 had clearly failed. Lack of faith in the Oslo process—and its institutions, personnel, and the Palestinian relationship with Israel—had reached a critical mass. Roy argued that "given the dysfunctional nature [of this system] people with either street or economic power began to form their own personal militias," leading to "an atomization of social relations," and suggesting that the "larger collective identity [had begun] to weaken."[67] It was within this precarious politicoeconomic setting that Ariel Sharon visited the Haram al-Sharif, or Temple Mount, prompting the first clashes of what became known as the al-Aqsa intifada.

The Intifada, Take Two

The "bubble" of Arafat and the core elite burst on 28 September 2000 with Sharon's visit to the Haram al-Sharif, which was probably more of a catalyst than a cause for the events that followed. Sharon's election as prime minister in March 2001, however, set the Palestinian-Israeli conflict on a new path. As violence escalated from clashes to shootings, from attacks on settlers to suicide bombings, and from air raids to land assaults, three significant processes changed the landscape of Palestinian elite politics: the systematic disempowerment of the governing protostate structures and its core elite; the diffusion of political power among alternative actors in the West Bank and Gaza Strip; and the push from various directions for internal reforms of the PA.

Israel's policy followed a simple logic: If the PA was unwilling or unable to stop attacks by Palestinians, especially suicide bombings, it would be punished or destroyed. As the stakes grew, and violence escalated, Israel increasingly targeted the nerve centers of the PA, cracking its core and pulling the political carpet from under Arafat.

Israel's refusal to transfer VAT and customs duties to the PA in fall 2000 brought the protostate to the verge of financial collapse within less than six months. The European Union's agreeing to pay an extra $10 million per month, coupled with additional funding from the Arab League, saved the PA at least financially at the time.[68] Israel's imposition of complete closures and curfews in major cities pushed the Palestinian economy to the point of breakdown. By October 2002 the United Nations reckoned that the economy was "near collapse" and estimated poverty levels to have reached about 55 percent in the West Bank and almost 70 percent in Gaza.[69] Unemployment skyrocketed, trade fell drastically, and production largely stopped. While the protostate struggled for survival, the potential for patronage decreased. The core elite now found itself squeezed between a shortage of funds and increasing economic demands from the broader population. According to UN assessments, donor aid could "not come close to covering [the] cumulative [economic] losses" caused by the second intifada.[70] The backbone of the core elite's economic power base had essentially been broken.

Israeli military incursions into the self-rule areas were equally detrimental to the core elite's control. These assaults appeared to peak in March and April 2002 in Operation Defensive Shield. The attacks significantly damaged the PA's political power base, targeting Palestinian security installations and civilian institutions, among them PLC offices, the Ministries of Education, Finance, Agriculture, Trade and Industry, and municipal buildings and chambers of commerce.[71] The World Bank and other agencies observed that "offices of PA ministries and agencies were entered and ransacked to varying degrees, with the destruction [focusing] particularly on office equipment, computers, and data storage facilities."[72] Those same agencies estimated that the damage to civilian institutions and infrastructure amounted to about $361 million.[73]

While dismantling the PA's institutional infrastructure, Israel also physically isolated the Palestinian leadership and stripped it of the privileges that VIP cards once brought it. Closures and curfew prevented the leadership and the core elite from meeting and devising or carrying out policies. The epitome of this elite paralysis was the Israeli army's repeated sieges of Arafat's headquarters in Ramallah or, more precisely, what was left of them. Arafat's incapacitation symbolized what Oslo had created: a regime that could quickly be stripped of its political power, its economic means, and its capacity to fulfill basic state functions. By April 2002 senior negotiator Saeb Erakat had come to the point of claiming that the "Palestinian Authority has ceased to exist."[74] He might have been exaggerating, but the core elite had been paralyzed economically and politically.

Proliferating Power and Calls for Reform

The al-Aqsa intifada opened a window of opportunity for contesting elites in the West Bank and Gaza Strip. With the PA's central institutions being dismantled and its leaders marginalized, various armed and organized groups came to the fore, fueling the uprising and thereby moving closer to the center of decisionmaking or, more precisely, creating alternative centers. Camille Mansour has argued that "given the voluntary, nongovernmental, and fractured nature of the militant groups most of the Palestinian actions—or reactions to Israeli action—were not the result of decisions emanating from a central, hierarchical commander."[75] In other words, the core of central decisionmaking had broken, and its constituent parts were scattering across the political spectrum. The strategic influence gained by these new actors, who called for demonstrations, attacked settlers and Israeli soldiers, and killed civilians inside Israel, was based on Israel's retaliation, attack on PA institutions, and dispatch of the Oslo formula. These developments represented a particular threat to the pro-Oslo elite around Arafat. People like Mahmoud Abbas, Ahmad Qurai, Nabil Shaath, or Saeb Erakat repeatedly called "for a return to the Oslo format of direct negotiations between Israel and the PA; an end to the intifada, especially of the armed variety; and a reconstruction of the PA around the spine of a unitary security force headed by Dahlan."[76]

The escalation of violence propelled a variety of groups into the center of the political arena so that Arafat and the core elite were, in a sense, confronted with and surrounded by new actors pushing toward their inner circle. Their leaders came, for the most part, from among inside activists. As Hammami and Tamari have argued, the "political vacuum created by the institutional breakdown of the PA has been filled by a variety of armed militias, [including] the now famous Fatah *tanzim,* the *shabiba* [Fatah's youth movement], members of the secular opposition, Islamic factions, [various] youth groups, students, and released prisoners."[77]

Although the groups were split along regional and factional lines, their political agendas overlapped to a certain degree, as they advocated armed struggle as the means for ending the Israeli occupation, largely considered Oslo dead, and called for internal reform of the political system that the PA had created.

Fatah's tanzim came to play a particularly important role in the diffusion of power. Under the leadership of Marwan Barghouthi, the tanzim virtually "logged out" of the protostate structures, formed a movement in its own right, and advocated a mixture of negotiations and armed struggle as a means to achieve Palestinian independence and statehood. As Barghouthi put it, "We can negotiate, but we must also have action on the ground."[78]

Like other armed factions, the tanzim leadership suffered retaliation by the Israeli army. Extrajudicial killings—a kind of "elitocide"—comprised one part of the Israeli strategy. By early 2002 Israel had carried out some sixty political assassinations of activist leaders from various secular and religious groups.[79] Harsher blows were dealt during the Israeli military invasions. "According to Fatah sources, many of the political and military activists Israel has killed or arrested in the West Bank invasions [were] its middle-rank cadre, the core of the Intifada leadership, including its West Bank general secretary and chief ideologue, Marwan Barghouthi. Their replacements [were] young, inexperienced, military figures whose loyalty is as much to the clan or their own ambition as to any central national leadership. The upshot [was a] movement in disarray, politically and strategically."[80]

One strategic political goal uniting the majority of Fatah and other inside activists, however, was the demand for internal PA reform. According to Barghouthi, "the intifada also poses a criticism of the internal situation."[81] This demand would later be echoed not only by broad segments of the Palestinian population, but also by Israel, the European Union, and the United States, be it for very different reasons.

By summer 2002, Sharon was insisting that Palestinian reform was a necessary precondition for a return to negotiations, an essential tool that the pro-Oslo elite needed to secure its political survival. He was backed up by U.S. president George W. Bush, who called for "new leaders, new institutions, and new security arrangements."[82] Secular factions from the West Bank and Gaza Strip, likewise, had expressed a clear "no to the continuation of the PA in its present from."[83] Without the support of these factions, especially those controlling the street, a return to the remnants of Oslo seemed impossible or, at least, meaningless.

Finally bowing to pressure, Arafat initiated a reform process, which, by early 2004, produced some changes but fell short of anything substantial. Although he signed the Basic Law and the Law on the Judiciary, the committees on reform and national reconstruction that he appointed were headed by Muhammad Rashid and Nabil Shaath.[84] In June 2002 he presented a new cabinet that "impressed no one."[85] Although Salam Fayad was appointed finance minister and, as a former IMF employee was seen as a technocrat fit for the post, the crucial position of interior minister, which Arafat relinquished, was given to Abd al-Razzaq Yahya, a returnee and former commander of the Palestine Liberation Army. In the discussions between the PLC and members of the Palestinian leadership that followed, it soon became clear that the cabinet would not receive the PLC's confirmation. As a result, the cabinet collectively resigned in September 2002, days before the PLC was to cast its vote. The parliamentary elite, its Fatah representatives in particular, could obviously no longer be convinced, co-opted, or bypassed as easily as they had been in the past. The corroding legitimacy of PA institutions was apparently taking its toll.

As external pressure for internal reform mounted—in particular from the Middle East Quartet, consisting of the European Union, Russia, the United States, and the United Nations—Arafat created a new post of prime minister in March 2003. While signaling that he was willing to hand over powers, he chose Mahmoud Abbas (Abu Mazen) to occupy this post. As Usher argues, "Arafat buckled and hedged . . . by appointing Abbas: a founding member of Fatah, acceptable to Israel and the world but one without any popular base in either the Occupied Territories or beyond. Unlike other real or perceived challengers, his legitimacy in Palestinian eyes derives solely from the fact that he is Arafat's appointment."[86]

The post of prime minister quickly developed into a focal point of conflict in the reform process, and Abbas soon found himself squeezed between conflicting pressures and seemingly incompatible interests.

First, he was caught in conflicts with Arafat over what powers the prime minister should have, how his cabinet was to be composed, and—perhaps most significant—who would control the security services. Despite a compromise hammered out between the two, Arafat managed to maintain control and to restrict the prime minister's powers. Second, the fact that Abbas was approved by Israel and the United States undermined his legitimacy in Palestinian society, especially among the armed factions. These groups essentially considered the installation of a Palestinian prime minister as a U.S.-led form of regime change through the back door. Third, Israel's repeated demands that the PA should disarm the militant groups and destroy their infrastructure presented Abbas with a serious dilemma: On the one hand, violent conflict with the armed factions would mean risking a civil war in the Palestinian territories, which could threaten the survival of the core elite. On the other hand, failure to keep the militant factions at bay would lead to more Israeli attacks, further undermining the remnant powers of the PA.

Abbas tried to resolve this quagmire by successfully negotiating a ceasefire between Israel and the armed factions. Simultaneously, he pushed for a swift implementation of the "roadmap to peace," which the Middle East Quartet had proposed in April 2003. However, the collapse of the ceasefire, the return to violent conflict, the resulting failure to implement the roadmap, and the continuous conflicts with Arafat ultimately led to Abbas's resignation in September 2003.

At the time of this writing, the Palestinian territories were thus witnessing perhaps the worst government crisis of the PA. The Israeli cabinet was now openly discussing Arafat's deportation, that is, the elimination of the center of Palestinian elite politics. At the same time, the core elite around Arafat was neither able to break the cycle of violence nor to initiate a return to the Oslo format. Direct negotiations between Israel and the PA had stopped. Instead of negotiating a final status arrangement with the PA, Israel began constructing a wall to separate large parts of the West Bank from Israeli territory. In addition, the hostile political environment, the damaged protostate infrastructure, and the worsening economic situation restricted the core elite's capacity to reassert its authority over the second and third circles it had once controlled. The militant factions now played a predominant role in determining the relationship with Israel, which was primarily characterized by armed conflict. The outcome has been a Palestinian core elite in turmoil. Ten years after the signing of the Oslo agreements, the process of state building had turned into a process of crisis management. In October 2003, Arafat declared a state of emergency and appointed an emergency cabinet under the leadership of Ahmed Qurai as prime minister. To some observers, however, this merely resembled a "disaster-management government," squeezed between a conflict of internal and external forces that it was no longer able to control. Clearly, the political and economic realities on the ground had made a meaningful democratic change and the continuation of the Oslo peace formula exceedingly difficult, if not impossible.

Conclusion

The politics of elite change in the Palestinian territories from 1994 to 2004 can be divided into two distinct phases. During the first phase of protostate building (1994 to 2000), a centralized neopatrimonial governance system was established and largely tolerated by Israel and Western donors. Arafat, at the center, dominated the elite circles within that system. In his immediate political orbit, a core elite consisting largely of loyal Fatah returnees circled, managing an informal politicoeconomic system of control, tying second and third elite circles to itself by means of patronage. Largely centralized control over coercive, representative, and administrative apparatuses enabled Arafat and the core elite to impose their mode of governance, counterbalance and marginalize competitors, and silence regime critics. Economic decline, a stalled peace process, and elitist rule, however, ultimately triggered a loss of legitimacy and nurtured criticism from individual and corporate actors.

The al-Aqsa intifada and Israel's military response to it significantly altered Palestinian elite circles. They cracked the walls surrounding the inner circle that had protected the core elite and stripped them of the institutional and patronage-based plexus that had affected control of a clientelist periphery. They also ejected some core elite members, although others tenuously remained within. They even temporarily vanquished Arafat from the political scene. At the same time, the second uprising created an opening for alternative, inside leaders to push their way into the third and second circles and sometimes to penetrate the first. Finally, it paved the way for internal political reform, which by spring 2004 had moved forward but had yet to produce ample results. As the core elite around Arafat was struggling for survival, the process of state building turned into a process of crisis management.

Thus, the Palestinian territories were witnessing—once again—a process of change, in which a semiformal core elite was trying to preserve its predominant role and to revive the political Oslo formula on which this predominance was based. As violence roamed the streets of Tel Aviv, Jerusalem, Ramallah, and Gaza, however, each Palestinian and Israeli life taken made a return to the Oslo formula more difficult—although a viable alternative to the central ideas of Oslo was not in sight.

Notes

1. *Israeli-Palestinian Interim Agreement on the West Bank and Gaza Strip,* annex I, art. II (1b, 2).
2. Said, *Peace and Its Discontents,* p. 2.
3. Jerusalem Media and Communication Centre, *Public Opinion Polls on Palestinian Attitudes Towards Politics, 1993–1997,* poll no. 3, accessible at www.jmcc.org/publicpoll/results.html.
4. Ibid.
5. Ibid.
6. Shikaki, "The Peace Process, National Reconstruction, and Transition to Democracy," p. 15.
7. Robinson, *Building a Palestinian State,* p. 175.
8. For example, Rex Brynen, "The Neo-Patrimonial Dimension of Palestinian Politics," *Journal of Palestine Studies* (spring 1995).

9. Haydar Abd al-Shafi, interview, 18 September 1997, Ramallah.

10. On the three-circle model used here, see the introductory chapter by Volker Perthes in this volume.

11. *Palestinian Authority's Political Programme,* art. 9.

12. Shikaki, "The Peace Process, National Reconstruction, and Transition to Democracy," p. 13.

13. World Bank, "Report on the Palestinian Civil Service: Issues and Recommendations," Washington, D.C., October 1996, p. 29.

14. Khalil Shikaki, interview, 6 September 1997, Nablus.

15. Calculations based on World Bank, "Palestinian Civil Service," p. 29; Palestinian Economic Policy Research Institute (MAS), *Economic Monitor,* vol. 1, Ramallah, 1996, p. 11.

16. Usher, "The Politics of Internal Security," p. 30.

17. Shu'aibe, "IPS Forum," p. 91.

18. Palestinian Legislative Council, "Report on the Findings of the General Comptrol Office," in Jerusalem Media and Communication Centre, *The Palestinian Council,* 2nd ed. (East Jerusalem: JMCC, 1996), p. 6.

19. Usher, "The Politics of Internal Security," p. 29.

20. Ibid.

21. Azmi Shu'aibe, interview, 9 September 1997, al-Bireh.

22. National Democratic Institute, *Report on the First Month of the PLC* (East Jerusalem: NDI, 1996), p. 58.

23. PLC Economics Committee member, interview, 7 October 1997, Ramallah.

24. Fatah PLC member, interview, 5 May 1998, al-Ram.

25. Hatem Eid, "The PLC and Civil Society," in Palestinian Academic Society for the Study of International Affairs (PASSIA), *Civil Society Empowerment: Policy Analysis* (East Jerusalem: PASSIA, 1998), p. 79.

26. "New Cabinet Appointed," *Jerusalem Times,* 7 August 1998.

27. World Bank, "Palestinian Civil Service," p. 5.

28. Palestinian Economic Policy Research Institute, *Economic Monitor,* vol. 2, p. 17.

29. Palestinian Independent Commission on Citizens' Rights (PICCR), *Third Annual Report,* Ramallah, 1997, p. 106.

30. Shikaki, interview, 6 September 1997, Nablus.

31. Hilal, "The Effects of the Oslo Agreements," p. 144.

32. Bishara, "Reflections on the Realities of the Oslo Process," p. 221.

33. Salim Tamari, interview, 4 May 1998, East Jerusalem.

34. Shikaki, interview, 6 September 1997, Nablus.

35. J. Baker, "Crackdown on Hamas," *Palestine Report,* 3 October 1997.

36. Ibid.

37. Marwan Barghouthi, interview, 5 October 1997, Ramallah.

38. Graham Usher, "Fatah's Tanzim: Origins and Politics," *Middle East Report* (winter 2000), p. 7.

39. Ibid.

40. Barghouthi, interview, 5 October 1997, Ramallah.

41. Usher, "Fatah's Tanzim," p. 7.

42. Tamari, interview, 4 May 1998, East Jerusalem.

43. United Nations Office of the Special Coordinator in the Occupied Territories (UNSCO), *Economic and Social Conditions in the West Bank and Gaza: Quarterly Report* (winter–spring 1997), p. 42.

44. Ibid., p. 20.

45. Ibid., p. 57.

46. Palestinian Economic Policy Research Institute, *Economic Monitor,* vol. 1.

47. United Nations Office of the Special Coordinator in the Occupied Territories (UNSCO), *The Impact of Closures and Other Mobility Restrictions on Palestinian Productive Activities* (January 2002–30 June 2002), p. i.

48. Ibid., p. 21.

49. United Nations Relief and Works Agency for Palestinian Refugees in the Middle East (UNRWA), *Annual Report of the Commissioner General, 1996,* p. 63.

50. Martin Beck, "Zur Misere der palästinensischen Autonomiegebiete," *Leviathan* 26, no. 1 (1998), p. 84.

51. Former undersecretary, Economics and Trade Ministry, interview, 7 August 1997, Ramallah.

52. Former undersecretary, Economics and Trade Ministry, interview, 7 August 1997, Ramallah.

53. Ghassan Khatib, interview, 9 May 1997, East Jerusalem.

54. PLC Economics Committee member, interview, 26 May 1998, Ramallah.

55. PLC Economics Committee member, interview, 7 October 1997, Ramallah.

56. Shu'aibe, "IPS Forum," p. 92.

57. PLC Economics Committee member, interview, 7 October 1997, Ramallah.

58. Ehud Ya'ari, "The Independent State of Arafat," *Jerusalem Report,* 5 September 1996.

59. Former undersecretary, Economics and Trade Ministry, interview, 7 August 1997, Ramallah.

60. John Immanuel, "PA Auditor Finds 40 Percent of Budget Wasted or Misused," *Jerusalem Post,* 25 May 1997.

61. Farsakh, "Under Siege."

62. Ibid.

63. PICCR, *Third Annual Report,* p. 111.

64. Roy, "Palestinian Society and Economics," p. 9.

65. JMCC, *Public Opinion Pulse,* June 2000, accessible at www.jmcc.org/publicpoll/opinion.html.

66. Roy, "Palestinian Society and Economics," p. 10.

67. Ibid., p. 9.

68. Hammami and Hilal, "An Uprising at a Crossroads," p. 3.

69. UNSCO, *Impact of Closures,* p. 2.

70. Ibid.

71. Hammami, "Interregnum," p. 19.

72. Local Aid Coordination Committee, press release, Jerusalem, 15 May 2002.

73. Ibid.

74. Graham Usher, "Palestine: Ending the Illusion," *Middle East International,* 19 April 2002, p. 4.

75. Mansour, "Impact of 11 September," p. 9.

76. Graham Usher, "Ashes to Ashes," *Middle East International,* London, 17 May 2002, p. 6.

77. Hammami and Tamari, "Second Uprising," p. 17.

78. Usher, "Fatah's Tanzim," p. 7.

79. Mansour, "Impact of 11 September," p. 6.

80. Graham Usher, "Shuffling Out Arafat," *Middle East International,* 14 June 2002, p. 4.

81. Hammami and Hilal, "An Uprising at a Crossroads," p. 7.

82. Speech by President George W. Bush, Washington, D.C., 24 June 2002.

83. Usher "Ashes to Ashes," p. 6.

84. Ibid.

85. Ibid.

86. Graham Usher, "The Other War," *Middle East International,* 21 March 2003, p. 19.

Part 5

Conclusion

11

Elite Change and Systems Maintenance

Volker Perthes

Elites matter. They certainly factor into the political and social developments that the Arab world will undergo in the coming decades. This may not be a particularly surprising conclusion—one would hardly expect a study focusing on elites to come to a different one—but it should be kept in mind theoretically and practically in regard to international cooperation with Arab countries. Although actors and their behavior cannot be examined in a meaningful way devoid of structural and institutional contexts, these "factors constitute at most constraints to that which is possible under a concrete historical situation."[1] Put somewhat differently, "institutional mechanisms do much to pattern the channels and ways in which elites compete and are recruited," but elites also "play a seminal role in shaping institutional designs."[2]

The structural and institutional contexts in most of the Arab world, as the case studies in this volume underline, are shaped by the prevalence of autocratic rule. This refers not so much to the more or less authoritarian constitutions, as to the underlying structures of dominance embodied in what is often referred to as the "security state," the political economy particular to the Arab world, regional structures (especially the prevalence of the Arab-Israeli conflict and other territorial conflicts), as well as, of course, the changing international environment (not the least of which currently involves the forces of economic globalization).

The availability of oil rents remains the most salient feature of the regional political economy; despite decreasing oil prices, oil revenues still amounted to between 48 percent and 59 percent of the cumulated budgets of *all* Arab states during 1995 to 2000.[3] Rent income enables core elites to establish clientelistic relationships with elites in the second or third circles, to buy-off contesting elites, and to maintain substantial autonomy from business and labor. Although the relation between rent income and political competitiveness is neither direct nor mechanical, it cannot be ignored: No one should be surprised that Bahrain (on which there is no case study in this book), the Gulf monarchy the least dependent on oil income, has advanced the furthest in pluralizing its system. The political opening in Algeria at the end of the 1980s was also linked to a steep decrease in oil income, and Saudi Arabia's gradual reforms are linked to the realization that the "days of abundant oil revenues are over and will not return," as Crown Prince Abdallah has stated.[4] A relative decline in oil income provides independent elites, primarily in the third circle, with the opportunity to make their voices heard, but it does not determine the balance of power within a given country's politically relevant elite .

Within these contexts, elites undergo change in their composition as well as in how they present themselves and in what actions they take. As noted, change has spread wider or deeper in some countries than in others. Young leaders who inherited their power have tended to liberate themselves from the influence of many of those people their fathers relied on while retaining some as long as they feel that they need their experience. In all of the Arab states examined, structural change has mainly occurred and—we suggest—will continue to occur primarily in the third circle, where members of political factions or social groups previously without representation in the PRE establish footholds. This is to be expected considering the rather gradual and controlled mode of elite circulation among Arab PRE at this stage. Here, in the third circle of influence, those who are co-opted by the core and those who try to force themselves on the incumbent elite through participation in elections, civil society activities, protest, or lobbying, meet. Here also, in most of the countries, one finds contesting elites and politicians, rather than technocrats or those politicos who "live from politics."

An increasing proportion of politicians in the PRE can generally be taken as a sign that a system is becoming more competitive. While this is not the case in most of the countries studied here, recruitment from parliament has increased in many cases. Given the debates in not a few countries about the importance of parliaments or consultative councils, such assemblies appear likely to increasingly become more important as elite incubators.

In all of the Arab countries, a large number of PRE newcomers bring with them new qualifications. In general, wherever changing economic, technical, or even political parameters, such as the spread of new communications technologies or the privatization of public services, open new fields of activity, doors are also opened to emerging elites. Economic elites will gain in importance as the countries of the Middle East and North Africa prepare to join the WTO, enter into association agreements with the European Union, and otherwise simply fulfill the need to encourage export-oriented industries in order to provide jobs to youthful majorities, fill state coffers with tax income, and obtain foreign exchange for imports.

Economic necessity thus becomes a major factor in elite change. In most of these countries, business elites currently coexist with the regime elites, rather than, for the time being at least, entering into struggles for political power. Gradually, however, they will become indispensable, so it seems, and will be asked to enter the fold rather than interjecting themselves into it.

At the end of the twentieth and the beginning of the twenty-first century, gradualism and, for the most part, peacefulness were and remain the prevalent modes of elite change in the Arab world. Certainly, the civil wars in Lebanon and Algeria contributed to sociopolitical changes in these two countries. In Lebanon, however, where the war ended more than a decade ago, most of the war elite—militia leaders recycled as politicians—have been quietly sidelined in the postwar transition period.[5] In Algeria, core and second-circle elites were rejuvenated, but not exchanged during the civil war. At any rate, although there are exceptions to the general mode of gradual and peaceful elite change in the Arab countries—the obvious case being that of regime-change-by-invasion in Iraq—this trend contrasts sharply with the historical experiences of the 1950s, 1960s, and 1970s, when revolutionary or putschist takeovers led to wide-ranging and structural changes of the core elite and its associated circles in so many Arab countries.

Gradualism, here, indicates that change, where it occurs, is steered and largely controlled from the core. In this respect, there is little difference between the republics and the monarchies of the Arab world. Rather, one could speak of signs of convergence: While the monarchies are broadening their societal base and their PRE through the establishment of parliaments or assemblies, not a few of the republican systems have tried to develop a hereditary legitimacy rooted, partly at least, in the blood relationship between would-be successors and long-standing leaders. This phenomenon has arisen at a time when the historical achievements of these regimes, or what has been celebrated as such over years and decades—Algeria's liberation, the 1952 revolution and others, the October War, and various "corrective" movements—have faded and fail to motivate the younger generations.

In the future, even where change at the top and in the core elite is mainly a matter of rejuvenation or generation change, new patterns of behavior and style are likely to emerge. Morocco, Jordan, and Syria all provide examples of top officials displaying more openness and transparency in dealing with the media and the public. These include such occurrences as the unprecedented public presentation of the wife of the Moroccan king or, somewhat ironically perhaps, the announcement by Syria's state news agency of the arrest of opposition figures. Socialized with satellite television and the Internet, younger members of these countries' political elite seem not to share the secretiveness of their predecessors with regard to issues of public interest. One can assume that such limited and symbolic steps toward transparency will create expectations for more openness.

Also, as noted, the biological rejuvenation of leadership elites has led to policy changes, particularly in the economic realm, and to a partial exchange of elite segments with others. Similar processes are likely to take place in countries on the verge of change at the level of the top decision-maker.

What one should not expect is that succession at the top—so much the focus of media attention concerning Egypt, Libya, Saudi Arabia, Tunisia, and other states—will lead to system change. In many cases, successions in Arab countries will bring about new *regimes*, but not a different regime *type*. Iraq under foreign occupation might take a different path, but the German or Japanese post–World War II model of a U.S.-led system transformation is not, in this author's judgment, the most likely scenario. A post-Arafat and independent Palestinian state may become a more democratic model than the one developed under the Oslo Accords because of the combination of external influences and changing balances within the domestic elite.

Most regime elites have so far managed to retain control of the mechanisms of domination established in the last three decades or so of the twentieth century. Through these the core maintains regime stability in part by orchestrating elite change—or, more precisely, the circulation and rejuvenation of the wider PRE. Thus co-optation prevails over competitive modes of elite recruitment. As a result, the political elites of most Arab states have become more representative; but what we are seeing emerge is a form of representation without (or with only limited and controlled) competition.

The co-optation and integration of aspirants to positions of (greater) responsibility and of some contestants may actually reduce or neutralize demands for more competition. Co-optation—in contrast to negotiated pacts, as in ideal-type democratic transitions—is of individuals, not of segments or entire networks that could establish themselves as alternatives to incumbents. Co-opted individuals are more easily integrated into the system and may thereby be neutralized as challengers.

Some regimes also resort to "fake competition,"[6] which is based around core-created or core-sponsored alternative parties or networks that give the impression of a competitive political system. This allows for a broadening of the PRE and the recruitment of new talent without threatening core elite control.

Almost all regimes will continue to seek new rent income in order to buy the allegiance or at least the consent of a silent majority (or maybe the silence of that majority). Although new and future regime elites must take into consideration somewhat heightened international sensitivities toward violence against political competitors and challengers, open repression remains an employable last resort. The instruments of the security state have been maintained all over the region.

Based on the empirical research in this volume, it is safe to assert that thoroughgoing institutional and political changes in Arab countries should not be expected, barring some sort of change in the relative influence among the PRE—specifically a decrease in the ability of the prime decisionmaker and core elite to control elite recruitment and hinder more competitive forms of elite circulation and change.

External interference and pressure may be successful if they are applied to elite strategies. They are likely to yield only limited success (at best) if their purpose is to bring about a change in leadership or the exchange of an entire elite. In both cases, such tactics create fears among incumbent elites about the stability of their regimes. Rather than encouraging political openings, these fears are likely to strengthen a prevalent autocratic elite consensus on the necessity of maintaining stability, or the status quo.

Such a consensus already exists in many Arab countries. As the case of Morocco illustrates, it may include some of the main opposition parties and thereby effectively marginalize the rest of the opposition.[7] Consensus on the rules of the game allow for economic adjustment and modernization, for the gradual rejuvenation of the elite—whereby new elements better equipped to respond to new challenges are brought in—and for successions and generation change, which can spare a country the types of divisions that can lead to major disturbances, including civil war. It is a consensus, however, that allows for modest institutional development at best, and is therefore likely to disappoint some constituencies, domestically and abroad, that expected deeper political systems change.

To date, such expectations, particularly in Western policymaking and media circles, have not been based on realism. Why, one might ask, should anyone expect a leader who has just inherited power to share it or risk it through democratic elections, unless forced to do so through constitutional or other constraints? Why should the advisors of that heir, and second-circle elites who owe their positions to him, urge him to open the political system and hold elections that would allow others to compete for the positions that they have just obtained?[8]

Conventional Western thinking may also have overrated the importance of youth and exposure to the West. First, exposure to the West is not a new phenomenon. Quite a number of elder technocratic elites obtained their expertise abroad; some of the prime decisionmakers of the outgoing generation were trained at Sandhurst or the École Supérieure de Guerre in Paris—as opposed to Harvard Business School or the École Nationale d'Administration more en vogue today. Second, time spent in the West, although an interesting and attractive subject to the media, obviously does not necessarily transform an heir apparent into a committed democrat. A future leader trained in, for example, a London clinic may well develop ideas about the efficacy of technology and efficiency and be inspired by British hospital organization; as head of state, however, he may then take the latter such forms of organization, rather than Westminster democracy, as a model for organizing "his" state.

Perhaps what must be realized is that elite change in autocratic systems should not be confused with "transition to" a new system. This applies not only to Arab states, but also to such cases as Turkmenistan, Belarus, the Democratic Republic of Congo, and others. In the Arab states, which provide an empirical basis for this book, the ruling elites have proved to be proficient at system maintenance. Although in many cases they have been less successful at providing services to citizens, their ability to preserve their regimes, which includes maintaining domestic stability, is a fact appreciated by many, including members of the business and intellectual elites and members of the wage-earning middle classes who in other respects may have second thoughts about these regimes and their policies.

Core elite strategies in most Arab countries have been increasingly influenced by inputs from and developments in their international environment. Consider, among others, the prospects of EU association or WTO membership; media globalization; international human rights campaigns; and more recently of course the geopolitical revolution brought about by the U.S. invasion of Iraq. While they could not escape the international context, these core elites have adapted to it, not least so by their management—or manipulation—of elite change. Elite circulation has thereby been used quite successfully for the modernization of policies and style, and the reproduction of power structures.

Research can be misleading if its analysis of Arab elites and change, or the potential for change in the Arab states, is gauged solely by the question of whether these elites have "succeeded" or will be able to succeed in bringing about a transition from autocratic rule to some form of democratic system. Such change may not be their goal. Arab PRE have proved themselves quite successful at developing a "type of political system whose institutions, rules, and logic defy any linear model of democratization,"[9] a type one might call liberalized autocracy or pluralistic authoritarianism[10] and is here to stay for some time.

The political role of elites remains crucial, nonetheless. During the 1990s hopes rose that in the Arab world democracies would emerge "without democrats."[11] There should today be little expectation of that happening if the "powerful" are not also "committed to the democratic project."[12] With limited external and societal pressures, and quite workable regime maintenance strategies, even emerging Arab elites will not automatically develop such a commitment. This is not to say that Arab countries are immune to democracy or addicted to despotism. The modernizing young and emerging elites are certainly not principally or ideologically antidemocratic. Given an uncertain future and a rapidly changing international environment, however, they may simply find their interests better served by not rocking the boat.

Notes

1. Przeworski, "Some Problems in the Study of Transition," p. 48.
2. Higley and Lengyel, "Elite Configuration After State Socialism," p. 8.
3. League of Arab States, Consolidated Arab Economic Report, 2001, p. 328.
4. *Financial Times,* 1 December 1999.
5. See Rola el-Husseini's chapter on Lebanon in this volume.
6. See Isabelle Werenfels's chapter on Algeria in this volume.
7. See Saloua Zerhouni's chapter on Morocco in this volume.
8. See, similarly, Carapico, "Successions, Transitions, Coups, and Revolutions."
9. Brumberg, "The Trap of Liberalized Autocracy," p. 56; see also Schlumberger, "Transition in the Arab World."
10. For more, see Perthes, *Geheime Gärten,* pp. 347–368.
11. Salameh, *Democracy Without Democrats.*
12. McFaul, "Fourth Wave of Democracy and Dictatorship."

Bibliography

Abdallah, Anwar. *Al-'Ulama wa-l-'arsh* (The scholars and the throne). London: al-Rafid, 1995.

Abdelnasser, Gamal. "Political Change in Egypt: The Parliamentary Elections of 2000 and Horizons of Reform." Working paper, SWP Study 19, Stiftung Wissenschaft und Politik, Berlin, 2001.

———. "Représentation syndicale et transition libérale en égypte: lecture des élections de 1996." *Égypte/Monde Arabe* 33 (1998): 181–221.

Abdel Nour, Ayman. "Syrian Views of an Association Agreement with the European Union." *EuroMeSCo Papers* 14 (December 2001).

Abdul Aziz, Muhammad, and Youssef Hussein. "The President, the Son, and the Military: The Question of Succession in Egypt." *Arab Studies Journal* 9/10 (fall 2001/spring 2002): 73–88.

al-Abed, Aref. *Lubnan wal Ta'if* (Lebanon and the Ta'if agreement). Beirut: Markaz Dirasat al-Wihda al-Arabia, 2001.

Abir, Mordechai. "The Consolidation of the Ruling Class and the New Elites in Saudi Arabia." *Middle Eastern Studies* 23, no. 2 (April 1987): 150–171.

Abu-Amr, Ziad. *Emerging Trends in Palestine: Strategic Political Thinking and Practice.* Jerusalem: PASSIA, 1996.

Abu Khalil, As'ad. "Determinants and Characteristics of Syrian Policy in Lebanon." In *Peace for Lebanon? From War to Reconstruction,* edited by Deirdre Collings. Boulder: Lynne Rienner, 1994.

Aburish, Saïd K. *Saddam Hussein: The Politics of Revenge.* London: Routledge, 2000.

Adam, Frane, and Matevz Tomšič. "Elite (Re)configuration and Politico-economic Performance in Post-socialist Countries." *Europe-Asia Studies* 54, no. 3 (2002): 435–454.

Alexander, Christoph. "Labour Code Reform in Tunisia." *Mediterranean Politics* 6, no. 2 (2001): 104–125.

Anderson, Lisa. *The State and Social Transformation in Tunisia and Libya, 1830–1980.* Princeton: Princeton University Press, 1986.

Arthur, Paul. "Elite Studies in a 'Paranocracy': The Northern Ireland Case." In *Research Methods for Elite Studies,* edited by G. Moyser and M. Wagstaffe. London: Allen and Unwin, 1987.

Asbach, Olaf. "Von der Geschichte politischer Ideen zur 'History of Political Discourse'?" *Zeitschrift für Politikwissenschaft* 12, no. 2 (2002): 637–667.

al-Atrash, Muhammad. "Hawl al-tawahhud al-iqtisadi al-'Arabi wa-l-sharaka al-Urubiyya" (On Arab economic unification and the European partnership). *al-Mustaqbal al-'Arabi* 24 (October 2000): 79–94.

Ayoub-Geday, Paul, ed. *The Egypt Almanac, 2001.* Cairo: Egypto-file, 2001.

Baaklini, Abdo, Guilain Denoeux, and Robert Springborg. *Legislative Politics in the Arab World: The Resurgence of Democratic Institutions.* Boulder: Lynne Rienner, 1999.

Bahout, Joseph. *Les entrepreneurs syriens: économie, affaires et politique.* Cahiers du CERMOC 7. Beirut: CERMOC, 1994.

———. "Les élites parlementaires libanaises de 1996." In *La vie publique au Liban: expressions et recompositions du politique,* edited by Joseph Bahout and Chawqi Douayhi. Cahiers du CERMOC 18. Beirut: CERMOC, 1997.

———. *La vie publique au Liban: expressions et recompositions du politique.* Cahiers du CERMOC 18. Beirut: CERMOC, 1997.

Barkey, Henri J., ed. *The Politics of Economic Reform in the Middle East.* New York: St. Martin's, 1992.

Batatu, Hanna. "The Egyptian, Syrian, and Iraqi Revolutions: Some Observations on Their Underlying Causes and Social Character." Inaugural lecture, Georgetown University, Center for Contemporary Arab Studies. Washington, D.C., 1983.

———. *Syria's Peasantry, the Descendants of Its Lesser Rural Notables, and Their Politics.* Princeton: Princeton University Press, 1999.

Baumgarten, Helga. "Ein palästinensischer Staat zwischen Demokratie und Neo-Patrimonialismus." Lecture delivered as part of "Probleme des Friedens im Nahen Osten," Münster, 30 January 2001.

Beblawi, Hazem. "The Rentier State in the Arab World." In *The Arab State,* edited by Giacomo Luciani, 85–98. Berkeley: University of California Press, 1990.

Beblawi, Hazem, and Giacomo Luciani, eds. *The Rentier State.* London: Croom Helm, 1987.

Beji, Hele. "La pédagogie des Lumières ou la réforme du système éducatif tunisien." In *Les États arabes face à la contestation islamiste,* edited by Bassma Kodmani-Darwish and Mary Chartouni-Dubarry, 255–269. Paris: Armand Colin, 1997.

Bellaire, Micheaux. "L'Administration au Maroc: le makhzen, étendues et limites de son pouvoir." *Bulletin de la Société de Géographie d'Alger* (1909).

Bellin, Eva. "Civil Society in Formation: Tunisia." In *Civil Society in the Middle East,* edited by Augustus Richard Norton, 1:120–147. Leiden: Brill, 1995.

———. *Stalled Democracy: Capital, Labor, and the Paradox of State-Sponsored Development.* Ithaca: Cornell University Press, 2002.

Bill, James A. "The Patterns of Elite Politics in Iran." In *Political Elites in the Middle East,* edited by George Lenczowski, 17–40. Washington, D.C.: American Enterprise Institute for Public Policy Research, 1975.

Bill, James, and Robert Springborg. *Politics in the Middle East.* New York: Harper Collins, 1994.

Binder, Leonard. *In a Moment of Enthusiasm: Political Power and the Second Stratum in Egypt.* Chicago: University of Chicago Press, 1978.

———. *Ethnic Conflict and International Politics in the Middle East.* Gainesville: University of Florida Press, 1999.

———, ed. *Politics in Lebanon.* New York: John Wiley, 1966.

Bishara, Asmi. "Reflections on the Realities of the Oslo Process." In *After Oslo:*

New Realities, Old Problems, edited by George Giacaman and Dag J. Lonning. Routledge: London, 1997.

Bligh, Alexander. "The Jordanian Army: Between Domestic and External Challenges." *MERIA* 5, no. 2 (summer 2001): 13–20.

Blin, Louis. "Les entrepreneurs palestiniens." In *L'Economie de la paix au Proche-Orient,* edited by Louis Blin and Philippe Fargues, 2:285–298. Paris: Maisonneuve et Larouse, 1995.

Bos, Ellen. "Die Rolle von Eliten und kollektiven Akteuren in Transformationsprozessen." In *Systemwechsel/1: Theorien, Ansätze und Konzeptionen,* edited by Wolfgang Merkel, 81–109. Opladen: Leske und Budrich, 1994.

Bottomore, Tom. *Elites and Society.* London: Routledge, 1993.

Boudahrain, Abdellah. *Le nouveau Maroc politique: quel avenir?* Casablanca: Al Madariss, 1999.

Boulding, Kenneth. *The Image: Knowledge in Life and Society.* Ann Arbor: University of Michigan Press, 1956.

Bouillon, Markus. "Walking the Tightrope: Jordanian Foreign Policy from the Gulf Crisis to the Peace Process and Beyond." In *Jordan in Transition, 1990–2000,* edited by George Joffé, 1–22. London: Hurst, 2002.

Bourdieu, Pierre. "Le capital social." *Actes de la Recherche en Sciences Sociales* 31 (1980).

———. "The Forms of Capital." In *Handbook of the Theory and Research for the Sociology of Education,* edited by John G. Richardson. New York: Greenwood, 1986.

———. *La réproduction: éléments pour une théorie du système d'enseignement.* Paris: Les Editions de Minuit, 1970.

———. "The Sentiment of Honour in Kabyle Society." In *Honour and Shame: The Values of Mediterranean Society,* edited by Jean G. Péristiany, 191–241. London: Weidenfeld and Nicolson, 1966.

Bourqia, Rahma. "The Cultural Legacy of Power in Morocco." In *In the Shadow of the Sultan: Culture, Power, and Politics in Morocco,* edited by Rahma Bourqia and Susan Gilson Miller, 243–258. Cambridge: Harvard University Press, 2000.

Boyan, Belev. *Forcing Freedom: Political Control of Privatization and Economic Opening in Egypt and Tunisia.* Lanham, Md.: University Press of America, 2000.

Brand, Laurie A. "Al-Muhajirin w-al Ansar: Hashemite Strategies for Managing Communal Identity in Jordan." In *Ethnic Conflict and International Politics in the Middle East,* edited by Leonard Binder, 279–306. Gainesville: University of Florida Press, 1999.

———. "In Search of Budget Security: A Reexamination of Jordanian Foreign Policy." Paper presented at "Politique et état en Jordanie, 1946–1996," Institut du Monde Arabe, Paris, June 1997.

———. *Women, the State, and Political Liberalization: Middle Eastern and North African Experiences.* New York: Columbia University Press, 1998.

———. "Economic and Political Liberalization in a Rentier Economy." In *Privatization and Liberalization in the Middle East,* edited by Iliya Harik and Denis J. Sullivan, 167–188. Bloomington: Indiana University Press, 1992.

Bratton, Michael, and Nicolas van de Walle. "Neopatrimonial Regimes and Political Transitions in Africa." *World Politics* 46, no. 4 (July 1994): 453–489.

Brown, Leon Carl, et al. *Tunisia: The Politics of Modernization.* New York: Praeger, 1964.

Brown, Michael E., Sean M. Lynn-Jones, and Steven E. Miller, eds. *Debating the Democratic Peace*. Cambridge: Cambridge University Press, 1996.

Brown, Nathan. *The Palestinian Reform Agenda*. Peace Works 48. Washington, D.C.: United States Institute of Peace, 2002.

Brumberg, Daniel. "The Trap of Liberalized Autocracy." *Journal of Democracy* 12, no. 4 (October 2002): 56–68.

———. "Survival Strategies vs. Democratic Bargains: The Politics of Economic Reform in Contemporary Egypt." In *The Politics of Economic Reform in the Middle East*, edited by Henri J. Barkey, 73–104. New York: St. Martin's, 1992.

Brynen, Rex. "The Dynamics of Palestinian Elite Formation." *Journal of Palestine Studies* 25, no. 3 (spring 1995): 31–43.

———. "Economic Crisis and Post-Rentier Democratization in the Arab World: The Case of Jordan." *Canadian Journal of Political Science* 25, no. 1 (March 1992): 69–97.

———. "The Neopatrimonial Dimension of Palestinian Politics." *Journal of Palestine Studies* 25, no. 1 (autumn 1995): 23–36.

Burton, Michael, and John Higley. "The Study of Political Elite Transformations." *International Review of Sociology* 11, no. 2 (2001): 181–199.

Burton, Michael, Richard Gunther, and John Higley. "Introduction: Elite Transformations and Democratic Regimes." In *Elites and Democratic Consolidation in Latin America and Southern Europe*, edited by John Higley and Richard Gunther, 1–37. Cambridge: Cambridge University Press, 1992.

Butter, David. "Beyond Mubarak." *Middle East Economic Digest* 43, no. 40 (1999): 7–23.

Camau, Michel. "D'une République à une autre: Refondation politique et aléas de la transition libérale." *Maghreb-Machrek* 157 (1997): 3–16.

———. *Pouvoir et Institutions au Maghreb*. Paris: Berger-Levrault, 1978.

———, ed. *La Tunisie au présent: une modernité au dessus de tout soupçon?* Paris: CNRS, 1987.

Cantori, Louis. "The Dual Middle Eastern State and Political Succession." *Middle East Policy* 9, no. 3 (September 2002): 105–123.

Cantori, Louis, et al. "Political Succession in the Middle East." *Middle East Policy* 9, no. 3 (September 2002).

Carapico, Sheila. "Foreign Aid for Promoting Democracy in the Arab World." *Middle East Journal* 56, no. 3 (summer 2002): 379–395.

———. "NGOs, INGOs, GO-NGOs and DO-NGOs: Making Sense of Non-Governmental Organizations." *Middle East Report* (spring 2000): 12–15.

———. "Successions, Transitions, Coups, and Revolutions." *Middle East Policy* 9, no. 3 (September 2002): 109–110.

Cassarino, Jean-Pierre. "The EU-Tunisian Association Agreement and Tunisia's Structural Reform Process." *Middle East Journal* 53, no. 1 (1999): 59–74.

Chabal, Patrick, and Jean-Pascal Daloz. *Africa Works: Disorder as Political Instrument*. Oxford: James Currey, 1999.

Chahal, Nahla. "Etat et confessions: la formidable capacité d'intégration du système libanais." In *Nationalismes en mutation en Méditerranée orientale*, edited by Alain Dieckhoff and Riva Kastoryano, 113–131. Paris: CNRS Editions, 2002.

Charfi, Mounir. *Les ministres de Bourguiba, 1956–1987*. Paris: L'Harmattan, 1989.

Cherifi, Rachida. *Le Makhzen politique au Maroc: Hier et aujourd'hui*. Casablanca: Afrique Orient, 1988.

Chesnot, Christia. "La Jordanie entre deux crises." *Politique Internationale* 96 (summer 2002): 129–143.

Cheurfi, Achour. *La classe politique algérienner de 1900 à nos jours. Dictionnaire biographique.* Algiers: Casbah, 2001.

Claisse, Alain. "Le Makhzen aujourd'hui." In *Le Maroc actuel,* edited by Jean-Claude Santucci, 285–309. Paris: CNRS, 1992.

Cohen, Samy. *L'Art d'interviewer les dirigeants.* Paris: Presses Universitaires de France, 1999.

Collings, Deirdre, ed. *Peace for Lebanon? From War to Reconstruction.* Boulder: Lynne Rienner, 1994.

Craissati, Dina. "Social Movements and Democracy in Palestine: Politicization of Society or Civilization of Politics?" *Orient* 37 (1996): 111–136.

Cunningham, Karla J. "Factors Influencing Jordan's Information Revolution: Implications for Democracy." *Middle East Journal* 56, no. 2 (spring 2002): 240–256.

Cunningham, Robert, and Yassin Sarayrah. *Wasta: The Hidden Force in Middle Eastern Society.* Westport, Conn.: Praeger, 1993.

Daoud, Zakya. "Maroc: les élections de 1997." *Monde Arabe-Maghreb Machrek,* no. 158 (October–December 1997): 105–128.

Dekmejian, Richard Hrair. "The Rise of Political Islamism in Saudi Arabia." *Middle East Journal* 48, no. 4 (autumn 1994): 627–642.

———. "Saudi Arabia's Consultative Council." *Middle East Journal* 52, no. 2 (spring 1998): 204–218.

Denoeux, Guilain, and Robert Springborg. "Hariri's Lebanon: Singapore of the Middle East or Sanaa of the Levant?" *Middle East Policy* 7, no. 2 (October 1998).

Dieterich, R. "The Weakness of the Ruled Is the Strength of the Ruler: The Role of the Opposition in Contemporary Jordan." In *Jordan in Transition, 1990–2000,* edited by George Joffé, 127–148. London: Hurst, 2002.

Dillman, Bradford. "Facing the Market in North Africa." *Middle East Journal* 55, no. 2 (spring 2001): 198–215.

———. "The Political Economy of Structural Adjustment in Tunisia and Algeria." *Journal of North African Studies* 52, no. 3 (1998): 1–24.

Droz-Vincent, Philippe. "Syrie: la nouvelle génération au pouvoir." *Monde Arabe-Maghreb Machrek,* no. 173 (July–September 2001): 14–38.

Drysdale, Alasdair. "The Succession Question in Syria." *Middle East Journal* 39 (1985): 246–257.

Dunn, Michael Collins. "The al-Nahda Movement in Tunisia: From Renaissance to Revolution." In *Islamism and Secularism in North Africa,* edited by John Ruedy, 149–165. New York: St. Martin's, 1994.

———. "The Coming Era of Leadership Change in the Arab World." *Middle East Policy* 5, no. 4 (January 1998): 180–187.

Dupont, Hubert [pseud.]. "La nouvelle armée libanaise: instrument du pouvoir ou acteur politique?" *Confluences Medierannées,* no. 29 (spring 1999).

Economic Consultative Council. Tahdith wa tatwir al-qita' al-'amm (Modernization and development of the public sector). Unpublished paper, Amman, June 2000.

Economic Intelligence Unit. Country Profile 2002. Jordan, London, 2002, 21f.

Eisenstadt, Shmuel. *Traditional Patrimonialism and Modern Neopatrimonialism.* Beverly Hills: Sage, 1973.

Eisenstadt, Shmuel, and René Lemarchand, eds. *Political Clientelism, Patronage, and Development.* Beverly Hills: Sage, 1981.

Entelis, John P. "Algeria: Technocratic Rule, Military Power." In *Political Elites in Arab North Africa: Morocco, Algeria, Tunisia, Libya, and Egypt,* edited by William I. Zartman, 92–143. New York: Longman, 1983.

————. *Comparative Politics of North Africa: Algeria, Morocco and Tunisia.* Syracuse: Syracuse University Press, 1980.

————, ed. *Islam, Democracy, and the State in North Afric*a. Bloomington: Indiana University Press, 1997.

Entelis, John P., and Mark A. Tessler. "Republic of Tunisia." In *The Government and Politics of the Middle East and North Africa,* edited by David E. Long and Bernard Reich, 435–458. Boulder: Westview, 1986.

Etzioni-Halevy, Eva. "Elites and the Working Class." In *Classes and Elites in Democracy and Democratization: A Collection of Readings,* edited by Eva Etzioni-Halevy, 310–325. New York and London: Garland, 1997.

Faath, Sigrid, ed. *Konfliktpotential politischer Nachfolge in den arabischen Staaten.* Hamburg: Edition Wuqûf, 2000.

Fandy, Mamoun. *Saudi Arabia and the Politics of Dissent.* New York: St. Martin's, 1999.

Farsakh, L. "Under Siege." *Middle East Report* (winter 2000).

Feldner, Yotam. "Egypt's Succession, Part I: Will Egypt Follow Syria's Precedent? Part II: Does Gamal Mubarak Have a Chance?" *MEMRI Inquiry and Analysis,* 24 and 25 July 2000.

Fields, G. Lowell, John Higley, and Michael Burton. "A New Elite Framework as Political Sociology." *Revue Européenne des Sciences Sociales* 28 (1990): 149–182.

Figuie, Gérard. *Le Point sur le Liban.* Beirut: Anthologie, 1994.

al-Fiqi, Mustafa. *The Copts in Egyptian Politics: Makram Ebeid and His Role in the National Movement* (in Arabic). Cairo: Dar al-Hillal, 1985.

Frey, Frederick W. *The Turkish Political Elite.* Cambridge: MIT Press, 1965.

al-Gauwadi, Mohammed. *The Egyptian Political Elite from 1952 Until Today* (in Arabic). Cairo: Dar al-Madbouli, 2001.

Ghadbian, Najib. "The New Asad: Dynamics of Continuity and Change in Syria." *Middle East Journal* 55, no. 4 (autumn 2001): 624–641.

Gill, Graeme J. *The Dynamics of Democratization: Elites, Civil Society and the Transition Process.* Basingstoke: Macmillan, 2000.

Goldschmidt, Arthur, Jr. *Biographical Dictionary of Modern Egypt.* Cairo: American University in Cairo Press, 2000.

————. "The Butrus Ghali Family." *Journal of the American Research Center in Egypt* 30 (1993): 183–188.

Gotowicki, Stephen H. "The Military in Egyptian Society." In *Egypt at the Crossroads: Domestic Stability and Regional Role,* edited by Phebe Marr, 105–125. Washington, D.C.: National Defense University Press, 1999.

Granduillaume, Gilbert. *Nédroma: l'évolution d'une médina.* Leiden: Brill, 1976.

Gurny, J. N. "Female Researchers in Male Settings." In *Experiencing Fieldwork: An Inside View of Qualitative Research,* edited by William B. Shaffir and Robert A. Stebbins. Newbury Park, Calif.: Sage, 1991.

Hachemaoui, Mohammed. "La représentation politique en Algérie: médiation clientélaire et prédation, 1997–2002." *Revue Française de Science Politique* 53, no. 1 (February 2003).

Hakimian, Hassan, and Ziba Moshaver, eds. *The State and Global Change: The Political Economy of Transition in the Middle East and North Africa.* Surrey: Curzon, 2001.

Halpern, Manfred. *The Politics of Social Change in the Middle East and North Africa.* Princeton: Princeton University Press, 1963.

Hamladji, Noura. "Co-optation, Repression and Authoritarian Regimes' Survival:

The Case of the Islamist MSP-Hamas in Algeria." EUI working paper, SPS 7, 2002.

Hammami, R. "Interregnum: Palestine After Operation Defensive Shield." *Middle East Report* (summer 2002).

Hammami, R., and J. Hilal. "An Uprising at a Crossroads." *Middle East Report* (summer 2001).

Hammami, R., and S. Tamari. "Second Uprising: Beginning or End?" *Journal of Palestine Studies* (winter 2001).

Hammond, Andrew. "Egyptians Question Whether Syrian Example Will Set Precedent for Mubarak Succession." *Washington Report on Middle East Affairs* (August/September 2000): 51–52.

Hammoudi, Abdellah. *Master and Disciple: The Cultural Foundations of Moroccan Authoritarianism.* Chicago: University of Chicago Press, 1997.

Hanafi, Sari, and Linda Tabar. "On the Way to Nakba II." *Between the Lines* (October 2002): 31–36.

Hanf, T. *Coexistence in Wartime Lebanon: Decline of a State and Rise of a Nation.* Translated from German by J. Richardson. London: Centre for Lebanese Studies/I. B. Tauris, 1993.

Harbi, Mohammed. *Une vie debout: mémoires politiques, 1945–1962.* Algiers: Casbah, 2001.

Harik, Iliya. "Maronite Church and Political Change in Lebanon." In *Politics in Lebanon,* edited by L. Binder. New York: Wiley, 1966.

———. "Political Elite of Lebanon." In *Political Elites in the Middle East,* edited by George Lenczowski. Washington, D.C.: American Enterprise Institute for Policy Research, 1975.

Harik, Iliya, and Denis Sullivan, eds. *Privatization and Liberalization in the Middle East.* Bloomington: Indiana University Press, 1992.

Harik, Judith. "The Public and Social Services of the Lebanese Militias." Papers on Lebanon, Centre for Lebanese Studies, Oxford, 1994.

Heller, Mark Allen, and Nadav Safran. *The New Middle Class and Regime Stability in Saudi Arabia.* Cambridge: Harvard University, 1985.

Henderson, Amy, and Paul Pasch. "Jordan." *FES-Analyse.* Amman: Friedrich Ebert Foundation, January 2001.

Henderson, Simon. *After King Fahd: Succession in Saudi Arabia.* Policy Paper 37. Washington, D.C.: Washington Institute for Near East Policy, 1994.

Heradstveit, Daniel. *Arab and Israeli Elite Perceptions.* Oslo: Universitetsforlaget, 1974.

Hermassi, Mohammed Elbaki. *Leadership and National Development in North Africa: A Comparative Study.* Berkeley: University of California Press, 1972.

Hidouci, Ghaci. *Algérie: la libération inachevée.* Paris: Editions la Découverte, 1995.

Higley, John, and Michael G. Burton. "The Elite Variable in Democratic Transitions and Breakdowns." *American Sociology Review* 54 (February 1989): 17–32.

Higley, John, and Richard Gunther, eds. *Elites and Democratic Consolidation in Latin America and Southern Europe.* Cambridge: Cambridge University Press, 1992.

Higley, John, and György Lengyel. "Elite Configuration After State Socialism." In *Elites After State Socialism: Theories and Analysis,* edited by John Higley and György Lengyel, 1–21. Lanham, Md.: Rowman Littlefield, 2000.

Higley, John, and Glenn Moore. "Political Elite Studies at the Year 2000: Introduction." *International Review of Sociology* 11, no. 2 (2001): 175–180.

Hilal, Jamil. "The Effects of the Oslo Agreements on the Palestinian Political System." In *After Oslo: New Realities, Old Problems,* edited by George Giacaman and Dag J. Lonning. London: Routledge, 1997.

———. *Takuin al-nukhba al-filastiniyya mundhu nushu' al-haraka al-wataniyya al-Filastiniyya ila ma ba'd qiyam al-Sulta al-Wataniyya* (The formation of the Palestinian elite: From the emergence of the national movement until after the establishment of the National Authority). Ramallah and Amman: Muwatin and al-Urdunn al-Jadid Center for Strategic Studies, 2002.

Hinnebusch, Raymond. "From Nasir to Sadat: Elite Transformation in Egypt." *Journal of South Asian and Middle Eastern Studies* 7, no. 1 (fall 1983): 24–49.

Hourani, Hani, and Ayman Yassin. *Who's Who in the Jordanian Parliament, 1997–2001.* Amman: al-Urdunn al-Jadid Center for Strategic Studies, 1998.

Howe, Marvine. "Morocco's Democratic Experience." *World Policy Journal* 17, no. 1 (spring 2000): 65–70.

Hudson, Michael. "Lebanon After Ta'if: Another Reform Opportunity Lost." *Arab Studies Quarterly* 21, no. 1 (winter 1999): 27–40.

———. "The Problem of Authoritative Power in Lebanese Politics: Why Consociationalism Failed." In *Lebanon: A History of Conflict and Consensus,* edited by Nadim Shehadi and Dana Haffar Mills. London: I. B. Tauris, 1988.

———. *The Precarious Republic: Modernization in Lebanon.* New York: Random House, 1968.

Hunter, Albert. "Local Knowledge and Local Power." In *Studying Elites Using Qualitative Methods,* edited by Rosanna Hertz and Jonathan Imber. Thousand Oaks, Calif.: Sage, 1995.

Huntington, Samuel. "Will More Countries Become Democratic?" *Political Science Quarterly* 99 (summer 1984): 61–98.

Hurewitz, J. C. *Middle East Politics: The Military Dimension.* London: Pall Mall, 1969.

Imam, Abdallah. *Sadat's Coup d'Etat: The Path to the Presidency* (in Arabic). Cairo: Ruz al-Youssef, 2000.

International Crisis Group. "The Meanings of Palestinian Reform." Middle East briefing, Amman and Washington, D.C., 12 November 2002.

International Institute for Strategic Studies. "Mapping Egypt's Future: The Fading of Old Certainties," no. 7, August 2000.

Israeli-Palestinian Interim Agreement on the West Bank and Gaza Strip. Occasional Document Series 7. East Jerusalem: Jerusalem Media and Communication Centre, 1996.

Joffé, George, ed. *Jordan in Transition, 1990–2000.* London: Hurst, 2002.

Johnson, Michael. *Class and Client in Beirut.* London: Ithaca, 1986.

Karabadji, Faycal. "L'Economie algérienne menacée par la mafia politico-financière." *Le Monde Diplomatique* (September 1998): 10–11.

Karl, Terry Lynn. "Democracy by Design: The Christian Democratic Party in El Salvador." In *The Central American Impasse,* edited by Giuseppe Di Palma and Laurence Whitehead, 195–217. New York: St. Martin's, 1986.

Kechichian, Joseph A. *Succession in Saudi Arabia.* New York: Palgrave, 2001.

al-Khafaji, Isam. "War as a Vehicle for the Rise and Demise of a State-Controlled Society: The Case of Ba'thist Iraq." In *War, Institutions, and Social Change in the Middle East,* edited by Steven Heydeman, 258–291. Berkeley: University of California Press, 2000.

Khalaf, Abdulhadi. "The New Amir of Bahrain: Marching Sideways." *Civil Society* 9 (April 2000): 6–13.

Khan, Mushtaq. "State Failure in Developing Countries and Strategies of Institutional Reform." Paper presented to the ABCDE Conference, Oslo, 24–26 June 2002.

Khashan, Hilal, and Simon Haddad. "The Coupling of the Syrian-Lebanese Peace Tracks: Beirut's Options." *Security Dialogue* 31, no. 2 (June 2000): 201–214.

Khatibi, Abdelkébir. *L'Alternance et les partis politiques*. Casablanca: Eddif, 2000.

al-Khazen, Farid. *Intikhabat Lubnan ma ba' da al-Harb* (The postwar Lebanese elections). Beirut: Dar an-Nahar, 2000.

al-Khazen, Farid, and Paul Salem, eds. *Al-Intikhabat al-ula fi Lubnan ma ba' adal Harb* (The first postwar parliamentary elections in Lebanon). Beirut: Dar an-Nahar/LCPS, 1993.

Khiari, Sadri, and Olfa Lamloum. "Le Zaïm et l'Artisan ou de Bourguiba à Ben Ali." *Annuaire de l'Afrique du Nord* 37 (1998): 377–395.

al-Khouri, Riad. *Qualifying Industrial Zones as a Model for Industrial Devlopment: The Case of Jordan and Its Implications for the Middle East Region*. Amman: Freidrich Ebert Foundation, 2001.

Kially, Majid. "Nahu bina'a thakafa siasiya jadida fi al-saha al-Filistiniya" (Toward building a new political culture in the Palestinian arena). *Adab* (September 2002).

Kienle, Eberhard. *A Grand Delusion: Democracy and Economic Reform in Egypt*. London: I. B. Tauris, 2001.

Knoke, David. "Networks of Elite Structure and Decision Making." *Sociological Methods and Research* 22, no. 1 (August 1993).

Krämer, Gudrun. *Ägypten unter Mubarak: Identität und nationales Interesse*. Baden-Baden: Nomos, 1986.

———. "Liberalization and Democracy in the Arab World." *Middle East Report* (January–February 1992): 22–25.

———. "The Integration of the Integrists: A Comparative Study of Egypt, Jordan, and Tunisia." In *Democracy Without Democrats? The Renewal of Politics in the Muslim World*, edited by Ghassan Salamé, 200–226. London: I. B. Tauris, 1994.

Laarif-Beatrix, Asma. *Edification étatique et environnement culturel: le personnel politico-administratif dans la Tunisie contemporaine*. Paris: Publisud, 1988.

Lamloum, Olfa, and Bernard Ravenel, eds. *La Tunisie de Ben Ali: La société contre le régime*. Paris: L'Harmattan, 2002.

Lasswell, Harold. *Politics: Who Gets What, When, How*. Cleveland: Peter Smith, 1958.

League of Arab States, General Secretariat. *Al-Taqrir al-iqtisadi al-'Arabi al-muwahhad, 2001* (Consolidated Arab economic report, 2001). Cairo and Abu Dhabi, 2002.

Legrain, Jean-François. "Les 1001 successions de Yasser Arafat." *Monde Arabe-Maghreb Machrek*, no. 160 (April–June 1998): 3–29.

Leila, Ali, Monte Palmer, and Yassin el-Sayed. *The Egyptian Bureaucracy*. Syracuse: Syracuse University Press, 1988.

Lenczowski, George, ed. *Political Elites in the Middle East*. Washington, D.C.: American Enterprise Institute for Public Policy Research, 1975.

Leveau, Rémy. *Le fellah marocain: défenseur du trône*. Paris: Presses de la Fondation Nationale des Sciences Politiques, 1985.

Lijphart, Arend. "Typologies of Democratic Systems." *Comparative Political Studies* (1969).

Lipset, Seymour Martin. "Some Social Requisites of Democracy: Economic

Development and Political Legitimacy." *American Political Science Review* 53 (1959): 69–105.

Longuenesse, Elisabeth. "Ingenieurs et médecins dans le changement social: Egypte, Syrie, Jordanie." *Monde Arabe-Maghreb Machrek*, no. 146 (October–December 1994): 3–6.

Lowell Fields, G., John Higley, and Michael Burton. "A New Elite Framework for Political Sociology." *Revue Européenne des Sciences Sociales* 28 (1990): 149–182.

Luciani, Giacomo. "Allocation vs. Production States: A Theoretical Framework." In *The Arab State,* edited by Giacomo Luciani, 65–84. Berkeley: University of California Press, 1990.

Lust-Okar, Ellen. "The Decline of Jordanian Party Politics: Myth or Reality?" *International Journal of Middle East Studies* 33 (2001): 545–569.

Maghraoui, Abdesslam. "Depoliticization in Morocco." *Journal of Democracy* 13, no. 4 (October 2002): 24–32.

———. "Political Authority in Crisis." *Middle East Report* (March 2001).

Magnuson, Douglas K. "Islamic Reform in Contemporary Tunisia: Unity and Diversity." In *Tunisia: The Political Economy of Reform,* edited by I. William Zartman, 169–192. Boulder: Westview, 1991.

Maila, Joseph. "L'Accord de Taef deux ans après." *Les Cahiers de l'Orient,* no. 24 (1991): 13–69.

———. *The Document of National Understanding: A Commentary.* Oxford: Centre for Lebanese Studies, 1992.

Mainwaring, Scott. "Transitions to Democracy and Democratic Consolidation: Theoretical and Comparative Issues." In *Issues in Democratic Consolidation: The New South American Democracies in Comparative Perspective,* edited by Scott Mainwaring, Guillermo O'Donnell, and Samuel J. Valenzuela. Notre Dame, Ind.: University of Notre Dame Press, 1992.

Makdisi, Jean Said. "The Mythology of Modernity: Women and Democracy in Lebanon." In *Feminism and Islam,* edited by Mai Yamani, 231–250. New York: New York University Press, 1996.

Mannheim, Karl. "The Problem of Generation." In *Essays in the Sociology of Knowledge,* edited by Paul Kecskemeti, 276–322. London: Routledge and Kegan Paul, 1952.

Mansour, Albert. *Al-Inqilab 'ala al-Taef* (A revolution on Ta'if). Beirut: Dar al-Jadid, 1993.

Mansour, C. "The Impact of 11 September on the Israeli-Palestinian Conflict." *Journal of Palestine Studies* (winter 2002).

Mantzavinos, Chris, Douglass C. North, and Syed Shariq. "Learning, Change and Economic Performance." Paper presented to the 5th Annual Conference of the International Society of New Institutional Economics, Berkeley, California, 13–15 September 2001.

Martinez, Luis. *La guerre civile en Algérie.* Paris: Karthala, 1998.

Marzuq, Nabil. "Al-Batala wa-l-faqr fi Suriya" (Unemployment and poverty in Syria). Damascus: Syrian Economic Society, 2001.

McFaul, Michael. "The Fourth Wave of Democracy and Dictatorship: Noncooperative Transitions in the Postcommunist World." *World Politics* 54, no. 2 (January 2002): 212–244.

Merkel, Wolfgang, ed. *Systemwandel 1/Theorien, Ansätze und Konzeptionen.* Opladen: Leske und Budrich, 1994.

Migdal, Joel S. *Weak States and Strong Societies: State-Society Relations and State Capabilities in the Third World.* Princeton: Princeton University Press, 1988.

Milton-Edwards, Beverly, and Peter Hinchcliffe. "Abdallah's Jordan: New King, Old Problems." *Middle East Report* (winter 1999): 28–31.
————. *Jordan: A Hashemite Legacy.* London: Routledge, 2001.
Moore, Clement Henry. *Politics in North Africa: Algeria, Morocco, and Tunisia.* Boston: Praeger, 1970.
Moyser, George, and Margaret Wagstaffe. *Research Methods for Elite Studies.* London: Allen and Unwin, 1987.
————. "Studying Elites: Theoretical and Methodological Issues." In *Research Methods for Elite Studies,* edited by George Moyser and Margaret Wagstaffe. London: Allen and Unwin, 1987.
————. "The Threatened Elite." In *Research Methods for Elite Studies,* edited by G. Moyser and M. Wagstaffe. London: Allen and Unwin, 1987.
Murphy, Emma C. *Economic and Political Change in Tunisia: From Bourguiba to Ben Ali.* New York: St. Martin's, 1999.
————. "Economic Reform and the State in Tunisia." In *The State and Global Change: The Political Economy of Transition in the Middle East and North Africa,* edited by Hassan Hakimian and Ziba Moshaver, 135–155. Richmond, Surrey: Curzon, 2001.
————. "The Foreign Policy of Tunisia." In *The Foreign Policies of Middle East States,* edited by Raymond Hinnebusch, 235–256. Boulder: Lynne Rienner, 2002.
————. "The State and the Private Sector in North Africa: Seeking Specificity." *Mediterranean Politics* 6, no. 2 (2001): 1–28.
al-Najjar, Ghanim. "Waqi' wa-mustaqbal al-awda' al-siyasiyya fi fuwwal al-Khalij" (Reality and future of the political situation in the Gulf states). *al-Mustaqbal al-'arabi* 24, no. 268 (June 2001): 90–112.
Nassif Tar Kovacs, Fadia. *Les rumeurs dans la guerre du Liban: les mots de la violence.* Paris: CNRS Editions, 1995.
Nezzar, Khaled, and Mohamed Maarfia. *Un procès pour la vérité: L'armée algérienne face à la désinformation.* Algiers: ANEP/Marinoor, 2002.
North, Douglass C. "Economic Performance Through Time." *American Economic Review* 84, no. 3 (June 1994): 359–368.
Norton, A. R. *Hizballah of Lebanon: Extremist Ideals vs. Mundane Politics.* New York: Council on Foreign Relations, 1999.
Obeidi, Amal. "Elitenstruktur in Libyen: Neue Institutionen und aufstrebende Eliten." In *Elitenwandel in der arabischen Welt und Iran,* edited by Volker Perthes. SWP Study 41. Berlin: Stiftung Wissenschaft und Politik, 2002.
O'Donnell, Guillermo, Philippe C. Schmitter, and Laurence Whitehead, eds. *Transitions from Authoritarian Rule: Tentative Conclusions About Uncertain Democracies.* Baltimore: Johns Hopkins University Press, 1986.
Ofeish, Sami. "Lebanon's Second Republic: Secular Talk, Sectarian Application." *Arab Studies Quarterly* 21, no. 1 (winter 1999).
Oxford Business Group. *Emerging Syria, 2002.* London: Oxford Business Group, 2002.
The Palestinian Authority Political Programme. Documents on Palestine. Vol. 2. East Jerusalem: PASSIA, 1997.
Pawelka, Peter. *Herrschaft und Entwicklung im Nahen Osten: Ägypten.* Heidelberg: Müller, 1985.
Peeler, John A. "Elites, Structures, and Political Action in Latin America." *International Review of Sociology* 11, no. 2 (2001): 231–246.
Perkins, Kenneth J. *Tunisia: Crossroad of the Islamic and European Worlds.* Boulder: Westview, 1986.

Perthes, Volker. "Bourgeoisie and the Ba'th: A Look at Syria's Upper Class." *Middle East Report* (May–June 1991): 31–37.
———. *Geheime Gärten: Die neue arabische Welt.* Berlin: Siedler-Verlag, 2002.
———. "Myths and Money: Four Years of Hariri and Lebanon's Preparation for a New Middle East." *MERIP* (spring 1997).
———. *The Political Economy of Syria Under Asad.* London: I. B. Tauris, 1995.
———. "The Private Sector, Economic Liberalization and the Prospects of Democratization: The Case of Syria and Some Other Arab Countries." In *Democracy Without Democrats? The Renewal of Politics in the Muslim World,* edited by Ghassan Salamé. London: I. B. Tauris, 1995.
———. "*Si vis stabilitatem, para bellum:* State Building, National Security, and War Preparation in Syria." In *War, Institutions, and Social Change in the Middle East,* edited by Steven Heydeman, 149–173. Berkeley: University of California Press, 2000.
———. "Syria's Parliamentary Elections of 1990: Remodeling Asad's Political Base." *Middle East Report* (January–February 1992).
———. "Syria Under Bashar al-Asad: Modernisation and the Limits of Change." *Adelphi Paper.* London: IISS, forthcoming 2004.
———. *Vom Krieg zur Konkurrenz: Regionale Politik und die Suche nach einer neuen arabisch-nahöstlichen Ordnung.* Baden-Baden: Nomos, 2000.
———, ed. *Elitenwandel in der arabischen Welt und Iran.* SWP Study 41. Berlin: Stiftung Wissenschaft und Politik, 2002.
———, ed. *Scenarios for Syria: Socio-Economic and Political Choices.* Baden-Baden: Nomos, 1998.
Perthes, Volker, and Stefania Spapperi. "The Young Entrepreneurs of the Arab World: New Attitudes to Politics and Business? Some Remarks on the Regional Forum for Young Entrepreneurs, Jordan, 10–12 May 2001." Manuscript on file. Later published in *al-Urdun* (in Arabic), 5 January 2003.
Peterson, J. E. "Succession in the States of the Gulf Cooperation Council." *Washington Quarterly* 24, no. 4 (autumn 2001): 173–186.
Picard, Elizabeth. "Arab Military in Politics: From Revolutionary Plot to Authoritarian State." In *The Arab State,* edited by Giacomo Liuciani. Berkeley: University of California Press, 1990.
Piro, Timothy J. *The Political Economy of Market Reform in Jordan.* Lanham, Md.: Rowman and Littlefield, 1998.
Pollack, Josh. "Saudi Arabia and the United States." *Middle East Review of International Affairs* 6, no. 3 (September 2002).
Przeworski, Adam. *Democracy and the Market: Political and Economic Reforms in Eastern Europe and Latin America.* Cambridge: Cambridge University Press, 1991.
———. "The Games of Transition." In *The New South American Democracies in Comparative Perspective,* edited by Scott Mainwaring, Guillermo O'Donnell, and J. Samuel Valenzuela, 105–152. Notre Dame, Ind.: University of Notre Dame Press, 1992.
———. "Some Problems in the Study of Transition to Democracy." In *Transitions from Authoritarian Rule: Tentative Conclusions About Uncertain Democracies,* edited by Guillermo O'Donnell, Philippe C. Schmitter, and Laurence Whitehead. Baltimore: Johns Hopkins University Press, 1986.
Quandt, William B. "Algeria's Uneasy Peace." *Journal of Democracy* 13, no. 4 (2002): 15–23.
———. *Revolution and Political Leadership: Algeria, 1954–1968.* Cambridge: MIT Press, 1969.

Rabe, Hans-Joachim. "Palestinian Elites After the Oslo Agreement (1993–1998)." Ph.D. diss., School of Oriental and African Studies, University of London, 1999.

Rabil, Robert. "The Maronites and Syrian Withdrawal: From 'Isolationists' to 'Traitors'?" *Middle East Policy* 8, no. 3 (September 2001): 23–43.

al-Rasheed, Madawi. *A History of Saudi Arabia.* Cambridge: Cambridge University Press, 2002.

Reinhardt, Ulrike J. "Civil Society Co-operation in the EMP: From Declarations to Practice." *EuroMeSCo Papers* 15 (May 2002).

Robinson, Glenn E. *Building a Palestinian State: The Incomplete Revolution.* Bloomington: Indiana University Press, 1997.

———. "Can Islamists Be Democrats? The Case of Jordan." *Middle East Journal* 51, no. 3 (summer 1997): 373–387.

Roy, Olivier. "Patronage and Solidarity Groups: Survival or Reformation." In *Democracy Without Democrats? The Renewal of Politics in the Muslim World,* edited by Ghassan Salamé, 270–281. London: I. B. Tauris, 1995.

Roy, Sara. "Palestinian Society and Economics: The Continued Denial of Possibility." *Journal of Palestine Studies* (summer 2001).

———. "Why Peace Failed: An Oslo Autopsy." *Current History* (January 2002): 8–16.

Ruedy, John, ed. *Islamism and Secularism in North Africa.* New York: St. Martin's, 1994.

Rugh, William. "Education in Saudi Arabia: Choices and Constraints." *Middle East Policy* 9, no. 2 (June 2002): 40–55.

———. "Emergence of a New Middle Class in Saudi Arabia." *Middle East Journal* 27, no. 1 (winter 1973): 7–20.

Rustow, Dankwart A. "Transitions to Democracy." *Comparative Politics* 3 (April 1970): 337–363.

Ryan, Curtis. "Peace, Bread and Riots: Jordan and the International Monetary Fund." *Middle East Policy* 7, no. 2 (1998): 54–66.

Sadiki, Larbi. "Bin Ali's Tunisia: Democracy by Non-Democratic Means." *British Journal of Middle Eastern Studies* 29, no. 1 (2002): 57–78.

Said, Edward. *Peace and Its Discontents: Essays on Palestine in the Middle East Process.* New York: Vintage Books, 1995.

Sakijha, Bassem, and Saeda Kilani, eds. *Towards Transparency in Jordan.* Amman: Arab Archives Institute, 2000.

———. *Wasta—The Declared Secret: A Study on Nepotism and Favouritism in Jordan.* Amman: Arab Archives Institute, 2002.

Salamé, Ghassan, ed. *Democracy Without Democrats? The Renewal of Politics in the Muslim World.* London: I. B. Tauris, 1995.

Salem, Paul, and Abi Saab, eds. *Al-Intikhabat an-niyabia wa azmat al-dimuqratiya fi Lubnan* (Lebanese legislative elections and the crisis of democracy). Beirut: LCPS, 1998.

Saliby, George. *Za'amat wa 'a'ilat* (Leadership and families). Vol. 1. Beirut: Dar an-Nahda al-Arabia, 2001.

Sasley, Brent E. "Changes and Continuities in Jordanian Foreign Policy." *MERIA* 6, no. 1 (March 2002): 36–48.

al-Sayed, Galal. *Parliament or Volcano?* (in Arabic). Cairo: N. P., 2001.

Sayegh, Daoud. *Al-Nizam al-Lubnani fi thawabitihi wa tahawulatihi* (The Lebanese political system). Beirut: Dar al-Nahar, 2000.

Sayigh, Yezid. "Armed Struggle and State Formation." *Journal of Palestine Studies* 26, no. 4 (summer 1997): 17–32.

Scham, Paul E., and Russell E. Lucas. "'Normalization' and 'Anti-Normalization' in Jordan: The Public Debate." *MERIA* 5, no. 3 (September 2001): 54–70.

Schlumberger, Oliver. "Arab Political Economy and the European Union's Mediterranean Policy: What Prospects for Development?" *New Political Economy* 5, no. 2 (2000): 247–268.

———. "Transition in the Arab World." EUI Working Papers, RSC Mediterranean Programme Series, no. 2002/22, 2002.

———. "Jordan's Economy in the 1990s: Transition to Development?" In *Jordan in Transition, 1990–2000,* edited by George Joffé, 225–253. London: Hurst, 2002.

Schlumberger, Oliver, and André Bank. "Succession, Legitimacy, and Regime Stability in Jordan." *Arab Studies Journal* 10, no. 1 (spring 2002): 50–72.

Schmitter, Philippe C., and Laurence Whitehead. "Prospects for Democracy." In *Transitions from Authoritarian Rule: Tentative Conclusions About Uncertain Democracies,* edited by Guillermo O'Donnell, Philippe C. Schmitter, and Laurence Whitehead, 47–63. Baltimore: Johns Hopkins University Press, 1986.

Schwedler, Jillian. "Don't Blink: Jordan's Democratic Opening and Closing." *MERIP* Press Information note 98, 3 July 2002.

Schwingel, Markus. *Pierre Bourdieu.* Hamburg: Junius, 2000.

Seaver, Brenda. "The Regional Sources of Power-Sharing Failure: The Case of Lebanon." *Political Science Quarterly* 115, no. 2 (2000).

Segev, Tom. *The Seventh Million: The Israelis and the Holocaust.* New York: Henry Holt, 2000.

Sha'ban, al-Sadiq. *'Udat Hannabaal . . . aw Tajdid 'Ahd.* [The Return of Hannibal . . . or the renewal of an era]. Tunis: CERES, 1997.

Shehadi, Nadim, and Dana Haffar Mills, eds. *Lebanon: A History of Conflict and Consensus.* London: I. B. Tauris, 1988.

Shehata, Samer. "Political Succession in Egypt." *Middle East Policy* 9, no. 3 (September 2002): 110–113.

Shikaki, Khalil. "Palestinians Divided." *Foreign Affairs* 81, no. 1 (January–February 2002): 89–105.

———. "The Peace Process, National Reconstruction, and the Transition to Democracy in Palestine." *Journal of Palestine Studies* (winter 1996).

Shlaim, Avi. *The Iron Wall.* New York: W. W. Norton, 2000.

Shu'aibe, Azmi. "IPS Forum—A Window on the Workings of the PA: An Inside View." *Journal of Palestine Studies,* 30, no. 1, iss. 117 (autumn 2000): 88–97.

al-Shubayli, 'Abd ar-Rahman. *Al-Shaykh Muhammad bin Ibrahim bin Jubair.* Riyadh: Majlis al-Shura, 2002.

Sinclair, Brady. "Studying Members of the United States Congress." In *Research Methods for Elite Studies,* edited by George Moyser and Margaret Wagstaffe. London: Allen and Unwin, 1987.

Singh, Ranjit. "Precluding Transition Politics: The Durability of Post-Colonial Arab Authoritarianism." Paper delivered at the annual meeting of the Political Science Association, Boston, August 2002.

Skovgaard-Petersen, Jacob. "Religious Heads or Civil Servants? Druze and Sunni Religious Leadership in Post-War Lebanon." *Mediterranean Politics* 1, no. 3 (1996).

Soltan, Gamal. "The Military and Foreign Policy." In *Armée et nation en Egypte: pouvoir civil, pouvoir militaire,* edited by May Chartouni-Dubarry, 107–121. Paris: Institut Français des Relations Internationales, 2001.

Sonbol, Amira el-Azhary. *The New Mamluks: Egyptian Society and Modern Feudalism.* Syracuse: Syracuse University Press, 2000.

Souaidia, Habib. *La sale guerre*. Paris: La Découverte, 2001.

Springborg, Robert. "The Arab Bourgeoisie: A Revisionist Interpretation." *Arab Studies Quarterly* 15, no. 1 (winter 1993): 13–39.

———. *Family, Power, and Politics in Egypt: Sayed Bey Marei—His Clan, Clients, and Cohorts*. Philadelphia: University of Pennsylvania Press, 1982.

———. "The President and the Field Marshal: Civil Relations in Egypt Today." *MERIP* (July–August 1987).

Stone, Russell A. "Tunisia: A Single Party System Holds Change in Abeyance." In *Political Elites in Arab North Africa*, edited by I. William Zartman, 144–176. New York: Longman, 1982.

Tachau, Frank. *Political Elites and Political Development in the Middle East*. Cambridge, Mass.: Schenkman, 1975.

Taheri, Amir. "Les átouts d'Abdallah." *Politique Internationale* 83 (spring 1999): 209–224.

Tayyara, Muhammad Najati. "Al-Muthaqqafun al-Suriyun: Adwar wa-As'ila" (The Syrian intellectuals: Roles and questions). *al-Adab* (March–April 2001): 58–65.

Teitelbaum, Joshua. *Holier Than Thou: Saudi Arabia's Islamic Opposition*. Policy Papers 52. Washington, D.C.: Washington Institute for Near East Policy, 2000.

Tessler, Mark. "Morocco: Institutional Pluralism and Monarchical Dominance." In *Political Elites in Arab North Africa: Morocco, Algeria, Tunisia, Libya, and Egypt*, edited by William I. Zartman, 35–91. New York: Longman, 1982.

———. "Morocco's Next Political Generation." *Journal of North African Studies* 5, no. 1 (spring 2000): 1–26.

Theobald, Robin. "Patrimonialism." *World Politics* 34, no. 4 (July 1982): 548–559.

Thompson, Eric. "Will Syria Have to Withdraw from Lebanon?" *Middle East Journal* 56, no. 1 (winter 2002): 72–93.

Tismaneanu, Vladimir, ed. *Political Culture and Civil Society in Russia and the New States of Eurasia*. London: Armonk, 1995.

Tlemcani, Rachid. *Etat, bazar et globalisation*. Algiers: Les Editions El Hikma, 1999.

Tozy, Mohammed. "Political Changes in the Maghreb." *CODESRIA Bulletin* 1 (2000).

Tripp, Charles. "States, Elites and the 'Management of Change.'" In *The State and Global Change: The Political Economy of Transition in the Middle East and North Africa*, edited by Hassan Hakimian and Ziba Moshaver, 211–231. Richmond, Surrey: Curzon, 2001.

U.S. Department of State. *World Military Expenditures and Arms Transfers, 1998*. Washington, D.C., 2002 (www.fas.org/man/docs/wmeat98/).

Usher, Graham. "The Politics of Internal Security." *Journal of Palestine Studies* 25, no. 2 (winter 1996): 21–34.

van Dam, Nikolaos. *The Struggle for Power in Syria: Politics and Society Under Asad and the Ba'th Party*. London: I. B. Tauris, 1996.

Vasil'ev, Aleksej M. *The History of Saudi Arabia*. London: Saqi Books, 1998.

Vermeren, Pierre. *Ecole, élite et pouvoir: Maroc-Tunisie, XX siècle*. Rabat: Alizés, 2002.

Vogel, Frank E. *Islamic Law and Legal System: Studies of Saudi Arabia*. Studies in Islamic Law and Society 8. Leiden: Brill, 2000.

Wagstaffe, Margaret, and George Moyser. "The Threatened Elite." In *Research Methods for Elite Studies*, edited by George Moyser and Margaret Wagstaffe. London: Allen and Unwin, 1987.

Waterbury, John. *The Commander of the Faithful*. London: Weidenfeld and Nicolson, 1970.

———. "Twilight of the State Bourgeoisie?" *International Journal of Middle East Studies* 23 (1991): 1–17.

———. "Whence Will Come Egypt's Future Leadership?" In *Egypt at the Crossroads. Domestic Stability and Regional Role*, edited by Phebe Marr, 17–28. Washington, D.C.: National Defense University Press, 1999.

Weber, Max. "Politics as a Vocation." In *From Max Weber: Essays in Sociology*, edited by H. H. Gerth and C. Wright Mills, 77–128. New York: Oxford University Press, 1946 (originally published in 1919).

Wenner, Manfred W. "Saudi Arabia: Survival of Traditional Elites." In *Political Elites and Political Development in the Middle East*, edited by Frank Tachau, 157–190. Cambridge, Mass.: Schenkman, 1975.

Werenfels, Isabelle. "Obstacles to Privatisation of State-Owned Industries in Algeria: The Political Economy of a Distributive Conflict." *Journal of North African Studies* 7 (2002): 128.

Wiktorowicz, Quintan. "Civil Society as Social Control: State Power in Jordan." *Comparative Politics* 33, no. 1 (October 2000): 43–61.

———. "The Political Limits to Nongovernmental Organizations in Jordan." *World Development* 30, no. 1 (January 2002): 77–93.

Williamson, Oliver. *The Mechanisms of Governance*. Oxford: Oxford University Press, 1996.

Willis, Michael J. "After Hassan: A New Monarch in Morocco." *Mediterranean Politics* 5, no. 3 (autumn 1999): 115–128.

Yamani, Mai. *Changed Identities: The Challenge of the New Generation in Saudi Arabia*. London: Royal Institute of International Affairs, 2000.

Yefsah, Abdelkader. "L'armée et le pouvoir en Algérie de 1962 à 1992." In *L'Algérie incertaine*, edited by Pierre R. Baduel, 77–95. Aix en Provence: Edisud, 1993.

Yizraeli, Sarah. *The Remaking of Saudi Arabia: The Struggle Between King Sa'ud and Crown Prince Faysal, 1953–1962*. Dayan Center Papers 121. Tel Aviv: Moshe Dayan Center for Middle Eastern and African Studies, Tel Aviv University, 1997.

Youngs, Richard. "The European Union and Democracy in the Arab-Muslim World." Working Paper 2, CEPS Middle East and Euro-Med Project, Brussels, 2002.

Zaki, Moheb. *Egyptian Business Elites: Their Visions and Investment Behavior*. Cairo: Konrad Adenauer Foundation/Arab Center for Development and Future Research, 1999.

Zartman, I. William. "Algeria: A Post-Revolutionary Elite." In *Political Elites and Political Development in the Middle East*, edited by Frank Tachau, 225–292. Cambridge, Mass.: Schenkman, 1975.

———. "The Algerian Army in Politics." In *Man, State and Society in the Contemporary Maghrib*, edited by William I. Zartman. New York: Praeger, 1972.

———. "King Hassan's New Morocco." In *Man, State and Society in the Contemporary Maghrib*, edited by William I. Zartman. London: Pall Mall Press, 1973.

———. *Political Elites in Arab North Africa: Morocco, Algeria, Tunisia, Libya, and Egypt*. New York: Longman, 1982.

Zartman, I. William, ed. *Tunisia: The Political Economy of Reform*. Boulder: Westview, 1991.

Zartman, I. William, and William Mark Habeeb, eds. *Polity and Society in Contemporary North Africa.* Boulder: Westview, 1993.

al-Zayat, Montasser. *Aiman az-Zawahir, As I Knew Him* (in Arabic). Cairo: Dar al-Mahrusa, 2002.

Zghal, Riadh. "Nouvelles orientations du syndicalisme tunisien." *Monde Arabe-Maghreb-Machrek,* no. 162 (1998): 6–17.

Ziadé, Khaled. "Tripoli: famille et politique." In *La vie publique au Liban: expressions et recompositions du politique,* edited by Joseph Bahout and Chawqi Douayhi. Cahiers du CERMOC 18. Beirut: CERMOC, 1997.

Ziyad, George. "After Mubarak." *Middle East,* no. 305 (2000): 17–18.

———. "Egypt's Diplomatic Dynamo Goes Regional." *Jerusalem Report* (April 2001): 32–33.

Zohny, Ahmed Y. "Toward an Apolitical Role for the Egyptian Military in the Management of Development." *Orient* 28, no. 4 (1987): 548–556.

Zoubir, Yahia H., and Daniel Volman, eds. *International Dimensions of the Western Sahara Conflict.* Westport, Conn.: Praeger, 1993.

The Contributors

Gamal Abdelnasser received his B.A. in trade and commerce from the University of Cairo. He worked for the Centre d'Etudes et de Documentation Economiques et Juridiques (CEDEJ) in Cairo and in the research project "Elite Change in the Arab World" at the German Institute for International and Security Affairs (SWP) in Berlin.

André Bank is currently doing his M.A. in political science, Islamic studies, and sociology at the University of Tübingen. He worked as an intern with the research project "Elite Change in the Arab World" at the German Institute for International and Security Affairs (SWP) in Berlin.

Steffen Erdle received his M.A. in Islamic studies, political science, and history from the University of Freiburg. He is currently finishing his doctorate at the Humboldt University, Berlin.

Iris Glosemeyer received her M.A. in political science, Islamic studies, and history from the University of Hamburg and her doctorate in Political Science from the Free University, Berlin. She has specialized on political developments in states of the Arabian peninsula, worked as a freelancer for a number of research institutions and participated in the research project "Elite Change in the Arab World" at the German Institute for International and Security Affairs (SWP) in Berlin. Currently she is a consultant to the German government.

Rola el-Husseini holds a Ph.D. in sociology from École des Hautes Etudes en Sciences Sociales, Paris. Between January 2001 and December 2003 she worked on the research project "Elite Change in the Arab World" at the German Institute for International and Security Affairs (SWP) in Berlin.

She is currently a postdoctoral associate at the Yale Center for Inernational and Area Studies and a lecturer in sociology at Yale University.

Volker Perthes holds a doctorate from the University of Duisburg. He worked as an assistant professor at the American University of Beirut (1991–1993) and has been with *Stiftung Wissenschaft und Politik (SWP)* the German Institute for International and Security Affairs since 1992. Currently, he is the head of the Middle East and Africa Division of SWP and the director of its research project on "Elite Change in the Arab World." Perthes is the author of numerous books and scholarly articles on Middle Eastern political economy and international relations.

Hans-Joachim Rabe received his Ph.D. in Middle East politics from the School of Oriental and African Studies (SOAS) in London. He is currently working for a German development agency, where he coordinates public relations in one of its developments.

Oliver Schlumberger is a research officer at the German Development Institute (GDI), Bonn, and continues to lecture at the Institute of Political Science, Eberhard-Karls University of Tübingen, where he served as an assistant professor at the time of writing. His current research focuses on issues of governance in the MENA region, on economic reform and order in the Arab and developing world, and on methods of comparative research on political regimes and nondemocratic regime change. He is the author of several articles on Middle Eastern and international political economy and Arab politics.

Isabelle Werenfels received an M.Sc. in development studies from the School of Oriental and African Studies (SOAS), London. After working as a journalist on social and political developments in the Middle East for several years, she joined the project "Elite Change in the Arab World" at the German Institute for International and Security Affairs (SWP). She currently holds a research position at SWP and is finishing her doctorate in political science at Humboldt University, Berlin.

Saloua Zerhouni received her Ph.D. in political science from Hassan II University, Casablanca. She has worked on parliamentary elite and democratic transition in Morocco. She held a previous research position at Georgetown University and is currently working in the research project "Elite Change in the Arab World" at the German Institute for International and Security Affairs (SWP) in Berlin. She is an assistant professor at Mohammed V University, Rabat, Morocco.

Index

Abbas, Mahmoud (Abu Mazen), 276, 290, 292–293

Abdallah, Abdelwahhab, 215

Abdallah, Crown Prince: as head of royal family faction, 149–151; on political participation, 161, 163; political reforms, 302; religious influence on, 146; religious radicalism, 154; as SANG commander, 143, 149; as SEC chair, 143

Abdallah II, King of Jordan: Battikhi resignation, 40; as central figure in elite, 44, 46*fig*, 49, 58*n29;* challenges in establishing primacy, 37, 39; economic reforms, 51–53; generational influences on, 19; modernization by, 11; policies under, 49–54; political influence of business elite, 13–14, 24, 54–56; political reforms delayed by, 52–53; succession to throne by, 35; Syrian-Jordanian relations, 53

Abdel-Hadi, Aisha, 128

Abdelnasser, Gamal, 10, 28, 117

Aburish, Saïd, 18

'Adl wa-l-Ihsan, al-, 67, 79

Adly, Habib al-, 119

Adritec Group, 41

Afghanistan, 147–148, 153

Ahardan, Mahjoubi, 78

Ait-Ahmed, Hocine, 6, 187, 194, 203*n53*

Ala, Abu (Ahmad Qurai), 277

Alawites, 110

Algeria: Arab-Israeli conflict, 22; Arab Maghreb Union membership, 225;

bureaucratic authoritarian system in, 173; circles of influence, 176–179, 181*tab*, 182–189, 192–196; clientelism, 189, 195–197; Concorde Civile, 177, 186, 201*n21;* continuity through elite change, 174–175, 189–190, 198–200; coup d'etat (1992), 173, 198; decisionmaking style, 9; dynamics within elite, 180*fig;* economic factors, 196–198; economic reform, 25; education, 190–193; elections, 179, 186–188, 191, 211; elite change in, 14; EU relations, 177, 199; generational change in, 190–196; Islamists in, 173–174, 177–178, 186–187, 192; Kabyle protest movement, 179, 185–188, 192, 197, 201*n23;* labor unions, 183, 204*n72;* leftists in, 186–188; media, 186, 188, 190, 203*n55;* military role in, 175–179, 188, 191–192, 199–200, 303; NGOs, 194–195; oil production, 174, 178, 198–199, 205*n89;* parliament in, 182, 185; political reform, 26, 29, 104, 173, 302; politicians in, 16; as rentier state, 189, 199, 205n88; September 11 attacks, 188; sociocultural factors, 196–197; technocrats, 182; unemployment in, 191; U.S. relations, 177; WTO membership, 179, 184, 199

Al-Qaida, 148, 163

Al Saud family, 142, 148–152

Alternance, 65, 83*n24,* 84*n25*

329

Amazighs, 68
Amr, Abdel Hakim, 123
Amr, Yasir, 273
Anderson, Lisa, 27
Annan, Kofi, 247
Aoun, Gen. Michel, 243, 250, 257, 265n48
Arab-Israeli conflict, 88, 106, 133
Arab-Israeli War: (1948), 117; (1973), 18, 117, 128
Arabization, 175, 191–192, 199
Arab League, 128
Arab Maghreb Union (UMA), 225
Arab world, 1, 3–7
Arafat, Yasser: Camp David summit (2000), 288; as center of power, 271–272, 274, 293; decisionmaking style, 9; disempowerment by Israel of, 268; economic influence of, 282, 286; elite change after, 14; Fatah elections, 281–282; Israeli siege of, 290; leadership struggles around, 19; passing of power from, 21, 304; return to Palestine, 267; state of emergency, 293; strength and weakness in, 23
Aramex, 41
Armenians, 260
Arouch, 5, 187–188, 192, 194, 203n49
Asad, Bashar al-: Arab-Israeli conflict, 22; corruption, 92, 112n30; democratization, 25–26; economic reform, 98–99, 111; first government of, 91–93; foreign relations, 106–108; generational influences on, 19; installation as president of, 87, 130–131; Jordanian-Syrian relations, 53; limits to reform by, 87–88; modernization by, 11; political authority of, 88–89; political reform, 103–106, 108–109; pre-succession positions of, 88–89, 92; second government of, 91
Asad, Basil al-, 257
Asad, Hafiz al-: death of, 4, 87, 91, 129; diplomacy under, 108; economic reform, 99–100; Hariri ties with, 250; Jordanian-Syrian relations, 53; ossification of elites and, 8; as presidential monarch, 9
As'ad, Kamel al-, 246
Asad, Mahir al-, 90
'Atiya, Mamduh, 121
Auda, Shaikh Salman al-, 158, 162

Australia, 262
Awadallah, Bassem, 41, 45, 46fig
Awakening Shaikhs, 134, 143–144, 153–154, 158, 162
Azhar, Shaykh al-, 127

Badr, Prince, 151–152
Badran, Mudar, 45
Badran, Rim, 45, 46fig
Bahouth, Sima, 46fig, 48
Bahrain, 19, 25–26, 302
al-Bahr Company, 285–286
Bakri, Mustafa, 122
Bandar bin Sultan, Prince, 167n27, 168n68
Bank, André, 28, 35
Banking, 100
Barak, Ehud, 31n51, 288
Barcelona process, 121, 124, 132, 222
Barghouthi, Bashir, 273
Barghouthi, Marwan, 19, 281–282, 291
Bashir, Salah al-Din al-, 41, 45, 46fig
Basri, Driss, 58n32, 68, 71
Batatu, Hanna, 109
Battikhi, Samih, 39–40, 44–45, 58n30
Baz, Abd al-Aziz bin, 153–155, 158
Baz, Osama al-, 119
Beck, Martin, 284
Belarus, 306
Belhadj, Ali, 186
Belkheir, Larbi, 176, 178
Bellaire, Micheaux, 62
Bellin, Eva, 219
Ben Achour family, 221
Ben Ali, Zin al-Abidine: Algerian reformers view of, 204n79; consultative unilateralism of, 236n42; dimensions of change under, 229; elite change, 14; end of term limits for, 212; extended family of, 214, 234n20; on future conflict, 235n38; on human rights, 223; liberal phase, 210–211; neutralization of politics by, 230–231; ongoing phase, 211–212; opposition views of, 224; as outsider, 212, 234n17; ouster of Bourguiba by, 207, 227, 233n1; palace's influence, 214, 216; politicians' roles, 16; recruitment of RCD officials, 217; repressive phase, 211
Bendjedid, Chadli, 173, 175, 200n2
Benflis, Ali, 17, 179, 182, 200n8, 201n28

Benzekri, Driss, 68
Berbers, 68, 187, 198, 203*n53*
Berri, Nabih, 245–246
Betchine, Gen. Mohamed, 188
Bin Laden, Usama, 148, 159, 164–165,
  168*n66*
Bishara, Azmi, 279–280
Bottomore, Tom, 5
Boudiaf, Mohamed, 176, 191, 204*n69*
Boumedienne, Houari, 173
Bourdieu, Pierre, 193
Bourguiba, Habib: divide-and-rule lead-
  ership style, 230; ouster of, 207,
  233*n1;* as supreme decisionmaker,
  209, 233*n8;* weaknesses in rule of,
  209–210
Bouteflika, Abdelaziz: army's relations
  with, 177–179, 196, 201*n28;* avoid-
  ance of reforms by, 197; election of,
  176–177, 201*n14;* shadow cabinet of,
  201*n30;* trade unions, 183
Boutlilis, Leila, 193
Boutros Ghali, Youssef, 121, 125,
  137*n26,* 138*n40*
Boycotts, 112*n21,* 122, 243–244, 273,
  280
Burton, Michael, 2, 174, 243
Bush, George W.: calls for PA reform,
  291; forced regime change, 23; Saudi
  letters to, 162, 167*n39;* Syria
  Accountability Act (2003), 262
Business elites: in Egypt, 124–127;
  emergence of, 14–15; increased
  influence of, 302–303; in Jordan,
  13–14, 24, 54–56; in Lebanon,
  249–250; in Morocco, 71; in Saudi
  Arabia, 144, 156–157; in Syria,
  97–98, 109; in Tunisia, 208,
  218–219, 224, 228, 236*n46*

Cairo Post, 126
Camp David Accords, 121, 123, 128,
  132
Camp David summit (2000), 288
Canada, 262
Caucasus region, 2
Center of Strategic Studies (CSS),
  University of Jordan, 40
Central Asia, 2
Chabal, Patrick, 196
Chafik, Mohammed, 68
Chaouch, Ali, 215
Charfi family, 221

Chebbi, Ahmed Nejib, 220
Chiboub family, 214
Christians; 240–245, 252–254, 260. *See
  also specific groups*
Citibank, 41
Civil society, 220–221, 227, 256
Clergy, 254–255, 261. *See also*
  Religious leaders
Clientelism: in Algeria, 189, 195–197; in
  Jordan, 36, 38, 48; in Lebanon,
  248–249, 261; in Palestine, 279; rent
  incomes and, 301; in Tunisia, 230
Clinton, Bill, 288
Co-optation, 304
Committee for the Defense of
  Legitimate Rights (CDLR), 159
Computer literacy, 100–101
Confessionalist system, 12, 259–261
Congo, Democratic Republic of, 306
Consociationism, 240–241, 243
Coordination des Arouch, des Dairas et
  des Communes (CADC) (Algeria), 5,
  187–188, 192, 194, 203*n50*
Copts, 126, 130, 136*n13*
Corruption: in Jordan, 49, 51; in
  Lebanon, 248, 261; in Morocco, 70,
  85*n39;* in Palestine, 277–278, 284,
  287; in Saudi Arabia, 156, 162; in
  Syria, 92, 104–105, 112*n30;* in
  Tunisia, 235*n33*
Council of Senior Ulama, 153–155, 160

Dabbas, Suhayr al-Ali, 41
Dahlan, Muhammad, 274, 290
Dalila, Arif, 105
Damascus Spring, 94, 104–105
Dead Sea Retreat, 40
Debt rescheduling, 174
Decisionmaking, 9–10
Democratic pole, 224
Democratization: in Algeria, 174, 191,
  197, 199, 200*n2;* authoritarian view
  of, 25–26; in Eastern Europe, 2;
  elites' role in, 2; and Islamists, 25; in
  Morocco, 25–26, 61, 65–66; in
  Palestine, 304; prospects for,
  306–307; in Tunisia, 207, 210–211,
  223
Dependency theory, 102
Dhia, Abdelaziz Ben, 215
Diplomats, 121, 127–128
Discourse analysis, 12
Dissenters, 6

Divorce, 127, 136*n13*
Diwaniyyas, 12
Djaballah, Abdallah, 197
Djilani, Hedi, 214, 218–219
Donor aid, 284
Driss, Rachid, 221
Druze, 245, 260

Eastern Europe, 2
Ebeid, Atef, 119, 123–124
Economicization, 52–53
Economic reform: in Algeria, 174, 195;
    in Bahrain, 25; effect on elites of,
    24–27; in Jordan, 24–25, 41–42,
    50–52; in Saudi Arabia, 145; in
    Tunisia, 210, 212, 218, 227, 232
Education: in Algeria, 190–193; among
    elites, 16–17, 31*n41*, 72–73; reli-
    gious influence on, 152–153; in
    Saudi Arabia, 146–147, 152–153,
    158, 166*n19;* in Tunisia, 213,
    216–217; of women, 146
Egypt: age groups of leaders, 17–19;
    Arab-Israeli conflict, 22; business
    elites, 124–127; circles of influence,
    119–123, 126; consumer boycott of
    U.S. and Israeli goods, 122; econom-
    ic reform, 24, 26; elections, 121–122,
    125–126, 135, 136*n17;* elite change
    after Mubarak, 14; EU relations, 22,
    132; Free Officers Revolution
    (1952), 117; Iranian relations, 128;
    Iraqi relations, 128; Islamists, 122,
    129, 134; Israeli peace treaty, 117,
    121; Jordanian relations, 53; journal-
    ists, 122; judiciary, 119, 122; July
    generation, 117; labor unions, 122,
    125, 128; leadership succession,
    129–133, 135, 138*n46;* Libyan rela-
    tions, 128; mapping the elite in,
    118–123; military role in, 15,
    120–121; NGOs in, 122; October
    generation, 117, 128; ossification of
    elites in, 8; parliament in, 10,
    121–122, 185; patterns of elite circu-
    lation, 123–124; political parties' role
    in, 9; political reform, 26–27; politi-
    cians in, 16; as presidential monar-
    chy, 9; privatization, 122; scenarios
    for elite change, 133–134; Supreme
    Constitutional Court (SCC), 122,
    129; technocrats, 119, 123; U.S. rela-
    tions, 128

Egyptian Trade Union Federation
    (ETUF), 122
Eid, Hatem, 277
Elections: in Algeria, 179, 186–188,
    191, 211; boycotts of, 243–244, 273,
    280; in Egypt, 121–122, 125–126,
    135, 136*n17;* in Israel, 281; in
    Jordan, 52; in Lebanon, 242–244,
    247, 255–256, 259–260; in Morocco,
    65–66, 72, 81; in Palestine, 272,
    281–282; in Saudi Arabia, 161, 165;
    in Syria, 114*n57;* in Tunisia, 211,
    224, 233*n12*
Elite change: age and, 165, 169*n71;*
    context of, 7–8; continuity through,
    80–82, 174–175, 189–190, 198–200;
    cultural perspective of, 76–77;
    defined, 119; economics of, 75–76,
    196–198, 282–287; effect by country
    of, 13–14; Egyptian scenarios for,
    133–134; by force, 23; identifying
    agendas of actors in, 11–12; in
    Jordan, 13–14, 35, 54–56; in
    Morocco, 13, 68–72; outside pressure
    for, 305; under "outsider" leaders,
    212; in Palestine, 14; patterns of
    dynamics in, 118, 123–124; political
    perspective of, 74–75; as product of
    outside events, 145, 163; regional
    and international factors, 19–24, 177;
    in Saudi Arabia, 14, 141; sociocultu-
    ral factors in, 196–197; steering, 141;
    in Syria, 13, 91–97, 108–111
Elite circulation: in Jordan, 57*n12;* in
    Lebanon, 243, 261; patterns of,
    123–124, 229
Elite reshuffling: in Jordan, 39–40,
    57*n12;* in Morocco, 72–74, 78–79; in
    Syria, 91
Elites: circles within, 6–7; conjunctural,
    239, 252–255; contesting, 213, 220,
    290–293; convergence of, 243–245,
    264*n26;* definition, 2, 165*n2;* disuni-
    fied, 263*n7;* economic, 284–287;
    education among, 16–17, 31*n41*,
    72–73; emerging, 239, 255–258;
    families traditionally belonging to,
    42–43, 142, 148–152, 214; formaliz-
    ing informality, 40–44; generation as
    influence among, 17–19, 73,
    190–196; globalization and, 21; iden-
    tifying, 119; implementing, 213, 219;
    importance of, 301; issues and

approaches in study of, 7–8; journalists as, 5–6; modernity as goal of, 24–29; perception of change among, 74–77; politically relevant (PREs), 5–7, 8–13; power shifts within, 36–37; recruitment patterns, 38–44; redefined, 239, 245–252; regime, 234*n18;* religious leaders as, 5; social backgrounds of, 68, 84*n33;* stasis in, 61; struggles among, 173; temporary, 5; youth as members of, 124–125. *See also* First circle of influence; Second circle of influence; Third circle of influence
Elitocide, 291
Emigration, 191
EMP. *See* Euro-Mediterranean Partnership
Entelis, John, 193
Entrepreneurs. *See* Business elites
Erakat, Saeb, 276, 290
Erdle, Steffen, 16, 29, 207
Euro-Mediterranean Partnership (EMP): challenge to elites of, 7; complementary initiatives, 235*n37;* Jordanian membership, 50; membership of, 112*n22;* Syrian role, 89, 101, 112*n22;* Tunisian role, 211, 226
European Union (EU): Algerian relations, 177, 199; association agreements' influence on economic elites, 302; Egyptian relations, 22, 132; Maghreb dependence on, 21; Middle East Quartet membership, 292; stability valued over democracy by, 232; Syrian relations, 89, 101; Tunisian relations, 211, 225–226, 233*n14*

Fahd, King of Saudi Arabia: Basic Law of Government, 144, 150; business elite's appeals to, 156; health of, 152; as Sudairi brother, 149
Faisal, Toujan, 46*fig,* 49
Fake competition, 304
Faluji, Imad, 273
Fanek, Fahd, 46*fig,* 48
Faqih, Sa'd al-, 159
Fares, Issam, 257
Farsakh, Leila, 288
Fatah Central Committee, 281
Fatah Higher Council (FHC), 281

Fatwas, 153, 158
Fayad, Salam, 17, 292
Faysal, King of Saudi Arabia, 142, 148–149, 151, 160
Feldner, Yotam, 130
First circle of influence: in Algeria, 176–179, 189; in Egypt, 119–121; in Jordan, 44–45; in Lebanon, 239–240; in Morocco, 61, 69, 77, 81; in Palestine, 272–276; in Saudi Arabia, 141; in Syria, 90, 94; in Tunisia, 213–216
Foreign direct investment, 50, 284
Forum des Chefs d'Entreprise (FCE), 183
Fouché, Joseph, 248, 264*n36*
France, 89
Fuleihan, Bassel, 17
Future Generation Foundation, 125, 130

Gamaa Islamiyya, 123
Ganzuri, Kamal al-, 123–124
Gauwadi, Mohammed al-, 121
Gaza: Israeli sealing of, 268; PA authority over, 267, 272; poverty in, 284, 288–289; truck restrictions, 285. *See also* Palestine
Gemayel, Amin, 244, 253
Gemayel, Pierre, 244, 253
Gemayel, Pierre, Jr., 253–254
General Agreement on Tariffs and Trade (GATT), 225
General Union of Tunisian Students (UGET), 209, 220
General Union of Tunisian Workers (UGTT), 209, 218–220, 226, 228, 235*n27*
"Generation entelechy," 190
Gerrymandering, 243
Ghandour, Fadi, 41, 46*fig,* 47
Ghannouchi, Mohamed, 215
Ghannouchi, Rachid, 207, 220
Ghazzala, Abdel Halim Abu, 123, 131–132, 133*tab*
Globalization, 21, 101–102
Glosemeyer, Iris, 16, 28, 141
Gradualism, 303
Greek Catholics, 241
Greek Orthodox Christians, 241, 263*n14*
Groupement Islamique Armés (GIA) (Algeria), 187
Groupe Salafiste pour la Prédication et le Combat (Algeria), 187

Guevara, Che, 194
Gulf states, 53
Gulf War (1991): anti-Western feelings
   from, 211; Egyptian role, 117,
   139n50; invasion of Kuwait, 145,
   147; Saudi role in, 147; Syrian role
   in, 262

Halafawy, Jihan al-, 127
Halayqa, Muhammad, 43
Hamarnah, Mustafa, 40, 46fig
Hamas (Palestine), 58n30, 270, 280
Hamdi, Hachemi, 221
Hammami, Hamma, 220, 290
Hanoune, Louisa, 187
Harakat al-Mahrumin, 246
Haram al-Sharif, 288
Harbi, Mohammed, 190, 197
Hariri, Bahia, 250
Hariri, Rafiq al-: biography of, 249–250;
   as businessman-turned–political
   leader, 15, 197; family of, 250, 257;
   liberal economic policies of, 22, 24;
   as Sunni leader, 255; Syrian-
   Lebanese relations, 259
Hariri Foundation, 250
Hashemite monarchy, 37, 48, 56
Hassan bin Talal, Prince, 35
Hassan II, King of Morocco: death of, 4,
   28, 61; military relationship with, 70;
   and parliament, 65; personification of
   authority under, 67–68, 81; political
   acumen of, 62–65; political reform,
   64, 83n14; state of emergency,
   83n21
Hawali, Shaikh Safar al-, 162
al-Hayat, 103, 162
Heirs, 257
Higley, John, 2, 174, 243
Hikayat, 119
Hilel, Jamil, 279
Hizballah (Lebanon), 22, 246–248, 259
Honor, 197
Humaid, Shaikh Salih bin, 155, 161
Human rights: in Algeria, 179, 187–188,
   199; in Jordan, 53; in Morocco, 68,
   80; in Tunisia, 223, 232
Husaynids, 209
Husein, Muhammad, 100
Hussein, King of Jordan, 4, 35, 50, 53
Hussein, Saddam, 23
Husseini, Hussein el-, 257
Husseini, Rola el-, 10, 16, 29, 239

Hydrocarbons, 174, 178, 198–199. See
   also Oil

Ibrahim, Saad Eddin, 130, 138n37
Ibrahimi, Ahmed Taleb, 186
Ideal Group, 41
Ikhwan, 154
Illiteracy, 75
Ilves, Tom, 197
Imbaba, State of, 132
Immobilisme, 61, 72
Infitah, 120–121, 227
Informality, 40–44
Institut Arabe des Chefs d'Entreprise
   (IACE) (Tunisia), 218
Int@j, 41
International Court of Justice, 19
International Crisis Group (ICG), 129,
   138n46
International Monetary Fund (IMF):
   Algerian program, 174; Jordanian
   agreements with, 50, 55; Lebanese
   loan requests, 259; Tunisian attitudes
   toward, 226
International Parliamentary Union, 160
Internet, 100, 303
Intifada: effect on PRE of, 267–268,
   282, 288–290, 294; as generational
   influence, 19, 23; Jordanian demonstrations in support of, 45, 47, 52;
   Jordanian government responses to,
   52, 55, 58n34; as opportunity for
   contesting elites, 290–294; Sharon
   visit to Haram al-Sharif, 288
Iran, 128, 161
Iraq: age groups of leaders, 18; difficulty
   of field research in, 32n65; Egyptian
   relations, 128; elite change, 14, 23;
   invasion of Kuwait (1990), 145, 147;
   Jordanian interests in, 42; Jordanian
   relations, 53; oil sales to Syria, 107,
   110; regime change, 23, 303–304;
   Syrian relations, 107, 113n50, 262
Iraq war: core elite strategies influenced
   by, 306; elite change from, 14;
   regime change, 23, 303–304; Saudi
   views, 162
Isa, Amir of Bahrain, 4
Islam: in Morocco, 69–71; Shi'a, 147,
   161–162, 164, 242, 246, 260; Sunni,
   109–110, 240, 242, 255; in Syria,
   110; in Tunisia, 222; Wahhabi, 142,
   154

Islambouli, Khalid, 133–134
Islamic Action Front (Jordan), 48–49
Islamic awakening, 134
Islamic Jihad (Palestine), 270
Islamic Research Academy, 127
Islamist reformers, 181*tab,* 193–195
Islamists: in Algeria, 173–174, 177–178, 186–187, 192; alternate routes to power for, 18–19; Arab-Israeli conflict, 22; cooptation of, 48; as decisionmakers, 9; democratization and, 25; in Egypt, 122, 129, 134; in Jordan, 48, 52; in Lebanon, 246–248; in Morocco, 66, 71; repression of, 52; in Tunisia, 211, 222–223. *See also* Religious leaders
Israel: closure of access to Palestinians, 268, 283; control over PA, 268; Egyptian peace treaty, 117, 121; election campaign bombings, 281; elections, 281; generational influence on leaders, 20–21; invasion of Lebanon (1982), 128; Jordanian relations, 52, 55; Mubarak visit, 137*n32;* Palestinian economic dependence on, 283–284; PLO relations, 267; Shebaa Farms, 253, 259; siege of Arafat, 290; Syrian relations, 89, 106–107; taxation of Palestinians by, 268, 289; withdrawal from Lebanon (2000), 259. *See also* Intifada
Izz, Ahmad, 124, 138*n40*

Jaafar, Mustapha Ben, 220
Jamal al-Atasi Forum (Syria), 104
al-Jazeera, 105, 145
Jebali, Tehani el-, 127
Jettou, Driss, 16–17, 24, 66–67, 74
Jordan: age groups of leaders, 18–19; Arab-Israeli conflict, 22; business elites' political influence in, 13–14, 24, 54–56; circles of influence, 44–45, 47–49; civil unrest in, 45, 47, 49; clientelism, 36, 38, 48; composition of elites in, 44–45, 46*fig,* 47–49; corruption in, 49, 51; Economic Consultative Council (ECC), 11, 39–43, 50–51; economic reform, 24–25, 41–42, 50–52; Egyptian relations, 53; elections, 52; elite change in, 13–14, 35, 54–56; elite circulation, 39–40, 57*n12;* Euro-Mediterranean Partnership, 50;

Executive Privatization Commission Council, 43; foreign policy, 53–54; General Intelligence Department (GID), 39; Gulf states relations, 53; human rights in, 53; IMF agreements, 50, 55; Iraqi relations, 53; Islamists, 48, 52; Israeli relations, 52, 55; legislature of, 37–38, 47; military role in, 37; neopatrimonialism, 35–36, 38; NGOs in, 40, 48; openness in, 303; Palestinians in, 12, 55; political parties' role in, 9, 38; political reform, 42, 52–53; politicians in, 16; power shifts within elites, 36–37; privatization, 41–42, 50–51; recruitment of elites in, 38–44; responses to intifada, 45, 47, 52, 55, 58*n34;* royal succession, 35; security services, 37, 52; Syrian relations, 19–20, 53; Turkish relations, 53; WTO membership, 50
Jordan First (Al-Urdunn Awwalan), 48, 53
Jordan parliament in, 52
Jouini, Mohamed Nouri, 215
Journalists: as decisionmakers, 9; in Egypt, 122; as elites, 5–6; killing of, 203*n55;* in Morocco, 71, 73, 80. *See also* Media
Jubair, Shaikh Muhammad bin, 155
Judiciary: in Egypt, 119, 122; in Lebanon, 251, 265*n56;* women as members of, 127
Jumblat, Wallid, 245

Kabariti, Abd al-Karim, 45
Kabyle protest movement (Algeria), 179, 185–188, 192, 197, 201*n23*
Kafi, Ali, 176
Kallel, Abdallah, 215
Kana'an, Taher, 48
Karameh, Omar, 250
Ka'war, Karim, 41, 45
Khaddam, Abd al-Halim, 90, 104, 108, 257
Khafaji, Isam al-, 18
Khair, Maj. Gen. Sa'd, 39, 44, 46*fig*
Khalid, King of Saudi Arabia, 148, 151
Khalid bin Faysal, 166*n23,* 167*n35*
Khalid bin Sultan, Prince, 162, 167*n32*
Khalil, Chakib, 197
Khalil, Mustafa, 123
Khatib, Ghassan, 285

Khreish, Antoine, 254
Kilo, Michael, 105
Kuwait, 145, 147

Laanigri, Col. Maj. Hamidou, 70, 85*n39*
Labor unions: in Algeria, 183, 204*n72;*
    in Egypt, 122, 125, 128; in Syria, 97;
    in Tunisia, 208–209, 218–219, 224,
    228, 235*n27*
Lahoud, Emile, 250–252, 259, 261,
    264*n38*
Lahoud, Emile, Jr., 252, 257
Lahoud, Jamil, 251
Lahoud, Nasri, 252
Lakakh, Rami, 126, 137*n26*
Lamari, Gen. Mohamed, 177–178,
    201*n16*
Lamari, Smail, 176
Lasswell, Harold: defining elites, 2
Latin America, 2, 5
Leaders, 3, 5, 30*n15. See also*
    Succession, leadership
Lebanese Forces (LF), 243–244, 257,
    264*n47*
Lebanese-Syrian relations: elite circula-
    tion in Lebanon, 243, 261; Lebanese
    opposition to, 257–258; Lebanese
    PRE support for, 258–259; selection
    of Lebanese presidents, 242; Syrian
    allies in Lebanese parliament,
    242–243; Syrian clients, 248–249;
    Syrian military presence in Lebanon,
    240, 263*n8;* Treaty of Brotherhood
    and Cooperation, 242; Tripartite
    Agreement, 248
Lebanon: age groups of leaders, 17;
    Arab-Israeli conflict, 22; business
    elites, 249–250; circles of influence,
    239–240, 255–258; civil war, 241;
    clergy in, 254–255, 261; clientelism,
    248–249, 261; confessionalist sys-
    tem, 12, 259–261; conjunctural
    elites, 239, 252–255; corruption, 248,
    261; decisionmaking structures, 9;
    economic reform, 24; elections,
    242–244, 247, 255–256, 259–260;
    elite change in, 14; emerging elites,
    239, 255–258; emigration from, 262,
    266*n66;* former warlords, 245–246,
    252–253; future of political system,
    259–260; IMF loans requested by,
    259; Islamists, 246–248; Israeli inva-
    sion (1982), 128; Israeli withdrawal

(2000), 259; judiciary, 251, 265*n56;*
    Maronites, 240–241, 254–255,
    263*n14,* 265*n55;* media, 265*n57;*
    military role in, 250–252, 261, 303;
    National Pact (1943), 240; National
    Reconciliation Conference, Ta'if,
    250; NGOs in, 256; notables in,
    252–254; parliament in, 10, 241–243;
    political opposition in, 6; political
    reform, 27, 29; population percentage
    by religion, 263*n16;* post–civil war
    stabilization, 239; prewar era,
    240–241; redefined elites, 239,
    245–252; religious leaders as elites,
    5; security services, 248–249; Shebaa
    Farms, 253, 259; Shiites in, 242, 246,
    260; Syrian relations, 12, 106, 240;
    Syrian role in, 29, 239, 242–243;
    Ta'if agreement (1989), 239, 241,
    243, 260; technocrats, 256–257. *See
    also* Lebanese-Syrian relations
Leftists, 186–188
LF. *See* Lebanese Forces
Liban Cell, 257
Libya, 128, 225
Lijphart, Arend, 241

Mabrouk family, 214
Madani, Abassi, 186
Maghraoui, Abdeslam, 52
Maghreb states, 21, 225
Magid, Wahid Abd al-, 131
Mahar, Ahmed, 119, 132, 139*n49*
Majali, Qaftan al-, 46*fig,* 47
Makhlouf, Muhammad, 90
Makhzan: defined, 82*n4,* 233*n3;* in
    Morocco, 62, 68, 73, 79; in Tunisia,
    207, 229–231
Mannheim, Karl, 31*n43,* 193
Mansour, Camile, 290
Marabouts, 197
Maronites, 240–241, 254–255, 263*n14,*
    265*n55*
Marzouki, Moncef, 220
Mas'ari, Muhammad al-, 159
Masharqa, Zuheir, 90
Masri, Mahir al-, 275
Masri, Sabih al-, 43, 46*fig,* 48
Masri, Taher al-, 48
Mass action, 2, 5
Mauritania, 83*n14,* 225
Mazen, Abu (Mahmoud Abbas), 276,
    290, 292–293

Media: in Algeria, 186, 188, 190, 203*n55;* in Lebanon, 265*n57;* in Morocco, 80; in Saudi Arabia, 145; in Syria, 95, 100; in Tunisia, 234*n23;* U.S.-Saudi relationship, 147. *See also* Journalists
Mediene, Mohamed "Tewfik," 176
Mediterranean Dialog, 199
Mestiri, Ahmad, 220
Middle East Airlines, 246
Middle East Quartet, 292
Military: in Algeria, 175–179, 188, 191–192, 199–200, 303; in Egypt, 15, 120–121; in Jordan, 37; in Lebanon, 250–252, 261, 303; in Morocco, 69–70, 85*n39;* role in elites of, 14–15; as source of elites, 11
Miru, Muhammad Mustafa, 92
Mohammed VI, King of Morocco: accession to power of, 61, 66; appointments of, 72–74; Basri dismissal by, 58*n32;* democratization, 25–26; economic reform, 75–76; elite change, 68–71; generational influences on, 19; institutionalization of royal power under, 67, 80; military relationship with, 70; political reform, 77; power sharing, 28
Monarchy: Al Saud family, 142, 148–152; control of elites by, 62–65; Hashemite, 37, 48, 56; presidential, 9. *See also individual rulers*
Monopolies, 285
Morocco: Arab Maghreb Union membership, 225; business elites, 71; change and continuity in, 80–82; circles of influence, 61, 69–71, 74–78, 81; consensus on stability, 305; corruption in, 70, 85*n39;* decisionmaking in, 9; democratization in, 25–26, 61, 65–66; economic reform, 24–25, 75–76; elections, 65–66, 72, 81; elite change in, 13, 68–72; elite reshuffling, 72–74, 78–79; human rights in, 68; Islam in, 66, 69–71; Islamists, 66, 71; journalists, 71, 73, 80; makhzan in, 62, 68, 73, 79; media, 80; military role in, 69–70, 85*n39;* monarchy as center of political elites, 62–65; parliament in, 10, 65, 71, 81; political reform in, 52, 64, 74, 76–80, 83*n14,* 303; politicians in, 16; tech-

nocrats, 16–17, 71, 73–75; Western Sahara conflict, 64, 70, 73, 83*n14*
Movement for Islamic Reform in Arabia (MIRA), 159
Movement of the Deprived, 246
Mubarak, Gamal, 15, 125–126, 130–132, 133*tab,* 138*n46*
Mubarak, Hosni: biography of, 128–129; conflict with Ghazzala, 123; education of, 124; elite change after, 14; military role in government, 120–121; ossification of elites and, 8; as part of October generation, 117; political authoritarianism of, 26; succession issues, 129–133, 135, 138*n46;* visit to Israel, 137*n32;* on youth in leadership roles, 125
Muhammad bin Fahd, Prince, 167, 167*n35*
Muhammad bin Nayif, Prince, 167
Muhammad bin Saud Islamic University (Riyadh), 160
Mukhabarat: Jordan, 37; Syria, 90, 95
Murr, Elias, 249, 257
Murr, Michel, 248–249, 251–252
Murr, Myrna, 249
Musa, Amr: biography of, 139*n48;* Egyptian education of, 124; as powerful figure, 121, 131–132, 133*tab,* 135; public image of, 139*n53*
Musawi, Abbas, 247
Muslim Brotherhood: Egypt, 123–124, 126–128, 133–134; Jordan, 48; Syria, 110
Muslim World League, 154, 166*n10*

Najd, 142, 147
Nashashibi, Muhammad, 273
Nasir, Izz al-Din, 97
Nasrallah, Hady, 264
Nasrallah, Hassan, 247
Nasser, Gamal Abdul, 120, 123, 135*n1,* 160
National Council for Liberty in Tunisia, 221
Nationalist rebels, 257–258
Nationalist reformers, 181*tab,* 193, 195–196
National Union of Tunisian Women (UNFT), 209
Nawaf, Prince, 150
Nayif, Prince, 147, 149–150, 165
Negotiators, 275

Neo-makhzan, 62–63
Neodinosaurs, 181*tab*, 192–194
Neopatrimonialism: defined, 56*n3;* in
    Jordan, 35–36, 38; in Palestine, 271,
    276, 279, 293–294; in Tunisia,
    229–230
Netanyahu, Benjamin, 20
New Jordan campaign, 50, 53
Nezzar, Gen. Khaled, 176–178, 188
Njeim, Gen. Jean, 251
Nongovernmental organizations
    (NGOs): in Algeria, 194–195,
    202*n45;* in Egypt, 122; in Jordan, 40,
    48; in Lebanon, 256; political change
    as goal for, 75; in Tunisia, 236*n46*
North Atlantic Treaty Organization
    (NATO), 199
Notables, 252–254
Nouira, Chakib, 218
Nouira, Hedi, 218
Nuqul, Ghassan, 41, 46*fig,* 47
Nuqul Group, 41

Oil: Algerian production, 174, 178,
    198–199, 205*n89;* as enabler of ren-
    tier states, 301; and generational out-
    look, 18–19; importance to Arab
    economies of, 301; Iraqi oil sales to
    Syria, 107, 110; political issues
    around, 12; Saudi reserves of, 147;
    Syrian production, 97, 99
Operation Defensive Shield, 289
Oppositions, political, 4, 6
Organisation Nationale des Enfants de
    Chouhada, 184
Organisation Nationale des
    Moudjahidine (OHM), 184
Oslo process: breakdown of, 131–133,
    293–294; Egyptian foreign ministry's
    rise and, 121; elite formation and,
    22–23, 29, 267; Fatah domination of
    Palestine and, 279; Islamic awaken-
    ing and, 134; and nature of
    Palestinian entity, 268–269, 271;
    Palestinian mistrust of, 288; support
    and opposition for, 270, 280–282,
    291
Osmane, Ahmed, 78

PA. *See* Palestinian Authority
Pakraduni, Karim, 253, 265*n52*
Palestine: age groups of leaders, 18;
    Arab-Israeli conflict, 21–22; circles

of influence, 272–280; clientelism,
    279; core elite rivalries, 275–276;
    corruption in, 277–278, 284, 287;
    decisionmaking style, 9; democrati-
    zation, 304; donor aid, 284; econom-
    ic dependence on Israel, 283–284;
    elections, 272, 281–282; elite
    change, 14; foreign investment in,
    284; identifying the PRE in, 9; Israeli
    closures, 268, 283; leadership succes-
    sion, 21, 304; legitimacy of elite,
    287–288; neopatrimonialism, 271,
    276, 279, 293–294; outside vs. inside
    leadership, 270–271, 274, 279, 282;
    parliament in, 272–273, 276–278;
    political reform, 29; post-Oslo politi-
    cal landscape, 269–271; presidential
    office, 274–275; public sector
    employment, 278–279; road map to
    peace, 293; Saudi support for, 149;
    security services, 271, 274–276,
    279–280, 292; taxation, 268, 289;
    unemployment, 283–284, 289
Palestine Liberation Organization
    (PLO): Executive Committee, 271,
    274; fading of, 271; Israeli relations,
    267; Lebanese role of, 241
Palestinian Authority (PA): areas of con-
    trol, 269; calls for reform of,
    291–292; Israeli control over, 268;
    prime minister post creation, 292;
    strength of, 271
Palestinian Company for Commercial
    Services (PCCS), 285–286
Palestinian leadership, 273–274
Palestinian Legislative Council (PLC),
    272, 276–278, 292
Palestinian National Council (PNC), 271
Pan-Arabism, 133
Pareto, Vilfredo, 2
Parliaments: in Algeria, 182, 185; in
    Egypt, 10, 121–122, 125; importance
    as elite incubators of, 302; in Jordan,
    52; in Lebanon, 10, 241–243; in
    Morocco, 10, 65, 71, 81; in Palestine,
    272–273, 276–278; in Saudi Arabia,
    160; in Syria, 93–94, 111*n6;* in
    Tunisia, 211, 234*n16*
Parrain, 183
Peeler, John, 5
Peres, Shimon, 20
Perthes, Volker, 1, 87, 165*n2,* 301
Platform of El Kseur, 187

PLC. *See* Palestinian Legislative Council
PLO. *See* Palestine Liberation Organization
Pluralism, state-controlled, 211
Pluralization, 26
Police, 37. *See also* Security services
Political entrepreneurs, 221
Politically-relevant elites (PREs), 5–7. *See also* Elites
Political parties: al-Wasat (Egypt), 19; Amal (Lebanon), 246–247; Ba'th (Syria), 88–89, 92–94, 111; Communist (POCT) (Tunisia), 220; Constitutional Democratic Rally (RCD) (Tunisia), 210, 216–217, 223; decisionmaking role of, 9; Democratic Forum for Work and Liberty (Tunisia), 220; Democratic Front for the Liberation of Palestine (DFLP), 270, 280; Democratic Socialist Movement (MDS) (Tunisia), 220; Destourian Socialist (PSD) (Tunisia), 209, 223; Fatah (Palestine), 269, 271, 279–282; Free Patriotic Movement (FPM) (Lebanon), 245, 257, 262; Front de Libération Nationale (FLN) (Algeria), 179, 182–183, 185, 190–192; Front des Forces Socialistes (FFS) (Algeria), 187, 190, 192, 197; Front Islamique du Salut (FIS) (Algeria), 173, 186–189, 191–192, 211; Hamas (Algeria), 182; Hizballah (Lebanon), 22, 246–248, 259; al-Islah (MRN) (Algeria), 186, 197–198; Islamic Tendency Movement (MTI) (Tunisia), 207, 210–211, 220; Istiqlal (Morocco), 64, 66, 69, 83*n18;* Justice and Development (Turkey), 134; Kata'ib (Lebanon), 244, 253–254, 264*n47;* Koutla al-Democratiya (Morocco), 65, 83*n18;* Lebanese Forces (LF), 243–244; Liberal (al-Ahrar) (Egypt), 124; membership as requisite for influence, 17; Mouvement de la Sociéte pour la Paix (MSP) (Algeria), 182, 186, 189; Mouvement Populaire (MP) (Morocco), 71, 78; Mouvment pour la Réforme Nationale (MRN) (Algeria), 186, 197; al-Nahda, 186, 197; Nasserite (Egypt), 124; National Democratic Party (NDP) (Egypt), 118, 122, 124–126; National Progressive Unionists (Al-Tagammu' a) (Egypt), 124; Neo-Destour (Tunisia), 208; New Wafd (Egypt), 124, 126; Organisation de l'Action Démocratique et Populaire (OADP) (Morocco), 83; Palestinian People's Party (PPP), 269; Parti des Travailleurs (PT) (Algeria), 187; Partie du Progrès et du Socialisme (PPS) (Morocco), 83*n18;* Party of Justice and Development (PJD) (Morocco), 66; Phalange (Kata'ib) (Lebanon), 244, 253–254, 264*n47;* Popular Front for the Liberation of Palestine (PFLP), 270, 280; Popular Unity Movement (MUP) (Tunisia), 220; Popular Unity Party (PUP) (Tunisia), 220; Progressive Democrats, 220; Progressive National Front (PNF) (Syria), 88–89, 92, 103, 114*n57;* Rassemblement National Démocratique (RND) (Algeria), 182, 185, 190; Rassemblement National des Indépendants (RNI) (Morocco), 71, 78; Rassemblement pour la Culture et la Démocratic (RCD) (Algeria), 187, 190; Renaissance (Tunisia), 211; Renewal Movement (Tunisia), 220; Republican Congress (Tunisia), 220; Social Liberal (Tunisia), 220; Union Constitutional (UC) (Morocco), 71; Union Nationale des Forces Populaires (UNFP) (Morocco), 64, 83*n17;* Union Socialiste des Forces Populaires (USFP) (Morocco), 64–66, 69, 78, 83*n18;* Unionist Democratic Union (Tunisia), 220; WAFA (Algeria), 186
Political reform: in Algeria, 26, 29, 104, 173, 302; economic development as argument for delay of, 52, 195; Egypt, 26–28; in Jordan, 42, 52–53; in Lebanon, 27, 29; in Morocco, 52, 64, 74, 76–80, 83*n14,* 303; in Palestine, 29; in Saudi Arabia, 161–163, 302; stability vs., 27–29; in Syria, 27, 103–106, 108–111; in Tunisia, 27, 29, 207–208
Politicians, 15–16, 93–97, 136*n6*

Popular Committee for the Support of
    the Intifada, 96
Populism, 13
Poverty, 284, 288–289
Power sharing, 28
PREs. See Politically-relevant elites
Preventive Security Services (PSS), 274
Privatization: in Algeria, 201n22; in
    Egypt, 122; in Jordan, 41–42, 50–51;
    in Saudi Arabia, 152, 156; in Syria,
    101–103, 109; in Tunisia, 210,
    227–228
Professionals, 38, 49, 158–161. See also
    Business elites

Qabbani, Muhammad, 254–255
Al-Qaida, 148, 163
Qaradawi, Shaikh Yusuf al-, 162
Qasim, Laith al-, 46fig, 48
Qatar, 19, 31n52, 32n52, 58n30
Qidweh, Khaled al-, 287
Qiyada filastiniyya, 9
Qualifying Industrial Zones (QIZs), 50,
    59n51
Qurai, Ahmad (Abu Ala), 277, 281, 290,
    293
Quran, 144
Qurnet Shahwan gathering, 253

Rabbo, Yasir Abed, 276
Rabe, Hans-Joachim, 23, 29, 267
Rabin, Yitzhak, 20, 134, 137n32, 267
Radical democrats, 181tab, 193–194,
    197
Raghib, Ali Abu, 17, 40, 45, 49
Rajoub, Jibril, 274, 276
Ramdane, Abane, 194
Ramdane, Omar, 183
Rashid, al-Fahda Al, 149
Rashid, Muhammad, 275, 286, 292
Rashid, Sayyid, 122
Rawabdah, Abd al-Ra'uf, 40
Regime types, 304
Rejectionists, 181tab, 193–194
Religious leaders: challengers and aspi-
    rants, 153–154; as decisionmakers,
    10; as effective outsiders, 280–281;
    as elites, 5; as political leaders,
    254–255; the ulama, 141–144,
    152–155, 183. See also Clergy;
    Islamists
Rentier states: Algeria, 189, 199,
    205n88; oil as enabler of, 301; Saudi

Arabia, 142, 156, 165; seeking of
    new income by, 304
Rifa'i, Ghassan al-, 17
Rifa'i, Samir al-, 39
Rifa'i, Zaid al-, 39, 45, 46fig, 48
al-Risala, 281
Robinson, Glen, 271
Roy, Olivier, 184, 288
Royal Institute of Amazigh Culture, 68
Russia, 292

Saadi, Said, 75
Sadat, Anwar: assassination of, 131;
    Camp David accords, 132; Israeli-
    Egyptian peace treaty, 117; Israeli
    war of 1973, 128; military role in
    government, 120; power consolida-
    tion by, 123; presidential terms of
    office, 137n31
Sadat, Jihan, 127
Sadr, Imam Musa al-, 246–247
Sahbani, Ismail, 218–219
Said, Abdelmajid Sidi, 183
Said, Edward, 269
Salah, Ahmad Ben, 220
Salam, Khalid, 275, 286
Salamah, Mahmoud, 105
Salman, Prince, 149, 151
Salons, 104–105
Sanqar, Ihsan, 94
Sant'Egidio community, 189
Saud, Ibn (Abd al-Aziz Al), King of
    Saudi Arabia, 142, 147, 150
Saud, King of Saudi Arabia, 153,
    167n37
Saud, Prince, 150
Al Saud family, 142, 148–152
Saudi Arabia: actors in elite of,
    142–144; Basic Law of Government,
    144, 151, 158; business elites, 144,
    156–157; circles of influence, 141,
    156, 163; Consultative Council (CC),
    143–144, 155, 157, 159–161,
    168n70; corruption in, 156, 162;
    decisionmaking style, 9; economic
    reform, 145; education, 146–147,
    152–153, 158, 166n19; elections,
    162, 165; elite change, 14, 141;
    Grand Mosque occupation (1979),
    154; Hariri activities in, 249–250;
    Iranian relations, 161; leadership suc-
    cession, 150–152; media, 145; oil
    reserves, 147; parliament in, 160;

peace initiative (2002), 107; political reform, 161–163, 302; politicians in, 16; privatization, 152, 156; Qatar relations, 32*n52;* religious leaders as elites, 5; as rentier state, 142, 156, 165; Royal Family Council (RFC), 151–152; September 11 attacks' affect on, 146, 156, 162; Shiites in, 147, 161–162, 164; shura council, 10; Supreme Economic Council (SEC), 143, 157; technocrats, 158–159; unemployment, 156, 168*n50;* urbanization, 143; U.S. relations, 145, 147–149, 164
Saudi Arabian National Guard (SANG), 143
"Saudization" program, 156
Sayf, Riad, 94, 104–105
Schlumberger, Oliver, 28, 35
Seale, Patrick, 88
Second circle of influence: in Algeria, 179, 182–184; in Egypt, 119–122, 126; in Jordan, 45, 47; in Lebanon, 240; in Morocco, 61, 69–71, 75–77, 81; in Palestine, 276–280; in Saudi Arabia, 141, 156, 163; in Syria, 90, 94–95; in Tunisia, 213, 216–219
Security services: in Jordan, 37, 52; in Lebanon, 248–249; in Palestine, 271, 274–276, 279–280, 292; in Syria, 90, 95; in Tunisia, 214
September 11 attacks: Algeria affected by, 188; causes of, 134; Saudi Arabia affected by, 146, 156, 162; Tunisia affected by, 227
Serageddin, Yassin, 131
Serfaty, Ibrahim, 67–68
Sfeir, Mar Nasrallah Butros, 243, 254–255
Shaath, Nabil, 273, 276, 281, 290, 292
Shabiba, 290
Shafa'ei, Hussein ash-, 128
Shafi, Haydar Abd al-, 272
Shaikh, Abd al-Aziz Al al-, 155
Sha'ir, Kamal al-, 43, 58*n25*
Sharaa, Farouk al-, 91, 108
Shari'a, 153, 162
Sharon, Ariel, 106, 288–289, 291
Shazli, Kamal al-, 119
Shebaa Farms, 253, 259
Sherif, Safwat, 119, 123, 126
Shihab, Fuad, 250

Shiites: in Lebanon, 242, 246, 260; in Saudi Arabia, 147, 161–162, 164
Shikaki, Khalil, 270, 274, 279
Shu'aibe, Azmi, 275
Shu'aibi, Shaikh Hamud al-'Uqla' al-, 153
Shura, 10, 159
Sidqi, Atef, 123–124
Singh, Ranjit, 123
Socialism, 189
Sonatrach, 179, 202*n38*
Sonbol, Amira el-Azhary, 126
Souaidia, Habib, 188
Special Economic Zones (SEZs), 50
Stagrosion, 218
State-controlled pluralism, 211
Structural adjustment, 174, 210, 232
Succession, leadership: in Egypt, 129–133, 135, 138*n46;* father-to-son, 129–131, 137*n36;* horizontal, 150; in Jordan, 35; in Palestine, 21, 304; in Qatar, 31*n52;* in Saudi Arabia, 150–152; in Syria, 130–131; in Tunisia, 207, 212, 233*n1, 233n10*
Sudairi, Hazza bint Al, 149
Suleiman, Omar, 119
Sulh, Riyad al-, 156
Sultan, Prince: at the Consultative Council, 161; religious influence on, 147; as SEC chair, 143; as Sudairi brother, 149, 151
Sunna, 144
Sunnis, 109–110, 240, 242, 255
Syria: age groups of leaders, 17–19, 96–97; Arab-Israeli conflict, 22; business elites, 97–98, 109; circles of influence, 90–91, 94–95; civil society movement, 103; computer literacy in, 100–101; corruption in, 92, 104–105, 112*n30;* dominance of Lebanon by, 29; economic reform, 25, 97–103, 111; elections in, 114*n57;* elite change in, 13, 91–97, 108–111; elite reshuffling, 91; European Union relations, 89, 101, 112*n22;* foreign relations, 106–108; French relations, 89; Iraqi relations, 107, 113*n50, 262;* Islam in, 110; Israeli relations, 89, 106–107; Jordanian relations, 19–20, 53; labor unions, 97; leadership succession, 130–131; Lebanese relations, 12, 106, 240; limits to reform in, 88; media, 95, 100; oil produc-

tion, 97, 99; oil purchases from Iraq, 107, 110; openness in, 303; ossification of elites in, 8; parliament in, 93–94, 111n6; political parties' role in, 9; political reform, 27, 103–106, 108–111; politicians in, 16; power distribution of elite, 89; as presidential monarchy, 9; privatization, 101–103, 109; security services, 90, 95; technocrats, 91, 93, 101; unemployment, 99; U.S. relations, 106–108, 262. *See also* Lebanese-Syrian relations
Syria Accountability Act (2003), 262
Syrian Computer Society (SCS), 11, 92, 108, 110
System maintenance, 306

Taba, 117, 128, 132
Talal, Walid bin, 152, 156–157, 161, 165
Talal bin Abd al-Aziz, Prince, 151–152, 154, 156
Taleb, Youssef Sabri Abu, 132
Taliban, 148
Tamari, Salim, 280, 282, 290
Tamazight (language), 187
Tantawi, Hussein, 119
Tanzim, 281–282, 290–291
Taoufiq, Ahmed, 70–71
Tarawneh, Fayez, 45, 48
Tawil, Samir, 43, 45, 46fig, 58n26
Taxation, 268, 289
Technocrats: in Algeria, 182; defined, 136n6; in Egypt, 119, 123; in Lebanon, 256–257; in Morocco, 16–17, 71, 73–75; in Saudi Arabia, 158–159; in Syria, 91, 93, 101; in Tunisia, 215, 229
Télé Liban, 246
Temimi, Abdeljelil, 221
Temmar, Hamid, 197
al-Thaura, 102, 105
Third circle of influence: in Algeria, 181tab, 184–189, 192–196; in Egypt, 119–120, 122–123; ideal types, 181tab, 192–196; in Jordan, 47–49; in Lebanon, 240, 255–258; in Morocco, 61, 71, 74, 76, 78, 81; in Palestine, 276–280; in Saudi Arabia, 141, 163; structural change in, 302; in Syria, 90–91, 95; in Tunisia, 213, 219–222

Tlass, Mustafa, 91, 104, 113n40
Touati, Mohamed, 176
Trabelsi, Hassan, 214
Trabelsi, Leila, 214
Transjordanians, 12, 47–48
Transparency, 303–304
Tribal chiefs, 48
Tripp, Charles, 2, 36
Troika, 242
Tunisia: Arab Maghreb Union membership, 225; attitudes toward IMF, 226; business elites, 208, 218–219, 224, 228, 236n46; circles of influence, 213–222; civil society, 220–221; clientelism, 230; corruption, 235n33; democratization, 207, 210–211, 223; economic policy, 227–229; economic reform, 210, 212, 218, 227, 232; education, 213, 216–217; elections in, 211, 224, 233n12; elite change in, 14; EU relations, 211, 225–226, 233n14; foreign policy, 225–227; human rights in, 223, 232; Islam in, 211, 222; Islamists, 211, 222–223; labor unions, 208–209, 218–219, 224, 228, 235n27; makhzan in, 207, 229–231; media, 234n23; neopatrimonialism in, 229–230; neutralization of politics in, 230–232; New Regime, 208, 210–214, 218, 227; NGOs in, 236n46; opposition parties, 220; ouster of Bourguiba, 207, 233n1; parliament in, 211, 234n16; political agendas of elites in, 222–229; political reform, 27, 29, 207–208; as presidential monarchy, 9; presidential succession, 207, 212, 233n1, 233n10; privatization, 210, 227–228; religious leaders as elites, 5; security services, 214; September 11 attacks' affect on, 227; the state as seen in, 226; technocrats, 215, 229; WTO membership, 211
Tunisian Association of Democratic Women, 221
Tunisian League for Human Rights (LTDH), 221
Tunisian Union of Farmers and Fishermen (UTAP), 209
Tunisian Union of Industrialists, Merchants and Artisans (UTICA), 209, 218–219, 226, 228

Turk, Riad, 105
Turkey, 53, 178
Turki, Shaikh Abdallah Al, 154
Turki bin Faysal, Prince, 150, 154
Turkmenistan, 306
Tyminski, Stanislaw, 197

UGTT. *See* General Union of Tunisian
  Workers
Ulama, 141–144, 152–155, 183
Umm al-Qura University (Mecca), 160
Unemployment: in Algeria, 191; in
  Palestine, 283–284, 289; in Saudi
  Arabia, 156, 168*n50;* in Syria, 99
Union Générale des Travailleurs
  Algériens (UGTA), 183, 185–186,
  191
Union Nationale de la Jeunesse
  Algérienne (UNJA), 185, 191
Union Nationale es Femmes Algériennes
  (UNFA), 191
United Nations (UN), 283, 289, 292
United Nations Relief and Works
  Agency (UNRWA), 284
United States: Algerian relations, 177;
  consumer boycott against, 122;
  Egyptian relations, 128; Middle East
  Quartet membership, 292; Saudi rela-
  tions, 145, 147–149, 164; Syrian
  relations, 106–108, 262; war on ter-
  rorism, 133, 177
Urbanization, 143
Uruguay Round, 211
al-Usbuaa, 122
Usher, Graham, 281, 292
'Utaibi, Juhaiman al-, 154
Utri, Naji al-, 92

al-Wafd, 130
Wahhabi sect, 142, 154
Wali, Youssef, 123, 126, 136*n15*
Walid, Prince, 152, 156–157, 161, 165
Warlords, 245–246, 252–253
Washington Consensus, 210
Wasta, 38

Waterbury, John, 72, 121, 126
Werenfels, Isabelle, 14, 29, 173
West Bank. *See* Palestine
Western Sahara, 64, 70, 73, 83*n14*
Women: Consultative Council role of,
  160; as delegates to party congresses,
  125; education of, 146; in Egypt,
  125, 127–128, 136*n13;* as judges,
  127; in Lebanon, 265*n56;* marriage
  to elite members, 124; in Morocco,
  66, 71, 73, 75; in Saudi Arabia, 146,
  158, 160; in Tunisia, 215
World Bank, 259, 289
World Trade Organization (WTO):
  Algerian membership, 179, 184, 199;
  exercise of authority by, 7; Jordanian
  membership, 50; membership's influence on economic elites, 302; preferential treatment among members,
  233*n13;* Tunisian membership, 211,
  225

Ya'ari, Ehud, 286
Yahya, Abd al-Razzaq, 292
Yassine, Abdessalam, 67, 84*n30*
Young Entrepreneurs Association
  (YEA), 41, 48, 57*n20*
Youssoufi, Abd al-Rahman: as dissident-
  turned-politician, 16, 65; political
  reform, 76; reelection as party leader,
  78; replacement of, 67
Youth, 124–125, 130, 255–256

Zahar, Taieb, 221
Za'im, 'Isam, 102
Zakat committees, 281
Za'noun, Riad, 273
Zarrouk family, 214
Zartman, William, 72
Zerhouni, Saloua, 11, 26, 28, 61
Zeroual, Liamine, 175–176, 188,
  202*n41*
Zghal family, 221
Zionism, 133
Zu'bi, Fawaz, 41, 45, 46*fig,* 48

About the Book

The recent deaths of four long-term heads of state in the Arab world heralded important changes, as political power passed from one generation to the next. Shedding light on these changes, *Arab Elites* explores the attitudes and political agendas of the emerging new leadership throughout the region.

A strong analytical framework informs the authors' discussion of elites in Algeria, Egypt, Jordan, Lebanon, Morocco, the Palestinian National Authority, Saudi Arabia, Syria, and Tunisia. The result is a portrait of the current state, and likely future, of politics in the Arab Middle East.

Volker Perthes is head of the Middle East and Africa Research Group at the German Institute for International and Security Affairs, Stiftung Wissenschaft und Politik. His extensive publications on the Arab World include *Geheime Gärten: die neue Arabische Welt* (*Secret Gardens: The New Arab World*).